Succeeding in the World of Work

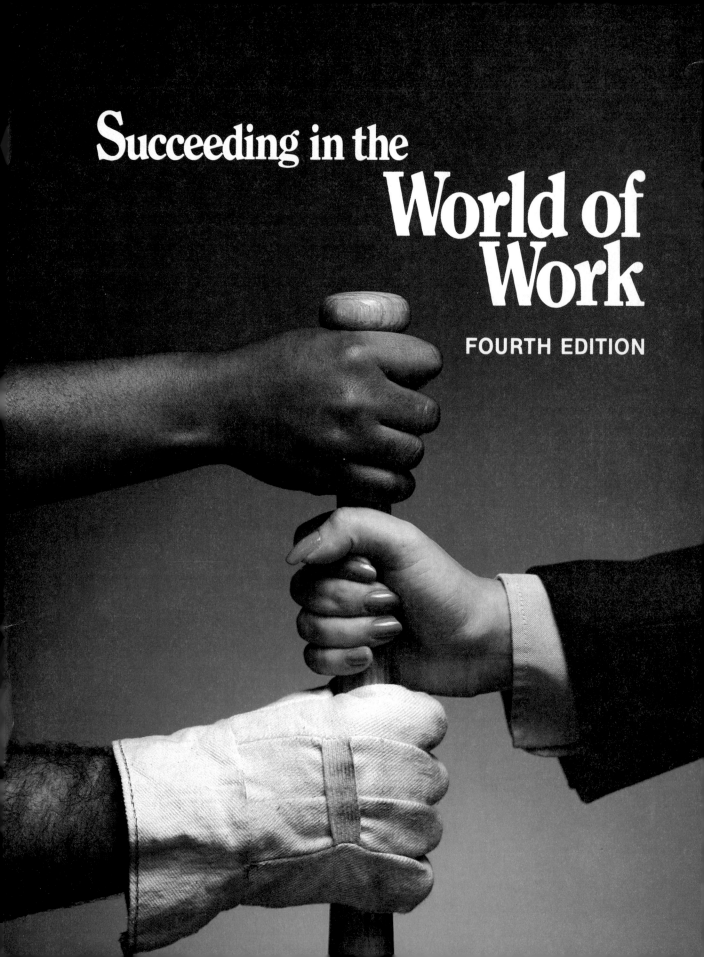

Succeeding in the
World of Work

FOURTH EDITION

Grady Kimbrell

Research Analyst
Santa Barbara School Districts
Santa Barbara, California

Ben S. Vineyard

Professor and Chairman Emeritus
Vocational and Technical Education
Pittsburg State University
Pittsburg, Kansas

Bennett & McKnight
a division of
Glencoe Publishing Company

Succeeding in the World of Work
Fourth Edition

Previous copyrights 1981, 1975, 1970

Glencoe Publishing Company
17337 Ventura Boulevard
Encino, CA 91316

ISBN 0-02-675550-5 (Student Text)
ISBN 0-02-675560-2 (Teacher's Annotated Edition)
ISBN 0-02-675570-X (Student Activity Manual)

2 3 4 5   89 88 87 86

Library of Congress Catalog Number: 85-71611

Printed in the United States of America

TABLE OF CONTENTS

TABLE OF CONTENTS

TABLE OF CONTENTS

TABLE OF CONTENTS

TABLE OF CONTENTS

Acknowledgments

The authors would like to express their sincere appreciation to their wives, Mary Ellen Kimbrell and Katherine Vineyard, for their assistance, support, and encouragement.

The authors also express their appreciation to the many associates, students, and friends who contributed to the revision of this book. Special recognition is given to Professors Donald W. Woolman, James Pappas, and Frank Slapar of Pittsburg State University, Pittsburg, Kansas; Mr. Rex Crowley and Mr. Bill Anderson of The National Bank of Pittsburg, Pittsburg, Kansas; Dr. Pauline Paulin, consultant for "Communication Skills;" Dr. Robert Carman and Mrs. Marilyn Carman, consultants for "Math Skills;" and Mr. Gary H. King, consultant for "Computer Literacy."

Introduction

You have probably been looking forward to getting out on your own for a long time. Well, the time has almost come. You will soon be "grown up," in charge of your own life, and free to come and go as you please.

Being an adult does have its advantages — you will enjoy being your own boss and making your own decisions. Along with the freedom and independence, however, come responsibilities, obligations, and lots of hard work.

As an adult, you will have to work to make enough money to support yourself and perhaps someday, a family. If you are like most people there will never be enough money for everything you want — you will have to learn how to manage your money carefully, to make sure that you get the most value for every dollar. You will also have voting, tax paying, and legal obligations as a citizen of the United States, your state, and your local community.

Are you ready for all of this? Do you have the knowledge, the skills, and the responsible attitude necessary to succeed? Will you be able to achieve and maintain the lifestyle that will make you happy? Do you feel confident that you know everything you'll need to know once you get out on your own?

If you are not 100 percent sure about your future, reading this book will help you. You will learn how to make some decisions and plans about your life so that you can get started in the direction you want to go. You will learn how to get the job you want and be successful at that job. You will review some basic skills and learn some new ones. You will learn how to manage your money wisely and how to meet your adult responsibilities. All together, you will learn the practical things you need to know now as you prepare to set out on your own.

PLANNING YOUR FUTURE

PART ONE

Have you decided what you are going to do with your life? Do you know what kinds of jobs are going to be available when you get out of school? Isn't it about time for you to establish a goal and start working toward it?

In this section you will read about the world of work — what it's like and how it affects every part of a person's lifestyle. You will spend some time getting to know yourself better so you can find a career that matches well with your interests and abilities. You will explore the thousands of occupations that make up the world of work and learn how to gather information about these careers. And finally, you will make a tentative career decision and develop a plan of action to reach your ultimate career goal. After completing this section, you should feel more confident and excited about your future.

The World of Work: Choices and Challenges

DO YOU KNOW . . .
- how your career affects your overall lifestyle?
- why people work—other than for money?
- how to use a strategy for making career decisions?

CAN YOU DEFINE . . .
- career?
- esteem?
- identity?
- job?
- lifestyle?
- self-realization?
- work?

When you were growing up, did you ever pretend that you were an astronaut? Did you ever think about being a movie star—or a truck driver—or a doctor? Most of us have daydreams in which we look and act like a famous, real-life hero, or a character in a favorite TV show. While our daydreams may not have been realistic, they started us thinking about the world of work.

Your place in the world of work will influence every part of your life for a big part of your lifetime. Your job will probably be the main activity in your life. This is why choosing the kind of work you will do is one of the most important decisions you will ever make.

In this chapter you will learn about work—why it is important and how it affects your life. You will also learn about the decision-making skills that everyone needs. Once you develop these skills, you can use them to choose the best career for you.

Lifestyles and Careers

A survey of high school seniors said, "Soon you'll be graduating. Each of you will be going in a different direction, making your own life. What, more than anything else, do you want out of life?" Do you know how you would have answered that question? Here are some typical answers from high school seniors.

- "To be able to travel and live wherever I want."
- "To make a better life for me and my family than my parents had."
- "To become rich and famous."
- "To grab all the gusto I can."
- "Just to enjoy life, wherever I am."

Although their answers differed, these seniors shared a common idea about the future. They all wanted, each in his or her own way, a happy, satisfying lifestyle.

You've probably heard the word *lifestyle* many times. Have you ever thought about what it means? Do you have any idea what it has to do with the world of work? Before we answer these questions, let's make sure we understand a few very basic terms from the world of work.

Job, work, and *career* are words that are often confused. We define **work** as any productive activity that results in something useful. People who work are usually paid for it, but not always. For most people work means having a job and getting paid for doing that job.

Does this diagram look like your present lifestyle? What elements would you add or subtract? Which elements should be bigger or smaller?

To a working person, a *job* may mean one particular task. Usually, though, people use the word **job** to mean the collection of tasks or duties that a person does to earn a living. This is what we mean when we talk about jobs—jobs like truck driver, housekeeper, and teacher.

The work a person does over a period of years is known as a **career**. Most people have many different jobs in their careers. We usually think of a career as a sequence of jobs in the same field of work.

Lifestyle, in simple terms, is the way we live. It's where we live, the kind of food we eat, the way we spend our free time. It is also the way we spend our work time.

In sum, a lifestyle is something we each create in the way we choose to use our time and resources. This means, of course, that each person's lifestyle is unique. No two lifestyles are exactly the same.

Lifestyle Patterns

Many things go into making up a person's lifestyle. Among other things, a detailed diagram of your lifestyle would include the following.

- The area in which you live
- The kind of house you live in
- The car you drive
- Your relationships with your family and friends
- Your favorite foods, movies, and leisure activities
- The school you attend

Your lifestyle pattern might look something like the diagram at the bottom of this page.

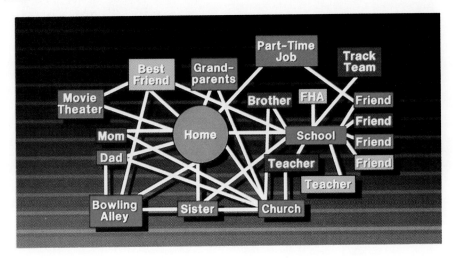

Another way of looking at lifestyles is to group related activities into major lifestyle categories. For example, you could put all the lifestyle elements into the five groups shown below.

Notice that each group of activities in the lifestyle pattern is the same size. This pattern assumes that the five parts of this person's lifestyle are of equal importance. In reality, of course, most people consider certain parts of their life more important than others. A lifestyle diagram for most people would show circles of various sizes, such as you see at the right.

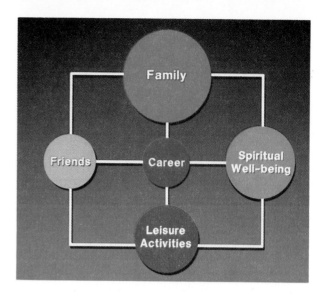

The diagram above represents the lifestyle pattern of a person whose family is by far the most important part of that person's life.

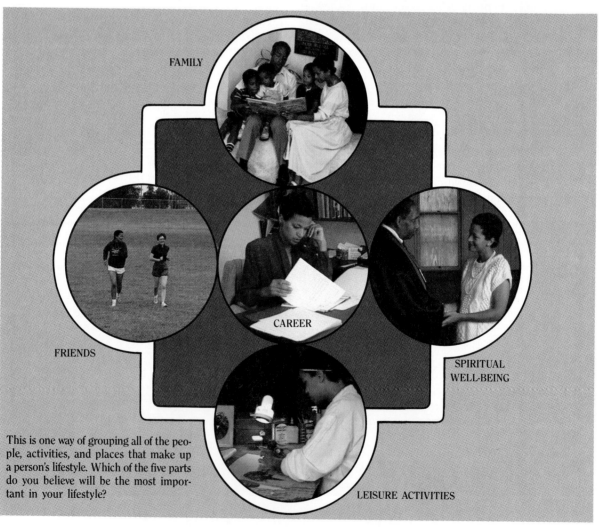

FAMILY

FRIENDS

CAREER

SPIRITUAL WELL-BEING

LEISURE ACTIVITIES

This is one way of grouping all of the people, activities, and places that make up a person's lifestyle. Which of the five parts do you believe will be the most important in your lifestyle?

Each major part of your lifestyle affects the others. This is particularly true of your work—your career. Maybe you noticed that *career* was placed at the center of each lifestyle pattern. This was done for a very good reason—for most people *work is the central activity around which they plan their daily lives.*

Are you beginning to see what a lifestyle pattern is? Even more important, do you see the connection between lifestyles and the world of work?

Make a Decision

Suppose that you just inherited $250,000 from a rich uncle whom you never met. In your uncle's will, he suggested that you use the money to make your lifestyle happier, and more satisfying. Think about the ways in which you could use the money? What's your decision—how will you spend your inheritance to improve your lifestyle? Give reasons for your decisions.

Your Identity—Your Work

As a student, your lifestyle is determined mainly by your role as a student. Being a student is probably the main activity in your daily life. Your **identity** (the personal quality or activity by which you are best known) is that of a student. When you are introduced to another person, you may be asked, "Where do you go to school?" or "What grade are you in?"

As an adult, you will have a new identity. It will be determined by the kind of work you do to earn a living. When you are introduced to another person, you may be asked, "What do you do?" or "Where do you work?"

Other things will help make up your total identity, but you will be known mainly by the work you do. Your work becomes your identity. We don't say, "Jim works as a teacher." We say, "Jim *is* a teacher." Sara doesn't work as a plumber. She *is* a plumber. Even the work you plan to do is used to identify you. For example, college students are sometimes identified as *pre-law* or *pre-med* students. They *plan* to work as lawyers or doctors.

As you start turning your dreams into reality, keep in mind the impact that your work will have on your overall lifestyle. The work you do to earn a living will

- largely determine your circle of friends.
- determine how much time you will have to spend with your family.
- probably determine your standard of living, as a result of how much you earn from your job.
- influence your political decisions.

Just by knowing the kind of work you do, other people will be able to guess a great deal about you. They'll probably know who some of your friends are, where you live, where you work, how much you earn, how much education you have, and how you spend your leisure time. Did you know that your work can affect your life in so many ways? Consider the following examples on the next page.

One of the questions people will ask you when they meet you for the first time is, "What do you do for a living?" Your identity will probably be determined by your career.

Neil was a mechanic in the service department of a Chevrolet dealership. While he worked in the service department, Neil became close friends with several of the other mechanics. He joined the company bowling team because George, another mechanic, was on the team. Since Neil was single and had no family, he spent most of his free time with his buddies in the service department.

Neil was not as interested in repairing cars as he was in selling them, and as soon as he got the chance, he moved out to the showroom as one of the dealership's regular salespeople. He made friends with the salespeople quickly and before long he was spending most of his time away from work with two or three of these salespeople. He still talked to his old friends in the service department when he got a chance, but there just didn't seem to be enough time. Neil even gave up his bowling nights so that he could work out with his new friends at the health club he joined.

Carol graduated from the University of Michigan with a master's degree in mechanical engineering. She had no trouble finding a job at a starting salary far above the starting salaries that many of her friends were getting in other fields. The pay got even better as Carol worked for several years, receiving hefty raises each year. Carol became used to the finer things in life—an expensive sports car, a luxurious apartment, dinners at the best restaurants.

Carol liked her job, but engineering did not provide the satisfaction she had hoped it would. She had always been interested in commercial art, but as a commercial artist she would only earn about half as much money as she was making as an engineer. That would mean some big changes in the lifestyle that she had become used to. She couldn't decide if the added job satisfaction would be worth the big drop in pay.

Women in the World of Work

How long will your work have such a powerful impact on your overall lifestyle? Consider this: After completing of high school, you can expect to live for about another fifty to sixty years. The average man entering the labor market today will work for about forty years. This hasn't changed much since the turn of the century. What has changed, though, is the amount of time women spend working outside the home.

During World War II many women went to work in America's factories, replacing the men going off to fight the war. These women proved themselves capable workers, but most gave up their factory jobs and resumed their homemaker roles after the war.

Then, in the 1960s, many women began moving back into the labor force. The cost of living, especially housing, had risen sharply. In many families, both husband and wife had to work to support their chosen lifestyle.

At first, women were satisfied with the traditional jobs for women—secretaries, nurses, teachers. By the 1970s, however, more women were delaying marriage until they had established careers. The divorce rate was up, and there were more women heads-of-households than at any time in the past. Many women needed and wanted jobs that paid well. But the best-paying jobs—especially in management—were almost always filled by men.

In the 1980s there is still some prejudice against placing women in management and some other high-paying jobs. The opportunities for women are, however, much better than ever before—and they're getting better all the time.

More than 1.5 million women are entering the world of work each year. It is estimated that by 1990 at least half of all employed people in the U.S. will be women (in 1983, over 43 percent were women). Single or married, for many years to come, most women will work about as long as men. Many women will leave the working world only for brief periods when their children are born.

Kathy graduated from high school when she was eighteen. She began working as a data-entry operator in a local computing firm. Kathy worked for the same company for five years and was promoted twice during that time.

She met many new friends at work and in her leisure activities. She dated several young men, but not steadily. When she began a new job with another firm, she met Phillip. Kathy and Phillip liked one another very much and soon began to go out often. Two years later, when Kathy was twenty-five, they were married.

Phillip was also twenty-five. He had a good job, but his income was hardly enough to cover all their expenses. They decided that Kathy should continue working so that they could afford a nice apartment and trade in Kathy's old Chevy for a newer model. With Kathy working, they were also able to save some money each month toward a down payment on a house.

A month before their first child was born, Kathy quit her job. She did not begin working again until after their second child was in the first grade. By then the family had moved to another city, and Kathy had found a part-time job as a typist at the local high school. She had also begun taking night classes in data processing.

Soon Kathy was offered a full-time job as a computer operator with a large insurance firm. Through the years, she changed jobs two more times to accept better positions. She continued to work until her son had completed two years of college, moved to his own apartment, and begun his first full-time job. At this point Kathy decided to quit her job and stay at home.

Kathy has spent the last two years as a full-time homemaker. But she is now thinking about taking additional classes in data processing. She hopes to begin a new career as a computer programmer or analyst.

Kathy's story would have been an unusual one a few years ago. Today, though, most women spend as much time working outside the home as Kathy did. In the years to come, more and more women will be filling positions that have traditionally been labeled "men only."

Women are now doing many of the jobs that used to be considered "men's work." Don't let outdated traditions prevent you from pursuing the career that you want.

Working Women in the 80 s			
	% Women in the Field		
Occupation	1980	1985	Change
Designer	27.3	52.7	+25.4%
Economist	22.9	37.9	+15.0%
Health administrator	46.2	57.0	+10.8%
Psychologist	48.1	57.1	+ 9.0%
Chemist	14.4	23.3	+ 8.9%
Architect	5.8	12.7	+ 6.9%
Drafter	11.1	17.5	+ 6.4%
Attorney	9.4	15.3	+ 5.9%
Engineer	2.8	5.8	+ 3.0%

This chart shows only a small sampling of the occupations in which women are finding more jobs every year.

Why People Work

You probably have a good idea about why most people work—to earn money, right? Yet lots of people with more money than they could ever spend, continue to work. Why? To understand all the reasons that people work, it will help to look briefly at the ideas of a famous psychologist.

Dr. A. H. Maslow was a respected psychologist who studied many things, including the basic needs of human beings. From his studies, Dr. Maslow developed a list of needs. According to Dr. Maslow, each level of needs must be satisfied before the next level becomes important.

Survival and Safety Needs. Maslow's list begins with the most basic needs—the needs for food, water, and good health. These are survival needs. We all must satisfy these needs if we are to continue living.

After our survival needs are met, we become concerned about safety. We need protection from physical danger. We need to know that we are safe at home, at work, and wherever we travel.

How do we satisfy our survival and safety needs? Most of us satisfy these needs by working. We work to earn money so that we can buy food, clothing, and shelter. Many people must work long and hard for the money they need to buy groceries and pay the bills. For millions of people this is the main purpose of work—to earn enough money for survival and safety needs.

You will need a great deal of money to pay for all the things you need, and want, in your lifetime. You will probably have to work hard to earn your money.

Of course, if you are like most people, you will want more money than you need to buy just the essentials. You will also want to buy some of the extras—stereos, automobiles, movie tickets—that make life enjoyable. The more extras you want, the more money you will need to earn.

Social Needs. After our safety needs are met, we look for companionship and affection. Sometimes this need is called a "sense of belonging." It means that someone cares about us, that we've been accepted by people we respect.

Our social needs are often met by our family and close friends. Companionship and meeting people may seem like strange reasons for working, but isn't social contact one of the things you enjoy most about going to school? You probably like to be with other people. Work, like school, gives you a chance to meet and be with people.

The people you spend your workday with will be important in your life. You will socialize with them on the job and sometimes after hours. Thus, your place of work will be a source of social contacts and possibly one or two close friends.

According to Dr. Maslow, these are the basic needs. All human beings have these needs, from the most basic survival needs to the ultimate needs for self-realization. You can satisfy all of these needs through your career.

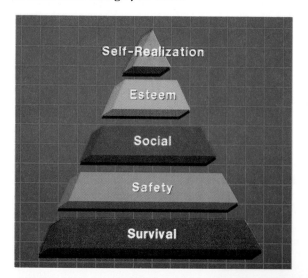

I n 1985 Buddy Ebsen was added to ABC's weekly "Matt Houston" series. Buddy, who was seventy-six years old at the time, had been in show business most of his life. He had appeared in dozens of movies and had starred in "The Beverly Hillbillies" and "Barnaby Jones" on television. As a result of his acting success, Buddy was financially secure. It wasn't necessary for Buddy to ever work again. So why did he return to the daily grind of a weekly TV series?

"I'm used to getting up at dawn and going to the studio to be with my pals on the set," Buddy said. "It's my lifestyle and I wouldn't trade it for any other."

Esteem Needs. After social needs are met, we seek esteem, both self-esteem and esteem from others. What is esteem? Esteem is your worth or value as seen by others. Self-esteem is your worth or value as seen by you—it's the credit you give yourself for being a good, worthwhile person.

The esteem that others feel for you determines how they will treat you. When others hold you in high esteem, it bolsters your self-esteem. This self-esteem is a special feeling, rather like the one you get when the team you're on wins a game. Self-esteem doesn't come and go, though, like the feeling you get with games won and lost. Self-esteem stays with you as long as you feel good about yourself.

Self-esteem is an important reason for working. If you do your work well, others will respect you for it. When this happens, you'll feel proud and respect yourself. For most people the chief source of both esteem from others and self-esteem is success in the world of work.

Many people work, not because they need the money, but because they need the companionship. You will meet lots of people and make many new friends through your work.

Self-Realization Needs. According to Maslow, self-realization is the highest level of needs you are capable of reaching. If you achieve self-realization, you have reached all the important goals in your life. Very few people ever reach this level. But of those who do, more than 90 percent credit their career as being responsible. It is through their work that they achieve self-realization.

Make a Decision

Imagine you have a job that pays $20,000 a year. You have been doing the job for six months, and you have not received one minute of enjoyment or satisfaction from the job. Someone has just offered you a job paying $14,000 a year that you know you would love. It's the type of job that makes you feel good about yourself at the end of the day because you've really accomplished something worthwhile. What's your decision—do you keep your present job or take the new one? Give reasons for your decision.

Career Decision-Making

You have seen that the work you do will

- influence every part of your lifestyle.
- provide your identity as a person.
- continue for most of your adult life.
- help satisfy your basic human needs.

It should be obvious that your career choice is one of the most important decisions you will ever make. Not just a job, but your entire lifestyle, for many years to come, is at stake. Making a career decision is the first step in achieving the lifestyle you want.

Knowing this, you would think that most people would choose their careers very carefully. Yet it is estimated that half of all employed people do *not* choose the jobs they want. Most people simply "fall" into one job or another depending on what's available at the time they're looking. Some people get lucky, but many end up with careers, and lifestyles, that they don't really enjoy.

How does this happen? Lack of knowledge about how to make decisions, and lack of planning. You see, most people don't bother with a plan for their lives. They'll spend lots of time making decisions about a six-week trip to Europe, or even a one-night party. If they want to drive from Chicago to Los Angeles, they'll make decisions and plans about their trip. They'll look at a road map and call ahead for motel reservations. But plan their lives? Most people don't bother. As a result, half of all Americans are not very well satisfied with their lives.

Of course, chance happenings are not always bad. A blind date can turn out to be someone you want to marry. A part-time summer job can lead to a satisfying life career. But the odds are against it. Research shows clearly that the happiest, most satisfied people shift the odds in their favor. They take control of their lives and make things happen.

Decision-Making Strategy

None of us remembers our earliest decisions in life. They may have been choices between orange juice and milk, or who should rock us to sleep. We had only to cry to make our choices known.

As young children we made decisions about which games to play. As we grew older we began deciding which clothes to wear. Those were simple decisions. If we made bad choices, we probably didn't have too many regrets the next day.

When we began to spend money, our choices seemed more important. If we bought a sweater that didn't match our other clothes, or a record that we didn't care for, we felt bad. We felt as though we had made a big mistake.

You still make routine, simple decisions every day. In the months and years just ahead, you will be making some major decisions. Some decisions, such as which car you will buy, will affect your life for several years. Others—such as who you marry, whether or not you continue your education, and which career you will choose—will affect you for your whole life.

Decisions that will affect your life for many years should be made carefully and logically. Using a decision-making process can help you with these important decisions. Here is a seven-step, decision-making process that works.

1. Define your need or want.
2. Analyze your resources.
3. Identify the choices.
4. Gather information on each choice.
5. Evaluate the choices.
6. Make your decision.
7. Plan how you will reach your goal.

No matter what kind of decision you are making, the decision-making process will increase your chances of making the right choice. For example, suppose you want to buy a car. You have already defined your want—a car. That's step one.

Step two is to analyze your resources. This means studying your finances to see how you will pay for the car. If you need a loan, you must check around for the best interest rate and terms for paying off the loan.

In step three you will identify your choices. To do this you will need to check out all the available sources of cars. These might include new-car dealers, used-car dealers, and owner-advertised cars in the classified ads. The result of this step will be a list of all the cars you can choose from.

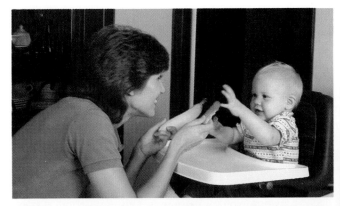

Do the decisions seem to be getting harder and harder to make? Using a decision-making strategy will help you make some of the most important decisions of your life.

In step four you will gather information. For each car on your list, you will need to know such things as cost, condition, insurance, and warranty.

In step five you will evaluate the choices. You will review the information you have gathered and determine which factors are the most important. You might even establish a system of pluses and minuses to rate your choices.

In step six you will decide which car best satisfies your need for the price you are willing to pay. You will decide to buy that car knowing it was the best choice you could make.

In step seven you will make plans to buy the car. You will list all the things you need to do, such as arrange for a loan, inform the car dealer, and buy some insurance. By planning ahead you make sure that nothing will prevent you from getting your car as quickly as possible.

Making Your Career Decisions

The steps in the decision-making process just described will be a little more complex when you choose your career. You can follow the same steps, but some will have several parts.

The first step is to define your future needs and wants. Where will you want to live? How much of your time will you want to spend at your job? Will you want to do a lot of traveling, or will you prefer to stay close to home? How much money will you need?

These are just a few of the questions you'll need to answer in determining your needs and wants. How do you go about answering these questions? A good place to begin is with your daydreams and your lifestyle goals. In Chapter 2 you will read about how you can use your dreams and goals to identify your future needs and wants.

Step two, analyzing your resources, involves much more than it did in the car-buying example. Your "resources" for choosing a career are the things that make you *you*. Such things as your values, interests, skills, and personality go together to make up your personal resources.

You can study your resources through observation, testing, and experience. A thorough study will provide a good understanding of yourself. In Chapter 2 you will also learn a great deal about how to study and analyze yourself.

Step three in the decision-making process is to identify the choices. In career decision-making this means picking several careers that you think might fulfill your needs and wants. If you're like many teenagers, you are probably not sure what you want to do when you graduate from high school. You may not even know what sorts of careers there are to choose from.

This is why it's so important to spend some time exploring careers. The more careers you are aware of, the better your chances of finding one that's right for you. Reading the first part of Chapter 3 will increase your awareness of available careers.

After you have identified several interesting careers, you are ready for step four in the decision-

making process. In step four you will gather information on each possible career. You will need to find out about such things as job duties and responsibilities, work relationships, required skills, and much, much more. The last part of Chapter 3 explains how to go about doing your career research.

In step five you will evaluate your career choices. At this point you will understand yourself, and you will have all the information you need about your chosen careers. You will now be able to match your values, interests, and skills with the career information you've gathered. This evaluation process should prepare you for making a decision. Chapter 4 has suggestions that will help you evaluate your choices.

In steps six and seven you will actually make your career decision and plan how to reach your career goal. You may change your goal several times, but it's still important to make a decision and plan. You need something to work toward while you are learning more about yourself and the world of work. If your decision becomes unrealistic or undesirable, you can repeat the decision-making process to arrive at a new goal. Chapter 4 will help you make a decision and a plan of action.

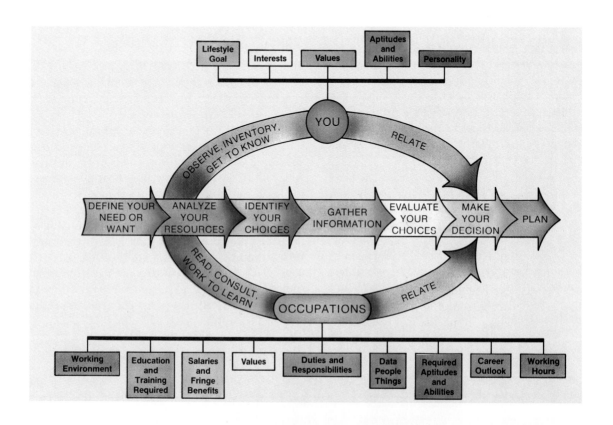

REVIEW YOUR LEARNING   CHAPTER 1

CHAPTER SUMMARY

Like everyone else, you will want to live the lifestyle that will make you happy. Of all the things that will make up your lifestyle, your career will probably be the most important. As an adult you will probably be identified by the kind of work you do. Your work will determine, at least in part, your circle of friends, where you live, and how you spend your leisure time.

People work for several reasons. They work for money to pay for necessities such as food, clothing, and housing. They also work to satisfy their needs for social contact, esteem, and self-realization. In many families, both husband and wife must work to support their chosen lifestyle. Opportunities for women are better than ever before, and getting better all the time.

Your career choice is one of the most important decisions you will ever make. Using the decision-making process will increase your chances of making a choice that is right for you. The seven steps in the decision-making strategy are 1) define your needs and wants, 2) analyze your resources, 3) identify the choices, 4) gather information, 5) evaluate the choices, 6) make your decision, and 7) plan how you will reach your goal.

WORDS YOU SHOULD KNOW

career
esteem
identity
job
lifestyle
self-realization
work

STUDY QUESTIONS

1. What are the five major parts of a person's lifestyle?
2. What are the five basic needs in Maslow's Pyramid of Needs?
3. What is the main reason most people work?
4. What is the identity of most school-age people?

REVIEW YOUR LEARNING

5. How are adults usually identified?
6. Name four things that you can often guess about a person by knowing the kind of work he or she does.
7. Why are half of all Americans not very well satisfied with their lives?
8. What is the most important first step in achieving a lifestyle that will be satisfying in five, ten, or twenty years?
9. What are the seven basic steps in the decision-making process?
10. Give one reason why many women began entering the work force in the 1960s.

DISCUSSION TOPICS

1. Think of the adults you know who are working. Do they work only for money, or do they get other satisfactions from their work? How does their work affect the other parts of their lives?
2. What things do you expect will be most important in your lifestyle ten years from now?

SUGGESTED ACTIVITIES

1. Pretend that the date is ten years from today. Describe, in 500 words or less, your lifestyle. Include the city and state where you are living. Also include descriptions of the following.

   - The area where you live
   - Both the outside and inside of the building in which you live
   - The person or persons who live with you
   - The car(s) and any other vehicles that you own

   Tell about your favorite leisure activities, your relationships with family and friends, and anything else that will be important to you ten years from now. Then describe the place where you work and the kind of work you do to provide this lifestyle.
2. Write a short report on the changing role of women in the world of work.

Getting to Know Yourself

DO YOU KNOW . . .
- how your values will affect your career choice?
- what your major interests are?
- how aptitudes and abilities affect success?
- how to match your personality with a suitable career?

CAN YOU DEFINE . . .
- ability?
- aptitude?
- data?
- interests?
- personality?
- self-concept?
- values?

As you know from reading Chapter 1, a satisfying lifestyle depends greatly on a satisfying career. For that reason, you've probably decided not to be among the 50 percent who "fall" into a career. Instead, you will use the career decision-making process to choose a career that's right for you. In doing this you will take a big step toward controlling your own lifestyle.

Before you start exploring careers, get to know yourself a little better. You should have a good understanding of your own values, abilities, and personality. Then you can match yourself with a realistic, satisfying career. This chapter will help you get to know yourself better.

Your Lifestyle Goal

Your lifestyle goal is the way you see yourself living in the future. Thinking about your lifestyle goal is like daydreaming. This kind of daydreaming can tell you a lot about yourself. As you read in Chapter 1, it can help you identify your strongest needs and wants.

Daydreaming how you want to live will help you decide certain things about your career goal. Will you want a comfortable lifestyle that requires a good income? Or will you be satisfied with a simpler, less expensive lifestyle?

Some of your daydreams are probably pure fantasy, not likely to ever come true. An example would be a tall, heavyset person dreaming of being a professional jockey. Another example would be an extremely awkward, uncoordinated person dreaming of being a ballet dancer.

Many of your daydreams, though, are good indications of realistic lifestyle goals. A character in the play *South Pacific* sings "You've got to have a

The first step in planning a satisfying lifestyle is to daydream about it. Your dream can provide important information as you get to know yourself better.

dream. If you don't have a dream, how you gonna have a dream come true?" The point is—if you have no idea about where you want to go, how will you ever get there?

Many of your daydreams will give you clues about what sort of lifestyle you will want five, ten, or twenty years from now. So start paying attention to your daydreams. When you realize that you've just dreamed about a lifestyle goal, get a pencil and paper. Write down the lifestyle that you've just imagined for yourself. Later, when you identify and research careers, you can look for careers that will make this lifestyle dream come true.

Your Values

The ideas, relationships, and other things that are important to you are your **values**. If you believe money is important, then money is one of your values. If your family and friends come first in your life, then you value them above all else.

While you were growing up, you probably shared most of your parents' values. For example, if your parents placed a great deal of importance on education, chances are you did, too. If their religion was very important to them, you most likely shared many of their religious beliefs.

As you got older, you began to question many of the values you grew up with. You may have hung onto the values that made sense to you and forgot about those that didn't. You probably placed less emphasis on some and more emphasis on others. You may have even added some values of your own.

Make a Decision

You are driving home from a party late one night. Several of your closest friends are in the car with you. You start to slow down when you see someone with car trouble waving for you to stop. Your friends begin to laugh and kid around as you all notice the person in trouble is someone whom everyone makes fun of at school. Your friends are saying things like, "You're not going to stop for *him*, are you?" But you think maybe you should stop. What do you do—stop or keep going? You must make a quick decision. Give reasons for your decision.

It is important to know what your values are when you make career decisions. For example, if you place a high value on helping others, you won't want a job that seems socially useless or harmful—no matter how big the salary. If spending time with your family is important to you, you won't want a career that requires a lot of out-of-town travel.

Ten general values are listed below. Think about which of these values are most important to you.

- **Fame**—Do you want a career that will make you famous? If you don't expect to be famous throughout the country, do you want to at least be well known in your state or town?
- **Money**—Is it important to you to earn a lot of money?
- **Power**—Do you like having power over other people? Would you rather be a boss than someone who takes orders?
- **Religion**—Will your religion come before all other areas of your lifestyle? Will the demands of your job take second place to your religious activities?
- **Humanitarianism**—Is helping other people one of the most satisfying things you do? Will you insist on a career in which you do something for people and society?
- **Family**—Do you want to stay close to your family members? Would you turn down career opportunities that take you away from your family?
- **Health**—Is your physical and mental health more important than anything else? Must you work only in the most healthful environments?
- **Aesthetics**—Do you value art, music, and drama? Would you prefer a career in which you can appreciate and add to the beauty in the world?
- **Creativity**—Do you feel the need to create new things? Would you sacrifice security for a chance to create?
- **Social Contact**—Is it important to you that you work with other people? Do you always try to avoid situations in which you will be working alone?

Give some thought to what your values are before you choose a career. As you read and learn about a career, think about how that career would match your values. Don't choose a career that would cause you to go against your values.

Your Interests

You can get to know and understand yourself better by looking at your **interests**. Your interests are the things that you enjoy doing the most. You will want to consider your interests carefully when choosing a career.

Your Favorite Activities

Think for a moment—what activities do you like doing the most? Think about your hobbies. What do you do in your spare time? Your hobbies are probably things you do well, that give you satisfaction. Did you know that many successful photographers first took pictures only as a hobby? Many people earn a living doing something that they used to do only as a hobby.

Which classes in school have been your favorites? Your favorite subjects are good indications of your interests. Do you like math? Have you taken any vocational classes? Perhaps you have developed a strong interest from one of these classes. If you really enjoy one of your classes, there is a good chance you could be successful pursuing a career in that area.

This lady's hobby is refinishing furniture. She would probably enjoy a career in one of the many occupations related to the furniture business.

POWER

HUMANITARIANISM

MONEY

RELIGION

FAME

FAMILY

HEALTH

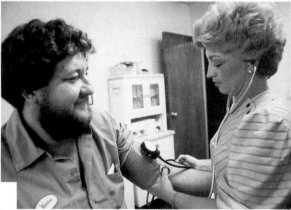

AESTHETICS

CREATIVITY

SOCIAL CONTACT

If you have taken part in school and social activities, you probably have a lot of interests. If you haven't been involved in many of these activities, you may want to start getting involved. It's impossible to know if you'll be interested in something until you try it. The more interests you develop, the better your chances of finding a career that will satisfy you.

Preference for Data-People-Things

Would you enjoy working with **data** (facts, such as numbers, words, and symbols)? How would you feel about doing most of your work with **people**? Or are you a person who likes to work with **things**—putting parts together, sewing clothes, or repairing machines? To find a career you will enjoy, you will need to know if you are most interested in data, people, or things.

Of course, very few jobs are limited to just one of these three categories. Most jobs involve combinations of the three. It is possible, though, to identify jobs as being *primarily* involved with one or two of these.

For example, accountants, secretaries, and counselors work primarily with people and data. Salespeople deal mostly with people and things, while house painters work mainly with things. Graphic designers and computer operators work mainly with data and things.

As you research a career to see which of the three categories is primarily involved, look beyond the surface. To a patient, for example, it may seem that nurses work primarily with people. But a lot of their time is spent working with data and things. A mechanic, who appears to deal solely with things, may spend a lot of time keeping records, ordering parts, and figuring charges.

Another important factor is the difficulty of the work in each of the three areas. For example, waiters and ministers both work with people. The waiter probably works with more people, but the "people" part of the waiter's job is less difficult. It requires fewer people skills.

The people skills the waiter uses are serving food efficiently and making people feel welcome. The minister counsels and guides people, often when they are distressed and troubled. This means that the level of people skills required for the minister's job is much higher than that required for the waiter's job.

Here's another example. Cashiers and math professors both work with data. The cashier probably deals with data more times in a given day than does the math professor. But consider the difficulty of the two data jobs. The cashier simply adds numbers on a machine or piece of paper and makes change. The math professor works with complex math formulas and equations. A much higher level of data skills is required for the math professor's job.

Most jobs involve work with all three — people, data, and things. You should look for a career, however, that deals *primarily* with your preference.

PEOPLE

DATA

THINGS

The U.S. Department of Labor, in a book called the *Dictionary of Occupational Titles,* has rated every job according to its difficulty in each of the three categories—data, people, and things. With this book you can find out the data-people-things difficulty for any career you wish to research.

Interest Surveys

If you need help in finding out what your interests are, you should take an interest survey. There are many different surveys available. One of these, the *World of Work Career Interest Survey,* is similar to a test, but there are no right or wrong answers. From a long list of work activities, you decide how much you would like to do each one. Then you can see which career groups (and jobs) you might enjoy. Your teacher, counselor, or work-experience coordinator can arrange for you to take one of these surveys.

Aptitudes and Abilities

It takes more than an interest in a career to be successful in that career. You must also have the necessary **aptitude** or **ability.** An aptitude is a knack, or a potential, for learning certain skills. An ability is a skill that has already been developed.

J ane wanted more than anything in the world to be a singer. Her family arranged for her to take singing lessons. She practiced faithfully for several years. But she never learned to sing on key. Her voice wasn't very good either. Even her own mother didn't like to hear her sing.

Being a singer was not a realistic goal for Jane. She just didn't have the aptitude to become a good singer.

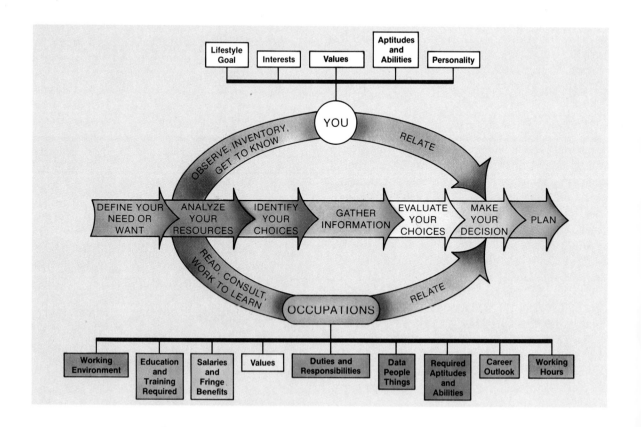

In many careers, especially those such as music, art, and sports, a great deal of natural aptitude or ability is needed. This does not mean, however, that ability alone is enough to be successful. Hard work, in the form of practice, training, and experience, is also necessary.

Davis began playing baseball when he was only four years old. His father, a semiprofessional player who loved the game, practiced with him. David could run fast and was well coordinated.

In grade school David was always the first person chosen when it came time to choose up sides. In high school David played center field on the school team. He batted .390 during his three years in high school and was also an outstanding fielder. When he graduated, he signed with a major-league team.

Learning to play baseball was easy for David because of his aptitude. He was born with the natural talent to become a great baseball player. As a professional player he had several years of training to develop his aptitude into outstanding ability.

Simply being interested in a career isn't enough. You must also have an aptitude for it.

To choose a career in which you can be successful, you must know your aptitudes and abilities. You don't want to choose a career only to find that you cannot do the tasks that you'll be expected to do.

How do you find out what your aptitudes and abilities are? You can do several different things.

A good place to begin is with yourself. What do *you* think your strongest abilities are? Are you good at expressing ideas? Are you a skilled mechanic? Do you paint pictures that people praise and admire? Can you do math problems faster than anyone in your class?

Your grades usually give a good indication of your mental aptitudes and abilities. Your overall grade point average should tell a great deal about whether or not you have the ability to do well in college. Your grades in individual courses should suggest your strongest mental abilities.

Of course, if you don't try very hard in school, you may have more aptitude for certain kinds of work than your grades indicate. Developing your aptitudes into useful abilities will be difficult unless you make the effort.

Usually your teachers can let you know whether or not you have the aptitude for certain kinds of work. For example, suppose you are taking shorthand this semester. Your shorthand teacher can probably tell whether or not you have the aptitude to develop good shorthand skills. The same is true for other skills courses, such as auto mechanics, electronics, drafting, typing, and bookkeeping.

Make a list of what you believe are your strongest abilities. Don't be modest—give yourself credit for the things you do well.

Your school counselor can also help you learn about your strengths and weaknesses. Just as there are tests to determine your interests, there are tests to measure your abilities and aptitudes. Some tests show how easy or difficult it would be for you to develop skills in a special field. The tests predict your potential for learning such things as clerical skills, radio code, and playing a musical instrument.

If you have not taken an aptitude test, ask your counselor to give you one. The chart on this page shows you some of the aptitudes measured by aptitude tests. While different tests measure different aptitudes, the chart will give you a good idea of the kinds of aptitudes that can be measured.

You may not have the physical ability needed to succeed in certain kinds of work. You read, for example, about the girl who wanted to become a singer, but whose voice wouldn't cooperate. Many young people would like to become professional athletes. Very few people, however, have the necessary natural talent.

If you are considering a career that requires special ability, be sure you have an aptitude for it. Try to be realistic. A goal is worthwhile only if there is a possibility of reaching it.

You have some strengths—and weaknesses. We all do. Everyone has both. Look toward your future and plan your career with a positive, realistic attitude. Plan to do the best you can with what you have. You will be a happier worker and a more satisfied human being if you choose a career that does not ask too much, or too little.

Your Personality

How would you describe your own personality? What words would you think of if someone asked you to talk about your personality? Do words like *friendly, shy, outgoing, happy,* and *quiet* come to mind? Can you think of any others?

It is important that you try to understand your personality better than you probably do now. The more you know about your personality, the better your chances of finding a career that you will enjoy.

Understanding your personality can help you find jobs with co-workers who have similar personalities. This will make your work more enjoyable. Understanding your personality will also help you find jobs that are done in environments that match up well with your personality. Again, this will make you happier.

Employers are very concerned about personality. Many say that they look for employees with "pleasing personalities." When employers call schools to discuss the kinds of student workers they want, the employers often make remarks like the following.

What Are Your Aptitudes?	
Aptitude tests indicate your strengths and weaknesses in areas such as those shown in the chart below. Taking an aptitude test may help you pick a career at which you can be successful.	
Type of Aptitude	**Description**
General	Good understanding of facts, opinions, concepts, and reasoning; related to school achievement
Verbal	Good understanding of words and ideas and their meanings; able to use words and ideas easily and clearly
Numerical	Good at doing arithmetic and problems; work quickly and accurately
Spatial	Good at visualizing shapes, heights, widths, depths mentally; can visualize in three dimensions
Form Perception	Good at observing detail in objects and drawings; can distinguish between shapes
Clerical Perception	Good at observing all details and noticing errors in spelling, punctuation, etc.; accurate in recording details
Motor Coordination	Good at moving eyes and hands or fingers together to do a job rapidly and smoothy
Finger Dexterity	Good at moving the fingers quickly and accurately to work with small objects
Manual Dexterity	Good at working with hands
Eye-Hand-Foot Coordination	Good at moving the hands and feet together as needed quickly and accurately
Color Discrimination	Good at noticing differences and similarities between colors and shapes of colors

- "Send me someone with a nice personality."
- "Send me someone with a clean-cut personality."
- "I want someone who can type and who has a good personality."

When employers explain why they hired one person rather than another, they make comments like the ones below.

- "I hired Antonio because he had such a nice smile and a pleasing personality."
- "I didn't hire Lorna. She was a whiz at typing, but she didn't have much personality."
- "I hired Ruby because she had more personality than the others."

Before you can examine your own personality more closely, you must know what personality is. What are we talking about when we talk about personality?

There are many different ways to define personality. Here we will say that **personality** is the combination of all the attitudes, interests, values, behaviors, and characteristics that make you the person you are. You are unique—different from every other person on earth. Your personality is that unique combination of things that makes you different.

Many psychologists have developed complex theories trying to explain personality. When they talk about personality, they use words like *self-concept, extravert, introvert, dominant, submissive, impulsive, structured, hostile,* and *secure.* Looking more closely at a few of the ways in which psychologists talk about personality may help you understand your own personality better.

Self-Concept

Your **self-concept** is the way you see yourself—your feelings about your own worth and value. Your self-concept changes from day to day. When you do something really well, or when someone else pays you a compliment, your self-concept improves. You tend to think of yourself as a good, worthwhile person. But when you fail at something, or someone points out a fault, your self-concept goes down. At this point you might have a very low opinion of your own worth.

Although you experience highs and lows, you do have a consistent, ongoing self-concept. In general, you either like yourself, dislike yourself, or feel something in between. You have ideas about what you can and cannot do. You have a picture in your mind of the kind of person you are.

How you see yourself provides important clues to your personality. This, in turn, suggests careers you would probably enjoy and in which you would be successful. If you see yourself as a very attractive person, perhaps you should consider careers in modeling or entertainment. If you see yourself as a friendly person who can communicate easily, you may be successful selling products or providing people with a service.

Take some time to examine your own feelings about yourself. Do you have a realistic opinion of yourself? Do you give yourself the credit you deserve, without exaggerating your good points? You may want to compare your own ideas about yourself with the opinions other people have of you. . If it looks as though you see yourself clearly, use your self-concept to guide you in your career decision-making.

Personality Types

Some of the most respected ideas about personalities and how they relate to career choices were developed by Dr. John Holland. A quick look at Dr. Holland's ideas may help you learn more about your personality.

Your personality will help you or prevent you from succeeding in your chosen career, depending on how well you match yourself with the right career. Do you know what sort of career your personality is best suited for?

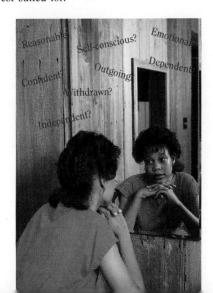

Dr. Holland says that there are six basic personality types. He also says that people resemble, more or less, one of the personality types. The six types are listed and described briefly.

- **Realistic**—Realistic people like to work with objects, tools, and machines. They avoid educational activities and social situations. They value money, power, and status.
- **Investigative**—Investigative people like to examine physical, biological, and cultural situations and happenings so that they can understand and control them. Investigative people do not like persuasive, social activities. They usually develop strong mathematical and scientific skills.
- **Artistic**—Artistic people like to be involved in free, unregulated activities so that they can create new art forms and products. Artistic people avoid rigid, unchanging systems and activities. Artistic people develop skills in languages, art, music, drama, and writing.
- **Social**—Social people like to help, teach, train, cure, and enlighten other people. Social people avoid working with materials, tools, and machines. They are usually skilled at getting along with others, and they value social and ethical activities.
- **Enterprising**—Enterprising people like to manipulate other people in order to achieve their goals and make money. Enterprising people avoid scientific and investigative activities.

They value political and economic achievement and prefer to be leaders rather than followers.
- **Conventional**—Conventional people like to keep records, file materials, and organize information, often with the use of business machines. Conventional people avoid free, unregulated activities. They value business and economic achievement and have clerical and numerical abilities.

In Holland's book, *Making Vocational Choices: a Theory of Careers,* (Prentice Hall, 1973), you can read more about the six personality types. You can also look at a test called *The Self-Directed Search* that Holland developed to help people find out what unique mixture of personality types they happen to be. The scores from this test can help you match your personality to appropriate occupations.

Personality and Career Choices

Many psychologists other than Holland have developed methods of helping people match their personality to suitable careers. Like Holland, many have developed personality tests and inventories. If you would like to find out more about your personality, talk to your counselor. He or she will discuss with you the various personality tests available.

Of course you may not need to take a test to find out about your own personality and how it relates to careers. You may already have a good idea of what your personality is like. You may know what sort of career would match well with your personality. For example, you may know that you are a generally nervous person who would not like a career making high-risk decisions in business management. Or you may be a highly social person who needs to be around people and could not spend long hours working alone. Another possibility is that you are the independent type who will need to be your own boss, rather than someone who takes orders.

It might help to make a long list of words that describe you. You could also make a list of words that describe the opposite of you—all the things that you are not. Then, as you research careers, find out whether or not people with your characteristics usually enter and succeed in each career.

If you enjoy working with tools and machines, you probably *don't* enjoy attending lectures and seminars on historical and scientific topics. Some personality tests can give you clues about careers you would probably like and dislike.

REVIEW YOUR LEARNING   CHAPTER 2

CHAPTER SUMMARY

Do not explore occupations until you have a good understanding of yourself. You need to know all about yourself—your dreams, values, interests, abilities, aptitudes, and personality. Only by knowing all these things about yourself can you be sure to find a career that you will enjoy and in which you will be successful.

You need to pay attention to your daydreams to find out what kind of lifestyle you would like to have in the years to come. It's important to know what your values are so that you don't pick a career that conflicts with your values. You also want to take a close look at your main interests—the activities you enjoy doing and your preferences for working with people, data, or things.

Being interested in a career will not, however, make you successful in that career. It's also necessary to have the aptitudes and abilities needed to perform the duties of that career. Matching your personality with an appropriate career will also contribute to your success and happiness.

WORDS YOU SHOULD KNOW

ability
aptitude
data
interests
personality
self-concept
values

STUDY QUESTIONS

1. How can dreaming help you in your career decision-making process?
2. Name at least five things that many people value.
3. In making a career decision, why is it good to have many interests rather than just a few?
4. What book rates jobs in terms of their data-people-things difficulty?
5. What is the difference between *aptitude* and *ability?*
6. How can your school counselor help you identify your aptitudes and abilities?

REVIEW YOUR LEARNING

7. Employers say that they want employees with what kind of personality?
8. List at least five words that psychologists use to describe personalities.
9. What are the six personality types as identified by John Holland?
10. Which of Holland's personality types would you expect a high school English teacher to be?

DISCUSSION TOPICS

1. How well do you know yourself? Do you know yourself well enough to choose a career for which you are suited?
2. Have you ever thought about your values? Of the ten values described in this chapter, which two or three are the most important to you?
3. Do you think people can be grouped into personality types? If so, which type are you?

SUGGESTED ACTIVITIES

In this activity, each person in your class will make a collage. A collage is made by pasting a variety of materials on a sheet of cardboard. Pictures from magazines and other materials are arranged so that they tell a story. The class will discuss all of the finished collages. This will be done in five steps.

1. Collect the materials you will need to make your collage. Useful materials include the following.
   - A large piece of cardboard or poster board
   - Colored pens, crayons, or poster paint (with brushes)
   - Scissors
   - Some old magazines (at least a dozen)
2. Make a collage that represents you. Try to show some of your values, interests, relationships with others, your personality, and your lifestyle goals. Make your collage at home, then give it to your teacher without letting other students see it.
3. Pass all of the collages around the class so everyone can see them. Then your teacher will show each collage. The class will try to guess who made each collage, giving reasons for their guesses. The more discussion of each collage, the better. The person who made the collage will get to see if other people see him or her in the same way.
4. Following the discussion of all the collages, each student should pick up his or her collage and explain the meaning of each part.
5. When you pick up your collage, you may then ask the class some questions. You may ask them to explain comments they made in the discussion of your collage. This will help you understand how others see you.

Researching Careers

DO YOU KNOW . . .
- how exploring career areas can help you identify careers you want to research?
- what to look for when researching careers?
- where to find information on careers?
- how work experience can help you learn about careers?

CAN YOU DEFINE . . .
- career cluster?
- career consultation?
- career interest areas?
- fringe benefits?

You learned in Chapter 1 how the decision-making process can be used to reach a career decision. The first step was to begin dreaming about how you would like to live in five, ten, even twenty years. The next step was to analyze your resources, which meant getting to know more about your own values, interests, abilities, and personality. After reading Chapter 2 you should have a good idea of who you are.

This chapter will help you with the third and fourth steps in the career decision-making process. In step three you will identify several careers that you believe will fulfill your needs and wants. Then, in step four, you will research these careers to see if they match up with your lifestyle goals and personal resources.

Exploring Careers

Maybe you already have some ideas about careers you would enjoy. If so, make a list of these careers and start your research. The second part of this chapter will show you how to do a thorough job of researching careers.

On the other hand, you may have no idea which careers would interest you the most. Like many people, you may not even be aware of the many different kinds of jobs that are available. In this case, you would need to explore the various career possibilities before making a list and starting your research.

In fact, even if you already have several careers in mind, you might want to do some exploring. Perhaps you'll find one or two careers that you didn't know about. You may want to add these to your list. Remember—the more careers you research, the better your chances of finding one that's right for you.

Where do you get ideas about careers you might like? You can talk to your friends and members of your family. You can start noticing to the jobs people are doing as you go about your daily routine. While you read, do your school work, and watch television, you can be thinking of possible careers.

You can also get some career ideas in the next few pages of this book. Spend some time reading through the general career information that follows. Don't rush through this material. Take your time and imagine yourself in many of these careers. As you explore and daydream about yourself in all kinds of jobs, list the careers that you want to learn more about.

Career Clusters

The U.S. Office of Education organized all jobs into fifteen career clusters. Each of the clusters is a group of careers that have certain things in common. Looking at these few clusters, rather than thousands of separate jobs, will make it easier for you to explore careers.

The fifteen clusters, and a few of the careers within each cluster, are listed below. Both your school library and the public library should have books that list hundreds of careers in each cluster.

- **Agriculture**—includes grain and dairy farmers, beekeepers, fruit harvesters, and others who work with plants and animals
- **Arts, Humanities, and Sciences**—includes librarians, teachers, editors, musicians, psychologists, chemists, and economists
- **Business and Office**—includes typists, accountants, computer programmers, secretaries, and general clerical workers
- **Communications and Media**—includes TV announcers, sound and video engineers, telegraph operators, line and instrument installers, and many other radio and TV careers
- **Construction**—includes architects, carpenters, building contractors, plumbers, and many others involved in the construction of buildings, roads, and bridges

Be on the lookout for career possibilities. You will notice people working at jobs you never knew existed. One of those jobs might be just the one for you.

- **Health**—includes physicians, nurses, dentists, veterinarians, medical assistants, medical technicians, and lab workers
- **Home Economics**—includes homemakers, dietitians, clothes designers, and nutritionists
- **Hospitality and Recreation**—includes restaurant and hotel managers and workers, athletic coaches and trainers, and airline flight attendants
- **Manufacturing**—includes mechanical and electrical engineers, tool designers, market analysts, and factory workers
- **Marine Science**—includes marine biologists and engineers, fish farmers, lab technicians, divers, and others who work with marine life and ocean resources
- **Marketing and Distribution**—includes sales and advertising managers, salesclerks, truck drivers, and others involved in selling and distributing goods
- **Natural Resources and Environment**—includes petroleum and mining engineers, miners, oilfield workers, foresters, loggers, and wildlife workers
- **Personal Services**—includes hairstylists, butlers, domestic workers, and funeral workers
- **Public Service**—includes fire fighters, police officers, street cleaners, probation officers, prison guards, and social service workers
- **Transportation**—includes airline pilots and mechanics, ship captains, bus and truck drivers, and others involved in transporting people and goods.

AGRICULTURE

ARTS, HUMANITIES, AND SCIENCES

BUSINESS AND OFFICE

COMMUNICATIONS AND MEDIA

HEALTH

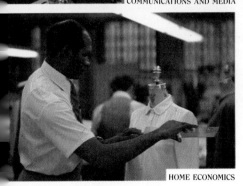

HOME ECONOMICS

CONSTRUCTION

HOSPITALITY AND RECREATION

MARINE SCIENCE

MARKETING AND DISTRIBUTI

MANUFACTURING

NATURAL RESOURCES
AND ENVIRONMENT

PERSONAL SERVICES

PUBLIC SERVICE

TRANSPORTATION

Do two or three of the clusters sound more interesting to you than the others? If so, find out more about the jobs in those clusters.

Several reference books with information about careers organize career information into these fifteen clusters.

Make a Decision

You just read about fifteen career clusters. Some of the clusters probably sound more interesting to you than others. Narrow the choices to your three favorites. Then use the decision-making strategy to choose the one cluster that sounds most appealing. What's your decision—which cluster would you most like to explore further? Give reasons for your decision.

Career Areas

Another way of grouping similar jobs for easier career exploration is to organize occupations by career interest areas. Each interest area is a category of jobs that are similar according to interests. This means that a person interested in one job in that area will probably be interested in the other jobs in that area. By learning about the general interest areas, you may get a better idea of the *kinds* of jobs that you would enjoy.

On each of the twelve pages beginning with page 31, you will read a brief description of one of the career interest areas. The skills and abilities most needed for jobs in that area are listed, along with some questions. The questions will help you decide whether or not you would be interested in this area of work.

This information on career areas is condensed from the *Guide for Occupational Exploration (GOE)*. If you need more information about a particular career area, refer to the *GOE*. The *Worker Trait Group Guide* (Bennett & McKnight, Peoria, IL) also has more detailed information on these interest areas.

ARTISTIC

Careers in the artistic interest area would give you a chance to express your creativity. The artistic area includes literary arts, visual arts, performing arts (drama, music, and dance), crafts, and modeling.

People who work in the literary arts like to write and edit (correct and improve). Some write plays, movie scripts, short stories, and novels. Others edit the work of creative writers to make the books and articles more interesting and easier to read.

Workers in the visual arts may paint portraits or landscapes, design scenery for plays, or sculpt statues. Others work as photographers, taking pictures for magazines, newspapers, and books.

People in the performing arts like to perform in front of others. They may act in plays, movies, or on TV. Others sing, play musical instruments, or dance.

Skills and Abilities Needed

Writers must be able to express themselves well with words. A good imagination is helpful for almost any kind of writing. Some writers must also be skilled at gathering and organizing information. Others must have a sense of humor or a great deal of knowledge about a certain subject.

Artists, photographers, and sculptors must understand and apply artistic techniques. They need to "see" how the final product will look from rough sketches. Of course they must be able to use their brushes, pens, or sculpturing tools with skill.

Actors and actresses must be able to express ideas and emotions through facial expression, voice inflection, and body motion. They also must be able to memorize lines, speak clearly, and perform with poise.

Most musicians must be able to read music. They also must be able to sing or play an instrument with skill. Dancers must move with grace and rhythm, coordinating body movements to the music and to the movements of other dancers. Singing, dancing, playing instruments—all of these occupations require a natural talent and usually many years of training.

Many people who work in performing arts are talented in all three areas: they act, sing or play a musical instrument, and dance. Modeling requires poise similar to that needed by an actor.

Is This Work For You?

- Have you written an original story, poem, or newspaper article?
- Can you create original characters and situations in stories and plays that entertain others?
- Have you taken courses in drawing or sketching? Was your work selected for display?
- Have you taken photographs of your family and friends, activities, or landscapes? Were they of good quality?
- Do you enjoy creating designs in clay?
- Have you performed in a play? Do you enjoy performing before an audience?
- Have you memorized long passages of poetry? Can you recite them before an audience?
- Have you spoken on radio or TV? Can you control your voice, and is it pleasing?
- Have you sung or played a musical instrument in school programs? Have you had lessons in singing or playing a musical instrument?
- Can you read music? Have you ever written a song?
- Have you taken dancing lessons? Have you performed as a dancer before an audience?
- Have you modeled for an artist or photographer?

SCIENTIFIC

The scientific area can be divided into four groups: physical sciences, life sciences, medical science, and laboratory technology. Workers in these careers discover, collect, and analyze information about the natural world. They solve problems in medicine, life sciences, and natural sciences.

People who work in the physical sciences may help solve pollution problems or study the causes of earthquakes. Some conduct experiments to develop new metals. Many use advanced math to solve very complex problems.

Workers in the life sciences may do research to find better ways of processing food. Others experiment with growing bacteria to learn about diseases.

People in the medical sciences are involved in the prevention, diagnosis, and treatment of disease. Laboratory technology workers perform tests in chemistry, biology, or physics.

Skills and Abilities Needed

Workers in the physical and life sciences must use logic and the scientific method to investigate many kinds of problems. They must be able to make decisions based on their own judgments or information that can be measured. Most need highly developed math skills.

People in the medical sciences must also use a great deal of logic and scientific reasoning to diagnose and treat injuries and illnesses. They must be able to deal with people or animals who are in pain or under stress. Great skill and accuracy in the use of eyes, hands, and fingers are all important.

Laboratory technology workers must understand and use scientific and technical language and symbols. This work requires great accuracy in conducting scientific tests.

Is This Work For You?

- Have you taken and enjoyed courses in earth science or astronomy?
- Have you collected rocks or minerals as a hobby? Can you recognize differences in ores and minerals?
- Have you owned a chemistry set or microscope? Do you like testing new ideas with this equipment?
- Have you taken courses in biology or zoology? Do you like conducting experiments with plants or animals?
- Have you studied plants in a garden, forest, or laboratory? Can you identify different kinds of plants?
- Have you had any first-aid training?
- Do you enjoy watching medical shows on TV? Can you understand the technical terms used?
- Can you skillfully handle small instruments, such as tweezers?
- Have you taken algebra or geometry? Can you read and understand charts and graphs?

PLANTS AND ANIMALS

Workers in the plants and animal area are involved primarily in farming, forestry, and fishing. The types of jobs included are management, supervision, planting and harvesting of crops, and the care and training of animals.

The people in management may plan and oversee the sale and shipment of farm crops or animals. Some study market trends to plan the type and quality of crops to plant. Others plan and direct projects for cutting timber and replanting forests.

Supervisors oversee workers who plant and harvest crops. The supervisors often work right along with the workers they're supervising. Many of these workers live and work in rural areas on farms, ranches, or forest preserves.

Among those who care for and train animals, some train horses for racing. Others feed, exercise, and groom pets. Some train and care for animals used in entertainment acts.

Skills and Abilities Needed

Managers must understand and apply procedures related to the kinds of work they are managing. For example, farm managers must understand the necessity of rotating crops so that the farm soil will stay fertile. Managers of cattle ranches must know how to feed cattle so that they can produce beef of prime quality. All managers must know how to keep accurate financial and production records.

Supervisors must understand and give directions well. They must get a clear picture of the work to be done from their manager, then pass the information along clearly to the workers they supervise. Many supervisors must demonstrate the use of tools and equipment to workers. Basic arithmetic skill is needed to keep records for workers.

Those involved in the care and training of animals must understand the habits and physical needs of the animals under their care. The ability to work quickly and skillfully with one's hands is necessary for many jobs. Typical tasks include trimming the nails of dogs and cats, fastening shoes to horses' hooves, or helping a veterinarian give shots to sick animals.

Is This Work For You?

- Have you raised or cared for an animal? Do you like the responsibility of caring for an animal?
- Have you taken care of a sick or injured animal? Can you tell if an animal is getting sick or better by the way it looks or acts?
- Have you raised plants? Would you like to take a course to learn more about how plants grow?
- Have you been a member of the FFA or 4-H? Did you complete any projects that required planning, budgeting, and record-keeping?
- Have you worked all day mowing lawns, planting or trimming trees, or picking fruit? Are you interested in supervising this kind of work?
- Do you like to camp, fish, or hunt? Would you like a full-time job doing these things?

PROTECTIVE

The protective career area includes workers in safety and law enforcement, and those in security services. Workers in these careers protect people and property. Most workers are employees of the federal, state, or local governments. Most work in departments such as the police department or fire department.

Careers in safety and law enforcement involve making sure that people obey laws and regulations. Some workers patrol certain areas, issue tickets, investigate disturbances, provide first aid, and arrest suspects. Others patrol an area to observe fishing or hunting activities and to warn or arrest persons violating fish and game laws. Some manage or supervise the work of others.

Those in security services protect people and animals from injury or danger. They may guard money and valuables being transported by an armored car. Some guard inmates and direct their activities in prison. Others respond to alarms to fight fires, give first aid, and protect property.

Skills and Abilities Needed

Safety and law enforcement workers must work well under pressure and in the face of danger. They must use guns, fire-fighting equipment, or other safety devices with skill. Investigators must be able to use practical thinking to conduct or supervise investigations.

Security workers must use reason and judgment in dealing with all kinds of people in different ways. They must think clearly and react quickly in emergencies. They must be willing to work in physically demanding and dangerous situations.

Is This Work For You?

- Do you enjoy watching television detective shows? When you read detective stories, do you try to solve the mysteries?
- Have you taken courses in government, civics, or criminology? Did you find these subjects interesting?
- Have you worked as a camp counselor or other group leader? Do you like helping people?
- Have you been a member of a volunteer fire or rescue squad? Can you stay calm in emergencies?
- Have you taken a first aid course? Can you treat injuries quickly and skillfully?

MECHANICAL

People who work in the mechanical career area apply mechanical principles to practical situations using machines and hand tools. There are several thousand different jobs in the mechanical area. People in engineering careers plan, design, and direct the construction of buildings, bridges, roads, airports, and dams. Workers in management careers manage industrial plants where technical work is done. Engineering technology workers collect and record technical information. Other workers operate vehicles such as airplanes, ships, trucks, vans, locomotives, or ambulances.

Craft technology workers do highly skilled hand or machine work, and systems operation workers operate and maintain equipment. Quality control workers inspect or test materials and products, while materials control workers receive, store, or ship them.

Crafts workers use their hands and hand tools skillfully to make or repair products. Equipment operation workers operate heavy machines or equipment.

Skills and Abilities Needed

Engineers must understand the principles of chemistry, geology, physics, and related sciences. They use involved and complex mathematics to solve complicated problems.

Management workers must plan and direct the work of others, either directly or through lower level supervisors. They must react quickly in emergency situations to make important decisions. These decisions often involve the safety of others and great amounts of money.

Engineering technology workers must use math to solve problems and clear language to write technical reports.

Pilots must coordinate the use of hands, feet, and eyes to control the ship or airplane. They must react quickly in emergencies and use judgment to make decisions that affect the lives of passengers.

Craft and craft technology workers must read blueprints or sketches and picture how a finished product will look.

Skills and abilities needed by many other workers in the mechanical area include good math skill, good judgment in making decisions, and skillful use of eyes, hands and fingers to operate or adjust equipment.

Is This Work For You?

- Have you taken algebra, geometry, and advanced math? Can you solve practical problems using math?
- Have you taken physics courses? Do you like to study energy and matter?
- Have you built or repaired a radio, TV, or amplifier? Do you understand electrical or electronic terms or drawings?
- Have you served as a leader in school activities? Have you directed the work of other students?
- Have you taken courses in mechanical drawing? Do you like this kind of activity?
- Do you like to read airplane or boat magazines? Do you like and understand technical articles?
- Have you made minor repairs around the house? Do you like working with your hands?
- Have you repaired or installed parts on an automobile? Do you like this work?

INDUSTRIAL

Industrial careers include production technology, production work, and quality control. Some industrial workers do skilled machine work to make products. Some set up machines and teach others to operate them. Others check the quality of products. Most industrial work is done in factories.

Production technology workers set up production machines and make sure they are operating correctly. They may use precision measuring devices to find defects in the production process. Production workers set up and use many kinds of machines. Some make paper or plastic products, others make products from metal. Other workers use power screwdrivers or riveting machines to fasten the parts of a product together. Quality control workers check products for defects.

Skills and Abilities Needed

Most industrial workers need basic math skills for measuring, planning schedules, and keeping production records. Production technology workers must be able to read and understand blueprints. This is required for setting up and adjusting machines and equipment. Production workers must read and follow instructions on setting up machines and equipment. An important skill in many factories is detecting differences in the shape, size, and texture of materials. Many industrial workers must adjust to doing the same thing over and over according to a set procedure.

Is This Work For You?

- Have you taken industrial arts or machine shop courses? Did you learn to use measuring devices, such as gauges and micrometers? Do you like to set up machines according to written standards?
- Have you taken general or applied math courses? Do you like subjects that use math skills, such as measuring?
- Have you assembled a bicycle or toy by following drawings or written instructions? Did you have a fairly easy time doing this?
- Have you held a part-time job where mechanical equipment was used? Do you like working around mechanical equipment?
- Have you sorted paper, metal, or glass for recycling? Were you able to tell the difference between similar types of materials?
- Would you like to work in a factory?

BUSINESS DETAIL

Workers in the business detail area perform clearly defined activities requiring accuracy and attention to details. Most work is done in an office setting.

Administrative workers may prepare correspondence and keep records for a company. Some organize and oversee clerical operations in an office. Jobs in this group are found in offices of businesses, industries, doctors, lawyers, and other professionals.

Workers dealing with mathematical detail often use a calculator to compute answers and keep records. Some compute wages for payroll records, while others compute the cost of labor and materials for production records. Jobs in this group are found wherever record keeping is important. Many of the jobs are in banks, finance companies, accounting firms, or the payroll and inventory control departments of businesses and government.

Those in financial detail may compute payments and interest on loans. Some operate cash registers in grocery stores. Others record bids for items and collect deposits at auctions. Jobs in this group are found wherever money is paid to or received from the public.

Workers in oral communications may operate a telephone switchboard or register guests in a hotel. Others receive callers at an office and direct them to the proper area. Some interview people and compile information for surveys. Other business detail workers sort and deliver mail, take dictation, and type letters and reports. Some workers operate checkwriting or billing machines. These jobs are found in private businesses, schools, hospitals, and government agencies.

Skills and Abilities Needed

Business detail workers must get along well with all kinds of people. They must be able to change work activities often, but also be able to keep doing the same thing for hours at a time. The ability to speak clearly is important in most jobs involving business detail.

Administrative detail workers must follow instructions without close supervision. Those in mathematical detail work must use a calculator, record numbers correctly, and follow procedures for keeping records. Financial detail workers must use math to figure the cost of things and make change. Workers in oral communications must speak clearly and listen carefully.

Is This Work For You?

- Have you taken courses in business math and typing? Is your work accurate?
- Have you taken courses in bookkeeping or accounting? Do you like working with numbers?
- Have you balanced a checking account or figured interest rates? Are you able to spot errors quickly?
- Have you been in charge of records for a club or social group? Do you like organizing files?
- Have you worked part-time in an office? Did you enjoy this work?
- Have you sold tickets, candy, or other items? Can you make change rapidly and accurately?
- Have you given directions to others for finding your home? Were they able to follow your directions?

SELLING

Workers in the selling career area sell products or services. Some spend all of their time in a single location, such as a department store or an automobile agency. Others travel regularly, calling on businesses or individuals in many different locations. Some workers in this group are known as *vendors*. Vendors work at stadiums, street fairs, restaurants, or wherever crowds gather for entertainment or recreation.

People in sales technology may call on businesses to sell radio or TV advertising time. Others sell computers or professional supplies to dentists, doctors, or engineers.

Those in general sales may call people on the telephone to sell products. But most of the people in this area work in retail stores selling clothing, sporting goods, jewelry, furniture, and household appliances. An auctioneer sells goods to the highest bidder at an auction. Vendors may sell popcorn, peanuts, sandwiches, and drinks.

Skills and Abilities Needed

People involved in selling must be able to express themselves well. Salespersons must keep up their enthusiasm in all meetings with buyers. They must persuade others to make decisions to buy, and this often means helping customers make up their minds. While doing this, customers must be treated with courtesy and respect, even in difficult situations. Salespeople must also be able to keep up their confidence when many potential buyers decide not to buy.

Those involved in selling must also have a thorough understanding of the product or service that they are selling. Customers won't buy from a salesperson who doesn't seem to know much about the product or service being offered.

Basic math skills are needed to compute markup of prices, cost of installing equipment, or quoting special rates on large sales. Accurate records must be kept on contracts, sales, and purchases.

Those in vending jobs may need to be able to speak clearly and loudly, perhaps singing or calling out to attract attention. They may need to stand or walk for long periods at a time. They must often climb stairs or push through crowds while carrying heavy containers or pushing a cart.

Is This Work For You?

- Have you taken sales-related courses? Did you enjoy them?
- Have you sold things to raise money for a school or civic project? Do you like this activity?
- Have you attended auctions? Can you guess, in advance, the selling prices of items?
- Have you made speeches or been in debates? Do you like presenting ideas to people?
- Have you worked as a salesperson in a store? Do you enjoy sales work?
- Have you taken basic math courses? Can you compute percentages in your head?

ACCOMMODATING

Workers in the accommodating group attend to the wishes of others, usually on a one-to-one basis. Everyone in this group provides a service. Some provide hospitality, barber, and beauty services. Others provide passenger, customer, and attendant services.

Hospitality workers may greet guests and answer questions about social and recreational activities in a hotel. Some greet and seat customers in a restaurant. Others provide personal services to airplane passengers, such as answering questions or serving meals.

Those in barber and beauty services may cut, trim, shampoo, curl, or style hair. Some give hair and scalp-conditioning treatments or facial treatments. Some clean, shape, and polish fingernails.

Others in this cluster may serve meals to customers in a restaurant, work as chauffeurs, or carry baggage.

Skills and Abilities Needed

Everyone who works in this cluster must be able to get along well with all kinds of people. Those in hospitality need to speak clearly and put others at ease. Workers in barber and beauty services must understand written instructions for applying hair coloring and permanent waving solutions. They must use a variety of tools, such as scissors, tweezers, combs, curlers, and hair blowers.

Those in passenger services must read maps to locate addresses and select the best routes. They must judge distances and speeds to avoid accidents. Customer service workers must talk with different kinds of people to find out what services they want or to provide them with the information they want.

The ability to move fingers and hands easily and quickly to handle dishes, money, and merchandise is important in many jobs.

Some attendant services require lifting and carrying things such as luggage, trays of dishes, and bags of golf clubs. Many of these jobs require one to do the same task over and over, often in the same way.

Is This Work For You?

- Have you taken courses in speech? Do you like to speak to groups?
- Have you planned or organized a party? Can you lead others in games and group activities?
- Have you cut someone's hair? Do you style your own hair? Do you like to try new and different hair styles?
- Have you applied theatrical make-up? Do you enjoy changing the appearance of others?
- Have you worked at a health spa or athletic club? Do you enjoy helping others?
- Have you driven a vehicle in heavy traffic? Did you stay calm?
- Have you given directions to anyone who was lost? Did you make the directions clear?
- Have you served food or beverage at a party? Can you do this without spilling or dropping things?
- Have you collected tickets or ushered at a play? Do you remain courteous when others are rude to you?
- Have you had a part-time job as a waiter or waitress in a local restaurant? Did you enjoy waiting on people?

˙HUMANITARIAN

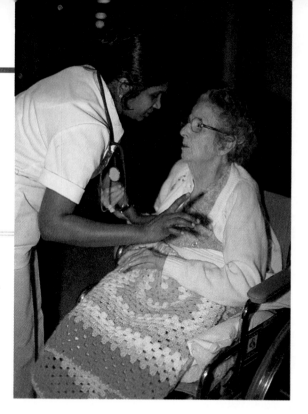

Workers in the humanitarian career area help people with mental, spiritual, social, physical, or vocational concerns. They provide social services, nursing care, and therapy. Some do specialized teaching, and others care for children and adults who need special care.

Social service workers help people deal with their problems. They may help people overcome emotional or social problems. Some of these workers help prison parolees find jobs and adjust to society, and others help parents with child-rearing problems. Some help people with educational and career plans. Many social service jobs are in schools, mental health clinics, guidance centers, welfare offices, and churches.

People in nursing may provide general nursing care to patients in a hospital. They may give medications to patients as prescribed by a doctor. Some plan and carry out school health programs. Therapy workers may direct and help patients in physical therapy exercises. Others train the physically handicapped in daily routines, such as grooming, dressing, and using the telephone. Many of these jobs are in hospitals, nursing homes, and rehabilitation centers.

Child and adult care workers help the elderly, the very young, and the handicapped. These workers may help elderly persons bathe, feed, or dress themselves. Some use electronic equipment to collect medical data. Others entertain and supervise children in a nursery. Many of these jobs are in hospitals, clinics, schools, day care centers, and private homes.

Skills and Abilities Needed

Social service workers must care a great deal about people, their needs, and their welfare. These workers must be sincere and honest enough to gain the confidence of those they are trying to help. Counselors must use logical thinking to help others define and solve personal problems.

People in nursing careers must follow instructions exactly and record information accurately. Many need special medical skills to care for or treat sick or handicapped people. Those in nursing and therapy, and those who care for children and adults, must work fast in emergencies.

Is This Work For You?

- Have friends come to you for advice or help with personal problems? Did you help them?
- Have you taken courses in psychology, sociology, or other social sciences? Do you like to study human behavior?
- Have you worked as an aide in a hospital, day care center, or nursing home? Do you like helping people who are ill or injured?
- Have you taken a first-aid course? Do you remember actions you should take in an emergency?

LEADING-INFLUENCING

People who work in leading-influencing careers influence others with their high-level verbal or numerical abilities. These careers include jobs in education, law, business administration, finance, and social research. There are also jobs in math and statistics, communication, promotion, and many related careers.

Workers may use advanced math and statistics to solve problems or conduct research. Some design or write computer programs. Others teach in public or private schools.

Social research workers study human behavior. They may analyze information on jobs or interpret information on economic conditions. Others research the mental development of people.

Those in law careers advise and represent persons in legal matters. They may represent clients who are suing or being sued for money or legal action. Some prepare wills, deeds, and other legal documents. Lawyers are often elected to public office.

Business administrators direct activities in private companies or government agencies. Those in services administration manage programs and projects in health, education, welfare, and recreation.

Communication workers write, edit, and report facts. Most of these jobs are with radio or TV stations, newspapers, and publishing firms. Promotion workers raise funds, advertise products and services, and influence people in their actions.

Skills and Abilities Needed

All workers in the leading-influencing area must be able to speak and write clearly. Good language and math skills are needed to analyze and interpret information. Those dealing with math and statistics use advanced logic and scientific thinking to solve complex problems. More and more, they must be able to use computer technology.

People in education must understand and use basic principles of effective teaching. Social research workers use various theories and methods of research, then organize research notes and write reports and findings. Those in law careers must understand, interpret, and apply legal principles and laws.

Those in business and finance must interpret statistics and financial reports. Many need to understand and use computers. Administrators must think logically to make good decisions.

Communication workers must use words that give readers and listeners a clear picture. The ability to speak clearly and easily is especially important.

Is This Work For You?

- Have you taken courses in advanced math? Do you like solving difficult problems?
- Have you had experience using a calculator? Can you use many of the functions?
- Have you helped friends or relatives with homework? Can you explain things well?
- Have you done research projects or surveys? Do you enjoy these activities?
- Have you taken debate or speech courses? Do you feel at ease presenting a point of view in front of a group?
- Have you supervised activities of others? Were their jobs done well?
- Have you been a treasurer of a school or community group? Can you keep accurate financial records?
- Have you worked on a school newspaper? Can you report events accurately?
- Have you worked for a political campaign? Can you understand and influence the public?

PHYSICAL PERFORMING

Workers in the physical performing area either participate in sports or perform physical feats. Those in sports may play on professional teams, coach players, or officiate at games. Some instruct or recruit players. Others regulate sporting events. Most of these jobs are in football, baseball, basketball, hockey, golf, tennis, or horse racing. Most players practice five or six days a week for about six to nine months a year. Football games are played once a week during a season of about five months. Baseball and basketball games are played several times each week. Golf and tennis events are on a less regular basis. Horse racing is daily, four to six days a week during the season. Jockeys may ride in several races each day.

Workers who perform physical feats often work in circuses, carnivals, theaters, and amusement parks. Some show their gymnastic skill on a high wire or trapeze to entertain audiences. Some juggle and balance things, such as balls, knives, or plates. Others perform acrobatic stunts on a horse in a circus. Stunt performers are also used in movies and TV shows.

Skills and Abilities Needed

Professional athletes and those performing physical feats need exceptional eye, hand, and body coordination. In most sports, superior speed and strength are needed. The ability to judge distance, speed, and movement of objects or people is important, too. Of course all athletes must have the highly developed skills needed for the particular game they play. Coaches and umpires must understand the rules of the game. Some jobs in this career area, such as jobs involved with regulating sports events, do not require athletic skills.

Is This Work For You?

- Have you competed in sports? Do you know the rules of any sport well enough to be a referee, judge, or umpire?
- Have you been an umpire or official in informal games? Can you make decisions quickly and firmly?
- Have you coached a team or individual in athletic events? Were you effective?
- Have you competed against others in athletic events? Do you remain calm and alert during competition?
- Have you won any special sports events? Do you excel in any athletic skill?
- Have you performed stunts that required daring and skill? Do you perform them without great fear?
- Have you had a hobby or specialty act such as juggling, acrobatics, or wire walking? Do you perform well before an audience?

What To Research

You should now have a list of careers that you think you might enjoy. You are ready to research these careers thoroughly. But before you start, think about what you'll be looking for. What things will you want to find out for each career?

Below is a list of nine factors to consider as you do your research. Use this list as a checklist for each career you research. Try to gather information on each of these factors for each career. This will help you compare careers and make a wise career decision. Here are the nine factors to consider.

- Values
- Duties and responsibilities
- Working environment
- Working hours
- Aptitudes and abilities
- Education and training
- Data—people—things
- Salaries and fringe benefits
- Career outlook

Values

Some careers require the people entering them to hold certain values. For example, the pastor of a church would need to place religion high on a list of personal values. An artist would have to rank creativity high, while a politician would probably need to feel that power is an important value. Unless you have certain values, success in some careers is unlikely.

In Chapter 2 you considered your own values. When you research a career, think about whether or not that career requires certain values. Then decide how well the values related to that career will match up with your own values.

Duties and Responsibilities

Duties and responsibilities are different for every job. One job may involve lots of lifting, pushing, and pulling, but no responsibility for the work of others. Another job might involve continual supervising and management of lower-level workers,

with almost no physical activity. The number of different duties and responsibilities is almost limitless.

You will find that some work activities would actually be fun. Others would be okay, some would be boring, and some you would dislike very much. If you're going to spend as much as two thousand hours a year at work, it's worth the time it takes to choose carefully—and pick a job you will enjoy doing.

Working Environment

Closely related to work activities is the working environment. The working environment is made up of the working conditions, such as the sounds, smells, sights, and temperature surrounding the worker. The environment also includes the physical demands placed on the worker.

You will want to find out about the working environment and the duties and responsibilities for each career you research. During your research you will see workers engaged in a wide variety of activities, in a wide variety of environments.

A major factor in determining working environment is whether the work is done indoors or outdoors. A lot of people don't like to be confined indoors during their working hours. They prefer to work in the sun and fresh air.

Do you like to spend a lot of time outdoors? Do you plan to live in an area that is very hot in the summer and cold in the winter? If so, you may prefer indoor work, where the temperature is controlled.

There are several questions to keep in mind about the working environment. Is the work done mainly indoors or outdoors? Is it done sitting down or standing up? Will you have to endure extremes of heat and cold? And perhaps most important, is the work environment dangerous in any way? If so, you must decide whether or not any extra pay would make working in a dangerous environment worthwhile to you.

Working Hours

The average work week is about forty hours. The most common working hours are from eight to five, Monday through Friday. Some jobs, though, require less than eight hours of work a day. A short workday is sometimes referred to as *banker's hours* because banks used to close early in the afternoon. (Actually, most bank employees work several hours after closing time.)

Other jobs require many more than eight hours of work in a day, and many require working on weekends. For example, most retail stores are open on Saturday, and many are open on Sunday. This means that many salespeople must work on weekends. These people usually get a day off during the week, but in some cases they may work more than forty hours.

Some jobs require working nights. For example, hospitals must be staffed through the night—so some nurses work from three in the afternoon until eleven at night. When they leave, the next shift comes on duty and works until seven the next morning. Many factories also employ people to work night shifts.

Do you have a preference for which hours, and how many, you will work? As you research each career, find out the usual hours of work.

Aptitudes and Abilities

You already know that it takes more than an interest to succeed in a career. Each career has its own set of required skills. In most careers, workers need many different skills.

Some skills are easy to learn, but others take a long time to develop. It takes years to learn the diagnostic skills needed to be a medical doctor. The math skills required of an engineer also take years to develop. As you know, skills and abilities, for any kind of work, are more easily learned if you have an aptitude for learning them.

In Chapter 2 you analyzed your own aptitudes and abilities. As you do your research, find out which aptitudes and abilities are needed for each career. You can then match your natural talents with careers that require those same skills and abilities.

Education and Training

Different careers require different kinds and levels of education and training. You will need to know the minimum requirements for each career. Depending on the career, this could mean a grade school, high school, or college education. It could mean two years of training at a business, technical, or community college or school.

Be sure to find out how much education and training is required for each career that you research. You wouldn't want to choose a career requiring five or six years of college unless you were willing to spend lots of time studying.

You may have already decided that you do not want to continue schooling of any kind after you leave high school. If so, you need to find out the educational requirements for each career you research so that you can eliminate those careers that require additional education.

If you haven't made any educational decisions, your research will help you. You may find a career that you think would be just right for you. If that career requires a college education, you will know what you need to do to pursue that career. You will read more about the importance of education and training in the next chapter.

Data-People-Things Relationships

You have thought about whether you would prefer working with data, people, or things. Of course almost every job requires that you get along with people. Some jobs, such as sales jobs, require working with *lots* of people—some of them complete strangers. For such careers, you would need a strong people preference. Other careers require more interest in working with data or things.

As you read in Chapter 2, the *Dictionary of Occupational Titles* is a good source of information on data-people-things functions for thousands of jobs. Your teacher or librarian can help you find the data-people-things ratings in this book.

Salaries and Fringe Benefits

One of the main reasons for working is to support your chosen lifestyle. You will want to check the average salary for each career that seems interesting to you. Don't make the mistake of looking at just the beginning salary. Find out how much the people earn who have been working in that career for five, ten, or fifteen years. Are they earning a lot more than beginning workers? It is important to find out what kind of salary increases you can expect.

In a few years you may have a family to support. Would you be able to support a family with the income from this career? Since most beginning workers don't have to support a family, they sometimes forget to look at the earnings of those who do.

Fringe benefits are the "extras" provided by many employers. They include such things as paid vacations, health and life insurance, bonuses, and retirement plans. Some careers offer more fringe benefits than others.

As with pay increases, fringe benefits will become more and more important as you get older. A retirement plan may be the farthest thing from your mind now, but you will soon be very interested in such plans. Health insurance is also an extremely important concern, especially if health costs continue to rise. A company that offers lots of fringe benefits is often preferable to one that offers a high starting salary and no benefits.

Both Paula and Bob continued working after they were married. They both had good jobs, and together they earned enough for a very comfortable lifestyle.

After Paula and Bob had been married for two years, Paula learned that she was pregnant. Six months later she quit her job. Bob and Paula soon realized that it would be very hard to live on just one salary. But by watching their money very carefully, they were able to get by for a while.

Paula knew she would have to go back to work soon after the baby was born. She wanted to stay home with the baby, but she had no choice. Bob's salary alone would not be enough for the three of them.

Keep your lifestyle goals in mind as you research careers. Do you like to do things that cost a lot of money? If so, make sure you choose a career that pays well. And remember—fringe benefits will become more and more important as you get older and begin supporting a family.

Make a Decision

Lots of people just go out and look for any job and take the first one they get. Other people do some exploring, get to know themselves better, and research the careers they think they might like. Career exploration and research take time and effort. It's much easier to just take the first job that comes along. Unfortunately, the chances of finding a job that you really enjoy are greatly reduced without career research. What's your decision—will you do some research or take whatever job comes along? Give reasons for your decision.

Career Outlook

Suppose you find a career that you think you would enjoy. Suppose this career pays well and that it fits with your data-people-things preferences. There's only one problem with this career—there aren't many jobs available.

The long-term outlook for a career is very important. If the outlook is poor, there probably won't be many jobs available. You might have to move a long way from home to get a job. You certainly don't want to spend lots of time and money on education for a career that may not exist.

Check the outlook for each career you research. You probably won't want to choose a career if the outlook for jobs is too limited.

How To Research

Researching careers means carefully gathering and studying information about several different careers. There are three main sources of career information. To do the best job of career research, you will need to make use of all three sources.

- **Libraries**—Carefully check all books, pamphlets, magazines, directories, films, computerized guidance systems, and video cassettes available in your school and public libraries.
- **Career consultations**—Talk directly with workers in various careers.
- **Work**—Work at jobs in the career areas that appeal to you. This is the most effective way to do your research.

Occupation	Growth Rate	New Jobs
Computer service technicians	97%	53,000
Legal assistants	94	43,000
Computer systems analyst	85	217,000
Computer programmers	77	205,000
Computer operators	76	160,000
Office machine repairers	72	40,000
Physical therapy assistants	68	26,000
Electrical engineers	65	209,000
Civil engineering technicians	64	23,000
Peripheral electronic data-processing equipment operators	64	31,000
Insurance clerks, medical	62	53,000
Electrical and electronics technicians	61	222,000
Occupational therapists	60	15,000
Surveyor helpers	59	23,000
Credit clerks, banking and insurance	54	27,000
Physical therapists	54	25,000
Employment interviewers	53	30,000
Mechanical engineers	52	109,000
Mechanical engineering technicians	52	25,000
Compression and injection mold machine operators, plastics	50	47,000

Some experts have predicted that the twenty occupations listed above will be the fastest growing occupations in the years from 1982-1995. Although growing rapidly, these occupations still make up only a small part of the total labor force.

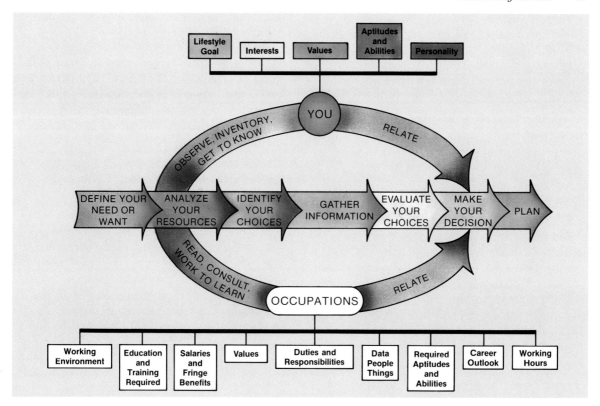

Libraries

It is easier to research careers now than ever before. More information on careers has been printed in the last ten years than in the previous three hundred.

Your school and public libraries are both excellent sources of career information. Some school libraries have a special section devoted entirely to career information. These sections are often called *Career Information Centers.*

If your school has a career information center, that is the place to start your research. If there is no career center, start with the library's card catalog (your library may have a microfilm reader or data bank in place of a card catalog).

Books. Looking up *careers* in the card catalog will give you a list of all the available books on careers. If you want information on a particular career area, such as business, science, or engineering, look up that topic in the catalog.

The U.S. Department of Labor publishes three books that will be especially helpful in your career research. These three books are the *Dictionary of Occupational Titles,* the *Occupational Outlook Handbook,* and the *Guide for Occupational Exploration.* Most school and public libraries will have these books.

The *Dictionary of Occupational Titles (DOT)* describes the work activities of more than 20,000 jobs. Although it contains a lot of information, the *DOT* is well organized and easy to use. Simply look up the name of the job you want to research in the alphabetical index of occupational titles. There you will find a nine-digit code number for that job. You can then turn to the front section of the book and find the job description you want.

It's a good idea to write down the *DOT* numbers for the jobs you are researching. The reason for this is that many other sources of information use the *DOT* numbers to organize their information.

The *Occupational Outlook Handbook (OOH)* is one of the most helpful resources available for career information. Updated every two years, the *OOH* provides information on more than two hundred occupations. The *OOH* provides detailed, accurate information about

- how much education and training are required,
- usual hours of work,
- working conditions,
- expected earnings,
- job outlook, and
- sources of additional information.

You should know that such things as salaries and job outlooks change from time to time. When you use the *OOH,* try to get the most recent edition. Don't waste your time gathering old information.

A supplement to the *OOH,* the *Occupational Outlook Quarterly,* is published four times a year. The *Quarterly* is probably the most up-to-date source of information on the latest employment trends.

The *Guide for Occupational Exploration (GOE)* is organized into twelve interest groups. Each group is further divided into subgroups called *worker trait groups.* Each worker trait group (there are sixty-six in all) has descriptive information, a listing of jobs within the group, and answers to questions about

- the kind of work done,
- skills and abilities needed,
- interests and aptitudes, and
- how to prepare for this kind of work.

The twelve career areas described on pages 31—42 are the twelve areas used to organize the *GOE.*

Magazines. Since most magazines are published weekly and monthly, magazine articles provide the most up-to-date information on careers. Use the *Reader's Guide to Periodical Literature* to find ar-

---

Millions of musical instruments already are in use and the number will increase as the population grows and as people have more leisure time. The large number of instruments in use will assure a demand for repair work. However, opportunities for untrained workers in these occupations are few. Most music store owners and self-employed tuners and repairers are reluctant to train persons who do not have at least a basic understanding of instrument repair. Training such people requires time that could be more profitably spent doing tuning or repair work. Individuals with some familiarity of the trade may find it easier to get a trainee job.

Because musical instrument tuning and repair are a luxury for most consumers, these occupations are sensitive to the downturns in the economy. During poor economic conditions, tuners and repairers may lose income because their customers put off tuning and repairing instruments. People wishing to enter the trade usually find music store owners and self-employed repairers and technicians especially reluctant to hire trainees when business is slow.

Earnings

Median annual earnings of most musical instrument repairers were $14,500 in 1982; the mid-

Office Machine Repairers

(D.O.T. 633, 706.381-010 and -030)

Nature of the Work

Office or business machine repairers maintain and repair the machines that are used to process paperwork in business and government. These machines include typewriters, adding and calculating machines, cash registers, dictating machines, postage meters, and duplicating and copying equipment. (Computer service technicians, who work on data processing equipment, are discussed in a separate statement elsewhere in the *Handbook.*)

Office machine repairers (often called field engineers, customer engineers, or service technicians) make regular visits for preventive maintenance to the offices and stores of customers in their assigned area. The frequency of these service calls depends upon the type of equipment being serviced. For example, an electric typewriter may require preventive maintenance only three or four times a year, while a complex copier probably may require more frequent attention. During these calls, the engineer inspects the machine for unusual wear and replaces any worn or broken parts. Then the machine is cleaned, oiled, and adjusted.

isolated, repairs can be made. Minor repairs generally can be made on the spot since most repairers carry a complete line of repair parts; more serious repairs, however, may require that a component or the entire machine be taken to the repair shop.

Office machine repairers generally specialize in one type of machine. Those employed by manufacturing companies or dealers usually are familiar only with the brand produced or sold by their employer. Repairers who work for small independent repair shops must be able to work on equipment from several different manufacturers.

Repairers use common handtools, such as screwdrivers, pliers, and wrenches, as well as other tools especially designed to fit certain kinds of business machines. In addition, they use meters, oscilloscopes, and other types of test equipment to check for malfunctions in electronic circuits.

Working Conditions

Servicing office machines is cleaner and less strenuous than the work in most other mechanical trades. Repairers generally wear business clothes and do most of their work in the customer's office.

Workers travel a great deal because they usually visit a number of customers each workday.

One of the most useful books in your career research will be the *Occupational Outlook Handbook.* The OOH, as it is called, is revised every two years. Make sure you're reading the most recent edition. The world of work is constantly changing.

ticles on careers you want to research. The *Reader's Guide* is an index of major magazines and journal articles. It is available in either book form or on microfilm. Articles are listed alphabetically by subject.

Files. Many libraries and career information centers also have pamphlet files. These files store pieces of information other than books and magazines. Occupational briefs, brief summaries of specific jobs, are examples of the kind of information you can find in a file on a certain career.

The information in these files is usually indexed in the card catalog. If you're not sure where the files are located or how to use them, ask your librarian for help.

Audiovisuals. Most libraries and career centers also have a collection of audiovisual materials. Audiovisuals are all the things you watch and listen to, such as films, slide presentations, listening cassettes, and videotapes. Chances are your library has some filmstrips and films that tell and show you what it's like to work in certain careers.

Check with your librarian to find out what audiovisuals are available. Once you know where the materials are located and how to operate the equipment, you will be able to research careers as you have time. It is often helpful to follow up your reading with a visual presentation of a certain career.

Career Consultations

A career consultation is a meeting with someone in a certain career to obtain information about that career. You can learn a great deal about a career by talking to someone who has worked in that career area for many years.

Computerized Guidance Systems. Your school library may have a computerized career guidance system. Most computerized systems help you determine your career interests and provide you with lists of suitable careers. Many systems also provide up-to-date information on such topics as salaries, duties, job outlook, and educational institutions. Be sure to ask your librarian about computerized career information.

After you have researched several careers, arrange career consultations for the two or three careers that seem most interesting to you. If possible, meet at the place where the person works. This will help you get a first-hand feel for the working environment. You may get an opportunity to watch people doing their work.

What questions should you ask? You want to learn all you can about the demands and rewards of that career. The list on page 53 will serve as a checklist for the types of questions you should ask.

Next to actually working, a career consultation is the best way to learn about careers. Most successful people are happy to talk about their work. Ask your teacher, counselor, or work experience coordinator to help you. They can probably suggest names of successful people who will talk with you about careers that interest you.

Part-Time Work

The best way to learn about a career is by working on a part-time job. You can work during the summer, after school, or on weekends. Your job should be one that you can do well and that you find interesting. It should give you an opportunity to observe other jobs in that career area. Most part-time jobs provide the following benefits.

A career consultation with someone who has been successful in a certain career is a good way to learn about the demands and opportunities of that career.

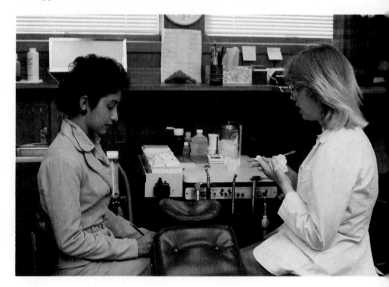

- An opportunity to explore careers that interest you and decide whether or not they are right for you
- A chance to broaden your understanding of the working world
- A good time to develop work habits that will help you succeed in a full-time job
- A way to make the transition from student to full-time worker more easily

Working part-time, you will be able to see the difference in work environments. You will be able to try a variety of work activities. Summer and after-school jobs can lead in many directions —depending on your interests, aptitudes, and personality.

Between their junior and senior years in high school, Alan and Lisa began working at Charter Motor Company, a local garage and service station. They were hired as service-station attendants and worked full time until school began in the fall. They pumped gas, cleaned windshields, and checked tire pressure. They made change for cash customers and wrote out credit slips for credit customers. When there were no gasoline customers, they helped the shop mechanics. Alan and Lisa made minor repairs, installed fan belts and batteries, and sometimes helped with oil changes and tune-ups.

At the end of the summer, Alan and Lisa went back to school. A full-time worker replaced them during school hours. But Alan and Lisa continued working part-time after school.

By this time Alan knew that he didn't care much for the direct contact with customers. He preferred helping the mechanics, and he mentioned this to his boss. Because there was an increase in the repair business, Alan became an assistant to one of the shop mechanics.

Lisa liked the contact with customers more than any other part of her job. She enjoyed talking with them, and soon she was selling them tires, batteries, and other accessories.

After graduating, Alan stayed with Charter Motor Company as a full-time mechanic. Lisa began a sales training program. She worked for the oil company that supplied Charter.

Lisa and Alan started with the same part-time job. Through this job they both learned what sorts of work activities they liked and disliked. This self-discovery feature of part-time jobs is often more valuable than the money they bring in.

Work Experience Programs. Does your school have a work experience or career development program? Such a program can help you select realistic career goals and find part-time work related to these goals. The programs are known by several names. They may be called *Cooperative Education, Cooperative Work Experience, Work Study,* or *Diversified Occupations,* just to name a few.

Many of the vocational work experience programs are called *cooperative* programs because of the cooperation that goes on between the school and employers. A teacher-coordinator teaches a class related to the job and supervises the students on their jobs. Employers pay students at least the minimum wage, and the school usually grants credits for time spent on the job.

Probably the most common type of work experience program is the *vocational* program. Vocational work experience provides specific career preparation. Students in vocational programs get jobs related to the careers they are preparing for in school.

Make a Decision

Suppose you work after school and on Saturdays in a fast-food restaurant. You earn a few cents more than the minimum wage. One day your work experience coordinator comes to you and asks you if you would like to "explore"—on a non-paid basis—exactly the kind of work that you have been wanting to try. Unfortunately, the exploratory job is at the same hours you've been working at the restaurant. What's your decision—will you keep your paying job or take the exploratory work experience? Give reasons for your decision.

You wouldn't buy a car without trying it out. The best way to try out a career is with a part-time job, while you are still in school. Your school probably has several programs that make it possible for students to work and attend school at the same time.

Another common type of work experience program is *general* work experience. General work experience provides useful experiences for young people through school-supervised, part-time employment. This work does not need to be related to a specific career goal. It is part of the total school program.

Students successfully completing a general work experience program receive school credits. These students are also paid the minimum wage. The program's goals are to develop desirable attitudes and to help students see the relationship between their schooling and job success.

A third type of work experience program is the *exploratory* program. Exploratory programs provide students with an opportunity to try several different kinds of jobs. In most of these programs students receive credits but no pay.

While the lack of pay is a disadvantage, there are some advantages to jobs in exploratory programs. The main advantage is that there are more kinds of work experiences available in exploratory programs. In exploratory jobs you can try out work activities in careers not available on a paying basis. Another advantage is that when employers are not paying you, they are more willing to take the time to show you a greater variety of jobs. You will get more chances to talk to different kinds of workers and to "explore" the work environment.

Volunteer Work. If you can't get a part-time job through a school program, you might try volunteer work. Most areas offer many chances to do volunteer work. You can volunteer at hospitals, the American Red Cross, schools, YMCA/YWCA, and humane societies. Your counselor or work experience coordinator can probably refer you to organizations that need volunteer help.

Many schools give credits for volunteer work done through a work experience program. Most volunteer work involves office, health, recreation, or education jobs. Some examples are listed below.

- **Office jobs**—bookkeeper, receptionist, typist, and switchboard operator
- **Health career jobs**—animal caretaker, blood-pressure screener, candy striper or junior volunteer, first-aid instructor, laboratory aide, and x-ray aide
- **Recreation jobs**—camp counselor, crafts instructor, dance teacher, and referee/umpire
- **Education jobs**—teacher aide and tutor

Working On Your Own. Even without a work experience program or the possibility of volunteer work, you may still find part-time work. You could go into business for yourself. Many people are willing to pay students to wash cars, paint walls, weed lawns, or any number of other jobs that need doing.

If you are interested in starting your own business, be sure to read Chapter 14. This chapter explains many of the things a person needs to know about starting a business.

REVIEW YOUR LEARNING

CHAPTER SUMMARY

The third and fourth steps in career decision-making are to identify some careers that interest you and then to explore those careers. If you don't have any career ideas of your own, exploring the U.S. Office of Education's Career Clusters or the Department of Labor's Career Interest Areas are good ways to find some careers that you might enjoy.

In researching careers you must find out many things about each career. For each career you must learn how much education and training required; what aptitudes and abilities are needed; whether the work is primarily with data, people, or things; and much, much more.

There are several effective ways to research careers. You learn a lot by reading the many books, magazines, and pamphlets at your school and local library. You can also learn about specific careers by conducting career consultations with people who have been successful in those careers. The best way to research a career, though, is to get a part-time job in that career.

WORDS YOU SHOULD KNOW

career clusters
career consultation
career interest area
fringe benefits

STUDY QUESTIONS

1. Why should you research several careers?
2. Where are at least two places you can get career ideas in your day-to-day living?
3. What are two methods of organizing career information as developed by government offices?
4. Name at least three occupations in the same career cluster as the occupation of tool designer.
5. According to what factor are all jobs in a career interest area similar?
6. If creativity is one of your values and one of your abilities, what career interest area might you want to explore?
7. If you enjoy watching television detective shows, what career area might you be interested in?
8. Name at least three things a person must be able to do to be successful at selling.
9. If you value helping other people more than any other activity, which career area should you be sure to explore?
10. What nine factors should you consider for each career that you research?
11. What are four types of fringe benefits?

REVIEW YOUR LEARNING

12. What are the three major sources of career information?
13. What is the best way to learn about a career?
14. Name four types of work experience programs.
15. Which type of work experience program would be most helpful for you if you did not need any extra money but wanted to find out as much as possible about different kinds of jobs?

DISCUSSION TOPICS

1. Suppose you have a choice between two jobs that you think you would enjoy. One has a high starting salary, but beginning workers are paid almost as much as those who have been working for five years. The other job has a lower starting salary, but those who have been working for five years earn more than the five-year workers on the other job. Would you take the job with the higher or lower starting pay?
2. Describe your perfect work environment and ideal working conditions. Ask other students if they agree with your description.

SUGGESTED ACTIVITIES

1. Select two careers that you would like to learn more about. Find one successful person in each of these careers. Ask your family, teachers, work experience coordinator, and counselor to suggest names of successful workers.

   Call each person. Ask if you may come to their place of work to talk briefly about the work that they do. If the person you call says he or she will not be able to talk with you, call someone else.

   During your consultation, ask all the questions you can think of. You want to learn as much as you can about that career. The following list of questions may help you.

   - How do you spend most of your time on the job? Which work activities do you like most? Which do you dislike?
   - What skills are needed for this work? Are there other skills that are helpful for advancement in this career?
   - What education or training is needed to begin working in this career? What other education is helpful for advancement?
   - Is work in this career mainly with people, data, or things?
   - Are there personal qualities that contribute to success?
   - How many hours a day do people in this career work? How often must a person work overtime? Do many people in this career work nights or weekends?
   - Is the work mostly done indoors or outdoors? Is the working environment sometimes uncomfortably hot or cold? Is the noise level sometimes unpleasant? Is the work dangerous?
   - Will there be a need for workers in this field in the next five, ten, or even fifteen years? Will the need be great or small?
2. Prepare a collage on one career cluster or career interest area that you would enjoy. Show some of the different workers in that cluster or area. Include pictures of the various work environments.

CHAPTER FOUR

Planning for Success

DO YOU KNOW . . .
- how to evaluate your career information?
- why it's important to make a career decision?
- what kind of education and training you will need to reach your career goal?
- how to make a career plan?

CAN YOU DEFINE . . .
- apprentice?
- profession?
- trade?
- tuition?
- vocation?

Did you follow through on the suggestions in the first three chapters? If so, you have completed the first four steps in the career decision-making process. If not, you may need more time to 1) define your needs and wants, 2) analyze your resources, 3) identify your choices, and 4) gather information on each choice.

When you have done all of the above, you are ready for the last steps in the decision-making process. These steps involve evaluating your choices, making a decision, and planning how you will reach your ultimate career goal. This chapter will help you with each of these important steps.

Evaluating Your Choices

The fifth step in the decision-making process is to evaluate your choices. In this step you will match what you've learned about yourself with the career information that you've gathered. You will do this to find the best possible match between yourself and a career.

A good tool to use in evaluating your career choices is a *personal career profile,* such as you see on the next page. This profile will help you summarize your information. It will also help you compare yourself to your career choices.

Prepare a profile for each of your final career choices. Write the information about yourself just once. Then duplicate this personal information for each profile. This will make it easy for you to compare yourself with each career.

After completing each profile, go back and read through all your information very carefully. Then ask yourself the nine career questions.

1. Does this career match up well with my values?
2. Will I find the duties and responsibilities of this career interesting?
3. Will I be happy with the working environment?
4. Will the number of hours and the time of day worked be acceptable for my desired lifestyle?
5. Do I have the skills needed in this career, or the aptitudes to develop them?
6. Am I willing to continue my education and training as long as necessary to work in this career? If so, will I be able to afford the necessary training and education?
7. Do the data-people-things requirements in this career match up well with my own preferences?
8. Will this career pay well enough for me to live the lifestyle I want to live in five, ten, or twenty years? Will all the fringe benefits that I'll need be available?
9. What is the career outlook? Will there be jobs available in this career when I am ready to begin work? Is the long-term outlook good?

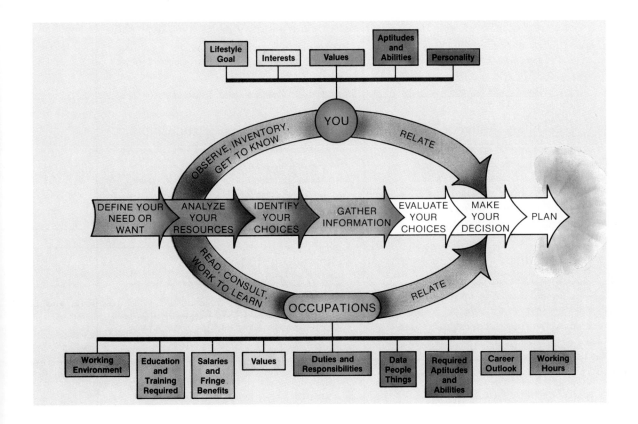

Personal Career Profile

Name *Susan James*   **Date** *May 12, 1986*   **Match**
(1-5, with 5 being
the best match)

Personal Information	Career Information	

Your Values:

The value scales I took showed that I like to help other people (humanitarianism). I like having "power" over others -- I like to be a leader. Doing creative things is fun too.

Values:

As a teacher I would have a chance to help others -- that's what it's all about. Teacher's certainly have plenty of opportunities to be leaders, too. And teacher's need to be creative!

4

Your Interests:

My hobby interests have always been photography, reading, tennis, and most outdoor sports. After flying with Dan last summer, I'd dearly love to take flying lessons. My career interest survey showed that I might like a career in leading/influencing, science, or maybe a "humanitarian" career.

Career Duties and Responsibilities:

As a teacher, I would present information, direct student discussions and activities in class. I would help each student individually, too. (Maybe I could teach P.E. sports or science in a high school.)
A teacher's working conditions would be good in most schools. (Summer's off!)

4

My Personality:

I like people, and I have a good attitude toward learning. I have an "open" mind. I'm enthusiastic, too. But I don't have the energy and drive that some people have. I don't know if I could work night after night.

Type of Personality Needed:

A teacher must like kids! Even when they aren't very likeable. I would have to prepare my lesson every day -- couldn't just forget about it. Teacher's need to be organized, too, not like Mr. Jackson! And they need to treat all their students alike.

4

Data-People-Things Preferences:

I think I like working with people most of all. I wouldn't want to be stuck in an office all day with only "data" to talk to. And I wouldn't like working only with things. Some data would be O.K. though.

Data-People-Things Relationships:

Teachers work mostly with people -- their students, other teachers, the principal, parents. They work with data (information), too, though. I don't think they work much with things.

4

Skills and Aptitudes:

I may have some "natural" teaching skills -- the kids at the YMCA always come to me for help. I helped several kids in Miss Moore's class. Math and science are easy for me. And I am the best softball player in 4th period PE!

Skills and Aptitudes Needed:

Being able to present information so students can understand it is a very important skill. And, of course, you must know your subject. An appetite for learning new approaches to teaching is important too.

4

Education/Training Acceptable:

I sure never thought I would go to college - I never even liked doing the homework in high school! But here I am a senior with no real prospects of a good job. Maybe college is the answer.

Education/Training Required:

Four years (it sounds like forever, but I guess it does go fast) - four years of college is required before you can begin teaching in most states. Some states require course work beyond that.

2

Making a Decision

You are now ready for step six in the career decision-making process. It's time to make your choice. Which career do you want to pursue?

You may feel that you're not ready to make a career decision. It's such an important decision. You may feel that you need more time—that you just don't know what you want to do.

It is only natural to hesitate at this point. If you choose a career now, you may work in that career for years—for a lifetime even. You want to be sure you're making the right choice. You may think that you should take several more months, or even several more years, to make this important decision.

Career decisions *are* important decisions—perhaps the most important you'll ever make. This does not mean, though, that you should wait until you are absolutely sure what you want to do to make a decision. Try to make a decision now, even if it's one you may change later. In any case, make a decision before you graduate from high school.

You may know some recent high school graduates who have not yet made a career decision. What are these people doing? Are they making any progress toward achieving their lifestyle goals? Or are they wasting their time, waiting until they "find" themselves and know what they want to do? Some of these people may be using the "I need more time" excuse to avoid making a difficult decision. Some people get to be thirty years old and still have not made their first career decision.

It's far better to make a *flexible* decision now. A flexible decision is one that you know you may change later. It's not always a final decision, but it's the best decision you can make at the time.

Making a career decision, even a flexible one, will have a positive influence on your life. This decision will give you a sense of direction in life—something to work toward. For perhaps the first time in your life, you will know where you're going.

Six months, or a year from now, you may find that your choice was not a good one for you. Maybe you overlooked some important information or misjudged your willingness to continue your edu-

cation. Whatever the reason, you may want to go through the decision-making process again.

Changing a career decision is not necessarily a bad thing, especially if you make the change before you begin working or early in your career. Changes made after you've been working for a few years can be more costly in terms of both time and money. Many people do, however, change their careers even later in life. Government studies show that the average American changes careers five times. With career planning you may not have to change careers so often.

The thing to remember is that changing a decision is better than never making a decision. By making a decision, you will find out whether or not you like a certain career. If it turns out that you don't like that career, you'll at least have eliminated one possibility. You'll be that much closer to the right career for you. And who knows—that first decision may turn out to be the right one!

Be open-minded. Listen to any suggestions that your family and friends might have about careers in which you would be happy and successful. You must be the one, however, to make the final decision.

A Plan of Action

Have you made a career decision? Did you decide which of your career choices is the best match for your particular interests and abilities? If so, you should begin planning how you will reach your goal.

There is no substitute for planning if you want to be successful and happy. Having a plan doesn't guarantee success, but it greatly improves your chances.

In planning to reach your ultimate career goal, you will first need to establish some intermediate, planning goals. In establishing these planning goals you will make decisions about what kind and how much education and training you will need. The following section will help you establish your planning goals and learn more about the importance of education and training. You will then be ready to make a plan and get started toward achieving your ultimate career goal.

Planning Goals

Planning goals are all the small steps you must take to get from where you are now to where you want to be. As you achieve these goals, you gain confidence. Your life seems to have a sense of direction. You move steadily toward your ultimate career goal.

Specific Goals. To know whether or not you are making progress toward your ultimate career goal, make your planning goals specific. A statement such as "I want to be a success" is too general. It doesn't give you much to aim for. "I want to be accepted by a college with a good journalism program," is much more specific. It is a planning goal that will help you.

Set Specific Goals	
Once you have a general idea of what you want to do, make your career goals as specific as possible. The more specific your goal, the easier it will be for you to plan how you will reach that goal.	
General	**Specific**
I want to be involved in publishing.	I want to edit science magazines and journals for high school and college students.
I want to drive a truck.	I want a steady job driving a delivery truck for a large department store.
I want to have something to do with food.	I want to be a cook in a hotel restaurant.
I want to work with computers.	I want to be an electronics technician specializing in the repair of business computer systems.
I want to work with tools and machines.	I want to be a tool and die maker for an automobile manufacturer.

Having specific goals makes it much easier to figure out what you need to do to succeed. Try writing out statements of all your planning goals. Then read the statements to see if you could make them more specific. The more specific the statements, the faster you will progress toward your ultimate career goal.

Realistic Goals. Besides being specific, your planning goals should be realistic. Not everyone can be a rock star or a professional athlete. If you are 5'3", you will probably never play basketball for the Lakers or Celtics. If you are color blind, you may as well accept the fact that you probably won't be a famous painter. If you have looked closely at your aptitudes and abilities, you should be able to set realistic planning goals.

Do not confuse *realistic* with *traditional*. For example, most truck drivers, carpenters, airline pilots, doctors, lawyers, and politicians have traditionally been men. These traditions have been changing, however. Young women today have many choices. It is very realistic for girls to consider the careers listed here, or any other for that matter.

Short- to Long-Term Goals. When you set your planning goals, think in terms of short-range and medium-range goals. These short- and medium-range goals will be stepping stones on your way to meeting your long-range goal. In other words, they will help you know that you are on the right track —and on schedule.

Let's say your ultimate goal is to open your own restaurant by the time you are forty. A medium-range goal might be to become the chef at a good restaurant by the time you are thirty. Your short-range goal might be to go to cooking school and to get a part-time job this summer (in a restaurant of course) to save money for the cooking school.

The short- and medium-range goals will also help you determine whether or not you need to change your ultimate goal. Suppose your long-range goal is to be a surgical nurse. You may set a short-range goal to work as a candy striper. Working as a candy striper will help you decide if you really like nursing. If you find out that you don't like nursing, you will be able to change your ultimate goal. In this case your short-range goal will have prevented you from wasting many years of hard work and training.

Set short-, medium-, and long-range planning goals for yourself. These goals will help you determine whether or not you are making progress toward your ultimate career goal.

Christine and George grew up as next-door neighbors in a Chicago suburb. Their birthdays were only a month apart, and they attended the same schools from kindergarten through high school. They were good friends, but they didn't date each other.

During their senior year, both George and Christine discussed their career goals with their counselor, Mr. Johnson. He helped them work through the decision-making process, and both chose tentative goals.

George decided he wanted to become an engineer. He knew it would be a difficult college program, that engineering would require a lot of math. Many of the colleges that Mr. Johnson recommended for engineering had five-year programs, which sounded like a lot of work to George. But George had a vision of his future lifestyle. This lifestyle would require the good income that a career in engineering would provide.

Christine chose accounting as her career goal. She had always enjoyed working with numbers. Her career profile showed accounting to be a good match.

After several months researching colleges, both Christine and George applied to the University of Illinois and both were accepted. They both enjoyed college life—it was fun to be out on their own. The choice of whether to study or socialize was theirs alone. There were no parents around to ask if their homework was done. Christine made several close friends and spent some time talking with them almost every day. But she remembered her lifestyle goals because she wanted to reach those goals very much. She kept a good balance of study and social activities, and she graduated with an A− average in the spring of 1985.

George's college life took a different turn. There were parties in the dorm almost every weekend, and George went to most of them. The parties were a lot more fun than studying for a test. After two years George had a C− grade average, which was not good enough to continue in engineering.

George changed his career goal, thinking he would like to be a science teacher. He thought that education courses might be a little easier than engineering courses. Changing his college program meant that it would take him five years of study to graduate with a four-year degree.

When someone asked him how changing career goals would affect him, George was philosophical. "Oh, I won't have as luxurious a lifestyle as I had planned—teachers don't make as much money as engineers. I probably won't be able to do all the things I wanted. I guess I didn't want them badly enough to work for them. Not too many people really get what they want out of life anyway."

George and Christine responded to their career goals in different ways. The important point is that they both set some goals. Even George, who had to change his ultimate goal, benefitted from having a plan. What sort of career might George have found if he had never made a plan?

The Value of Education and Training

As you set your goals, you probably began to realize the importance of education and training. Almost all jobs, in any career, require some special training. The amount of training can vary from a few days of on-the-job experience to several years of college work. This means that at least one of your goals should involve getting the education and training that you will need in your chosen career.

Graduation from high school has become the minimum requirement for most jobs. Although you can get a job without a high school diploma, your opportunities would be very limited. The jobs available for people without a high school diploma are usually the jobs no one else wants.

Labor Department surveys show a close relationship between job security and education. It is also true that most careers requiring more education and training pay higher salaries in the long run.

Make a Decision

You have already made your flexible career decision. You know what you want to do, but you are not yet sure how you are going to go about reaching your goal. You could go to school full-time for two years, or four years, or even six years, and then enter your career field. Or, you could get an entry-level job, save some money, and go to school later. You could even combine these two approaches. What's your decision—full-time school now, work later; work now, school later; or, one of the combinations in between? Give reasons for your decision.

There is no doubt about it. The more education and training you have, the greater your chances of getting and keeping a job. In most cases, more education and training means more money.

Education and training do not guarantee success in the world of work. They do, however, greatly improve your chances for success. The more education and training you have, the more career opportunities you'll have to choose from. This is why it is so important for you to select the program you need—and get started learning.

On-the-Job-Training. Many companies offer workers on-the-job training. This training can last from a few days to two or three years. The starting pay for on-the-job training is low, but it increases gradually. Some industries offer in-plant training programs that include formal classroom instruction. Other companies send workers to junior colleges and other schools.

To find the type of on-the-job training you want, apply to your area's Job Service Office of the State Employment Service. You may also apply directly to company personnel offices and private employment agencies.

Apprenticeship. An **apprentice** is someone who learns how to do a certain job through experience and guidance from a skilled worker. There are apprenticeship programs for more than four hundred occupations.

The most popular apprentice programs are in the trades. A **trade** is an occupation that requires manual or mechanical skill. Trade occupations are those such as machining, plumbing, carpentry, painting, and sheet metal work.

In an apprenticeship you would learn a trade from a person who is already skilled in that trade. Most of your learning would take place on the job. You would probably also do some classroom work.

An apprenticeship offers several advantages to young workers entering the world of work. First, training through experience is an excellent way to learn trade skills and job-related information. Another advantage is that your training does not cost a lot of money. In fact, you can earn money while you are an apprentice. You would be paid less than skilled workers, but as your skills increased so would your pay.

The length of time required to complete an apprenticeship program varies. It can take up to six years. The average, though, is about four years.

Most apprenticeship programs are registered with the federal or state government. Apprentices who complete these programs receive certificates from the U.S. Department of Labor or the state apprenticeship agency. For more information on apprenticeship programs in your area, contact your local state employment office or write to the Department of Labor. Your teacher may have addresses and phone numbers.

As an apprentice, you can earn money while you learn a trade. It usually takes from two to five years to complete an apprenticeship.

Vocational Schools. The work that a person does to earn a living is said to be that person's *vocation*. The Vocational Education Act of 1963 established a system of schools to help people learn a vocation. These schools offer work-related programs for high school students and most young adults just out of school. Most vocational schools also offer evening programs for adults.

Vocational-technical schools have two purposes. First, they try to provide programs in which people can learn skills that will meet the labor needs of the community. Second, they give students a chance to learn the skills they need to get a job.

Vocational schools are not expensive to attend. Some charge as little as sixteen dollars per year for basic fees. Class fees for tools and materials depend on the course, but are low in most schools.

You can take a variety of courses at a vocational school. Business, health, industry, and agriculture, are just a few of the career areas included. Some of the larger schools offer training for more than forty industrial occupations.

The vocational school in your area may have a program that will help you reach one of your career goals. How much longer will you be in high school? You may still have time to complete the program you need. If not, you can attend the area vocational school after graduation. See your counselor for more information.

Trade Schools. Private trade schools provide training and teach students how to solve real work problems in job-like settings. These schools often have programs that are not available in public vocational schools. Trade schools are, however, more expensive than vocational schools. The costs range from a few hundred dollars to several thousand dollars for a complete program.

The length of time needed to complete a trade program depends on the skills you want to learn. Since you would take only courses in your chosen field, you can complete most programs in less than two years.

Have you chosen a career in the trades? Do you want to begin work as soon as possible? If so, you should ask your school counselor about trade schools. For a directory of trade schools, write the National Association of Trade and Technical Schools, 2021 K Street NW, Washington, D.C. 20006.

Community Colleges. Community colleges are sometimes called *junior colleges* or *city colleges*. These colleges offer two years of college-level work in vocational and academic areas.

Many of the same vocational and technical courses offered in trade schools are also available in community colleges. In fact, community colleges offer instruction in more than sixty occupational areas. These areas include agriculture, restaurant management, business, health, industry, and service occupations. The credit you earn in many of these courses can be transferred to a four-year college and be counted toward graduation.

Many community colleges offer courses at night. These courses make it possible for you to work during the day and go to school in the evening. In this way you can acquire needed education and training while earning some money.

Community colleges are much less expensive to attend than private trade schools and four-year colleges. If you attend a local junior college, you may

Attending a community college can be the perfect way to get the extra training and education you need if you don't want to spend four years in college. An important advantage to community colleges is the extremely low cost.

not pay any **tuition** (cost of attending the school) at all. Your only expenses would probably be for books and perhaps a small student activity fee. If you live at home, you won't have to pay room and board costs.

You probably have a community college near you. Talk to your school counselor about the college. Your counselor probably knows what programs are available. If the community college offers the courses you want, you may want to enroll.

Colleges and Universities. A **profession** is a career that requires specialized training and a long period of academic preparation. Some examples of professions are the medical, legal, and teaching professions. If you plan to enter a profession, you will probably need a college degree.

Most professions require a bachelor's degree, which usually means four years of college. Other professions require six to eight years of college. Over two thousand colleges and universities offer professional and technical training to qualified high school graduates.

Every college will require you to take a certain number of general education courses. You will also be required to take a certain number of courses in your area of specialization. Beyond these requirements, you may choose the courses you take.

Selecting a college is much like making a career decision. There are many factors to consider. To pick the best school for you, you will want to follow through with the complete decision-making process.

Not all colleges offer the same programs. Some colleges are especially good for one kind of program, but not as strong in another program. You will want to choose a college that offers a strong program in the area you will be studying.

Try to find several colleges with strong programs in your interest area. Then compare those schools. Compare them on the basis of size, location, cost, overall quality, and entrance and graduation requirements.

Location and size will probably be important considerations in your choice of colleges. You may want to stay close to home, or you may not. You may want to attend a very large state university. Or perhaps you'd be more comfortable in a small, private college.

The cost of a college education varies greatly, depending on which college you choose. State schools are usually less expensive than private schools. You must, however, be a resident of a state to take advantage of the lower costs. For example, if you live in Iowa you would pay much more to attend the University of Michigan than a student from Michigan would.

You may be able to get some help in paying your college expenses. You can apply for scholarships and grants, some of which may pay for almost all your costs. You can borrow money, sometimes without interest, to pay for your education. Many students work part-time while attending college to help pay their expenses.

Like costs, entrance and graduation requirements vary greatly from school to school. Some colleges accept only those students who were in the top 10 or 15 percent of their graduating class. Many colleges reject students who haven't had certain high school courses. You'll also find that once you are admitted, the number and variety of courses required for graduation will be greater at some schools than others.

Your chances of being successful and learning what you want to learn are greater if you pick the best college for you. To do this, you will want to carefully compare all of the factors.

There are many sources of information on colleges and universities. The best place to start is usually in your school guidance office. There you will find college catalogs, directories, and many other reference books.

Talk to your counselor. Your counselor knows a lot about most of the schools in your area and state. Your counselor also knows how to get more detailed information about any school in which you are interested. When it comes to choosing a college, your counselor will probably be your most valuable source of information and advice.

Adult Education. College is not the only road to a successful career. Another avenue is called *adult* or *continuing* education. This route may take longer, but the satisfaction is just as great.

A lot of attention is being given to adult education today. Most city high schools offer evening courses in business and industrial education. Some private schools have evening programs for people who work during the day. In many subjects, correspondence courses are also offered.

Colleges and universities encourage older people to return to college. They do this by offering evening courses of special interest to them. Anyone who wants to learn has many opportunities.

Many people have advanced their careers through adult education. The adult who has been in the working world for a few years usually knows the value of a chance to learn.

Make a Decision

Your counselor has just told you there are three colleges with good programs in the field you want to study. All three colleges are about the same distance from your home and with possible scholarships and loans, it looks as though they would all cost about the same. One is a large (30,000 students) state university, one is a medium-sized (8,000 students) university, and the other is a small (1,500 students) private college. So what is your decision—large, medium, or small? Give reasons for your decision.

Military-Service Training. People in the military often deal with very complicated equipment. Since World War II especially, the military services have provided specialized training in such areas as electronics, mechanical engineering, and computer technology. Many of the special skills you can learn in the armed services would be valuable after you left the service. In fact, the same training that some people receive free in the military would cost them a great deal as civilians.

Many people enjoy military life; others do not. If you think you might like serving in the military, talk to your counselor. Your counselor can help you find information about college programs for officer training. You can also get information from Army, Navy, Air Force, and Marine recruiting offices.

Making Your Plans

You have just read about many different ways you can get the education and training you need to reach your ultimate career goal. You now need to

Do not overlook the military as a source of education and training, especially if your ultimate career goal involves work in a highly technical area.

choose the program or school that will help you the most. If you will be in high school another semester or so, you can take some high school courses that will help you. If you will graduate soon, begin now to select the educational and training programs that you'll need after high school.

Answering the following questions will give you most of the information you need to prepare your career plan. You may have already answered some of the questions.

- What is my ultimate career goal?
- What high school courses can I still take to help me reach my career goal?
- What education and training must I acquire if I am to attain my career goal?
- Of the necessary education and training, how much must I get before I enter the career field in which I am interested?
- In what kinds of schools can I get this education and training?
- How much money will I need to get the necessary education and training?
- Where will I get the money I need for education and training?
- How much of the education and training I need can I get on the job?
- What part-time jobs will help me develop the knowledge and skills needed to reach my career goal?

After answering these questions, and any others that occur to you, start preparing your plan. Set up your plan in terms of the short-, medium-, and long-range goals you read about earlier in this chapter.

It's important that you write out your answers. The writing process will force you to come up with specific plans. Fill in dates by which you will have begun or accomplished each planning goal. This will help you check, from time to time, whether or not you are making progress toward your ultimate goal. Looking at Joe's career plan on this page may help you with your own plan.

Remember that your decisions and plans are flexible. You can always change them—in fact, you probably will. The advantage to having a plan, though, is that you will be moving ahead. Even as you change your goals, you will be getting closer to a career that is right for you.

After doing lots of career exploration and research, Joe wasn't entirely sure what he wanted to do, but he made the best decision he could at the time. He decided that he wanted to own his own airplane and have his own crop-dusting business. He had grown up working on farms, and he loved the outdoor farm life. He also liked machines, and speed, and excitement—and he had always dreamed of flying an airplane. What could be more perfect than making a living flying airplanes over farms?

The first thing Joe did after making his decision was to talk with his school counselor. The counselor was a big help. She answered lots of Joe's questions and told him where he could find more information. Joe left the counselor's office ready to write his plan of action.

Luckily, Joe had already taken several agriculture courses, and he belonged to the Future Farmers of America. During his last semester of high school, he would take all the math courses he could take—which would help with navigation problems. He would also see about getting a part-time job at the local fertilizer dealership. An airport job would have been great, but there were no airports nearby.

Joe did not have enough money to buy an airplane. He didn't even have money for the training program he would need to complete for his pilot's license. Since good-paying jobs were very scarce in Joe's area, it would be difficult to save any money. Joe decided that the best plan would be to join the Air Force. He didn't think he could handle the officer-pilot programs, but he could learn a lot about airplane maintenance—which would be helpful later. He could also save money for pilot training after he left the Air Force; and perhaps enough for a down payment on his own plane.

Joe thought that after finishing his time in the Air Force, he would take some business courses at the community college near his home. These courses would help him manage his own business. His savings from the Air Force would be enough to finance the college

(continued next page)

courses, as well as the flying lessons that he would take at the flying school affiliated with the community college.

With this general plan in mind, Joe wrote down his short-, medium-, and long-range planning goals. He also wrote down his ultimate career goal—crop duster. He then rewrote his goals to make them as specific as possible. He also adjusted them until he had them in order. His final list of planning goals looked like this:

Short-Term Goals

	Complete by
Take Algebra	December 1986
Talk to Air Force Recruiter	October 15, 1986
Have part-time job with fertilizer distributor— (substitute other ag-related job if not available)	November 1, 1986
Take Geometry 222	May 25, 1987
Graduate from high school	June 1, 1987
Join Air Force	July 1, 1987

Medium Range Goals

Acquire general experience and knowledge of airplane maintenance	1987–1993

	Complete by
Save 15-20 percent of pay	1987–1993
Use free time to read and study about airplanes and business management	1987–1993

Long-Range Goals

Take pilot training course	August 1993
Take business administration courses at Valley Community College	August 1993
Work part-time at Municipal Airport as airplane mechanic	October 1993
Graduate from training course	July 1994
Obtain associate's degree	May 1995
Full-time job as airplane mechanic	Fall 1995
Save more money and shop for plane	Winter 1995-1996
Buy plane	Spring 1996

Ultimate Career Goal

Begin doing business as crop duster	Summer 1996

The happiest and most successful people don't wait for things to happen. They make decisions and plan ahead.

REVIEW YOUR LEARNING   CHAPTER 4

CHAPTER SUMMARY

In this chapter you continued with the career decision-making process that you started in Chapter 1. First you evaluated your career choices by matching your knowledge about yourself with your career information. You then learned the importance of making a choice—even if it is a flexible one. This choice gives you something to work toward and prevents you from wasting time.

After making your career decision, you learned about the need to plan your career. This means establishing planning goals and choosing the kind and amount of education and training you will need. The education and training options include on-the-job training, apprenticeships, vocational and trade schools, community colleges, four-year colleges and universities, military service, and adult education.

Finally, you began to write out your career plan. You set planning goals for yourself and assigned time limits to these goals so that you could check your progress. You developed a plan of action that will take you to your ultimate career goal.

WORDS YOU SHOULD KNOW

apprentice
profession
trade
tuition
vocation

STUDY QUESTIONS

1. What is the main purpose of evaluating the career choices that you have researched?
2. What is a good tool to use in evaluating your career choices?
3. What often happens to high school graduates who have no idea what career they want to pursue?
4. How often does the average American change careers?
5. What are two words that describe the kinds of career goals you need to set for yourself?
6. What are the three kinds of goals, as far as time is concerned?
7. What is the minimum educational requirement for most jobs?
8. How long does it take to complete an average apprenticeship?
9. What are the two purposes served by vocational schools?
10. What is one advantage of attending a community college instead of a four-year college?
11. What is the minimum educational requirement for most professions?
12. Where is the best place to start finding information on colleges?

REVIEW YOUR LEARNING   CHAPTER 4

DISCUSSION TOPICS

1. Suppose your best friend wants to quit school at the end of the tenth grade. What reasons for staying in school would you give this friend?
2. Why is it difficult for most people to make a career decision— even a flexible one? Why do so many people avoid making a decision until they are a long way into their adult life?
3. At the present time, what career do you plan to enter? Why did you choose this career?

SUGGESTED ACTIVITIES

1. Ask your counselor to let you look through several catalogs of colleges that offer majors in areas related to your career goal. Choose three of these colleges and estimate the cost of attending for one year. Make a chart comparing costs for each school. Include costs for tuition, fees, books, and transportation. Include room and board only if you would be living away from home. Choose one of the colleges as your first choice, and be ready to explain your choice to the class.
2. Make a report on the adult-education programs in your community. Focus on the courses that would relate to your chosen career. If you decide not to attend college full time, you may be interested in taking some of these classes after graduation. Sources for this information are public and private high schools, vocational schools, two- or four-year colleges, and social-service organizations. Use the Yellow Pages in your phone book for addresses and telephone numbers of these agencies.
3. Suppose that you have a natural talent for some kind of work (pick a career). You are encouraged by your parents and your teachers to continue your education in this area. They feel you will have a great career if you develop your aptitude into abilities. The only problem is that the necessary education and training will cost a lot of money. You are broke, and your parents can't help you. Your boyfriend (or girlfriend) wants you to take whatever job you can get, so the two of you can get married when you graduate. Write a short essay explaining what you would do and why.

ENTERING THE WORLD OF WORK

PART TWO

The time will soon come when you need to find a full-time job. You will try to find a job that you enjoy and are good at. Once you find it, you will want to do everything possible to make sure that the employer hires **you**, and not one of the other applicants. And, if you are successful in getting the job you want, you will want to keep that job and progress toward your ultimate career goal.

This section will help you succeed at the activities mentioned above. You will learn all you need to know about finding and applying for a job — not just any job, but the one you want. You will also pick up lots of tips on what you need to do to meet your employer's expectations and to get along with your co-workers. Once you've learned how to accomplish these basic tasks, you can study methods for getting promotions and pay raises and being generally effective in your dealings with people. Since no career successes are really successes without good health, you will also learn the importance of being safe and healthy.

Finding and Applying for a Job

DO YOU KNOW . . .
- where to find job leads?
- how to apply for a job *successfully*?
- how to prepare for an interview?
- how to conduct yourself in an interview?

CAN YOU DEFINE . . .
- interview?
- job leads?
- personal data sheet?
- references?
- standard English?

If you have made your career decision, you should have some short-term planning goals. One of those goals is probably a part-time job in your chosen career area. You now need to find and successfully apply for such a job.

Even if you haven't decided on your career goal, you may want a part-time job. You may want to buy a car or some new clothes. Maybe you need to save money for more school and training after high school. Whatever your reasons for wanting to work, there are some proven ways to find and get jobs.

Finding Job Openings

Finding even a part-time job that you can do well and enjoy takes some planning. Some people don't bother with a plan at all. You may have heard friends talk about their luck in getting a job. "This was my day! I really lucked out. Summer vacation starts Friday, and my uncle offered me a job starting next Monday. I don't really know what it is, but at least I won't have to go out job hunting."

If it turns out to be the *right* job, then that friend is *really* lucky! Taking the first job that's offered is like trying to hit a target with your eyes closed—you've got a chance, but the odds are against you. Some people spend months, even years, doing a job they don't like very well. Then they hear of another job and try their "luck" again. With a little planning they could find a job they like and can do really well—a job they could take pride in!

A **job lead** is information about a possible job opening. In looking for a job, you want to find as many leads as possible. Doesn't it make sense that the more leads you have, the better your chances are of finding the job you want?

Where do you go to find job leads? Some of the best sources of leads are described in this section. From these sources you can build a long list of leads.

Make a long list of job leads before you start applying for jobs. The longer the list, the better your chances of finding the job you want.

School Counselors and Teachers

Your school probably has at least one counselor or teacher who helps students find jobs. Large high schools often have a work-experience or placement office with several counselors. These counselors specialize in career counseling and job placement. They are excellent sources of job leads.

The school personnel are there to help you. They can be very helpful because they know a great deal about you. They know your abilities, aptitudes, grades, and attendance record. They also have information on your attitudes and personality. With this information they have a good chance of finding the right job for you.

The fact that your school refers you to a job does not mean that you will be hired. Schools often refer several students for the same job. If this happens, you will have competition for the job from other students in your school. So make the best possible impression when you apply for the job—and continue to pursue other sources of job leads.

Family and Friends

Among your best sources of job leads are members of your own family. Friends of your family, and your personal friends, are also very good sources.

Family members and friends who have jobs are involved in the business world daily. They may know of job opportunities for which you are qualified. Perhaps you have a friend who recently began working. This friend may have heard about a job lead that is just right for you.

Make a list of family members and friends who might help you with job leads. Begin with members of your own family. Then add the names of friends of your family. It's especially important to include those people who are in business for themselves. They might be able to hire you. If they can't, they may know other business people who are looking for workers like you.

Add to your list any friends who work for companies where you think you might like to work. Then add the names of your own school friends and neighbors who might be connected with a business in which you are interested. A classmate's parent may work for a company that is looking for someone with your qualifications.

Don't hesitate to ask your father, mother, older brother, and all your friends and family members, if they can help you find a job. They may know of job openings not listed in the newspaper.

Some young people hesitate to ask their influential friends about job possibilities. These young people do not want to get a job by using "pull." Yet there is nothing wrong with having a friend or family member help you get a job, if you are qualified for it. The only kind of "pull" to be avoided is the kind that gets you a job for which you are not qualified. When this happens, both you and the company that hired you suffer.

Many jobs are never advertised in the paper or listed with a placement agency. These jobs are filled by friends and acquaintances of company employees. So don't limit your job search to answering ads. Ask family members and friends for job leads.

Employment Agencies

Employment agencies help people find jobs. Those who are looking for jobs submit their names to the agency. Businesses call the agency when they have job openings. The employment agency then serves as a sort of go-between, matching qualified job-hunters with the available jobs.

There are two basic kinds of employment agencies—public and private. Public agencies are operated either by the federal or the state government. Their services are free. Private agencies are managed by people who are trying to make a profit. This means that private agencies must charge a fee for their services.

Most large cities have both public and private employment agencies. The public agencies are identified by the names of the states in which they are located. *Minnesota State Employment Service* and *Texas State Employment Service* are examples. In California, the state employment service is known as the *Employment Development Department.*

Fill out an application form with the public employment agency nearest you. You will then be interviewed to determine your interests and qualifications. If and when a job is listed that seems right for you, someone from that office will notify you. If you are interested in the job, the employment office will refer you to the company.

Do not overlook the help that a private employment agency might give you. Private agencies often know about jobs that are not listed with the state employment service. Just remember—these agencies charge a fee for their services.

When you submit your name to a private agency, you will have to sign an agreement. This agreement will say that if the agency helps you find a job, you will pay the agency a fee. The fee is usually a certain amount, or a percentage of your first year's salary. You do not have to pay the fee unless the agency finds you a job that you accept. In some cases the employer will pay this fee for you.

Newspaper Advertisements

Read the help-wanted advertisements in the newspaper. These ads will help you learn a great deal about the job market. You will get an idea of the salaries being offered for different kinds of work and the qualifications needed for the kind of work that interests you. Follow up every newspaper ad that looks promising.

Be careful, though, when you respond to newspaper ads. Don't apply for jobs that require deposits of money. These "jobs" are usually not real jobs at all. They are often nothing more than attempts to sell you something—and take your money.

Other ads may require that you enroll in a course—for a fee—before you are hired. The people who place these ads generally take your money, but they have no jobs to offer.

General

IN BABYSITTER needed to for family of four children. be mature and flexible. Refer- s. call 780-2211.

DED-INSTRUCTORS for Mens ion. Apply in person at the .ry Health Spa, 7405 N. Uni- y, Tolona, IL.

ART IMMEDIATELY xperience necessary. Excel- training program. Full-time hours. Guaranteed wage plus ses in Telephone Magazine s Department. 685-9263.

TED FEMALE SINGER-Guitar er, mostly rock, some country R & B. Phone 602-3328.

Medical

★
MEDICAL TECHNOLOGIST
ASCP) or equivalent, with 6 s of experience, for clinic labo- y. Must meet IDPH require- ts for Supervisor. Part-time, 3- week, no weekends or nights. for appointment, Monday-Fri- 9-5, 671-7455.

APPRENTICE PHARMACIST computerized pharmacy. NE: 682-6631, 692-6338, ask

70. Office

EXECUTIVE Secretaries, Word Pro- cessors, Data Entry and Mail Room Clerks needed immediately. Con- tact Hope Temporary Services at 685-5055 for an appointment.

RECEPTIONIST/TYPIST
Position available in small down- town office for a mature self start- ing individual. Must be comfortable on the phone & dealing with the public. Position requires accurate typing. 70 wpm minimum. Must also be proficient with calculations. Excellent benefits available. Send resume to:
BOX AB8853
Astoria-Journal Star
1 News Plaza, Astoria, IL 61643

SECRETARY: Type 60, Ability to run office. $5.50 hr. + benefits. Men- dota Employment Service. 713 W. Lake. 682-4082. Pvt. Empl. Agcy.

SECRETARY
General office work. Accuracy in typing a must. High school gradu- ate. Send resume stating education and work experience to:
BOX BA 9943
Astoria Journal Star
1 News Plaza
Astoria, IL 61643

Your name on a Kelly pay-

77. Profess

MAJOR
MECHANIC/
Has several ope Plumbing, She Extimators. Mu perience of indu cial projects. E and salary histc Aurora Industri Bennett. 809 N IL. 60520

SHOP F

Manufacturer of cultural equipm person with a str service & superv should have at le rience in equip TROIT DIESEL, / ERPILLAR engine ful. Full line of c Contact by te resume to:
Rudy N
Big Whe
P.O. BC
Paxton,
PHONE: 21
Special Educ Part time Speech

You may find several good job leads in the help-wanted sec- tion of your local newspaper. While you're looking for a job, you should get in the habit of scanning these ads every day.

Government Offices

The U.S. government is the largest employer in the country. The federal government hires thousands of new employees each year for many kinds of jobs. Other government agencies—such as city, county, and state agencies—also hire many workers.

There are a number of advantages to government jobs. Most of these jobs are under a civil service or merit system. These systems protect workers from unfair dismissal. The pay and working conditions for government jobs are usually quite good.

Find out where the government offices are lo- cated in your area. Then call or visit these offices to find out about job openings.

Schools

In most cities the local school district is an impor- tant source of jobs. In addition to teachers, schools hire many kinds of workers. Among them are sec- retaries, file clerks, switchboard operators, library clerks, gardeners, custodians, cooks, and mainte- nance workers. Working conditions are usually very good. If you are interested in working in one of your local schools, check with the school district's personnel office.

Colleges, too, hire many workers besides teach- ers and professors. Many people enjoy working on a college campus. There they can associate with people who are interested in education and improv- ing themselves. If there is a college in your city and the work sounds interesting to you, apply at the college personnel office.

Direct Calls

In addition to following up leads from sources al- ready mentioned, you may want to make some di- rect calls on your own. Making direct calls means either telephoning or visiting potential employers. You will not be responding to an ad or following up a referral.

It takes a lot of work to find a job through direct calls. You don't know which companies have open- ings, and you don't know the people who work for companies that interest you. You will probably make a lot of phone calls and visits before you suc- ceed. But if you contact enough businesses directly, you will probably find some that are looking for workers with your skills.

Go through the Yellow Pages of your phone book looking for companies that interest you. Make a list of all these companies, including their addresses and phone numbers. Then call or visit each com- pany and ask if there are any job vacancies.

Make a Decision

You have exhausted every source of job leads —family, friends, newspaper ads, everything —and still no job. Making some direct calls appears to be your last hope at the moment. The problem with this is that you are not comfortable talking to strangers on the telephone—you're afraid you will embarrass yourself. You're thinking there must be an- other alternative. What's your decision— make some direct calls, wait and see if some- thing turns up, or . . .? Give reasons for your decision.

Job-Finding Summary

Remember—it is important to have as many job leads as possible. This is the only way you can choose the job that is right for you.

There are lots of other people looking for work! You may not be offered the job you want, and you may turn down some jobs offered you. In such cases you must continue to follow up every lead. This is another reason why it is a good idea to have as many jobs leads as possible. Putting all the information you have for each lead on a 3" x 5" card, such as you see at the right, will help you organize your information.

Also remember the following points.

- Don't rely on just one source of leads — use all available sources.
- Having a long list of potential employers will lessen the chance of your jumping at the first job offered.
- Be careful when responding to newspaper ads. Do not respond to those that require a deposit or fee.
- Do not hesitate to ask influential friends for job leads.
- Make use of both public and private employment agencies.

Applying for a Job

Once you have a list of job leads, you can begin applying for some jobs. The process of applying for a job is an important part of getting the job you want. Do not take it lightly.

Employers are looking for the best person to fill the job. They want to know whether or not you have the ability to do the work. They will be influenced by the way you dress and whether or not you are well-groomed. They will also notice if you use slang or any other language that is not standard English. In fact, they will want to know everything about you that relates to the job.

Employers have several ways of getting the information they need to choose the best person for the job. Most employers will have you fill out an application form. Some will have you write a letter of application and prepare a personal data sheet. For some jobs you will be asked to take a performance test. Almost all employers will want to interview you before they decide to hire you.

How you go about providing employers with the information they want often determines whether or not you get the job. Following the suggestions on the next few pages will increase your chances of being successful.

Why People Are Not Hired

Below are the ten most common reasons that applicants are not hired. The reasons are listed in order, with number one being the most common. This list is based on a survey of 153 companies.

1. Poor personal appearance
2. Overbearing—too aggressive—conceited superiority complex—"know-it-all"
3. Inability to communicate clearly—nonstandard English usage
4. Lack of planning for career—no purpose or goals
5. Lack of interest and enthusiasm—passive (waits for things to happen), indifferent (uncaring)
6. Lack of confidence and poise—nervous—ill-at-ease
7. Failure to participate in activities
8. Overemphasis on money—interested only in best dollar offer
9. Poor school record—just got by
10. Unwilling to start at the bottom—expects too much too soon

Before You Apply

If you are hired, there are certain things you will need to do. Take care of these things now—before you apply for a job. Doing so may make the difference in whether or not you get the job.

Social Security Card. As soon as you are hired, you will need a social security card. Without it you cannot be paid. If you do not already have a social security card, fill out an appliaction and mail it now!

Social security card application forms are available at your local social security office. You can find the address in the telephone directory. These applications may also be available in your school's work-experience office and at your local post office.

Work Permits. If you are under sixteen, you will probably need a work permit before you can start to work. Some states require work permits for all workers under the age of eighteen.

State and federal labor laws list jobs that are considered too dangerous for young workers. These laws also limit the hours that young people can work. A work permit shows that a young worker has been advised of these laws. In some states, work permits must specify the exact job duties and hours of work.

Work permits are usually issued by schools. Ask your counselor or work-experience coordinator if you will need a work permit. Doing this now may save you time, as well as help you get the job you want.

Standard English

In Chapter 10 you will learn about the importance of communication in the world of work. You will find out why employers always try to hire workers who can communicate effectively on the job. You will also learn how you can improve your communication skills.

Before you can demonstrate your communication skills on the job, you must get the job. You can increase your chances of getting the job by using **standard English** when you apply. Standard English is the use of words that mean the same thing to everyone. It means using proper grammar and spelling words correctly. This is the kind of English your teachers have always encouraged you to use.

Potential employers have several opportunities to notice your ability, or inability, to use standard En-

The young man meant to say, "This machine is broken." Don't use nonstandard English on the job.

glish. When they read your application form, they will see whether or not you can write and spell words properly. If you write a letter of application, employers will have another chance to determine whether or not you can write in standard English. And finally, in the interview, employers will listen carefully to the way you speak to make sure your vocabulary and grammar are acceptable.

To understand the importance of using standard English, suppose your application form or letter contained poor grammar or misspelled words. What would happen? Many employers wouldn't even bother to interview you. They receive lots of applications. They don't need to give anyone a second chance.

But suppose you do use good grammar and spell words correctly on the form and in your letter. You will probably be asked in for an interview. Using standard English in the interview will help you in two ways. First, the employer will take your proper use of the language as a sign that you are a well-educated person. Second, using standard English will show the employer that you can communicate clearly. Your chances of being hired are very good if the employer believes you are a well-educated person who can communicate effectively.

On the other hand, if you do *not* use standard English in the interview, the employer may think that you are not very intelligent. The employer may think that you did poorly in school. If your English is very bad, the employer may not be able to understand you. If this happens, the employer will certainly not offer you the job. This is especially true if you are applying for a job, such as salesclerk or receptionist, that involves dealing directly with customers.

Using standard English means more than using the accepted vocabulary and grammar. It also means *not* using phrases such as *you know, like,* and *okay* over and over. These phrases, and others, may slip into your speech pattern without your noticing it. They can be irritating to those listening to you. The last thing you want to do is irritate a prospective employer.

Think of it this way—you can use casual expressions in casual situations. Applying for a job, however, is not a casual situation, no matter how comfortable you feel about it. Your purpose—in your application and in your interview—is to show the employer that you are a competent person. Being a competent person involves communicating well with others. It also involves projecting an image that others will respect. So use your best English.

Application Forms

The employer's main purpose in having you fill out an application form is to obtain information about you. Employers may also use the application form to determine how neat you are and whether or not you can use standard English. If you remember this, you can gain an advantage over the many applicants who fill out their forms quickly and carelessly.

Follow the suggestions below for filling out application forms. These suggestions will help you sell yourself to the employer.

1. Complete the application form as neatly as possible! The employer will regard it as an example of your best work.
2. If you fill out the application form in the employer's office, use a pen. If you fill out the application at home and you can type, use a typewriter.
3. Answer every question that applies to you. If a question does not apply to you, write *NA*, for

Not Applicable or draw a short line in the space. This shows that you did not overlook the question.

4. Write your correct name—not a nickname—on the application form. Your first name, middle initial, and last name are usually all that is needed.
5. Spell all words correctly. If you are not sure of the spelling, use another word (one you can spell) with the same meaning.
6. Give your complete address, including your zip code.
7. If there is a question on marital status, simply indicate whether or not you are single or married. Do not supply any extra information about your marital status.
8. The questions about your place of birth refer only to the city and state where you were born. Do not write additional information, such as the name of the hospital.
9. The application may ask for your job preference. For example, it may say "For what job are you applying?" Answer with a specific job title or type of work. Do *not* just write "anything." Employers expect you to state clearly the kind of work you can do and want to do.
10. The application will include a section on education. Write the names of all the schools you

---

You Don't Have to Answer

Some applications contain questions you don't have to answer. You have the legal right to withhold information that is not related to your ability to perform the job in question.

Employers are not supposed to ask your race, religion, sex, or marital status. They may not ask if you have ever been arrested. They do not need to know if you have children, who takes care of your children, or if you are planning to have children. You are not required to provide information about your military or financial status.

If you are asked a question that you feel is illegal, decide what to do. If you are sure that your answer won't hurt your chances of getting the job, you may simply answer the question. Otherwise, you can point out that the question is illegal. You should realize, however, that this may lessen your chance of getting the job. Your third option is to ignore the question entirely.

have attended and the dates you attended each. If there are several, write them down for your own reference before you go to apply. By doing this you will be sure to remember all the information.

11. Be prepared to list several **references.** References are people who will speak on your behalf. They are people who will tell the employer you would be a good employee.

You should ask permission of the people you plan to list as references. Certain people are considered especially good references. The pastor of your church, a former employer, a teacher who knows you well, and friends who are established in business are some examples. Try to include some of these people as references.

An example of a correctly completed application is shown on the next two pages. Look it over carefully.

Letters of Application

The employer will probably not interview all the applicants for a job. You must convince the employer that you are one of the applicants who should be interviewed. This is why your application form and letter of application are so important. They are ways of selling yourself to an employer.

There are times when writing a letter of application is the only way of getting a personal interview. Write a letter of application in the following situations.

- When you wish to apply for an out-of-town job, especially if the job is a business or professional position
- When you answer a newspaper advertisement that asks you to apply by mail
- When you wish to be interviewed by business friends of your family
- When an employer asks you to write a letter of application

In many cases the employer gets his or her first impression of you from your letter of application. It is important that you make a good first impression. Unless you are specifically asked to write your letter in longhand, type it neatly. A neatly typed letter with all the words spelled correctly is impressive.

If you can't type, ask a friend to type your letter for you. If you do not know anyone who types, you can have a local typing service type your letter for a small fee. If you are applying for a job as a typist or stenographer, your letter of application is an excellent opportunity to show the employer how neatly you can set up and type a letter.

Here are some suggestions for writing an effective letter of application. If you follow these suggestions, your letter will make a favorable impression on the employer.

1. Write a first copy, then revise and develop this copy. Keep working on your letter until you say what you should say, in the way you should say it. You might ask a teacher or a friend in business to help you polish your letter. When you have the letter the way you want it, type it neatly.

2. Do not tell the employer how badly you need a job. Instead, concentrate on the contributions you could make to the company.

3. In your first sentence, establish a point of contact. This sentence should tell where or from whom you learned about the job. You might say, "At the suggestion of Mr. Oxford (a mutual friend), I am writing regarding the job as messenger in your office." If you are writing in answer to a newspaper ad, you might begin, "Your advertisement in today's *News Press* for a typist-clerk describes the work that I think I do best."

4. In the second sentence, state that you are applying for the job. You might say, "Please consider me an applicant for the position," or "I should like to be considered an applicant for this job."

5. In your second paragraph, begin describing the education and experience you have that qualify you for the job. If you have a lot to say about both your education and experience, use a separate paragraph for each. If you have little to say, describe both in the same paragraph. If you have no experience, don't make excuses. Instead, tell how your education in subjects related to the work (typing, bookkeeping, or auto shop, for example) will help you in this job.

6. In your last paragraph, ask for an interview at the employer's convenience. Be sure to include your phone number so the employer can contact you.

APPLICATION
FOR
EMPLOYMENT

(PLEASE PRINT PLAINLY)

To Applicant: We deeply appreciate your interest in our organization and assure you that we are sincerely interested in your qualifications. A clear understanding of your background and work history will aid us in placing you in the position that best meets your qualifications *and* may assist us in possible future upgrading.

PERSONAL

Date _January 2, 1986_

Name _Carson_ _Rebecca_ _Sue_
     Last   First   Middle

Social Security No. _987-65-4321_

Present address _21_ _West Third_ _Houston_ _Texas_ _75248_
    No.   Street   City   State   Zip

Telephone No. _207-868-9931_

Are you legally eligible for employment in the U.S.A.? _Yes_

State age if under 18 or over 70. _17_

What method of transportation will you use to get to work? _my own car_

Position(s) applied for _secretary_ Rate of pay expected $ _Open_ per week

Would you work Full-Time _No_ Part-Time _Yes_ Specify days and hours if part-time _3-10 p.m. Monday-Friday, weekends_

Were you previously employed by us? _No_ If yes, when? _NA_

If your application is considered favorably, on what date will you be available for work? _Immediately_ 19 _86_

Are there any other experiences, skills, or qualifications which you feel would especially fit you for work with our organization? _I have taken several business education courses including typing, shorthand, and data processing, and received excellent grades in all. I have also worked as a part-time typist for various companies during the past two years._

RECORD OF EDUCATION

School	Name and Address of School	Course of Study	Check Last Year Completed				Did You Graduate?	List Diploma or Degree
Elementary	Woodrow Wilson Elementary School 261 W. Hobsen Drive Morris, Texas 22576		5	6	7	8 ✓	☒ Yes ☐ No	
High	Central High School 1010 Arapaho Road Houston, Texas 75248	Business Education	1	2	3 ✓	4	☐ Yes ☒ No	
College			1	2	3	4	☐ Yes ☐ No	
Other (Specify)			1	2	3	4	☐ Yes ☐ No	

(Turn to Next Page)

List below all present and past employment, beginning with your most recent

I

Name and Address of Company and Type of Business	From Mo.	Yr.	To Mo.	Yr.	Describe the work you did	Weekly Starting Salary	Weekly Last Salary	Reason for Leaving	Name of Supervisor
Bidwell's Merchandise 2622 Reston Drive Houston, Texas (Dept. Store) Telephone 207-662-4593	10	85	12	85	typing and filing of customer correspondence.	$4.00 per hour	4.00 per hour	Not enough work — could only give me 10 hrs./wk.	Carolyn Smith

II

Name and Address of Company and Type of Business	From Mo.	Yr.	To Mo.	Yr.	Describe the work you did	Weekly Starting Salary	Weekly Last Salary	Reason for Leaving	Name of Supervisor
Industrial Systems Inc. 187 North Shore Road Galena, Texas (Manufact.) Telephone 207-711-1821	6	85	9	85	typing, short-hand, filing and some data processing	3.50 per hour	3.50 per hour	Return to school — end of summer job	Juanita Perez

III

Name and Address of Company and Type of Business	From Mo.	Yr.	To Mo.	Yr.	Describe the work you did	Weekly Starting Salary	Weekly Last Salary	Reason for Leaving	Name of Supervisor
Rogers Construction Co. 352 N. Mansfield Houston, Texas (Construction) Telephone 207-777-8998	10	84	2	85	Typed lengthy job proposals and bids for contractor	3.25 per hour	3.25 per hour	Job completed	Sam Warren

IV

Name and Address of Company and Type of Business	From Mo.	Yr.	To Mo.	Yr.	Describe the work you did	Weekly Starting Salary	Weekly Last Salary	Reason for Leaving	Name of Supervisor
Doug's Deli 908 Willow Avenue Crystal, Texas (Restau.) Telephone 600-383-5555	3	84	10	84	Took customer orders, washed dishes, helped prepare sandwiches.	3.15 per hour	3.50 per hour	To take job related to my career interests.	Doug Salazar

May we contact the employers listed above? ___Yes___ If not, indicate by No. which one(s) you do not wish us to contact ___NA___

PERSONAL REFERENCES (Not Former Employers or Relatives)

Name and Occupation	Address	Phone Number
Cindy Peters, Business Ed. Teacher Central High School, Houston, Texas	221 Highpoint Road Houston, Texas 22576	207-662-2323
Mildred Morgan, business owner Happy Child Day Care Center	897 University Avenue Crystal, Texas 56925	600-383-2121
Ralph Masterson, Pastor United Church	618 North Lawrence Houston, Texas 75248	207-868-8282

MILITARY SERVICE RECORD

Were you in U.S. Armed Forces? Yes_____ No__✓__ If yes, what Branch? ___NA___

Dates of duty: From ___NA___ To ___NA___ Rank at discharge ___NA___
       Month Day Year   Month Day Year

List duties in the service including special training ___NA___

Have you taken any training under the G.I. Bill of Rights? ___NA___ If yes, what training did you take? ___NA___

—2—

Some businesses receive dozens of application letters for each job. If they advertise in the newspaper, they may receive hundreds of letters. They usually interview only those applicants who are qualified for the job and whose letters are neat and well written. This means that if you are very careful about how you write your letter, you will have a big advantage. The letter on the next page is an example of a well-written letter of application.

After you have written one good letter, you can make it the model for other letters of application. Of course you will have to change the information in the first paragraph. Information about the specific job and how you learned about it will vary from letter to letter. But the paragraphs about your education and experience and the last paragraph will need little changing.

Before you type your actual letter, look at the sample letter on the next page. Then read the suggestions below. This will help you prepare a neatly typed, final copy of your letter, ready for mailing.

1. If you are typing your own letter, clean the characters in your typewriter before you begin. A letter typed on a dirty machine will show some letters (such as e) with blackened areas. Set your margins at about one and one-half inches.
2. The first part of your letter consists of three lines called the *heading*. The heading should include your address and the date you are writing the letter. You can place the heading either to the left or the right. It can either *begin* at the left margin or *end* even with the right margin. Type your street address two inches from the top of the sheet. On the next line, type your city, state, and zip code. On the third line, type the date.
3. The *inside address* (the name and address of the person or company to whom you are writing) *must* start from the left margin. The first line of the inside address should be about four or five spaces down from the last line of the heading. If your letter is very short, leave more space between the heading and the inside address. The purpose of leaving more space is to center your letter on the page. Check the spelling of the name of the person and company. Most people are particular about how their names are spelled! Also make certain that the address is correct.

This personnel director is reading an impressive letter of application. The person who wrote the letter has made a big step toward getting a job that many people want.

4. If you are addressing your letter to an individual, your *salutation* should be *Dear Mr. Fox:*, *Dear Miss Doe:*, *Dear Mrs. Winn:*, or *Dear Ms. Jones:*. Always follow the person's name with a colon. If you are writing to a company or personnel office and do not know the name of the person who will read your letter, use the salutation *Dear Sir or Madam:*.
5. Type the *body* of your letter very carefully. If there are no mistakes, it will make the best impression possible.
6. Your *closing* should be *Yours truly, Yours very truly,* or *Very truly yours,*. Always follow the closing with a comma. Only the first word of the closing should begin with a capital letter.
7. After the closing, space down four spaces and type your name.
8. Before you remove your letter from the typewriter, read it carefully to see if there are any mistakes. You can do a neater job of correcting mistakes if you do so before you remove the letter from the typewriter.
9. Sign your name in ink above the typewritten signature.

A Well-Written, Properly Typed Letter of Application

12 Spaces

Return Address and Date

638 Hollywood Drive
Santa Barbara, CA 93111
May 12, 1985

4 or 5 Spaces

Ms. Sally Kennedy, Personnel Director
Lectradynamics Incorporated
6255 Hollyfield Avenue
Santa Barbara, CA 93110

Inside address

2 Spaces

Dear Ms. Kennedy: *Salutation*

2 Spaces

State where you learned about job

Mr. Russel Smith, the work-experience counselor at Monroe East High School, suggested that I contact you about the clerk-typist position in your business office. Please consider me an applicant for this position.

State that you want to apply

I will graduate from Monroe East High School on June 12. I have majored in business education. My courses have included computer science, word processing, and two years of typewriting. I type seventy words a minute, and I am familiar with several types of office computers.

Body

State your education and experience

During my senior year at Monroe East High School, I have participated in the work-experience program. My work station has been in the accounting office of the El Dorado Oil Company, where I have further developed the skills I have been learning in school.

Ask for an interview

I plan to continue my education in night school and hope someday to become an executive secretary. May I have an interview? I shall be glad to call at your convenience. My home telephone is 964-9657.

2 Spaces

Yours truly, *Closing*

State your phone number

Anita Dobbins

4 Spaces

Anita Dobbins *Signature*

Personal Data Sheets (Resumes)

A good letter of application will probably convince an employer to call you in for an interview. You can, however, increase your chances of getting an interview by including a **personal data sheet** with your letter. Your letter will contain general information about your education and experience. Your data sheet will list details about you, your education, and your experience.

The personal data sheet, also called a *resume,* gives the employer more detailed information about you than can be included in the letter of application. The employer will be able to find the detailed information more quickly and easily on this data sheet. This information should help sell you to the employer.

Your personal data sheet may include detailed information about the courses you have taken in school; your work experience, if any; and your hobbies or interests related to the job for which you are applying. If you have no experience, don't mention this. Describe only the qualities and abilities you *do* have. You may also want to include the names of references on your personal data sheet.

Make several copies of your data sheet. Include one with each letter of application. Be as careful and neat in preparing your data sheet as you were in preparing your letter. Studying the sample data sheet on the next page will help you prepare your own data sheet.

Performance Tests

Depending on the type of job you are applying for, you may be asked to take a performance test. If you apply for a job as a secretary, for example, you will probably be given shorthand and typing tests. If you apply for a job as a welder, you will be asked to do some welding to demonstrate your welding skills.

The employer's main purpose in giving the tests is to find out whether or not you can do the job adequately. The employer may also use the test results to compare your skills with those of other applicants. How well you do on the test could determine whether or not you get the job.

If you believe you will have to take a test, ask someone who has taken a similar test what the test is like. It is a good idea to practice your skills be-

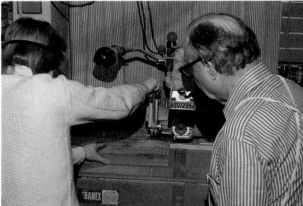

Doing well on a performance test is a must if you want certain kinds of jobs. Whenever possible you should practice before you take the actual test.

fore you go to take the test. In many cases you will be timed—so time yourself in your practice sessions.

The Interview

Application forms, letters of application, personal data sheets, and performance tests are all important parts of getting the job you want. You will probably not be hired, though, until you have had an **interview.** An interview is a formal meeting between an employer and a job applicant. For the employer, the interview is a way to find out whether or not the applicant is the best person for the job. For you, the applicant, the interview is a way to find out whether or not you would like the job.

An employment interview can be one of the most important experiences of your life! What happens in this twenty- to thirty-minute period may influence your whole career. Yet some job applicants give the

An Impressive Personal Data Sheet

SALLY BROPHY

PRESENT ADDRESS
510 W. Gibson
Towanda, IL 61702
(309) 442-1798

HOME ADDRESS
6219 Hill Farm Road
Peoria, IL 61614
(309) 683-6030

CAREER OBJECTIVE: To develop communication and organizational skills, and an awareness of the practical side of business in the fields of publishing, public relations, or advertising.

EDUCATION: Limestone High School, Bartonville, IL
Graduated June, 1981
Grade Point Average - 3.8 on 4.0 scale
College Preparatory Program

HONORS AND ACTIVITIES: Dean's Honor List
Student Council
Student Career Day Leader
Yearbook, sports editor
Swimming Team

WORK EXPERIENCE: Williams and Williams Publishing Company, Bloomington, IL
production coordinator, July 1981 - Present; responsible for variety of assignments dealing with production of textbooks, including photo acquisition and dummy layouts.

P.A. Bergner and Company, Peoria, IL
sales associate, part-time August 1979-June 1981; responsible for customer service and some ordering of merchandise.

Limestone High School, Bartonville, IL
swimming instructor, summers, 1978, 1979.

HOBBIES: reading, traveling, swimming

REFERENCES: On request

impression that they are at the interview simply because they have nothing better to do. A personnel manager for a large corporation on the West Coast told about a young woman who came to an interview wearing a bathing suit. She was on her way home from the beach! Of course, she didn't get the job.

The purpose of the interview is to allow the interviewer to learn several things about you. The interviewer will want to know such things as

- your attitude toward people and work,
- your education and work experience, and
- your career plans.

The interview also gives you a chance to learn more about the job. You will get a better idea of whether or not you would like the work. You will also have a chance to learn more about the company.

Before the Interview

There are several things you should do to prepare for the interview. The better prepared you are, the greater your chances for success once the interview begins.

If you call for an appointment, state your name clearly. Then tell how you learned of the job opening. Write down the exact time and place of the interview. Get the correct spelling of the interviewer's name and make sure you can pronounce the name correctly. Most often you will be interviewed by either the employer or the personnel manager.

Before the interview, study your personal data sheet. Be prepared to answer any questions you might be asked about the information on your data sheet.

Learn all you can about the company. What products or services does the company offer? How many people work for the company?

Some companies publish brochures and annual reports that give good information. Others print catalogs that describe their products. You can even learn about a company from reading about it in the Yellow Pages. You may also ask your family or teacher what they know about a company.

This information will give you something besides yourself to talk about during the interview. It will also show the interviewer that you are interested in the company. Your knowledge about the company will make a good impression on the interviewer.

You should take several things with you to the interview. Take a pen and pencil, your social security card, and a copy of your personal data sheet. Take a copy of your data sheet even if you have already mailed one to the employer. The employer may have misplaced it, or perhaps never received it.

Go to the interview alone! Do not take anyone with you. One high school girl took a friend along to her interview to boost her confidence. Her friend was also looking for work. As it happened, the employer liked the friend's qualifications better than those of the girl he was interviewing—so the employer hired the friend. Employers seldom hire applicants who bring other people with them to an interview.

Arrive five minutes early. If you drive to the interview, allow some extra time for the possibility of heavy traffic. If you are even one minute late—or rush in at the last minute—you will appear to be a careless person. But don't be too early either. Arriving five minutes before the time set for the interview is about right.

This young lady has come to her interview well dressed and well prepared. She knows how important an interview can be—the next few minutes could affect her entire life.

Rushing to an interview at the last minute makes a poor first impression. Allow yourself plenty of time—try to arrive about five minutes before your scheduled time.

Usually the first person you speak to when you arrive is a receptionist or the interviewer's secretary. Be very polite and cooperative with this person. The employer may ask for this person's opinion of you after you have gone!

Appearance

Your appearance is an extremely important part of the interview. Make sure your appearance is just right before you go to the interview. When you arrive, the employer's first impression of you will be based on how you look. Obviously you want to make a good first impression.

You should, of course, take a bath or shower before dressing for the interview. This may seem obvious, but some people fail to do this. As soon as these people walk into the interviewer's office, their body odor loses them any chance they had of getting the job. The strong smell of cigarettes has also lost many people jobs. This odor is very offensive to those who do not smoke.

Your hair should be freshly shampooed and neatly combed. Boys should be clean shaven. Few employers like extreme hairstyles and beards.

Beware of using too much perfume or cologne. Strong smells, even pleasing ones, can be very unpleasant.

It is also a mistake to wear a lot of jewelry, especially if it is large or jangly. Girls should use makeup sparingly. In short, don't wear anything that will draw attention to itself and away from you.

Many interviewers say they always notice an applicant's hands. Be sure that your hands and nails are clean and your nails neatly trimmed.

When you select your clothes for the interview, remember that you are looking for a job, not going to a party! The type of clothes you wear should depend on the type of job you are applying for. If you are applying for a factory or construction job, neat, clean work clothes are appropriate. Boys looking for a sales or office job should wear a dress shirt and tie with a suit or sport coat. Girls should wear a dress or a conservative blouse and skirt. Pant suits for girls are acceptable to most employers, but not all.

Your clothes should be conservative, not faddish. They need not be expensive, but they should be clean and unwrinkled.

Make a Decision

Suppose that you have three job interviews on Saturday. One interview is for a job as counter clerk in a fast food restaurant. Another interview is for a job as a sales clerk in a retail clothing store. The third interview is for a job as ditch digger for a plumber. You don't have time to change clothes between interviews so you must decide on one set of clothing for all three interviews. What's your decision—how will you dress for the interviews? Give reasons for your decision.

This fellow looks like he just "dropped in" for his interview. He has broken every rule of proper dress and grooming and probably has no chance of getting the job.

People who take the time to shine their shoes make a better impression than those who do not. Leather shoes are more impressive than tennis or canvas shoes. Matching dress socks should be worn to the interview, not white athletic socks. Hose and dress shoes are appropriate for girls.

The employer will look at you as someone who will represent the company. When two applicants have about the same qualifications, the employer will hire the one with the best appearance. So look your best!

During the Interview

You may be introduced to the interviewer by the receptionist or secretary. If not, the interviewer may introduce himself or herself to you. If this happens, say something such as "Hello, I'm John Jones, and I'm interested in the job as trainee in your bank." Speak clearly and loudly enough to be heard, and smile.

Do not offer to shake hands unless the interviewer offers first. When shaking hands, always grasp the person's hand firmly. A "limp fish" handshake can cause some people to think you have a weak personality. But don't prove how strong you are by grabbing the interviewer's hand and crushing it!

Stand until the interviewer asks you to sit. If you are not asked to sit down, then stand during the interview. If you do sit, sit alertly. Don't slouch!

Although you will feel nervous at first, you will become more relaxed as the interview goes along. It is normal to be a little nervous. But there is nothing to be afraid of.

Your eyes should meet the interviewer's eyes often. Some people do not trust a person who cannot look them in the eye.

Don't make the mistake of placing your purse, book, or any other possession on the edge of the interviewer's desk. The interviewer might think you are being disrespectful or too casual about the interview. If you are carrying something, keep it beside you.

Try to keep your hands still. Usually it is best to keep them in your lap. Don't lean on the interviewer's desk or try to read papers on the desk. Never chew gum or smoke during an interview.

There are two basic ways of interviewing. One method is for the interviewer to simply ask you to talk about yourself. If this happens, you must do most of the talking. Be sure to discuss all of your qualifications for the job. It is also a good idea to show that you are interested in the company. Give some specific reasons for wanting to work for that company. This is why it's important to learn as much as possible about the company before you go to the interview.

In the other type of interview, the interviewer finds out about your qualifications by asking specific questions. This is probably the most common type of interview. The following questions are some of the most frequently asked.

- "Why do you want to work for this company?"
- "What do you plan to be doing five years from now?"
- "Are you looking for permanent or temporary work?"
- "Which courses did you like best in school?"

Be prepared to answer such questions completely and honestly. If you do not know the answer to a question, say you do not know. If you try to fake it, the interviewer will probably know it. This makes a poor impression, and you will probably not be hired, even if your qualifications are good.

Two additional questions that are usually asked deserve special attention. These questions are

- "What kind of work would you like to do?" and
- "What salary do you expect?"

Too many young people answer the first question by saying "anything." This irritates many interviewers. They want to put you in the job for which you are best qualified. There is no job titled "anything."

If you are asked what salary you expect, do not mention a specific amount—it may be too low. If you give a low amount and are hired, you may be paid less than other people doing the same work. If you mention an amount that's too high, you may not be hired at all. The interviewer may feel that you would not be satisfied with a lower salary.

In answer to the salary question, say, "I'm sure you know better than I do what a fair salary would be. What do you usually pay for this kind of work?"

If the interviewer presses you for a specific answer, mention an amount that you believe others get for this kind of work.

Sometimes interviewers don't mention salary at all. In these cases, wait until the interview is almost over. Then ask what you would be paid if you were hired. Don't ask this question early in the interview. This might make a bad impression on the interviewer. He or she might think that you are interested only in what you will get out of the job.

If you are applying for a permanent, full-time position, it is all right to ask whether or not you will get a vacation. Again, wait until the end of the interview to ask this question. Part-time and temporary workers usually do not get paid vacations.

You may be asked to talk with someone in the company besides the interviewer. This person might be a department head or someone you would be working with if hired. Being asked to talk to a second person usually means that the interviewer is impressed with you. It usually means that your chances of being hired are very good.

Common Interview Questions

Listed below are some of the most frequently asked interview questions. You probably won't be asked all of these questions, but you'll be asked several. How will you answer them? It's a good idea to decide how you will answer the questions and then practice your answers.

- "Why would you like to work for our company?"
- "Are you looking for permanent or temporary work?"
- "What makes you think that you can do this job?"
- "What jobs have you had? Why did you leave?"
- "What subjects in school did you like best? Least?"
- "What extra-curricular activities did you participate in at school?"
- "What do you want to be doing in five years? In ten years?"
- "Do you prefer working alone or with others?"
- "What is your main strength? Your main weakness?"
- "How do you spend your spare time?"
- "What salary do you expect?"
- "Have you had any serious illnesses?"
- "Do you smoke?"
- "How do you feel about working overtime (beyond the scheduled hours)?"
- "What grades have you received in your schoolwork?"
- "When can you begin work?"
- "How did you become interested in this company?"
- "What questions do you want to ask?"

When the interview is over—go! You know it's over when you have described your qualifications and the interviewer has no more questions. Failing to leave immediately may cost you your chance of being hired.

If you have not been offered a job, it is all right to ask whether or not you will be called. Or you can ask if you may call back in a few days to find out the interviewer's decision. Thank the interviewer for his or her time, and leave. If you pass the receptionist or the secretary on your way out, thank that person, too.

After the Interview

After each job interview, take a few minutes to evaluate your performance. Which questions did you answer particularly well? Which could you have answered better? Did the interviewer ask any questions you weren't expecting? If so, you might want to jot them down so that you'll be ready if they're asked in another interview.

Can you think of any additional information about yourself that you should have provided? Evaluate your appearance and how well you presented yourself verbally. Did you use standard English?

If you evaluate yourself after each interview, you will learn from each experience. You will get better and better at making a good impression in an interview.

If the interviewer neither offered nor refused you the job, there's still time to make a favorable impression. Follow up the interview with a thank-you letter. Since few people do this, it will make the interviewer remember you.

Your thank-you letter need not be long. Just thank the interviewer for his or her time. Mention again that you are interested in the job. If you forgot to say something that you feel you should have said, include it in your letter.

Prepare your thank-you letter carefully. (See the suggestions for preparing letters, pages 77 and 80.) After you have completed your letter, mail it promptly.

If you make a good impression on the interviewer, you will have a good chance of getting the job.

REVIEW YOUR LEARNING   CHAPTER 5

CHAPTER SUMMARY

There are proven ways to find and get the job that you want. You begin by finding as many job leads as possible. Some good sources of job leads are school counselors and teachers, family and friends, employment agencies, newspaper ads, government offices, schools, and direct calls. By making use of all these job-lead sources, you will increase your chances of finding the best job for you.

As soon as you have a complete list of job leads, you can begin applying for jobs. It is very important that you put a great deal of serious effort into this process. How you go about applying may determine whether or not you get the job.

To successfully apply for a job, use standard English in all of your written and spoken communications with the employer. Prepare all application forms, letters, and data sheets as neatly as possible. When you are granted an interview, take some time to prepare for it and make sure your appearance is just right. Finally, you will want to practice and put to use all of the interviewing tips provided in this chapter. By doing all of these things you will increase your chances of being offered a job.

WORDS YOU SHOULD KNOW

interview
job leads
personal
references
standard English

STUDY QUESTIONS

1. Why is accepting the first job offered often not a good idea?
2. What are five good sources of job leads?
3. Why it is important to have as many job leads as possible?
4. Why is it important to use standard English in a letter of application and during an interview?
5. There will be questions on most application forms that will not apply to you. How will you show that you did not overlook these questions?
6. Why is it a bad idea to answer the question about job preferences with the word "anything?"
7. What four situations call for writing a letter of application?
8. What is the purpose of the first paragraph of a letter of application? The last paragraph?

REVIEW YOUR LEARNING

9. What kind of information should be included on a personal data sheet?
10. List three things you should do when setting up an appointment for an interview.
11. List three things you should take with you to an interview.
12. Why is it important to go alone when being interviewed for a job?
13. What are the two types of interviews?
14. What should you do after the interview if you are still being considered for the job?

DISCUSSION TOPICS

1. Suppose you were offered two jobs. One is a paying job in a fast food restaurant. The other is a non-paying job in a career you think you might like as an adult. You cannot take them both. Which would you choose and why?
2. If you were an employer and you had forty applicants for one job, would you interview them all? If not, how would you decide which ones to interview?
3. If you were an employer, what questions would you ask job applicants? Why did you choose these questions?
4. Explain some of your experiences with first impressions. How do first impressions change as you get to know a person? Can an employer usually get a true impression of an applicant in half an hour?
5. How will you convince an employer that you should be hired for a job?
6. Suppose you want to work in a city five hundred miles away. How would you go about getting a job there?

SUGGESTED ACTIVITIES

1. Select one job lead from the "Help Wanted" ads in your local newspaper. Write a letter of application. Carefully follow the instructions on writing application letters.
2. Divide into groups of three or four. Each group should then select one person to play the role of interviewer. The other students should take turns playing the role of the job applicant. After the interviews, discuss with the entire class the correct and incorrect behavior shown in the interviews.

You, Your Employer, and Your Co-Workers

Once you get a job, you will want to keep it. More than that, you will want to be successful on your job.

In this chapter you will learn several things that will increase your chances of being successful on the job. You will learn about the importance of having a positive attitude. You will learn what your employer will expect from you, and what you can rightfully expect from your employer. You will also learn what you can do to get along with your co-workers. After reading this chapter, you will be on your way to a successful job experience.

DO YOU KNOW . . .
- what factor is the most important in job success?
- what an employer will expect from you?
- what you can expect from an employer?
- what you need to do to get along with your co-workers?

CAN YOU DEFINE . . .
- attitude?
- commission?
- initiative?
- layoff notice?
- overtime?
- salary?
- severance pay?
- termination notice?
- unemployment compensation?
- wages?
- work evaluation?

Your Attitude

Perhaps the most important factor in your job success is your own **attitude**. Your attitude is your basic outlook on life. It is your way of looking at the world and the people in it.

Attitudes are often classified into two general types—positive and negative. People with positive attitudes tend to be optimistic, cheerful, and outgoing. They see life as exciting, worthwhile, and enjoyable. They usually get along well with other people and are happy most of the time.

People with negative attitudes complain a lot. They are often angry and withdrawn. They are unhappy a great deal of the time, and they do not seem to like other people much. They usually have a difficult time getting along with other people.

How well you get along with your employer and your co-workers will depend on your attitude. If you have a negative attitude, your employer and your co-workers will respond negatively to you. If you have a positive attitude, they will respond positively.

The main reason young workers lose their jobs is because they don't get along well with others. In fact, one study of beginning workers who had been fired showed that 82 percent lost their jobs because they did not get along with their fellow workers. The following story tells of one such worker.

Sara is nineteen. She has a job as a waitress in a restaurant known for its fine food and excellent service. Sara dresses neatly and is always well-groomed. She has a good memory and never makes mistakes on orders. Her arithmetic is always correct on customers' checks. But Sara does not smile easily and is often irritable. This makes the customers uncomfortable. As a result, Sara's tips are usually smaller than those of the other waitresses.

The busiest day of the year for the restaurant is Mother's Day. Every worker is expected to work on that day. However, Sara wanted to visit her own mother in Chicago on Mother's Day, so she begged the restaurant manager to let her off. Although the manager gave Sara the day off (without pay), he and the other waitresses felt that Sara had let them down. Everyone else had to work that much harder. For this reason, and because Sara finds it so difficult to get along with other employees and the customers, the manager has decided to fire Sara.

Sara is intelligent and a good worker, yet she is going to be fired. What could she have done differently to save her job?

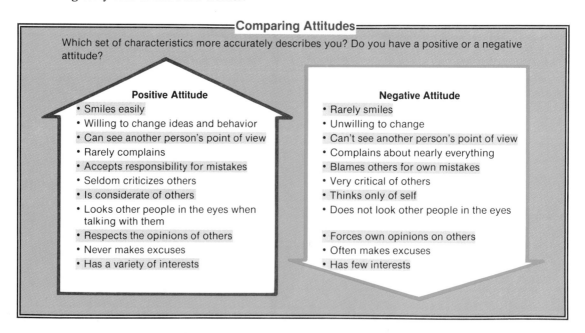

Comparing Attitudes

Which set of characteristics more accurately describes you? Do you have a positive or a negative attitude?

Positive Attitude
- Smiles easily
- Willing to change ideas and behavior
- Can see another person's point of view
- Rarely complains
- Accepts responsibility for mistakes
- Seldom criticizes others
- Is considerate of others
- Looks other people in the eyes when talking with them
- Respects the opinions of others
- Never makes excuses
- Has a variety of interests

Negative Attitude
- Rarely smiles
- Unwilling to change
- Can't see another person's point of view
- Complains about nearly everything
- Blames others for own mistakes
- Very critical of others
- Thinks only of self
- Does not look other people in the eyes
- Forces own opinions on others
- Often makes excuses
- Has few interests

This worker's positive, cheerful attitude will go a long way toward making her successful in the world of work.

Some general characteristics of people with positive and negative attitudes are listed in the box on page 92. Compare the characteristics. Are your own characteristics similar to those of people with negative attitudes or people with positive attitudes?

If you have a positive attitude, you are already on your way to success on the job. If you think you may have a negative attitude, you'll be happy to know that you can change your attitude. You can work at becoming the kind of person who likes other people. The younger you are when you start, the sooner you can develop a positive attitude—and the sooner you will be successful and happy on the job.

Your Employer's Expectations

Your employer will give you a paycheck regularly. In exchange, your employer will expect certain things from you. Your success on the job will depend on how well you meet your employer's expectations.

There is an old saying—"a day's work for a day's pay." At the very least, your employer will expect a

good day's work from you. In addition, your employer will expect you to have the qualities listed below.

- Cooperation
- Honesty
- Initiative
- Willingness to learn
- Willingness to follow directions
- Dependability
- Enthusiasm
- Ability to accept criticism
- Loyalty

Cooperation

The employer who pays your salary has a right to expect your full cooperation. Full cooperation means working well with everyone on the job to reach a common goal.

You can show your willingness to cooperate in many ways. One way is to do the tasks you don't like to do without complaining or trying to get someone else to do them for you. Another way to cooperate is to do your fair share of the work when you work with others. You can also cooperate by respecting your co-workers' ideas, even if these ideas differ from your own.

At the very least, your employer will expect you to give "a day's work for a day's pay."

Too many people have the attitude that each worker is responsible only for his or her own job. These people resent being asked to help others do their jobs. Don't make this mistake. Instead, pitch in willingly when a co-worker is behind or needs help. You may even want to volunteer your help when you see that a co-worker is having trouble. You will make a good impression on your employer and your co-workers when you demonstrate this kind of cooperation.

Honesty

Employers expect their workers to be honest with them and with the company. But some workers are not honest.

Probably the most common type of dishonesty on the job is stealing time. Your time during working hours doesn't belong to you. It belongs to your employer. Yet some people arrive at work a few minutes late every day. Others steal time from their employers by taking extra-long breaks or by stopping work before the end of the workday.

If your hours of work are eight to five, arrive a few minutes before eight. Then you can actually start working at eight. You should continue working, except for breaks and lunch, until five.

Stealing time costs the company a great deal of money. This type of stealing is probably the most costly form of dishonesty in business. Think of it this way—the money lost is money that might have been used to increase your salary or benefit you in some other way.

Another type of dishonesty on the job is stealing company property. Many employees have been fired for stealing materials and tools that belong to the company.

In one case a young man regularly used the office postage stamps for personal letters. He was not fired, but when it came time to select a new office manager, he was passed over. His dishonesty cost him a chance to advance in the company.

Be honest with your employer and your company. Don't steal company time or property. As an honest worker you will have a much better chance of being successful in your work.

Initiative

Suppose you have completed your job and no one has told you what to do next. What would you do

If you finish your work, don't sit down and wait for someone to tell you what to do. Find something to do. Show some initiative.

in a situation like this? Would you sit and wait for instructions from your boss, or would you find something that needed to be done—and do it?

Most employers expect their employees to take some **initiative**. Taking initiative means doing what needs to be done without being told to do it. After you have been on the job awhile, your employer will probably expect you to find things to do without being told.

Martha had just graduated from high school when she was hired as a secretary. Martha was a very pleasant person and a good typist, but she had never learned to use initiative. As soon as she completed her tasks, she always sat down and read a magazine. There was other work to do, but Martha never did it. She only worked when she was told exactly what job to do.

Because Martha never took the initiative to find something to do, her boss, Mrs. Wilson, had to supervise her constantly. This took so much of Mrs. Wilson's time that she could not get her own work done. She discussed the problem with Martha on two separate occasions. But Martha was either not able or not willing to change. Mrs. Wilson finally let her go. Martha's replacement kept busy and required little supervision, and Mrs. Wilson was able to do her own work.

You must use good judgment when taking initiative. Do not attempt to do work that you are not qualified to do.

Remember—if you never do any more than you get paid for, you will never get paid for any more than you do. Showing initiative will help you be successful on your job.

Make a Decision

Suppose that you have just finished everything your boss told you to do, and there are still two hours until quitting time. The boss left a few minutes ago, saying she wouldn't be back today. You've noticed several things that you could do during the remaining two hours, but you are also thinking you could do your homework assignment for English class tomorrow. It's an important assignment, and you won't have much time after work. What's your decision—will you do some extra jobs at work, your English assignment, or some of each? Give reasons for your decision.

Willingness to Learn

Employers expect their workers to learn the way things are done in the company. Learning a company's methods is usually not much of a problem for new workers.

You should make a special effort to learn everything you can about your job and your company. The more skills and knowledge you acquire, the better. Most workers who are promoted are workers who have taken the trouble to learn more than just their own daily tasks.

Willingness to Follow Directions

When you are given directions about how to do your work, you are expected to follow them *exactly*. That is why directions are given. You may not understand the reason for doing things in a certain way, but your employer or supervisor has a reason. Do the work as you are told.

After you have worked on the job awhile, you may make suggestions if you think your ideas will be well received. Be careful about this. Some people resent suggestions, even if they are good ones.

You may think you know more than your boss, but you should always follow directions. In almost all cases your employer or supervisor will know the right way to do the job.

Dependability

Employers expect their workers to be on the job every day, and to be there on time. Employees who come to work late can be fired. Even if they aren't fired, they are resented by the workers who do come to work on time. As a result, undependable workers will have problems working cooperatively with fellow workers.

If you are ill and can't go to work, call your employer or the person in charge. Say that you will be absent and explain why. Call as soon as you know that you can't go to work. Many workers have lost their jobs because they did not call their employers to report an absence due to illness.

Don't miss work unless you must. Be at work on time and work your full shift. Your employer will soon learn that you are a dependable worker, someone who can be counted on.

Enthusiasm

Employers know that the most productive employees are those who like their work and show enthusiasm for it. Your employer will expect you to be enthusiastic about your work. If you enjoy your work, this will be easy.

You may not, however, like some parts of your work. You would be fortunate if you found everything about your job interesting.

If there are certain things you don't like doing, don't dwell on how much you dislike these tasks. Instead, focus on the positive parts of the job. When other people ask how you like your job, tell them about the good things. This will help make the job more interesting and enjoyable. Your enthusiasm will grow, and you'll be a much happier person. You will also be a more productive and successful employee.

Ability to Accept Criticism

Constructive criticism is necessary on every job. Criticism is the employer's way of letting you know how the job is supposed to be done. Your employer will expect you to accept criticism without snapping back or sulking.

> Nancy was a bookkeeper in a bank. She was a good worker. She almost never missed a day of work, and she was always on time. Nancy's problem was that she could not accept criticism and benefit from it. On several occasions she made incorrect entries in her records. Each time this happened her supervisor told her she must give more careful attention to certain details on her job. Then Nancy sulked—she wouldn't speak or smile for the rest of the day. Nancy's sulking put a great strain on her supervisor because he could see the effect his criticism had on Nancy. Still, he felt the criticism was necessary. The supervisor finally had to let Nancy go because it took so much of his time to figure out how to approach Nancy without hurting her feelings.

Regardless of how you may feel when you are criticized, try to take it good-naturedly. Listen carefully and politely to your critic. Then thank him or her for trying to help you.

Accepting criticism means more than just listening politely and thanking the person. It means making use of the criticism. Think about your critic's comments and try to see how they can help you become a better worker.

Of course, there are employers and supervisors who are unfairly critical, and some lose their tempers. Short of quitting, however, there is nothing you can do about such things. You must listen politely without losing your temper. Regardless of how a criticism is delivered, it can be constructive or destructive depending upon how you use it.

If you were an employer and you had to correct some mistakes, which type of employee would you rather have—the kind that gets upset, or the kind that listens and tries to improve? Learning to accept criticism will help you progress in the world of work.

Loyalty

You have probably heard the expression "don't bite the hand that feeds you." This is certainly true in your relationship with your employer. You must be *for* your employer and the company, not against them.

No person is perfect, and neither is any company. You may not agree with everything your employer does. You may object to some of the company policies. But you should not complain to your friends or "run down" the company. Employers expect their workers to keep to themselves those things that pertain to the business.

You will never be happy working for an employer if you have only negative things to say about him or her. If for some reason you cannot be loyal, look for another job. If you must look for another job, resist the temptation to be critical of your present employer, especially when talking to other employers. No one wants to hire a complainer. Other employers also want loyal employees.

Don't bite the hand that feeds you. Be loyal to your employer. Your job and your chances for being successful depend on your employer's being successful. It's to your benefit to do all you can to help your employer.

What You Can Expect

After reading about what your employer can expect of you, you may feel that you are expected to give a lot without getting much in return. This is not so. You have a right to expect certain things from your employer. Some employers are more considerate than others, but you can expect your employer to provide the following things.

- Payments
- Safe working conditions
- Training
- Introductions to co-workers
- Explanations of policies, rules, regulations, and changes in your duties
- Evaluations of your work
- Discipline if you break rules
- Honesty

Payments

You can expect your employer to pay you for the work you do. You can also expect your employer to take care of various payments in your behalf. Your employer should deduct income taxes from your pay and set aside money for your social security and worker's compensation benefits. You will read more about these benefits in Chapter 23.

Your employer can figure your pay in several different ways. You will probably agree upon the type of payment when you are hired. In most cases the employer will calculate your pay the same way that he figures the pay for people who do jobs similar to yours. In a few cases, usually where sales jobs are involved, workers are given choices in how their pay will be figured.

Wages. Most beginning workers are paid a certain amount for each hour they work. Pay received for hourly work is usually referred to as **wages.** For example, your wage might be $4 an hour, $5.35 an hour, or if you're highly skilled, $20 an hour.

As a wage earner you will probably receive paychecks of varying amounts from one payday to the next. The reason for this is that you will probably not work the same number of hours every pay period. Even if you work the same number of hours every day, there may be more workdays in some pay periods than others.

If you work more than forty hours a week, you can expect your employer to pay you **overtime**. Overtime, also called *time and a half,* is a wage 50 percent more per hour than what you are normally paid. You can figure how much your overtime rate is by dividing your regular rate by two, and then adding that amount to your regular rate. For example, if you're making $4 an hour, your overtime rate would be $6 an hour ($4 ÷ 2 = $2; $4 + $2 = $6).

State and federal law requires that employers pay workers overtime for every hour they work over forty hours in a week. There are, however, some exceptions to this rule. For example, employers with fewer than four employees and employers whose businesses make less than a certain amount of money do not have to pay workers overtime.

If you have questions about whether or not you should receive overtime pay, first ask your employer. If you are still uncertain, call the nearest office of the Wage and Hour Division of the Labor Department. The number will be listed under United States Labor Department in the White Pages of the phone book.

Salary. Instead of paying you by the hour, your employer may pay you a **salary**. A salary is a fixed amount of pay for a certain period of time, usually a year or month. Salaried workers receive the same amount each paycheck, whether they work the same number of hours or not.

Most managers, supervisors, and company executives receive a yearly salary, rather than hourly wages. Whether they average eighty hours or thirty hours of work a week, they receive the amount agreed upon at the beginning of the year. They do *not* receive overtime pay.

Commissions. Most salespeople are paid a **commission**. A commission is a payment that is a percentage of the total amount sold by the salesperson. For example, suppose you have a job selling vacuum cleaners, and you are paid a 50 percent commission. If one week you sell $1000 worth of vacuum cleaners, your employer will pay you $500. If the next week you sell no vacuum cleaners, your employer will not pay you anything.

Most employers pay their beginning salespeople a wage or salary while they are learning how to sell the company's product. As these new salespeople gain experience, more of their pay is based on commissions and less on the wage or salary.

Safe Working Conditions

Your employer should provide safe working conditions for all workers. You should not be asked to use a machine that could be dangerous unless you have been taught how to operate it safely. You should not be asked to work in an unsafe environment. You have the right to expect your employer to fix faulty equipment and do anything else necessary to eliminate hazards on the job.

Training

Your employer should provide whatever training you need to learn the job. The way employers do this will differ from company to company. The amount and type of training you receive usually depend on the difficulty of the job.

You may simply be asked to watch an experienced worker do the job you will be doing. Or a worker may be assigned to teach you how to do the job. In some cases your employer may even send you to a training school.

Introductions

Your employer should introduce you to all of your co-workers. This common courtesy is one you can expect, but it is not always observed. If your employer does not show you this consideration, per-

You can expect your employer to teach you what you need to know to do your job. Usually an older, experienced worker or a supervisor will train you.

haps the other workers will make the introductions. If not, you will have to introduce yourself to your co-workers.

Explanations

Your employer should explain company policies, rules, and regulations so that you understand them. If you do not understand exactly how they affect you, ask for further explanation.

Your employer should also explain any changes that will affect you and your work. Your duties, working relationships, salary, and vacation schedules are some of the things that could change.

Your employer is probably very busy and may assume that you already understand such changes. If for some reason your employer does not explain the changes, ask him or her to explain them. You have a right to know why the changes have been made.

Evaluations

Your employer should evaluate your work and tell you how you are doing. He or she will probably watch you work and will notice how you get along with the other workers. Your employer may then write a **work evaluation**, a written report of your performance on the job. In many cases these evaluations are used to decide whether or not you will be promoted, given a raise, kept in the same position with the same pay, or fired.

After evaluating you, your employer will probably discuss the evaluation with you. This is up to your employer, though. Some employers choose not to discuss the evaluations.

If you do discuss the evaluation with your employer, you will probably discuss it in private to avoid any possible embarrassment. Your employer should discuss both your strengths and weaknesses. Some employers try to save time by discussing weaknesses only. This is not a good way to conduct evaluation interviews. Still, if your boss does it this way, try to profit from the criticism.

The employer's purpose in pointing out your weaknesses is to make you a better worker. It is to your advantage, as well as to the company's, that you improve in your job. If you follow your employer's recommendations, you will increase your chances of receiving more pay raises. Even more important, you will be able to take greater pride in your work. This should help make you a happier person.

If your boss points out your weaknesses but does not suggest how you can improve, ask for suggestions. Your boss should be able to help you. By asking questions you will also show your employer that you are genuinely interested in improving your work.

Study the employee evaluation form on the next page to get an idea of the kinds of things your employer will expect. When you know your employer's expectations, you can make sure you meet them. This will help you advance faster in the world of work.

Make a Decision

You've worked at your new job for six months now. You like the job and think you are doing it pretty well. You'd like to know what your supervisor thinks of your work, and what you can do to move up in the company. The problem is that your supervisor has never commented on your performance, and whenever anyone tries to talk to him, he gets upset because he's so busy. You want a work evaluation, but you don't want to anger your supervisor. What's your decision—speak up and ask for an evaluation, or keep quiet and wait? Give reasons for your decision.

After you have worked on the job for a certain period of time, your employer should let you know how you are doing. Unless you are perfect, your employer will probably point out some ways in which you can improve. Take advantage of this corrective criticism.

Discipline

If you do not follow company rules and regulations, you can expect to be disciplined. You can also be disciplined for failing to meet your employer's expectations. Most employers are fair in penalizing their employees. If you have not fulfilled your responsibilities, you should not resent being disciplined.

Honesty

Just as your employer can expect you to be honest, you can expect your employer to be honest with you. Your employer should pay you what he or she promised to pay you when you took the job. Your employer should not try to deny you any benefits or privileges to which you are entitled.

An Unfair Employer?

If you think your employer is being unfair in some way, you may want to discuss the problem with your employer. Whether or not you do this depends on your personality, your employer's personality, and your relationship with your employer. If you decide to talk about the problem with your employer, don't simply lay the blame on someone else. Be cooperative and understanding. You will then have a better chance of persuading the employer to see things your way.

If you and your employer cannot work things out, look for another job. Don't quit your present job, though, until you have found a job you like better. Some workers have quit their jobs, only to find that they are unable to get another one they like as well.

Getting Along with Co-Workers

Very few jobs are done by one person working alone. In your job you will probably have to work with several people. This means that in addition to meeting your boss's expectations, you must get along with your co-workers. You cannot become truly successful in your work all by yourself. To be successful you must have the friendly cooperation of your co-workers.

Very few people can be successful on their own—most of us need help from our co-workers. Try to get along with all the people on your job.

The reasons why you should try to get along with your co-workers are obvious. In the first place, you will be much happier and enjoy your work more if you have a good relationship with your co-workers. It is also true that if you and your co-workers enjoy working together, you will all get more work done. This will make your employer happy, which could result in pay raises and promotions.

Accept Differences

Getting along well with your co-workers is not always easy. No two people are exactly alike. People see things differently and react in different ways to the same situation. Different attitudes and beliefs can lead to conflicts.

To get along well with your co-workers, you must accept them as worthy individuals. You must accept them even if they are very different from you. Nobody is perfect, but everyone has some good qualities. Try to understand your co-workers' attitudes and behaviors. If you do this, you will be doing your part to encourage good working relationships.

If one of your co-workers is extremely difficult to get along with, do not judge him or her too harshly. There may be good reasons for that person's behavior. Perhaps a bad experience has had a negative effect on your co-worker. Maybe this person has serious problems at home. Whatever the cause, try to do *more* than your share in bringing about a good working relationship. You never know—someday you may be the one in need of some extra understanding and cooperation.

Remember—You're a Beginner

As a beginning worker keep your eyes and ears open. Don't spend a lot of time talking—just be friendly and ask questions about your work. You will probably find that your more experienced co-workers will be happy to help you get started. Some of them may point out your mistakes. If so, they are probably trying to do you a favor. Accept it as a favor, and thank them.

Some of your co-workers may offer suggestions for better ways of doing things. If their suggestions seem like good ones, and if they don't conflict with your boss's instructions, try them out. If they work well, use them.

Once you understand your job, do it yourself. Do not depend too much on others. Your co-workers have their own work to do.

Formality in Business Relationships

At first, you may be uncertain about how formal or informal you should be with your employer and your co-workers. It is better to be too formal than too informal. Of course you should smile and be pleasant to everyone. But don't get too chummy too soon.

If you are too eager, you may become close friends with a co-worker who is not really someone you want as a close friend. If this happens, it could put a great strain on your working relationship with that person. It is better to go slowly, getting to know everyone before you develop any close relationships.

On your job, employees may call each other by their first names. If so, it will seem only natural for you to call your co-workers by their first names. In many companies, though, beginning workers are expected to call older co-workers, and the boss, by their last names. Again, if you are not sure, it is better to be too formal than too chummy.

Don't get too chummy too soon when you start a new job. You can make some quick enemies by trying to act like a life-long friend after knowing someone for only a few days or weeks.

Stay Neutral in Disputes

One of the best ways to keep up a good working relationship with all of your co-workers is to mind your own business. No matter where you work, there will probably be disputes between some workers. If you get involved in such disagreements, you will lose every time! You may strengthen your friendship with one person for the moment. But you may well damage your working relationships with other workers for a long time. The best thing is to remain neutral.

Keep Your Sense of Humor

If you don't already have a good sense of humor, try to develop one. Try to laugh when the joke is on you. People tend to like people who can laugh at themselves.

If You Lose Your Job

You will probably be successful on your job. You should be aware, however, of the possibility of losing your job. The following information will help you understand why people sometimes lose their jobs and what they can do in such situations.

Termination

If for some reason your employer is not satisfied with your performance, your employer may give you a **termination notice**. In more common terms, this means you have been *fired*. A termination notice is a statement from your employer that you have been dismissed from your job with the company.

If you lose your job, don't place all the blame on your employer. Instead, think about what happened and how you could have prevented it. Learn from your mistakes. If you can see what you did wrong, there will be less chance of your being fired from your next job.

Begin immediately to look for the job that you think will be right for you. The places to go and the methods to use are the same as when you were looking for your first job. These were discussed in Chapter 5.

Layoff

Suppose that your company is not doing well and that you were one of the last employees hired. In this case, you may be given a **layoff notice**. A layoff notice is a statement from your employer that your period of employment is over, usually temporarily.

Being laid off is not the same as being fired. People are not laid off because of unsatisfactory work. They are usually laid off because there isn't enough work to do. In some cases they are laid off because their employers cannot afford to pay their wages.

It is customary for employers to notify you if you are to be laid off. Although they are not legally required to do so, some employers may give you **severance pay** when you are laid off. This means that because you are *severed* (cut off) from your job, you will receive a check. Depending on your situation and pay period, your check could be equal to one, two, or several weeks' pay.

Unemployment Compensation

If you are laid off or fired, you may be eligible for **unemployment compensation**. Unemployment compensation is money given to people who have recently become unemployed. Unemployment checks are provided for a limited time to those who are able to work and who are actively seeking work.

To qualify for unemployment compensation, you must have earned a certain amount of money prior to losing your job. Students working part-time do not usually qualify because their yearly earnings do not meet the minimum requirements. Your state unemployment office can tell you what the minimum is. You can read more about unemployment compensation in Chapter 23.

Be Optimistic

If you do lose your job, for whatever reason, try not to let this discourage you. Instead of seeing your termination as an end, look at it as a beginning. Many people who were disappointed and discouraged after losing a job have found new jobs that they like much better than their old jobs.

REVIEW YOUR LEARNING

CHAPTER 6

CHAPTER SUMMARY

The most important factor in your job success is usually your own attitude. The main reason young workers lose their jobs is because they don't get along with other people. If you have a positive attitude, you are on your way to success. If you have a negative attitude, you can and should change it.

Your employer will expect certain things from you: cooperation, honesty, initiative, a willingness to learn, a willingness to follow directions, dependability, enthusiasm, the ability to accept criticism, and loyalty. Your success on the job will depend on how well you meet your employer's expectations.

As an employee you have the right to expect certain things from your employer. Your employer should provide payments, safe working conditions, training, introductions, explanations, evaluations, and discipline. Your employer should also be honest with you. Most employers will be fair and honest.

You cannot be truly successful in your work unless you get along with your co-workers. You can encourage good co-worker relationships by accepting differences, remembering that you are a beginner, maintaining the proper formality, staying neutral in disputes, and having a sense of humor.

If you lose your job due to layoff or termination, be optimistic. Look at the lost job as a beginning to your future career rather than the end of your present one.

WORDS YOU SHOULD KNOW

attitude
commission
initiative
layoff notice
overtime
salary
severance pay
termination notice
unemployment compensation
wages
work evaluation

STUDY QUESTIONS

1. What are the two general types of attitudes?
2. How can you tell if someone else has a positive attitude?
3. What is the main reason that young workers lose their jobs?
4. Besides a day's work for a day's pay, name five things that an employer usually expects of workers.

REVIEW YOUR LEARNING CHAPTER 6

5. Why is it a good idea for a worker to do some of the tasks that he or she finds unpleasant?
6. What are two types of dishonesty on the job?
7. How should an employee deal with criticism of his or her work?
8. List five things that a worker can reasonably expect from an employer.
9. Name two reasons why it is important to get along well with co-workers.
10. Why isn't it a good idea to become close friends with a co-worker during the first week or two on the job?
11. Give two reasons why workers are laid off.

DISCUSSION TOPICS

1. Which do you think has a greater influence on attitudes—heredity or environment?
2. Of the things an employer expects of workers, which do you feel are most important? Rank them in order and compare your lists with the lists made by your classmates.
3. Of the things you can reasonably expect of an employer, which do you feel are most important? Rank them in order and compare your list with the lists made by your classmates.
4. Suppose that you work closely with a person who arrives late and doesn't do much after getting there. You seem to be doing a lot more than your share of the work. Your undependable co-worker and your supervisor are, however, close friends. Would you continue to do more than your share? Would you talk to your co-worker about it? Would you talk with your supervisor, go to the employer, or quit your job? What factors would affect your action?

SUGGESTED ACTIVITIES

1. Assume that you are not perfect. Pick a negative attitude you sometimes see in yourself. Spend a full week acting in the opposite way. Whenever you are tempted to behave negatively, act in a positive way. Act positively with as many persons as you can. At the end of the week, write a paragraph on your attempt to change a negative attitude into a positive one. List some of the people with whom you acted your part and tell of their reaction. Discuss this in class.
2. Ask a local employer to come to the class to discuss some of the problems of young, beginning workers. Ask this person to explain what the company expects of beginning workers. Find out if that company has a program to help new workers get started.

Progress Toward Your Career Goal

DO YOU KNOW . . .
- how to go about quitting a job?
- what employers look for when making promotions?
- what determines whether or not workers receive pay raises?
- how your appearance can increase your chances for success?

CAN YOU DEFINE . . .
- merit raise?
- minimum wage?
- promotion?
- seniority?
- supervisor?

Before you read this chapter, answer the three questions below.
1. Are you now working?
2. Are you meeting your employer's expectations?
3. Are you getting along with your employer and your co-workers?

If you answered Yes to each of these questions, you are already on your way to success in the world of work. If you want to advance further, read this chapter carefully. It will help you learn how to get a pay raise, a promotion, or both—it will help you move closer to your ultimate career goal.

Pay Raises

You may not have ambitious goals. You may be happy—for many years—doing the work you are doing right now. But one thing is almost certain—you would like to make more money. Even if you stay on the same job, you will want some pay raises.

What do you have to do to get a pay raise? Several factors are involved. In most cases your performance on the job is the most important factor. Two other important factors are the company you work for and the type of job you do.

Your Performance on the Job

You cannot expect a pay raise unless you are doing your job adequately. This means that to get a pay raise you must meet your employer's expectations as described in Chapter 6. It also means that you must get along well with all of your co-workers and your employer. Remember—you can't expect to be paid more for doing less!

You may get a raise by simply doing an adequate job—or you may not. Don't take this chance. If you want a raise, do more than what is expected of you.

More than any other factor, your performance on the job determines whether or not you get a pay raise. What chance do you think this young lady has of getting a raise?

This is where the initiative and enthusiasm discussed in Chapter 6 become important. The harder you work and the more you do, the better your chances for a pay raise.

If you have already had a work evaluation, you probably have a good idea of how well you are doing. If your employer pointed out weaknesses, you should be working to improve in these areas. If you haven't had an evaluation, ask your employer how you are doing. Let your employer know that you are interested in doing well and eventually earning a pay raise.

Company Policy

The company you work for probably has its own policy regarding pay raises. You may have asked about this policy during your interview. If not, schedule a meeting with your employer to discuss the company's policy.

Don't be afraid to ask for this explanation. You will not be asking for a raise, simply an explanation. As you learned in Chapter 6, all workers are entitled to an explanation of company policy.

Some companies have the policy of giving their employees automatic pay raises. These raises are given after employees have worked for the company for a certain period of time. The most common times to give automatic raises are at the end of six months and at the end of the first year. In almost all cases, though, workers must be doing at least adequate work to receive these raises.

Some companies give automatic raises to all workers, plus a bonus for outstanding work. This bonus is often called a **merit raise** to distinguish it from the automatic raises. Merit raises may be a small amount more or a lot more than the automatic raises. The amount usually depends on the quality of work.

In still other companies there may be no plan for automatic raises at regular intervals. In most of these companies the employer simply gives raises on the basis of merit. If at any time the employer feels that someone deserves a raise, the employer will raise that worker's pay. In these companies the best workers are usually given raises fairly often. The less productive workers may not receive raises for long periods of time, perhaps for years.

You can see that your company's policy plays a big part in determining whether or not you get a raise. In some companies, for example, no one gets a raise during the first year. In such a company, even the most outstanding workers must wait until their second year to get a raise.

The Job You Have

Whether or not you get a raise will often depend on the type of job you do. For most jobs there is a "going rate." This means that most of the workers who do a certain job receive about the same pay. There is usually a limit on how much employers will pay someone to do that type of job.

If you are working at an unskilled job, for example, the employer may not be willing to pay any more than **minimum wage**. Minimum wage is set by law. It is the lowest amount per hour that employers are allowed to pay. They must pay you at least minimum wage. Check with the state employment office in your area to find out what the minimum wage is at the present time.

The employer may not be able to afford paying more than minimum wage—even if you are doing an outstanding job. If you are working at such a job and want a raise, you will probably have to earn a promotion to make more money.

Some jobs are union jobs. This means that the pay for all workers doing a certain job is determined by the union contract. This contract states when raises will be given and the amount of the raises. In these cases the employer cannot give raises to certain workers even if he or she wants to.

If you have a union job, your pay scale is set for you. You cannot change it. If you want to know when you are supposed to get a raise, ask your union representative. You will read more about unions and union contracts in Chapter 13.

Promotions

Regardless of how well you perform on your present job, you may never receive enough pay raises to earn as much as you would like. You may never reach your ultimate career goal through pay raises alone. In either case, you will probably want to

For many unskilled, lower-level jobs, there is a limit to how much an employer will pay. If you want to make more than that limit, you will need to get a promotion.

work for a **promotion**, an advancement to a higher level job.

Almost everyone likes promotions. Promotions make people feel important and appreciated. These feelings contribute to a person's sense of worth and self-esteem. In almost all cases, promotions also mean more money.

The best time to find out about opportunities for promotions in a company is during the job interview. You should ask the interviewer what your chances are for advancement if you do well. After you have begun work, don't bother your employer by constantly asking questions about promotions.

Who Gets Promoted?

If you want a promotion, you must earn it. How do you know whether or not you have earned a promotion? Ask yourself these two key questions: 1) Have I increased my knowledge and skills in my present job, and 2) Have I done my work in the best possible way? You will need to do at least these basic things before you will be considered for a promotion.

In deciding who will be promoted, employers consider several factors. These factors usually include those described on the next few pages.

Seniority. Seniority is the privileged status that results from continuous service to one company. Those who have worked for the company the longest have the greatest seniority. The longer you stay with a company, the greater your seniority will be.

Workers who have achieved seniority have proven themselves to be steady, dependable workers. This is why most companies consider seniority when making promotions. Most companies do not, however, give employees promotions on the basis of seniority alone.

Knowledge of Job. Your knowledge of your present job is an important factor in whether or not you get a promotion. Your employer has probably noticed how much you know about your job. Are you very knowledgeable about your work? Are you always trying to learn as much as you can to improve your skills? Most employers feel that if you are both knowledgeable and open to learning more, you can probably do a more difficult job.

Quality of Work. The quality of your work is also considered by your employer. If you do your work well, you will probably perform well in a job with more responsibility.

Unless a younger worker demonstrates outstanding skills and knowledge, the worker with the most seniority will usually get the promotion. This is one advantage to staying with the same company for a long period of time.

Quantity of Work. Some employees do their work well, but they do it slowly. Employers are looking for workers who do their work well and do it quickly. Your employer will probably notice how much work you get done. From these observations your employer will determine how much work you would probably accomplish on a more responsible job.

Initiative. As you know, employers expect their workers to take some initiative. Your employer will watch to see how often you look for tasks that need to be done, and do them without being told. If you have initiative, you will require less supervision than someone without initiative. If you do your own work without much supervision, and then do whatever else needs doing, your employer may think you would make a good supervisor. This could mean a promotion for you.

Perseverance. Once you begin a task, do you always carry it through to completion? If you are a person with perseverance, you finish what you start.

Not everyone has perseverance. You probably know people who begin projects but never finish them. Being able to finish a job, even if it becomes tiresome and boring, is important to your career success. No employer will promote a worker with a history of uncompleted jobs.

Ability to Cooperate. The importance of being able to cooperate with others was discussed in Chapter 6. As you will remember, most beginning workers who lose their jobs lose them because they are unable to cooperate with their employers and co-workers.

Cooperation is necessary simply to keep your job. But it's even more important if you want a promotion. A promotion usually means greater responsibility, which often means getting along with more people. Some of these people may be difficult to work with. This is why employers want to promote only those people who have the ability to cooperate.

Ability to Think. A promotion often means taking a job that requires making decisions. For such a job, employers want someone who can think for himself or herself.

Employers are always looking for someone who can analyze problems. They want someone who can figure out the best way of doing a particular task. Always try to think for yourself. You will then have

Workers with perseverance see every job through to the end. These are the kind of workers that employers promote.

a better chance for a promotion than the employee who must always ask someone what to do.

Ability to Adapt. Do you have the ability to adapt to new situations? Can you learn to do things other than those for which you were originally hired?

Your employer probably expects you to do whatever needs to be done. This could mean doing some tasks that were not mentioned when you were hired. Jobs and duties change. If you can adapt to changes, you are a more valuable employee than one who cannot. Again, this makes you a more likely candidate for a promotion.

Education and Training. In considering you for a promotion, your employer will want to know whether or not you have adequate education and training for the new job. Of course, the more training you have had, the greater your chances for receiving the promotion.

It's up to you to see that you get the education and training you need for the job you want. If you haven't done so already, you need to find out what education and training you will need to reach your ultimate career goal. You may find that you will need several levels of education.

If you read Chapter 3, you know that the *Occupational Outlook Handbook* can help you decide what education and training you need. Your school's work-experience and counseling offices probably have copies of the *OOH*. Your public library may also have a copy.

You can also learn what education and training you need to reach your goals by asking your employer. Your employer may have an organizational chart. This chart will help you identify some of your medium-range goals. Once you know the specific positions you want to attain, you can better determine what education and training you need.

The more education and training you have, the sooner you will reach your career goal. If two employees have identical qualifications except for education and training, the promotion will go to the one with more education and training.

How do you get this education and training if you are working full time? Some companies provide their own courses for employees. These companies believe that money for education is well spent. Both the company and the employee benefit.

If there is a college or university in your city, night classes are probably available. Also, many public schools offer evening classes for adults. If such formal training is not available in your area, you can take correspondence courses and read trade magazines and books.

If you need more education and training, you can get it—even if you have a full-time job. These full-time workers are taking night classes at their local junior college.

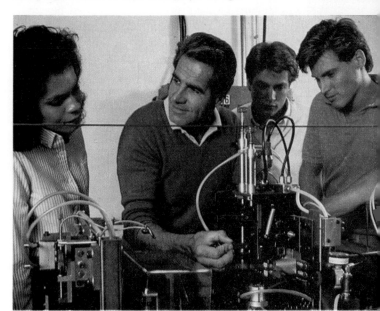

Appearance. In deciding who will be promoted, most employers consider appearance. Employers know that people who *look* successful, have a better chance of *being* successful. This is why employers promote people who are well-dressed and well-groomed.

A person who has carefully studied the reactions of people to clothing is John T. Molloy. He has been described by *TIME Magazine* as a "wardrobe engineer." His research show that those who dress neatly are *expected* to be successful. They generally receive better treatment both on and off the job. Those who dress in a sloppy manner or wear faddish styles or colors are not treated as well. In his book, *Dress for Success* (David McKay Co., Inc., 1975), Mr. Molloy describes how people react to various kinds of clothing. The following is a description of one of his experiments.

This fellow can probably forget about receiving any promotions. He apparently doesn't know that he must look successful to be successful.

To determine how people feel about tie-wearers in strictly economic terms, I took twin pictures of the same man. In one, he was wearing a gray suit and tie. In the other, he wore a similar suit, but with no tie and an open-collar shirt. Over one-hundred people picked at random were asked to estimate the yearly income of each of the two "twins." . . . the "twin" wearing the tie was generally awarded $3000 to $4000 more per year than his "brother."

Using the same set of photos, but questioning only women, I asked which of the men the women would trust enough to let into their homes, provided they didn't know him. Sixty percent of the women trusted neither, but of the forty percent who trusted one of them, they chose the man with the tie almost without exception.

Appearance is every bit as important as any other factor in determining who gets promoted. Often it is more important. If you and another employee are about equal in other areas, the employer may base the final decision on who has the best appearance.

Look at the other workers at your workplace. Do some wear shined leather shoes while others wear dirty tennis shoes? Do some wear slacks or dresses while others wear jeans? Do some of the men wear jackets and ties while others wear open-collar shirts?

If you notice these differences, ask yourself which of the workers have greater authority. You will probably find that those who dress in a neat, nonfaddish way have greater authority. They are probably paid more, too.

Of course the kind of work you do will affect your style of dress. For some jobs, such as construction and farm jobs, jeans are the accepted dress. Other jobs require uniforms. Even so, there is usually some small way in which you can make a better impression in your manner of dress.

On the job, dressing for success means dressing a little neater than the average employee. It means wearing what the person in charge believes is the look of success. For example, employers and supervisors expect their employees to have acceptable hairstyles. It doesn't matter how you like to wear your hair. If your hairstyle is offensive to the person in charge, that person will be a lot less likely to promote you or give you a raise.

We are all strongly influenced by how people look. It may not be fair, but it's true. Those who look well-groomed and well-dressed are given better treatment wherever they go. Shouldn't you let the look of success help you get the promotion you want?

Very small differences in appearance can make a big difference in the way people perceive you.
If they were equal in every way, which of these two workers would you promote?

Handling Responsibility

In almost all cases, promotions mean more responsibility. This often includes greater authority over other workers. Many people like authority and responsibility; many do not.

You don't have to accept a promotion just because it's offered. You may not think that you're ready to handle the added responsibility. Perhaps you feel that you'd be unhappy telling other people what to do. In either case, it might be better to turn down the promotion. This is not often done, but you may want to wait until you feel more comfortable about accepting greater responsibility.

Suppose that accepting a certain promotion would mean supervising other employees. In deciding whether or not you are ready for this promotion, consider both the advantages and disadvantages of being a **supervisor** (someone in charge of other workers).

Advantages of Being a Supervisor. One advantage of being a supervisor is higher pay. Most supervisors are paid more money than the workers they supervise. This is the way it should be since supervisors have more responsibility.

Another advantage is prestige (honor, respect, being well-known). Supervisory jobs usually carry a certain amount of prestige. Good supervisors are usually looked up to and respected by workers.

A third advantage of being a supervisor is that the work is usually more interesting. Supervisors are not normally required to do dull or routine work. Instead, they usually do a variety of more challenging and rewarding jobs. This means that there is a greater chance to be creative and to try new things.

Perhaps the most important advantage of being a supervisor is the chance to be a leader. The supervisor has greater influence in determining how the company will be run. By handling the extra responsibility and demonstrating leadership ability, the supervisor shows that he or she is worthy of further advancement.

Disadvantages of Being a Supervisor. Usually supervisors have a different kind of relationship with their employees than the employees have among themselves. The supervisor is the boss. People act and talk differently with the boss than they do with their co-workers. They usually are not quite so free in what they say. Many supervisors think of this as a disadvantage.

Another disadvantage is that a supervisor is often a target for criticism. Because the supervisor's paycheck is bigger, employees often feel that the supervisor should do more than they do. If the employees don't feel that the supervisor is doing enough work, they will probably be critical.

Being a supervisor may mean more money and prestige, but it can also mean isolation from the other workers and lots of extra work. Think about both the advantages and disadvantages before accepting a position as **supervisor**.

A third disadvantage of being a supervisor is the increased pressure to do a good job. A supervisor's mistakes are usually more costly to the company than the mistakes made by other workers. Many of the supervisor's mistakes are multiplied by the number of workers under his or her direction. This means added pressure to do everything right. Most supervisors see this pressure as a disadvantage.

Make a Decision

You have just been offered a promotion. If you accept the promotion, you will receive about $100 more each month in salary. Your new duties will include supervising about twenty-five other workers and attending two-hour management meetings after work once a week. In your present position you are responsible for your own work, and you are never asked to work more than the regular forty hours. What's your decision—accept the promotion, or decline it? Give reasons for your decision.

How to Be an Effective Supervisor

If you do accept a promotion that includes supervising the work of others, then learn to be a good supervisor. This is easy for some people but difficult for others. Consider the following situation.

During his senior year in high school, George worked at Walker's Auto Repair Shop each day after school. When George graduated, Mr. Walker asked him if he wanted to learn to be a mechanic. George accepted Mr. Walker's offer and quickly learned a great deal about being an automobile mechanic. George was a hard worker, and he was always willing to do something extra to help out a co-worker.

Three years later George was promoted to shop supervisor. He was now in charge of six mechanics. On the first day after his promotion, George noticed that Bob, one of the mechanics, was ten minutes late arriving for work. George felt that he must let Bob know that this would not be permitted. "Hey you!" he yelled when Bob walked into the shop. "Where've you been? You think we're paying you to sleep in all morning?" To Jack, another mechanic, George said, "If there's one thing I can't stand, it's somebody who leaves engine parts all over his bench. Where were you brought up? Learn to be neat and orderly if you want to keep working here!"

Perhaps George did need to say something to Bob and Jack. After all, George was responsible for their work. But couldn't George have handled these situations in a better way?

After attending college for one year, Ellen began working for the Maddox Company as a typist. One year later she was promoted to stenographer. Three years after this promotion, she became secretary to one of the vice-presidents of the company. She was an excellent worker, and everyone liked her very much.

When the office manager left the company to take another job, Ellen asked to be the new office manager. Company officials thought that Ellen would make a good office manager, although she had no experience at supervising other workers. Ellen was placed in charge of an office staff of sixteen employees. When several of these workers started coming to work late and leaving early, Ellen knew she should do something. But she was afraid she might make them angry with her. When some of the workers took a half-hour coffee break, Ellen didn't know what to do. So she did nothing—except worry about it. It wasn't long before some of the workers began talking back to Ellen when she gave them work to do. Finally, in frustration, Ellen went to the vice-president and asked to be relieved of her responsibilities as office manager.

Like most supervisors, Ellen tried to get along with the workers. But there are times when a supervisor needs to be critical. Shouldn't Ellen have exercised her authority, even if it meant making some of the workers unhappy with her?

If you have no supervisory experience, you will probably not be placed in charge of a large number of workers. Your first promotion to a supervisory position may place you in charge of only one or two workers. If so, you will have a better chance to learn how to be a good supervisor.

If being a supervisor seems difficult at first, don't be discouraged. You can improve if you work at it. Following are some guidelines for becoming an effective supervisor.

- Give clear directions.
- Train new workers.
- Be consistent.
- Treat workers fairly.
- Be firm when necessary.
- Consider the welfare of your workers.
- Set a good example.
- Delegate responsibility.

Give Clear Directions. Communication is often the biggest problem a supervisor has. Even the hardest workers will be unproductive if they don't understand what they are supposed to do. If they don't know what to do, it may be the supervisor's fault. The supervisor may have given too little direction or failed to make the directions clear.

As a supervisor you should give all the direction needed for each job. In some cases you may not be sure that the workers have understood your directions. If you're not sure, ask them some questions about what you've said. You will be able to tell from their answers whether or not they understood you. You can also improve communication by making the workers feel comfortable about asking you questions. If they know they can ask questions without being made to feel ignorant, they will ask when they are uncertain. This will make your job of giving clear directions much easier.

Train New Workers. If you are a supervisor, you may need to break in new workers. To make these workers as productive as possible, you will need to train them properly. You may do the actual training, or you may assign this task to one of your experienced workers. If you assign the training to someone else, choose someone who knows the work and has a flair for teaching. New workers trained by productive, enthusiastic workers are more likely to become productive, enthusiastic workers themselves!

The most successful supervisors are often the ones who know how to train employees.

Be Consistent. Be consistent in handling your supervisory duties. If you say that a certain job must be done in a certain way, make sure that it is always done in that way, by every worker. Another way of being consistent is to follow through on what you say. If, for example, you tell an employee that you will deduct part of his or her salary for being late, do it! If you do not follow through, your workers will not respect you and will tend to do as they please.

Treat Workers Fairly. If you expect the workers you are supervising to do their best work for you, you must treat them fairly. Do not let one worker come to work late or get by with sloppy work if you make everyone else arrive on time and do a good job.

Another part of being fair with your workers is being reasonable. Do not make demands that your workers can't meet.

If a worker tells you that you are being unfair, listen to the complaint calmly. Give the complaint careful consideration. If the employee is right, you may want to change your mind about the matter. If you think this person is wrong, explain your reasoning. You may not convince the worker that you are right, but he or she will appreciate your efforts to be fair.

Be Firm When Necessary. As a supervisor you must sometimes be firm with your workers. Do not let employees take unfair advantage of you, the company, or other workers. This doesn't mean that you should yell or lose your temper.

Every situation requiring discipline is different from every other. With some workers a friendly suggestion is all that's needed. With others you may have to be a bit more firm—"Do it this way!"

Sometimes problems result from the behavior of one employee toward another. Again, be firm when necessary. If the problem is a severe one, you may need to move an employee to another office or department.

Consider the Welfare of Your Workers. If possible, do what is best for your workers. This does not mean you should do whatever the employees ask. But you should be concerned about whether or not they are getting a fair deal. Do whatever you can to help them in their work without sacrificing the amount or quality of work done. If necessary, be willing to go to your boss and request changes that will benefit your workers.

Set a Good Example. Always try to set a good example for your workers. One supervisor was a bright young man who always came to work twenty to thirty minutes late. He dressed well and had a good appearance, but his work was sloppy. He seemed to have his mind on things other than his work. This set a bad example that was followed by some of his workers. They began showing up late for work and the quality of their work dropped off.

Finally, the young supervisor was replaced. The new supervisor was always on time and the quality of his work was top-notch. Soon the employees' work improved. One worker who had regularly come to work fifteen minutes late—just in time to beat the previous supervisor—started showing up five minutes before eight. The new supervisor hadn't said anything to this worker. He had simply set a good example.

If you are a supervisor, you must treat all your workers the same way. You can't give your favorite workers special treatment.

Delegate Responsibility. Some supervisors try to do too much. You may know people so "overworked" that they take work home every night. In some cases this is necessary. In many cases, though, the supervisors are simply not managing their time and employees efficiently. They are not delegating (giving) jobs and responsibilities to others. These supervisors probably have workers with light work schedules who are capable of doing more.

S ince she was a child, Arleen has always wanted things to be perfect. No matter what she did, it had to be exactly right. In school she never asked for help. She preferred to work alone. She prided herself on her ability to do things on her own.

For the past four years Arleen has been a computer programmer for a company in New York. Several months ago she was promoted to director of data processing. Arleen now supervises six other workers.

Naturally Arleen wants to make a good impression on the owner of the company. She wants to make sure that every program and every report is perfect.

Arleen knows that she can write programs and prepare reports better than any of the other workers. So instead of delegating this work to others, she writes the most important programs and prepares the major reports herself. Since the other workers often have nothing to do, they take long breaks. Arleen works late almost every night, but she still isn't getting all the work done.

Most effective supervisors work long and hard, but they also know their limits. When the workload becomes too heavy, they delegate some of their tasks to capable workers.

Why do some supervisors try to handle all the responsibilities themselves? Some are just poor organizers. Others may feel that no one else is able to handle the job. Still others want to feel important. They don't delegate responsibility because they want everyone else to depend on them.

If you are a supervisor, don't try to do everything yourself. Organize the work responsibilities and decide which ones you can delegate among your workers. Decide who can best handle each job and responsibility. In some cases you may even want to take time out to teach some workers how to do new tasks.

When you delegate responsibility, distribute the work fairly, according to each person's strengths and potential. But don't give away all of your work and responsibility. This would cause you to lose the respect of your workers—and perhaps your job, too!

Once you have turned over some responsibilities, you will be better able to handle the responsibilities left to you. In addition, your workers will appreciate the opportunity to show that they can be counted upon to handle important work. You, your workers, and the company will all benefit from your ability to delegate responsibility.

Changing Companies

You may find that there are no openings for promotions in your present company. All the higher positions may already be filled by qualified people. Or, it could be that a new company has offered you a job that you feel is a step up. The new job may bring you closer to one of your long-range goals. In either case, you may decide to change companies in order to advance toward your career goal.

Before you decide to leave your present company, though, consider how the change might affect you. Would the new job really increase your chances for further promotions? Does the new company usually give the more responsible jobs to its employees, or does it hire outsiders to fill the best jobs? How well do you think you would fit in with the new group of co-workers? Answer these questions before making your decision.

You may also want to make sure that the new job is related to your ultimate career goal. Don't leave your present company unless the new job will move you closer to your goal. Your long-range goal should be flexible, of course, but don't overdo it. It is usually not wise to job-hop.

Sometimes taking a new job with another company is the best thing to do. Sometimes it's not. But it is always best to have the new job before you quit the old one! People who quit their jobs to look for something better seldom find it. To make matters worse, they are without a paycheck all the time they are looking.

If you decide to quit your present company, you should observe certain courtesies in the way you quit your job. Unless company policy states otherwise, notify your immediate supervisor of your intent to leave the company. In large companies it is often necessary to notify the personnel office, too. You may be asked to make written notification. If this is the policy, follow it.

Don't wait until your last day on the job to tell your employer you are quitting. Give your notice far enough in advance for the employer to find a replacement before you leave. Courtesy requires that you give your notice of termination at least two weeks in advance. If you are paid once a month, it is customary to give at least a month's notice.

When you apply for new jobs, your next potential employers may get in touch with your former employer. If you failed to give proper termination notice, you may get a bad recommendation. This could cost you the job you want.

To reach your long-range career goal, you may need to change companies. It is not wise, however, to hop from job to job. Before you quit a job, make sure your new job will take you closer to your goal.

Ann Windsor was a high school senior who worked part time as a typist in a law firm. Ann assisted a legal secretary by typing letters and memoranda from a transcribing machine. One day Ann had difficulty adjusting the machine properly and asked Mrs. Allen, her supervisor, for help. Mrs. Allen, who was upset about the illness of 'her mother, quickly made the simple adjustment of the machine, but she spoke sharply to Ann about her not being able to do anything for herself. Ann was crushed. She soon developed a dislike for everything about her job and Mrs. Allen. Three weeks before school was out, Ann called Mrs. Allen and told her off. Ann quit her job without giving any advance notice. In the weeks following graduation, Ann looked everywhere for a job. It seemed that word had gotten around about her behavior in quitting her part-time job. Nobody wanted to take a chance on getting an employee like that. Ann finally did get a job, but it was in another city.

Make a Decision

You've gone about as far as you can go in your present company so you've decided to look for a better job elsewhere. You've had a great relationship with your employer, and you would like to use her as a reference. To do this, though, you would have to tell her you are looking for a new job—something you would rather not do. Her reference could make a difference, but you don't want to create trouble on your present job. What's your decision—ask for the reference, or do without it? Give reasons for your decision.

Several years ago, when he was just out of high school, the manager of this muffler shop got a minimum-wage job doing oil changes in a local service station. He worked hard, never stopped learning, and now he's his own boss.

REVIEW YOUR LEARNING

CHAPTER SUMMARY

As you progress in your career, you will want—and expect—some pay raises. Whether or not you receive pay raises will depend on your performance on the job, company policy, and the job you have. In most cases your performance on the job is the most important factor.

To earn more money and move closer to your ultimate career goal, you will probably need some promotions. Many factors, such as seniority, initiative, education, and appearance, determine who gets promoted. Before you accept a promotion, though, consider both the advantages and disadvantages. A promotion usually means more money and prestige, but it also means more responsibility and longer hours. If you do accept a promotion and become a supervisor, you can increase your effectiveness by doing such things as giving clear directions, treating workers fairly, and setting a good example.

Advancing toward your career goal may require changing companies. A decision to change companies should be made very carefully. Never leave your present company until you have a new job.

WORDS YOU SHOULD KNOW

merit raise
minimum wage
promotion
seniority
supervisor

STUDY QUESTIONS

1. What are three factors in determining whether or not workers receive pay raises?
2. How can an employer evaluation help you get a pay raise?
3. Give at least two reasons why an employer might not be able to give you a pay raise, even if he or she wanted to.
4. When is the best time to find out about opportunities for a promotion?
5. This chapter describes eleven factors that employers consider in deciding who will be promoted. What are these eleven factors?
6. Name two sources for finding out how much education and training you will need to advance toward your career goals once you have a job.

REVIEW YOUR LEARNING   CHAPTER 7

7. Name at least two ways you can get education and training while working full time.
8. What are four advantages of being a supervisor?
9. What are three disadvantages to being a supervisor?
10. List eight things a person can do to become a more effective supervisor.
11. Why is it very important to be courteous when quitting a job?

DISCUSSION TOPICS

1. Suppose you were offered a job where you were responsible for the work of others. Would you take it? Why or why not?
2. Suppose you had a good job, but you were constantly getting other job offers. Would you try to stick with one company, or would you take whatever job paid the most money? What other things would you want to consider before making a decision?
3. What do you consider the most important traits of a supervisor? Explain your reasoning.

SUGGESTED ACTIVITIES

Interview three people who supervise the work of others. Ask them the following questions.

- What are your biggest problems as supervisor?
- What do you like about being a supervisor?
- What don't you like about being a supervisor?
- What can a person do to get ready for a supervisory job?

Keep notes on their answers and discuss them in class. Do not give out the names of those you interview.

Your Personal Effectiveness

You can divide all the people in the world into two groups. One group consists of people who *let* things happen. The other group is made up of people who *make* things happen.

Which group do you think you are in? Are you a person who just takes things as they come? Or are you someone who makes things happen? You read earlier that people who plan ahead and *choose* their careers are the happiest and most satisfied. These people are the ones who make things happen their way. The ability to do this is called **personal effectiveness**. Personally effective people are the ones who progress quickly toward their career goal.

Personal effectiveness includes the ability to influence people. To be personally effective, you must be good at getting other people to see things your way. Improving your own personal traits and learning some persuasive methods are two ways you can increase your effectiveness with others. This chapter gives you several suggestions for doing both.

Self-Improvement

You are not as effective in human relationships as you could be—no one is. We all have room for improvement, and we *can* improve. Most people don't make the effort to become more effective, but it can be done. If you want to, you can learn to *make* things happen in your life.

Personal Traits

Many different traits go together to make up your personality. Which traits you have and the amount of each determine what your personality is like. You need to be aware of your traits before you can begin your self-improvement.

Below are brief descriptions of some common personal traits and qualities. You read about several of these in Chapters 6 and 7 because these traits are important to success in the world of work. The qualities described here are important in all human relationships, on the job and off.

- **Motivation**—The desire to achieve and succeed. This is often the most important factor in success. To be successful, you must *want* to be successful.
- **Attitude**—A key part of your personality. Your attitude can be generally positive or generally negative. You want it to be positive.
- **Self-Control**—Being able to control your emotions. You cannot be personally effective without controlling negative feelings, such as anger. Learn to express these feelings in ways that do not hurt others.
- **Loyalty**—Supporting family, friends, and employers in all situations, especially difficult ones. Loyalty will make you someone to be trusted. Like friendliness, if you are loyal to others, they will be loyal to you.
- **Sense of Humor**—Contributes to both your physical and mental well-being. Don't take life too seriously all the time. If you have a good sense of humor, people will tend to like you.
- **Common Sense**—Doing what is reasonable. Common sense also means using good judgment and learning from past experience.

- **Foresight**—The ability to look ahead. People with foresight make plans. They are always prepared.
- **Dependability**—The quality that makes you someone who can be counted on. Dependable people get the job done on time, every time.
- **Honesty**—"Honesty is the best policy." This is an old saying, but a good one. In the end you will be happier and more successful taking the honest route rather than the dishonest one.
- **Initiative**—Looking around to see what needs to be done. Don't wait for someone else to do it; do it yourself—now.
- **Open-Mindedness**—Trying to see both sides of a question or argument. Open-minded people are usually intelligent and happy because they keep their minds open to new, fresh ideas.
- **Tact**—Saying and doing things in a way that will not offend other people. Successful people know how to point out mistakes and problems without making people angry or unhappy.
- **Enthusiasm**—Happiness, excitement, and energy. Good things seem to happen to enthusiastic people. Everyone—co-workers, employers, friends—enjoys being around them.
- **Courtesy**—Good manners and a true concern for other people. Courtesy will do more than anything else to make others like you. Nothing so valuable costs so little.
- **Health**—Take care of yourself! Poor health makes everything just that much more difficult—if not impossible.
- **Friendliness**—Another key to being well liked. People will be friendly to you if you are friendly to them.
- **Punctuality**—Being on time. Your employer and your friends will not be able to depend on you if you get into the bad habit of being late.
- **Neatness**—Most people are bothered by dirtiness and sloppiness. A neat, clean appearance is essential to success.
- **Your Voice**—The tone and quality of your voice often affects people just as much as what you say. Listen to how you sound to others. Chapter 10 has more on how to make good use of your voice.

You have just read a brief description of nineteen qualities important to success. How well do you rate with each of these qualities? Make a chart like the one on this page, listing each of the nineteen personal traits. Then carefully consider how you stand with regard to each. Be honest with yourself. Do not write in this book.

How to Improve

Your personal traits have been developing since you were born. They have become "habits," and they can be difficult to change. But it will be easier to change these habits this year than next year, or five years from now.

You *can* change—and improve, if you want to. If you really feel that self-improvement is important, you can do it.

Do you have a good reason to improve? Is this reason really important to you? If not, you will probably go on being your same old self, bad habits and all. If, on the other hand, you have a good reason, you can achieve a great deal of self-improvement.

The following suggestions will help you make the self-improvements you want to make.

Take a Closer Look. You were asked to rate yourself on nineteen personality traits. If you rated your traits honestly, you probably found some that could be improved. It's not always easy to admit personal faults. If your rating shows weaknesses, don't be afraid to admit your shortcomings. No one is perfect.

Rating Your Personal Traits

Be as honest with yourself as possible. How do you rate on each of the traits listed below.

Trait	Excellent	Good	Fair	Poor	Very Poor
Attitude					
Common Sense					
Courtesy					
Dependability					
Enthusiasm					
Foresight					
Friendliness					
Health					
Honesty					
Initiative					
Loyalty					
Motivation					
Neatness					
Open-Mindedness					
Punctuality					
Self-Control					
Sense of Humor					
Tact					
Voice					

Take a close, hard look at yourself to see what traits are most in need of improvement. The first and most important step in any self-improvement plan is to recognize and admit weaknesses.

If you are having trouble seeing your faults, you may want to take a personality inventory. This is a type of test that shows strengths and weaknesses in your personality. If you feel such a test would be helpful, ask your counselor about taking one of these tests.

One at a Time. Choose one habit or trait for improvement. If you try to improve several traits at once, you will not be able to follow through on any of them. Devote all your effort to just the one trait. Start with the trait you believe is most in need of improvement.

How to Do It. Make a plan for improvement and stick to it—without excuses! One method for correcting bad habits is to develop a habit opposite the bad one.

Suppose you never have any enthusiasm. To correct this bad habit you might make a special point of noticing things that get you excited. You could concentrate on expressing your feelings about the things that you like. Every day you would go out of your way to find some things and express your enthusiasm for them. You would gradually find yourself getting enthusiastic about more things, with less effort.

A Self-Check. At first you will need to check your progress often. If possible, check yourself every day. After you have followed your plan for several weeks, you may find that you have indeed made progress. But keep checking yourself for weeks, even months. This checking will prevent you from slipping back into your old habits.

If you feel your friends will be honest, ask them if they think you are progressing. Knowing that others are checking on us from time to time helps us change our habits. This is one of the main reasons why many people who go to clubs such as *Weight Watchers* can lose weight and stay slim. The people in the club keep tabs on each other.

Moving On. Once you feel you have made real progress in improving one trait, begin working on another. At this point you will probably be feeling good about yourself. You will have confidence in your ability to improve. You will feel that you can change lifelong habits.

Other people will also notice your improvements. They will encourage you to keep up the good work. This will be the perfect time to begin working to improve another quality.

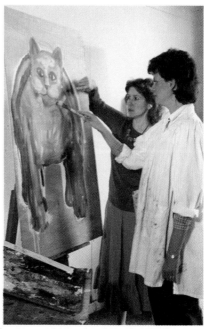

As soon as you reach one of your self-improvement goals, start working toward another. Each success will help motivate you in your future efforts.

Make a Decision

You know of several ways in which you can improve yourself. You realize that the best strategy for self-improvement is to concentrate on improving one bad habit or weakness at a time. The only thing that's preventing you from getting started is deciding which weakness or habit you should work on first. What's your decision—which area of self-improvement will you concentrate on first? Give reasons for your decision.

Influencing Others

There are times when being personally effective means convincing other people to see things our way. To be effective in these cases, we must get others to do what we want.

Being able to persuade people is more important in some careers than others. Managers and sales-people, for example, must be skilled at influencing others.

How good are you at getting others to see things your way? Would you like to improve your persuasive skills? In this section you will read about several things you can do to get your point across effectively. You will begin with the most important step—understanding other people.

Understanding Others

If you want someone to accept your way of thinking, you need to understand that person. You need to know what that person thinks and feels. The more you know about the person, the better able you are to pick the approach that will be most effective.

Since everyone is different, the right approach with one person may be the wrong approach with another. What makes one person love you may make another person hate you. When you're trying to persuade someone, you want to say and do the things that appeal to that person.

Of course, you can't make an in-depth study of every person you deal with. So how do you find out whether or not you are communicating with that person in the most effective way? There are several things you can do.

When you have the chance, get to know the person better. Consider the person's personality traits. Knowing more about these traits can help you understand other people, as well as yourself.

You can also notice a person's interests. What does that person do during his or her leisure time? These interests often provide clues to a person's values. Knowing someone's values can be a big help in finding the best way to persuade that person.

Another way to learn more about people is to observe their **body language**. Body language refers to the things people say through their physical actions. For example: picture in your mind someone with slouched shoulders walking head down and eyes to the ground. What is this person saying through body language? This person may be showing sadness or lack of confidence. On the other hand, a person who walks with shoulders back, head up, and arms swinging freely conveys a carefree, happy image.

Facial expressions are often the best indications of a person's emotions and feelings. Eyes, especially, tell a great deal about a person. When a person's eyes are opened wide, it usually means the person is surprised. The pupil of the eye becomes quite large when a person feels very happy.

If you are close enough to clearly see a person's eyes, you can learn a great deal. You can tell whether the person has a positive or negative feeling about what you are saying. If the pupils enlarge, the feeling is positive. If they become smaller, the feeling is negative. These changes occur quickly, though, so you have to watch closely. This is usually not a problem since looking the other person in the eye shows attentiveness.

Tightly closed lips usually mean disapproval. When people fidget (move restlessly) in their chair, you can often tell that they are bored with what you are saying.

There are many other ways people show their feeling through body language. In fact, several books have been written on this subject. By watching a person closely, you can learn a lot about his or her feelings.

Paying attention to body language will help you understand people better. You can tell a great deal about people just by watching them walk down the street.

Showing Interest

In 1936, Dale Carnegie wrote a book called *How to Win Friends and Influence People.* This book has now sold over ten million copies. It has been so popular because it explains Dr. Carnegie's techniques for getting people to react in a certain way.

In his book, Dr. Carnegie says, "You can win more friends in two months by becoming interested in other people than you can in two years by trying to get other people interested in you." Dr. Carnegie's point is that the most effective way to influence people is to be sincerely interested in them. The interest must, however, be genuine. Most people can spot a "phony" a mile away.

Smiling

An old song includes the words, "When you're smilin', the whole world smiles with you." The writer of that song must have known something about human relationships.

Other people react to you more favorably when you smile than when you don't. The expression on your face says more about you than the clothes you

wear or the company you keep. And a smile is a lot less expensive than a new wardrobe!

When you smile at a person, it's like saying "I like you." Your smile will attract others to you. It will smooth the way if you are trying to influence another person to do something. A pleasant smile can be very valuable.

Making Others Feel Important

In Chapter 1 you learned about Dr. Maslow's theory of basic human needs. You may remember that one need is the need for esteem. Some people meet all of their lower level needs, but do not have enough self-esteem. These people don't feel good about themselves—they don't feel important.

Everyone wants to feel important. You can win people over to your side by making them feel important. Think about your own feelings. When someone says something that makes you feel important, you probably have a good feeling toward that person.

One simple way of making a person feel important is to know and to use the person's name correctly. The sweetest sound in the world is the sound of one's own name. That sound means more to a person than the tune of a favorite song. Take advantage of this knowledge. Use the other person's name in your conversations.

Another way of making people feel important is to give them your sincere, undivided attention. Ask them questions to show that you are interested in their ideas. Be a good listener and concentrate on everything people say. When you think someone made an especially intelligent remark, tell them so.

Empathizing

Influencing other people does not mean that you must be a fast, convincing talker. In fact, you can earn someone's trust and respect faster by listening than you can by talking. A good listener gets along well with most people, especially if the listener empathizes with the speaker. To empathize means to

This is *not* the way to win friends and influence people. Being a good listener is the key to success in all human relationships.

see someone else's point of view, to sympathize with their situation.

Respect the other person's ideas, even if you don't agree with them. You may come to understand why that person feels as he or she does. You can't really be a good listener unless you are empathetic.

Henry Ford, the founder of Ford Motor Company, was asked the secret of his success. He said, "If there is any one secret to success, it lies in the ability to get the other person's point of view and see things from his angle as well as your own."

Giving Away Credit

Sometimes you should give up some of the things that make you feel important. In certain cases it is a good idea to let others take the credit for your ideas. Doing this will help you achieve your goals in human relationships.

Let's say you have an idea. It's an idea for a better way to do something at work. If you try to push a new procedure as your own idea, you may be successful, or you may not.

Remember, your supervisor is another human being. He or she needs attention and needs to feel important. If your supervisor has high self-esteem, he or she may help you with your ideas. But what should you do if your supervisor is insecure and does not have a high level of self-esteem? Then give away your idea—or at least the credit for it. Let your supervisor "discover" your plan.

Make a Decision

You mention to your supervisor an idea you have for a sales promotion at the store where you work. Later, you overhear your supervisor telling the idea to the store owner—but without even mentioning your name. The owner loves the idea immediately and praises the supervisor for being so creative. You would like to tell the owner that the idea was yours, but you believe this would make your supervisor angry. What's your decision—tell the owner, or let the supervisor receive credit for your idea? Give reasons for your decision.

You could work for months, even years, trying to convince people of the value of your own idea. If you give the credit to someone else, though, your goal may be achieved very quickly. You will probably gain a friend by making the other person feel important.

Of course there is a limit to the kind of ideas you should give away. If you come up with a new invention that might make you rich, don't give that idea away!

Avoiding Arguments

Have you ever tried to convince someone to see things your way? Did you end up in an argument? If so, you probably didn't really convince the other person of anything. And even when you win arguments, they often cause other people to have bad feelings about you. You may have trouble dealing with people after you've had arguments with them.

Jane Chen sells recording equipment for a large company. She is a very successful salesperson who never gets trapped into an argument.

One day she walked into an insurance firm in Los Angeles. She hoped to sell several different pieces of recording equipment. As she walked into the office of the vice-president to make her sales presentation, she was greeted with, "Oh yes, I should have canceled our appointment. I've decided to buy the equipment from the Brand-X Company."

Of course the vice-president was expecting an argument—or at least some negative comment about the other firm's equipment. But Jane simply said, "Brand X is an excellent product. I'm sure you'll be happy with it." The vice-president didn't know what to say. He was expecting an argument and instead, she complimented him and the competitor's product.

Jane smiled often. She showed a sincere interest in the insurance firm. She complimented the vice-president on the leadership of the company executives. After twenty minutes the vice-president asked for a demonstration of her equipment. The sale was made the same day!

The sooner you learn to control your emotions and avoid arguments, the better. There are no winners in most arguments.

Have you ever known people who like to argue? You may have noticed that nobody really wins. The more people argue, the more difficult it will be for them to work well with others. The only way to win in an argument is to avoid it.

Letting People "Save Face"

When people are wrong about something and know it, they have a temporary loss of self-esteem. After a while, they may admit their error, and even take pride in doing so. This won't happen, though, if someone else tries to force them to admit the mistake.

To refer to the error, to say "You were wrong" or "I told you so," makes people uncomfortable. When you do this, you "back people into a corner." You can guess how these people will feel about you after you point out their mistake.

It never pays to tell others about their mistakes (unless, of course, you are their supervisor). Let them "save face." Ignore the situation and talk about something else. You will keep an old friend, or possibly win a new one.

Admitting Your Mistakes

Never mention mistakes other people make, but you should always admit your own mistakes. In the long run, you gain nothing by giving excuses when you are wrong. On the other hand, there is something noble in quickly admitting your errors.

When you admit your mistakes, no one else has a chance to prove you wrong. In fact, other people are usually very understanding. They may even gain respect for you. This, in turn, makes it easier for you to influence them.

Giving Sincere Praise

Do you want to influence others? Do you want to change their behavior? If so, never begin with criticism. Criticism puts most people on the defensive.

Instead of criticizing, begin by looking for the things you sincerely feel are worthy of praise. Tell people what you like about them. Compliment them when they do or say something deserving of a compliment. Most people will respond to your praise by trying to do all they can to please you.

Being Positive

Have you ever known someone who complained constantly? Someone who had nothing good to say about anyone or anything? Some people are constant complainers. They can talk for hours about nothing but the bad things. These people have a negative attitude toward life.

People with a negative outlook are not very convincing. Happy people are much more persuasive. If you want to influence someone, be optimistic. Look on the bright side—emphasize the positive.

Let's listen to three different sales people. Try to decide which one will make the sale.

- Salesperson #1—"Hello! You don't want to buy this broom, do you?"
- Salesperson #2—"Hello! I would like to interest you in the unusual features of this broom."
- Salesperson #3—"Hello! I have two unusual brooms. Broom A is designed for heavy-duty work. Broom B is for sweeping small particles such as sugar and sand. Which broom would best meet your needs?"

All successful salespeople know the benefit of being positive. You will be much more effective in all your human relationships if you stay enthusiastic and positive even in the most difficult times.

Did you notice that the first salesperson makes it easy for the customer to say no? The second salesperson invites the customer to listen, and the answer could be yes or no. The third salesperson didn't ask for a yes or no, but rather for a choice between Broom A and Broom B. The third salesperson assumed that the customer's answer would be yes to one of the brooms. That salesperson emphasized the positive.

You've probably heard the old question about whether the glass is half full or half empty. You can often say what you think in either positive or negative terms. You will be much more effective with others if you choose the positive way.

Catching the Mood

Another important factor in influencing others is catching people in the right mood. People are much more agreeable if they are in a good mood.

How can you tell if someone is in a good mood? Sometimes you can tell by an answer to a greeting. Listen to the person's voice. Say, "Good morning. How are you?" The reply will likely be something like, "Fine, thank you." If the "Fine, thank you" is said with a *rising* pitch, that person is probably in a good mood. If it is said with a *lowering* of pitch, the person is probably not in a good mood. In this case, it might be wise to wait until later to discuss an important issue.

Do more than just listen to *what* someone says. Listen to *how* they say it. Listen for enthusiasm, anxiety, hesitation—any clues as to how the person feels.

Executives and the most successful salespeople know that the best time to talk anybody into anything is during a meal. We are all more open to influence from others while eating something we like. But this period lasts only a short time. It starts with the first bite and ends shortly after the meal has been eaten.

Being Assertive

People respect other people who are assertive without being *too* assertive. Being **assertive** means standing up for your rights, beliefs, and ideas. To be personally effective, you must be assertive without being too aggressive or "pushy."

Do you relate to others in a confident manner? To be assertive you must show confidence. One way to do this is to speak with authority. This does not mean you should talk like a "know-it-all." It just means that you should know what you are talking about. Then you will feel comfortable in your discussions with others.

It isn't easy to be assertive without being too aggressive. It is especially difficult for beginning workers, who have had little experience in human relationships on the job.

You can improve your self-confidence and become more assertive by spending some time visiting with co-workers. Let them get to know you. Talk about your likes and dislikes. Talk about your hobbies. Also show your interest in their likes and dislikes. As you get to know your co-workers better, you will feel more comfortable asserting yourself.

If you follow the suggestions made in this chapter for influencing others, people will probably like you. If you do you own job well, people will respect you. This will give you the confidence you need to speak up and assert yourself when necessary.

Being assertive is the happy medium between the scared, frightened type, and the pushy, aggressive type. You must be confident enough to speak up for what you want and believe without becoming selfish or overly aggressive.

Mary is a computer programmer for a large school district. She writes programs that tell the computer what it must do to print hundreds of different kinds of reports. After each program is written in a special computer language, Mary prints a practice report and checks it for errors. This is called *debugging*.

On Friday afternoon Mary was discussing the need for a new kind of report with the business manager and assistant superintendent. Mary's supervisor, Mrs. Caroll, walked into the meeting.

"Mary, I just ran the new attendance report and it's full of errors! I guess I'll have to come in this weekend and do it myself!"

How do you think Mary reacted to Mrs. Caroll's criticism? Here are three possible reactions.

Mary could have argued with Mrs. Caroll right there: "Mrs. Caroll, I just finished that program this morning. We've been discussing this other new

program since then. I didn't even go to lunch. At least give me a chance to correct it myself!"

Mary could have said nothing. If she hadn't said anything, though, the incident would have bothered her all weekend. In fact, if she never discussed the problem with Mrs. Caroll, Mary could have been unhappy for weeks.

Mary could have discussed the problem with Mrs. Caroll after the business manager and assistant superintendent left: "Mrs. Caroll, I'm sure there were errors in the attendance report. I only completed that program this morning and haven't had a chance to debug it. I'll make the corrections this afternoon. Your remarks in front of the business manager and assistant superintendent embarrassed me. Also, I'm afraid they will think that this department is not very efficient. If you have criticisms of my work in the future, I hope you will be kind enough to tell me in private."

Mary knows how to influence people. She used the third approach. She waited for the right moment, then she asserted herself, without being pushy or aggressive with her superior.

REVIEW YOUR LEARNING   CHAPTER 8

CHAPTER SUMMARY

You have a choice. You can be a person who *lets* things happen, or one who *makes* things happen. When you make things happen you are being personally effective. You are making decisions and planning ahead to ensure a happy, satisfying career.

Being personally effective means getting rid of bad habits and improving good ones. It's not easy, but if you want to badly enough, you *can* make self-improvements. By taking a closer look at yourself, working on one habit at a time, planning your improvement, and doing honest self-checks, you can eliminate negative traits. You can also improve yourself in areas such as motivation, friendliness, courtesy, and neatness.

Being personally effective also means influencing people. The most successful people in the world of work have learned to make other people see things their way. They've learned the importance of understanding and observing other people so that they can pick the most effective approach for each person. They've also learned effective tactics, such as making others feel important, being positive, empathizing, and giving away credit. By using these tactics and others, you too can win friends and influence people.

WORDS YOU SHOULD KNOW

assertive
body language
empathize
personal effectiveness
tact

STUDY QUESTIONS

1. List nineteen qualities about yourself that you need to examine to determine whether or not they need improvement.
2. What personality trait, more than any other, will make other people like you?
3. Which trait is often the first and most important in achieving success?
4. What quality are successful people using when they point out errors that others make, without making the other people angry or unhappy?
5. What are the five steps in the self-improvement plan presented in this chapter?

REVIEW YOUR LEARNING   CHAPTER 8

6. What is the most important thing for you to do when trying to influence people?
7. What is the title of one book you might read if you wanted to learn more about how to be personally effective?
8. Which of the methods described in this chapter for influencing people did Henry Ford believe to be the most important for success?
9. In only one type of situation is it to your advantage to point out someone's mistakes. What type of situation would this be?
10. List at least six things you can do to be more effective at influencing people.

DISCUSSION TOPICS

In this chapter you read about thirteen ways to influence people. Do one of two things. Either think about a situation in which someone used one or more of these methods, or a situation in which someone used the *opposite* of one of these. Explain the behavior of those involved (omit names). How did this behavior affect the other person? Was this behavior effective in influencing the other person? Discuss this in class.

1. Think of something reasonable that you would like a friend or family member to do. Then try to influence that person to do as you wish. Use as many of the keys for influencing others as seems appropriate. Don't rush the person. After a while, consider whether these approaches work better than your usual way of trying to influence others. You may wish to discuss your experiment in class.
2. Reread the discussion of body language in this chapter. Try to notice examples of body language. Make some notes and then discuss these with the class. Explain how you interpreted these examples of body language.

CHAPTER NINE

Your Personal Safety

In the United States an average of ten accidental deaths occur *each hour*. In that same time, about one thousand people are seriously injured.

Where do these accidents occur? About half of the deaths result from traffic accidents. One-third of the injuries occur in the home. Although the number of work-related accidents has been decreasing, close to two million people are injured at work each year.

In this chapter you will learn about injuries, accidents, and the importance of safety. You will read about the major causes and the true costs of accidents. You will find out what the United States government is doing to protect our health and safety. And most importantly, you will learn what *you* can do to make life safer for everyone—yourself included.

Any Place, Any Time

You are never totally free from the possibility of being involved in an accident. An accident can happen any place, any time.

I t was Gary's turn to make dinner. Lucy wasn't even home from work yet. As the stew bubbled on the stove, Gary gave it a final taste test. A bit more salt, he decided. He reached for the shaker, but it was empty. "Why do we keep the extra supplies in such a high cabinet?" he wondered as he dragged the swivel chair across the kitchen. "It's a good thing I have such great balance," he boasted to himself as he stretched from the chair to reach the salt.

As soon as Lucy got home, she had to drive Gary to the emergency room. He was very lucky. It was only a mild concussion. It could have been much worse.

At Home

Accidents in the home result in more injuries than either auto or work accidents. The National Safety Council reported that in 1983, twenty thousand deaths and three million disabling injuries occurred at home. A *disabling injury* is one that results in death, permanent physical damage, or the inability of a person to effectively perform regular duties or activities for a full day after the day of injury.

Falls (on stairs, ladders, and roofs, for example) caused most of the deaths. The next two greatest causes of accidental deaths in the home were fires and poisons. Twenty-five to forty-four year olds, and those over seventy-five, had the highest numbers of home-accident deaths.

Do you know anyone between the ages of fifteen and twenty-four who has died from drugs, medicines, or poisons? Chances are that you do. Compared to those under the age of fifteen, almost fourteen times as many people between the ages of fifteen and twenty-four died from poisons. Since most people over fifteen can read labels and follow directions, there must be other causes for the high death rate in this group. The possible causes will be discussed later in this chapter.

Accidental Deaths and Injuries

Accidents can happen anywhere, anytime. Each of us must do our part to reduce the number of deaths and injuries. The figures below show where the deaths and disabling injuries occurred in 1983.

	Deaths	Change from 1982	Deaths per 100,000 Persons	Disabling Injuries
All Classes	**91,000**	–3%	38.9	**8,800,000**
Motor-Vehicle	**44,600**	–3%	19.1	**1,600,000**
Public nonwork	40,400			1,400,000
Work	4,100			200,000
Home	100			less than 10,000
Work	**11,300**	–2%	4.8	**1,900,000**
Nonmotor-vehicle	7,200			1,700,000
Motor-vehicle	4,100			200,000
Home	**20,000**	–5%	8.5	**3,000,000**
Nonmotor-vehicle	19,900			3,000,000
Motor-vehicle	100			less than 10,000
Public	**19,500**	0%	8.3	**2,500,000**

In Motor Vehicles

Can you imagine a city of 44,600 people simply disappearing? In a sense that's what happens every year as a result of automobile accidents. Motor-vehicle accidents cause at least that many deaths every year.

In the chart on the preceding page, you can see that motor vehicles are the leading cause of accidental deaths in the United States. In 1983, automobiles were involved in almost half of the accidental deaths. It is estimated that these accidents cost 43.3 *billion* dollars. Here are some facts about cars and deaths.

- Drivers between the ages of fifteen and twenty-four have the highest accident rate of any age group.
- The accident rate for male drivers is two times higher than for females.
- Improper driving is responsible for 64 percent of all accidents.
- The use of alcohol is a factor in at least half of all the motor-vehicle deaths.
- The most dangerous time to drive is midnight to two a.m. on Saturday night.

- More motor-vehicle deaths are reported in July and August than in any other months.
- Labor Day is one of the most dangerous days to be on the road.

Despite these facts, there is some good news. The death rates from auto accidents have decreased slightly in the last five years. Better roads, lower speed limits, and the use of safety restraints are credited for the fewer number of deaths.

The driver is, however, still the key to reducing the number of automobile accidents. Driving is a privilege. All drivers must remember the dangers and responsibilities involved with driving a car. Safe driving is everyone's full-time job.

At Work

It is very important that all workers protect their health and safety. To protect yourself you must know how dangerous your work really is. Jobs in some industries are more dangerous than jobs in others.

Disabling injuries occur most often in trucking and railroad equipment jobs. The aircraft and communications industries have the fewest disabling injuries. In recent years, the construction industry has had a reduction in accidents. Agricultural and mining accident rates are still high, however. People who work in hazardous jobs must be especially careful.

Obviously more accidents are going to occur in some occupations than in others. Did you take the potential danger of different jobs into consideration when you made your career choice?

Work Accidents

Between 1912 and 1983, accidental work deaths per 100,000 population were reduced 76 per cent, from 21 to 5. In 1912, an estimated 18,000 to 21,000 workers' lives were lost. In 1983, in a workforce more than double in size and producing more than nine times as much, there were only 11,300 work deaths.

The 1983 accidental work death total of 11,300 was down 200 from 1982. Disabling injuries numbered 1,900,000, including 70,000 permanent impairments. Slight increases in employment and the average hours worked per week resulted in a small increase in exposure. The table below shows data by industry for 1983.

Industry Group	Workers (000)	Deaths 1983	Deaths % Change from 1982	Deaths Rates 1983	Deaths Rates % Change from 1982	Disabling Injuries 1983
All industries	100,100	11,300	− 2%	11	− 8%	1,900,000
Agriculture	3,400	1,800	0%	52	0%	180,000
Mining, quarrying	1,000	500	−17%	50	0%	40,000
Construction	5,400	2,000	0%	37	− 3%	200,000
Manufacturing	19,000	1,200	+ 9%	6	0%	330,000
Transportation and public utilities	5,300	1,300	− 7%	25	− 4%	140,000
Trade	22,700	1,200	0%	5	0%	350,000
Service	27,600	1,800	0%	7	0%	380,000
Government	15,700	1,500	− 6%	10	0%	280,000

Source: National Safety Council estimates (rounded) based on data from the National Center for Health Statistics, state vital statistics departments, and state industrial commissions. Numbers of workers are based on Bureau of Labor Statistics data and include persons aged 14 and over.

Costs of Work Accidents

Compensation paid to all workers in the nation who are under workers' compensation laws was approximately $16,145,000,000 in 1982 (latest figures reported by the Social Security Administration). Of this amount, $4,820,000,000 was for medical and hospital costs and $11,325,000,000 for wage compensation.

TOTAL COST IN 1983 .... **$33,400,000,000**

Direct Costs **$15,600,000,000**

Includes wage losses of $5,400,000,000, insurance administrative costs amounting to about $6,400,000,000, and medical costs of $3,800,000,000.

Indirect Costs **$15,600,000,000**

Includes the money value of time lost by workers other than those with disabling injuries, who are directly or indirectly involved in accidents. Also included would be the time required to investigate accidents, write up accident reports, etc.

Fire Losses **$2,200,000,000**

Cost per Worker **$330***

*This figure indicates the value of goods or services each worker must produce to offset the cost of work injuries. It is *not* the average cost of a work injury.

Source: Accident Facts, National Safety Council

Why do some companies have more accidents than others? Obviously some are involved in more dangerous work than others. Some use safer equipment; others provide more training programs. Accident-prevention and educational presentations (lectures, slides, films, and safety booklets) have also been successful in reducing accidents.

We don't always realize the importance of health and safety in our lives. We usually feel that nothing will ever happen to us, that it will happen to someone else. But accidents can and do happen to everyone. We must all think of the value of our health and safety. We must try our best to protect ourselves and others at all times.

The True Cost of Accidents

It is estimated that in 1983 the financial cost of accidents was 92.7 *billion* dollars. This is a huge amount of money, but money is only one small part of the cost of accidents. Since we cannot put a price tag on the other costs, it is impossible to determine the true cost of an accident.

In most jobs you must be able to work on a regular basis. If you miss time because of an accident, your job will suffer. You may even lose your job if you miss too much time.

S am thought he was very lucky when he signed a six-month contract to sing at the Valley Theatre. He was even happier when the audience liked his singing. Many people said Sam was good enough to be a star.

Next to singing, Sam's favorite activity was motorcycle riding. The speed thrilled him. On one of his days off Sam decided to ride to a city sixty miles away—he was a good rider and had no fear of traffic.

On the way home it began to rain. Four blocks from his apartment, a car turned in front of him. Sam's bike skidded on the wet pavement, and Sam was in the hospital for four weeks.

Sam's employer needed a singer, and the job couldn't wait until Sam got better. Sam probably hasn't lost his singing voice, but it may be hard for him to get another steady singing job.

A serious accident can cost you more than a job —it can cost you an entire career. An accident that prevents you from doing your chosen work can force you to change your personal goals. Consider what happened to Ralph.

E ver since he could remember, Ralph had wanted to be a carpenter. Two years ago he completed trade school and became an excellent carpenter. But one Friday afternoon a large beam fell from the crane and landed on Ralph's arm. His goals in carpentry vanished.

When Ralph left the hospital, he had lost the use of his arm. His career as a carpenter was over. Because of this accident, Ralph had to train for another type of work. His career goal had to be changed.

Perhaps the greatest cost of accidents is in the suffering and lost dreams.

- What was the cost to the seventeen-year-old who dived into a lake and hit bottom? Neck injuries paralyzed him for life.
- What was the cost to a young mother blinded by an explosion in her gas oven? She will never again see her husband or baby.
- What was the cost to a child who was injured in an auto accident? She can no longer walk.

If this young man has seriously injured his arm, leg, or back, he may need to find a job that is less physically demanding. Many people have had to make career changes as a result of accidents occurring on the job.

We cannot guess what "might have been" if these accidents had not happened. Think of all the athletes, plumbers, teachers, mechanics, and other workers lost because of accidents.

The cost of accidents is shocking. They cost money. They cost jobs. And they cost lives. We must all do our best to prevent accidents.

Causes of Accidents

Those who study accidents say that there are two main causes of accidents. The first is human error —everybody makes mistakes. The second major cause of accidents is an unsafe environment. Whether you are at home, at work, or at play, your environment may be unsafe.

Human Error

Most accidents, both on and off the job, are caused by human error. There are several types of human error, any of which can cause unsafe behavior. The types of human error are

- poor safety attitude,
- lack of knowledge,
- lack of skill,
- physical limitations, and
- fatigue.

Think about an accident you or someone you know has had. Chances are it happened because of one of the reasons listed in the first column.

Poor Safety Attitude. A person who does not care about safety has a poor safety attitude. Many accidents are caused by people with these attitudes.

Much research has been done to identify people with poor safety attitudes. It is likely that these people will be involved in an accident at some time. But researchers have not been able to find these people easily. Researchers *have* found that people with good safety attitudes are happy, responsible citizens.

A person's safety attitude can change. When you are excited, angry, depressed, or tired, you become less concerned with safety. Of course this makes you more likely to have accidents.

The use of drugs or alcohol can also lead to a poor safety attitude. This is part of the reason why alcohol is involved in at least half of all fatal automobile accidents. Another part of the danger from alcohol and drugs has to do with physical limitations.

The greatest number of deaths resulting from the combination of drugs, alcohol, and motor vehicles happens in the twenty-five to forty-four age range. The fifteen to twenty-four age group has the *next* highest number of deaths from these causes.

Emotions such as anger often create a poor safety attitude. A poor safety attitude usually means danger.

In what ways are these workers showing poor safety attitudes? Accidents like this can be avoided.

Lack of Knowledge. "I didn't know that machine was dangerous." These words are often heard after someone has had an accident. To prevent accidents at work you must have the necessary knowledge about machines and materials.

Workers are usually trained, but they cannot know everything about safe practices before they start to work. This lack of knowledge is especially dangerous in a shop. Things that a worker doesn't know often cause injuries.

Know your machines and tools. During shop class one student broke a finger. He had failed to clamp a vise on the drill table. He didn't know that the drill could spin a vise that wasn't clamped to the table.

When using machinery, *think safety*. Know what to do in an emergency. Study the instructions before using any machine.

Know about the materials you will be using. Many fires and explosions are caused each year by people who do not realize that certain liquids are flammable. Chemicals can be especially dangerous. Many chemicals that people used to think were safe are now known to be harmful.

Some products that people previously used freely are now thought to be possible causes of cancer. We are beginning to understand more about cancer-causing chemicals and dangers from radiation and asbestos. We need more knowledge about these chemicals and those that kill insects and weeds.

If not handled properly, some chemicals can destroy a worker's health. What can we do to protect ourselves? Be very careful when using any chemical. Learn what is in each substance. Then carefully follow the instructions on the container.

Lack of Skill. Lack of skill is the most common cause of accidents. A lack of skill shows up especially in emergencies. Consider what happened to Bill.

Bill finished truck-driving school a month ago. He had been driving an eighteen wheeler for two weeks. He had made a few panic stops, but he had had no serious emergencies.

Then it happened. The left front tire blew out. Bill could not control the truck, and it ran into the median strip of the highway.

Bill was lucky—there was little damage to the truck, and no one was hurt. But Bill's lack of driving skill could have caused a tragedy—the blowout could have happened in heavy traffic or on a bridge. Bill felt he had learned from this experience. He knew he had to improve his skill to better handle future emergencies.

There are many examples of accidents caused by lack of skill. Many people are injured while skiing. Some airplane pilots have crashed when landing because sudden changes in wind direction and speed require special flying skills. People learning to ride bicycles and motorcycles 'often lack skill. This sometimes leads to accidents.

Try to be as skilled as possible for your work, travel, and leisure activities. Try to notice when others lack skill—sometimes you can help them prevent accidents.

Having the necessary skill to do a job is probably the best way to prevent work-related accidents. When unqualified workers try to exceed their capabilities, the chance of an accident occurring rises sharply.

Physical Limitations. The inability to do certain physical tasks is called a *physical limitation*. Everyone has different physical limitations. Some, such as deafness, are usually permanent. A runner's pulled muscle is a temporary limitation. In many cases accidents occur because people are not strong enough or quick enough to prevent them.

Drownings rank second as the cause of accidental deaths for people fifteen to twenty-four years of age. Many of the victims lacked the strength to swim to safety. They were probably not aware of their physical limitations.

As mentioned, alcohol is a major cause of accidents. It slows the user's reflexes, making it impossible to react quickly to danger.

Fatigue. Many people suffer from **fatigue**, which is the physical condition of being very tired or exhausted. Fatigue is caused by extreme amounts of exertion, noise, heat, and humidity. Illness, lack of rest, and poor diet are also possible causes of fatigue. Avoid fatigue—it can cause unsafe behavior that may result in an accident.

John was very tired when he finished work Monday night at the Acme Machine Shop. He was so tired he didn't even shower and change clothes. He just started for home in his pickup truck.

John liked living on the little farm five miles from the city. It was only a twenty-minute drive to work. But that Monday night as John was driving home, the other cars seemed to be going much too fast. Suddenly, John felt a big bump. He saw he was off the road and headed straight toward a huge oak tree.

What do you think caused John to drive off the highway and into a tree? There were no skid marks to show that he tried to stop the truck. John probably went to sleep because he was suffering from fatigue. He had "run around" all weekend, and had slept and eaten very little. His body was tired. He had no energy left.

Besides causing a person to be sleepy, fatigue slows down movement. Studies show that there is a close relationship between good health and safety. If you are fatigued, you don't have good health, and you have a greater chance of being involved in an accident.

In the world of work, production goes down when workers are fatigued. Production on Mondays is often low because many workers are unfit for work. Their weekends have left them with little energy. And while fatigue causes production to go down, it causes the number of accidents to go up.

It is a worker's responsibility to be physically and mentally fit for work. Airline flight crews work only a few hours each week so they can be at their best before flight time. Should we expect less of other workers?

Lessening the Problem. Everyone must accept responsibility for their own safety, both on and off the job. For example, if you're ill or tired, pay special attention to safety. Know your limitations and overcome them if you can. If not, accept them. By pushing yourself beyond your limits, you invite injury.

A tired worker is a dangerous worker. Don't let fatigue reduce your effectiveness and attention to safety on the job.

Unsafe Environment

The second major cause of accidents is an unsafe environment. The accidents caused by an unsafe environment are not the fault of the victim. For example, Ann is a bus driver who is always very careful about her driving. One day there was an ice storm. Ann was approaching a corner when her bus slid on the ice and hit a truck. Avoiding this accident was probably impossible because of the unsafe conditions.

Machines are bigger, more complicated, and more powerful than ever. Yet the number of work-related accidental deaths is decreasing. Fewer workers are being injured on the job. Part of the reason for this good news is that **safety hazards** (potentially dangerous conditions) on the job are being reduced. Safety equipment, specially trained people, and new laws deserve much of the credit for this.

Safety Equipment. Safety equipment can help reduce accidents. Head protection for construction and factory workers has prevented many deaths and injuries, and safety glasses have reduced eye injuries. Safety padding and seat belts in automobiles and trucks have reduced injuries on the road. These are only a few of the many ways that accidents and their effects are being reduced. Of course no safety equipment will work if it is not used.

Make a Decision

You have a summer job working on a factory assembly line. You were told to wear safety goggles because of some grinding and drilling that is done at various places along the line. Many of the workers don't wear the goggles because the goggles are hot and very ugly—not at all "cool." You don't want to take a chance on seriously hurting your eyes, but you hate wearing the goggles. What's your decision—wear them all the time, or take them off when the supervisor isn't around? Give reasons for your decision.

Specially Trained People. Engineers are more capable now than ever before of predicting equipment failures. Safety engineers study the reasons for each accident. If an unsafe machine was at fault, the machine is redesigned or replaced. This helps to protect workers.

Inspectors work in factories, on construction sites, and in transportation. These people study conditions that might cause accidents. For example, inspectors are responsible for seeing that the equipment on airplanes, buses, and trains is in safe working order. Elevators are inspected regularly. By finding possible problems and having them corrected, inspectors prevent accidents.

New Laws. Today, most products must meet **standards** (acceptable levels) of performance and safety. This means companies must be certain that their products work well and work safely. Federal and state product-safety laws require this. The role that government plays in promoting safe practices will be discussed more fully in the next column.

Your Responsibility. Full control of the environment means removing anything in our surroundings that might be unsafe. It is not practical to think that we could ever do this. Trying to control the environment is expensive and inconvenient.

More control might include state or federal inspection of all transportation equipment, including privately owned automobiles. Other controls could mean more frequent closing of highways and city streets when the driving conditions are poor.

Since it is unlikely that we will ever totally control the environment, we must do what we can to prevent accidents. Making our environment safe is everyone's job.

Government Agencies

As mentioned earlier, accident prevention on the job has improved greatly. Companies are more aware of safe practices than ever before. Safety attitudes have improved through education.

Work in the nineteenth century was often very hazardous. Early railroads and industrial plants were especially dangerous, and there was very little safety engineering. There were few safety laws regulating dangerous occupations, such as mining. Miners had to deal with cave-ins, explosions, and a disease called *black lung.*

It became necessary for companies to prevent accidents and eliminate health hazards, so accidents were studied. Many new, safe practices were begun in order to reduce danger. Safety education programs were started by labor unions and management, especially in the larger industries.

The government makes and enforces laws that promote health and safety. As a result of these laws,

Today business people are more conscious of safety standards than ever before. Inspections and tests conducted by qualified engineers have reduced the amount of defective, and dangerous, products on the market.

The scientists and technicians at the Environmental Protection Agency have a big job—they are trying to make our country a safer place in which to live. Polluted water, polluted air, and toxic waste dumps are just a few of the hazards they are trying to eliminate.

two government agencies have been created to protect the health and safety of people. These agencies are the Occupational Safety and Health Administration and the Environmental Protection Agency.

OSHA

The **Occupational Safety and Health Act** was passed by Congress in 1970. The name of this act is usually shortened to **OSHA**. OSHA is legislation that determines safety and health standards for the world of work. OSHA decides what the lowest acceptable levels of safety will be. Inspectors can force company officials to appear in court when they find companies that do not meet the minimum standards.

Under the rules of OSHA, the employer and the employee have responsibilities and rights. The act says that each employer must provide a job site free from safety and health hazards. It also says that the employee must obey rules listed in the act. For example, where required, the worker must use protective equipment. For OSHA rules about your job, see the OSHA poster at your job site.

OSHA has been praised for saving lives. It has also been criticized as costing too much. It is expensive for industry to meet some of the OSHA standards and this cost is passed on to customers. Do you think OSHA should lower its standards?

The EPA

The **Environmental Protection Agency**, the **EPA**, is another governmental agency that makes our country safer for everyone. The EPA is an agency that tries to protect the environment. By doing this, it protects our health. Reducing air and water pollution is one of the main goals of the EPA.

Many scientific groups wrote reports that showed the need to protect the environment. These scientists studied air pollution in large cities. They analyzed water pollution in rivers and lakes, and found that pollution, which can cause serious diseases, had reached dangerous levels in some areas.

As a result of these studies, the EPA was given certain powers. Among them is the power to limit the amount of smoke and fumes released into the environment by autos and factories. These limitations help to reduce pollution.

REVIEW YOUR LEARNING

CHAPTER SUMMARY

Accidents can happen to anyone at any time. Each year the National Safety Council analyzes and reports many types of accidents. Human error is responsible for most accidents. The errors are caused by poor safety attitudes, lack of knowledge, lack of skill, physical limitations, and fatigue. Unsafe environments are the second main cause of accidents. Establishment of safety standards and government agencies, such as OSHA (the Occupational Safety and Health Act) and EPA (the Environmental Protection Agency) work to protect our health and safety.

Accidents can have serious consequences for victims, and the cost is great, both financially and personally. We are all responsible for the safety of ourselves and others.

WORDS YOU SHOULD KNOW

Environmental Protection Agency (EPA)
fatigue
Occupational Safety and Health Act (OSHA) ·
safety hazards
standards

STUDY QUESTIONS

1. Why is it impossible to figure the true cost of accidents?
2. What are the two main reasons for accidents?
3. When might someone who is usually safe have a poor safety attitude?
4. Why is it important to know about the machines and materials that you work with?
5. Give at least five causes of fatigue.
6. Why should workers avoid fatigue? Give two reasons.
7. What have been the three main factors in reducing the number of accidental deaths and injuries in recent years?
8. What has the government done to increase work safety?
9. What two government agencies are responsible for enforcing safety and health laws and regulations?
10. Give at least three reasons why some companies have fewer accidents than others.

REVIEW YOUR LEARNING   CHAPTER 9

DISCUSSION TOPICS

1. Discuss with your class the *true* cost of an accident that you know about.
2. Why do you think the number of job-related accidents is decreasing, while accidents at home are increasing?
3. Why are young people involved in so many accidents? Is there a solution?
4. Discuss ways in which you are personally responsible for your health and safety.
5. You must pay more for goods and services because of OSHA regulations. Is the extra cost worth it? Explain your reasoning.

SUGGESTED ACTIVITIES

1. Collect newspaper clippings about accidents. Try to answer the following questions.
   - What do you think was the cause of the accident?
   - Where or on whom would you place responsibility for the accident?
   - What might have been done to prevent the accident?
   - What can you learn from this accident about safety in your own life?
2. Write to OSHA and the EPA. Obtain all the information possible about how these agencies try to protect our health and safety.

PART THREE

DEVELOPING YOUR SKILLS AND UNDERSTANDING

Employers are looking for people who are still learning. They try to hire people with good, basic skills and a general understanding of what's going on in the world of work. They know that people who can read, write, speak clearly, and solve problems are people who can learn fast and make valuable contributions to their businesses.

The basic skills and knowledge that you will read about in this section are essential for every person in the world of work. How skilled and knowledgeable you become in these areas will have a big impact on your success. Much of what you read here will be a review of all the things you've been learning in school for the past twelve years. If your review reveals some weaknesses, you still have time to improve your skills before you enter the world of work.

Communication Skills

DO YOU KNOW . . .
- the common blocks to listening with understanding?
- how to organize a formal speech?
- four techniques that can help you to read for meaning?
- when a letter is the best form of communication?

CAN YOU DEFINE . . .
- communication?
- enunciation?
- feedback?
- inflection?
- jargon?
- previewing?
- pronunciation?
- skimming?

Communication is the process of exchanging information. It is how we transmit thoughts and ideas from one person to another.

Poor communication can cause all kinds of problems in the world of work. Suppose you just accepted a new job. Your boss will explain your duties and may even show you how to do them. But if your boss doesn't get the message across to you about how you are to do your job, you will probably make some mistakes. If this happens, your boss may think you are not capable of doing the work, or that you are not cooperative. You could even be fired. Your boss will probably not think that poor communication caused the mistakes.

There are four primary communication skills: listening, speaking, reading, and writing. These skills are necessary in almost every working situation. Almost without exception, those who rise to the top of any career are those who communicate well. Think about the people you admire and respect the most. Are they people who do a good job of getting their ideas across to others?

In this chapter you will learn about some things you can do to improve your communication skills. you can then begin working and practicing to become a better communicator. The work you do to improve these skills may be just as important as the work you do on the job.

The Communication Process

There are two parts to communicating a message. Every message must be sent, and it must be received. Even though a message is sent, no communication is going on unless someone receives it.

Receiving a message actually involves more than simply hearing or reading it. The receiver must be able to *understand* the sender's message. Communication means both the sender and the receiver understand the message *in the same way.*

Maybe that boss in the example mentioned earlier didn't give directions well. Even so, the boss could have done a better job of communicating with you by asking for **feedback**. Feedback is the receiver's response to the sender's message. Feedback makes it possible for the sender to determine whether or not a receiver understands a message. If your feedback indicated that you didn't understand the directions, the boss could repeat the message in different words until it was clear to you.

What if your boss doesn't ask for feedback to check on your understanding? Is there anything you can do to be sure that you understand the message? Yes, you may ask the boss to repeat and explain any part of the message that you feel you might have misunderstood.

In communication, both the sender and receiver of messages have responsibilities. The sender has the responsibility giving clear messages and asking for feedback to check on mutual understanding. The receiver has the responsibility for listening or reading intently and asking for more explanation on any parts that are not clear.

Some people think that just because they say something, they are communicating. They forget that unless someone listens to or reads their message, no communication has taken place. It takes at least two people to communicate a message.

Listening Skills

Did you know that we spend 70 percent of our waking hours communicating, either as a sender or receiver? We spend more time listening than we do speaking, reading, or writing. In fact, studies have shown that about 45 percent of our communication time is spent listening.

Listening—like speaking, reading, and writing—is a skill. Skillful listeners receive messages and understand them. These people are usually very successful in the world of work, and they often appear more intelligent than the rest of us. Those who develop high-level listening skills become far more knowledgeable than those who don't. How would you rate your listens skills? Are you a good listener?

Many people have never learned to listen well. Do you know anyone so interested in speaking that he or she hardly listens at all? There are people like that. They haven't learned the difference between *hearing* and *listening*. Hearing is just a physical process. Only our ears are involved. Listening is a mental process, requiring the use of your brain.

Basic Listening Skills

In one listening experiment, sixteen workers in a medical clinic listened to the same recorded message. Four hours later they were asked to explain in writing the main points of the message they heard. As you might expect, every response was different. Only three had fully understood the main points of the message. Nine understood most of what was said, but four interpreted the message quite differently than what the speaker had in mind.

It's so easy to misunderstand a message. You must work hard mentally to listen with understanding. There are some listening strategies, or skills, that can help you understand the messages sent to you. These strategies deal with what to listen for, or what to do—in your mind—while listening. These skills will also help you improve your reading.

Recognize Your Purpose. Sometimes you will know the purpose of a message before the person begins to speak. If so, think about how a clear understanding of that message may help you. If you don't know the purpose, make a quick mental note of how understanding might help you as soon as you realize the purpose. When you know how a clear understanding of the message can help you, you can better concentrate all your mental energy on the message.

Look for the Plan. In formal, structured speeches, there is usually some kind of plan. Informal talks may include a plan as well. Your boss's explanation of how to carry out your work responsibilities may have some organizational structure. You can greatly improve your understanding when you know the plan. You will also remember the message longer.

The speaker may list events or make generalizations, and then give evidence to support them. Cause-and-effect relationships and contrasts-and-comparisons are other common ways of organizing speeches. When you know how the speaker is organizing his or her thoughts, it is easier to understand the relationship of subtopics.

Give Feedback. You already read about one important listening skill—feedback. As a listener you can speed things up and improve understanding by sending signals back to the speaker. Nod your head to show that you are getting the message. A raised eyebrow or quizzical look will tell the speaker to slow down or repeat a complicated part of the message. With these small gestures and a quick summary of your understanding at the end, you can make sure that you and the speaker understand the message in the same way.

Take Notes. If you have a chance, make written notes on the speaker's main points. Then you can review them one at a time later. If you can't write down the main points, make mental notes. Say the

Communication is a difficult task to accomplish. Words have different meanings and people interpret words and gestures in different ways. Each of these listeners probably has a slightly different understanding of what the speaker is saying.

main points in your own words, in your mind. Try to relate the speaker's message to your own experiences. This rewording and repetition will help make certain things clearer and will also help you remember important items.

Distinguish between Fact and Opinion. Usually facts are more important than opinions. Listen to some radio and TV commercials. How much is fact and how much is opinion? Can you always tell the difference? Facts are truths. Opinions differ from one person to the next. Of course, "expert" opinion is often considered the next best thing to facts. When your boss gives you his or her opinions about how you should do your job, you will probably consider those opinions just as important as facts.

"Listen" for More than Verbal Content. There is much more to a speaker's message than the meanings of the words used. The way in which a speaker says what he or she says, and the speaker's body language are major parts of the message.

Inflection is the use of the voice to alter the meaning of a spoken message. By using inflection people can create several different meanings for the same sentence. They can say it loudly or softly. They can pick out one or two words and say them much louder than the others.

As a listener, you must pay attention to inflection. The speaker's inflection will give you valuable clues to the real meaning of the message. Anger, fear, and other emotions that are important to your understanding will come through inflection.

Observing the speaker's body language will also help you understand the message. You read about the importance of body language in Chapter 8. You don't "hear" gestures and body movements, but taking them into account makes you a better listener.

Distinguish between Important and Unimportant. You can't remember every word a person says. Try to sort out what is important and what is unimportant. Then discard what's unimportant.

Ask Questions. If you have a chance to ask questions, ask them whenever you don't understand. Some people are afraid they will embarrass themselves if they ask questions. Don't worry about that. On the job, especially, it's far better to ask questions and make sure you know what you are supposed to do than to risk doing your job wrong because of a misunderstanding.

Listen for a Conclusion. If no conclusion is given, mentally summarize the speaker's main points and draw your own conclusion. You may need or want to take some kind of action based on this conclusion.

Try to notice *how* people say what they say. You lose much of the meaning if you ignore body language, inflection, and gestures.

Use the Dictionary. We all hear words that are new to us. Often we need to know these words to understand the meaning of the message. Don't let yourself be confused twice by the same word. If someone uses a word you don't know, look up the meaning in a dictionary the first chance you get. If you make this a habit, you will improve your vocabulary. This will go a long way toward making you a better listener.

Blocks to Listening with Understanding

Some things commonly prevent people from being good listeners. We call them *blocks* to listening with understanding. If you can avoid these blocks, you can concentrate your attention on listening—and understanding.

Distractions. Distractions are noises, thoughts, anything that prevents you from concentrating on what the speaker is saying. Some people are bothered more by distractions than others. You may have noticed that the slightest interruption or noise can cause some people to "tune out." Other people seem to listen intently, to "hang on every word" and stay tuned-in regardless of interruptions.

Being able to block out distractions is mostly a matter of concentrated effort. You can do it if you focus all your mental energy on what the speaker is saying.

Emotional Blocks. If you don't like the speaker or strongly disagree with his or her ideas, you may find it difficult to listen. In the world of work, though, it you don't understand the message, you may not be able to do your job correctly. If you disagree with the speaker's ideas, it is especially important to listen and to understand. Otherwise you will be unable to respond in a meaningful way. When you know the value of listening in these situations, you can usually prevent emotional blocks.

Many people block out emotionally painful messages by hearing what they want to hear. The speaker says one thing, but the listener hears another. This may avoid the problem for a while, but it won't make it go away. It's better to listen and deal with the situation right away than to deal with a bigger problem later.

Planning a Response. One of the most serious blocks to listening is planning what you will say next. The mind works much faster than the mouth, and you can easily jump ahead of the speaker in many situations. When the speaker says something you want to respond to, it's tempting to think about your response and tune out the speaker. By doing this, however, you may miss out on a key piece of information. Then your reply will not be appropriate. Only by listening to and understanding the entire message can you make a good response.

Some people are able to listen intently without being distracted. This is a valuable skill for anyone. It is especially valuable in occupations where people must work in busy, noisy areas.

Make a Decision

Your boss is the slowest talker you have ever encountered, and he repeats every instruction over and over. You almost always know what he wants you to do after listening to his first few words, but he talks on and on. You find yourself thinking of other things, though you know you should pay attention. What's your decision—will you listen carefully to every word, or will you block out the boss and think of other things? Give reasons for your decision.

Speaking Skills

Your ability to communicate orally, to speak, will have considerable influence on your success in the world of work. Some careers require much greater speaking skills than others. Whatever your career, though, you will need to express yourself clearly so that your supervisor and co-workers understand the message you are sending.

Your Purpose in Speaking

Always keep in mind *why* you are speaking. In most cases, we speak to inform, to persuade, or to entertain.

Speaking to Inform. The main purpose of most conversations is to inform one or more of the people involved in the conversation. The participants exchange information, frequently changing roles from receiver to sender and back again.

When your purpose in speaking is to inform, get right to the point. Do not "beat around the bush," as they say. Be direct—say what you want to say clearly and quickly.

Few people make it to the top of their career areas without the ability to speak clearly and effectively. If you haven't taken a speech course, and there's still time, you might want to consider such a course.

We are called on occasionally to give directions. Giving directions was actually part of the job for Jennifer and Robert, who worked summers in an information office in a resort city in Colorado. When a visitor asked how to get to the local post office, Jennifer pointed north and said:

"Go nine blocks north to Main and turn right on Eighth Street. Continue on Eighth for three blocks, and the post office will be on your left."

Later in the day Robert was asked the same question. His reply was:

"Oh, go on up the street 'till you get to Eighth. Backus Drug Store is on the corner. If you have time, try some of their ice cream. It's out of this world! When I was in high school I used to stop by for a sundae every afternoon. The post office is about three blocks east from there."

Which directions would be easier to follow?

At first, Robert's directions may seem silly. But think about people you know who wander off the point when they are speaking. Robert's failure to stick to the main point is a bad habit that many people have. When you are speaking to inform people, get to the point.

Speaking to Persuade. In many careers it is necessary to persuade others to see or do things your way. In Chapter 8, you learned some methods for understanding and influencing others. Several of the hints in that chapter provide a good background for persuading others through spoken communication. To refresh your memory, look back to pages 124–130.

Use as many of these strategies as you can. Some are easy—is there any reason why you can't smile? If you use all of them, you can hardly fail. Perhaps the most important is learning the needs of the listener, then showing how you can satisfy at least one of those needs.

O ne day a man walked into the Auto Parts House and asked Laura, the salesperson, about buying some tires.

"Oh, my tires are wearing a bit thin. I'm on the road a lot, and I don't want to do any hydroplaning. What tires do you have for an '84 Buick for less than a hundred dollars apiece?"

Laura replied, "I think I'll have to look that up. So you don't like to hydroplane, huh? My sister rode a hydroplane across the English channel last summer and said it was totally breathtaking. I'd truly love to spend next summer in Europe.

"Yes, that would be wonderful. Have you found the prices?"

Laura interrupted, "I can't seem to find the list of cheaper tires. But if you ask me, you'd be better off spending a little more and getting some good radial tires. My boyfriend bought a set and he's put more than 30,000 miles on them without a single flat. Want to look at some radials?"

"No . . . thank you. I just remembered . . . I'm late for an appointment."

Late in the afternoon an older woman hurried in out of the rain.

"May I help you," asked Craig, one of the other salespeople working at the Auto Parts House.

"Well, my tires are getting a little thin."

"Is that your Olds?"

"Yes. Can you sell me a set of four for under $400?"

"Yes." Craig pointed to a tire on an overhead rack. "I've sold a lot of these tires, and most people get at least 30,000 miles wear. I can have a set of these spin balanced and on your car in about 40 minutes. The total for tires, installation, balancing, tax and everything is $386.45."

"Sounds good. Do it."

Craig listened to the customer and responded in a way that satisfied her need. How would you describe Laura's responses? Would you rather have Craig or Laura working for you?

Speaking to Entertain. Sometimes the purpose of a conversation is to entertain. In many careers, such as sales, it is necessary to entertain clients. Meeting with business associates, including your boss and those you supervise, provides other situations in which you will need to talk to and entertain others. Few of us are really comedians, but it is fun to talk, tell stories, and joke with friends. You may use slang expressions or even special words that only you and your friends know. This kind of speaking is usually quite informal.

A Plan for Speaking Formally

You may not give many formal speeches, but in the world of work many spoken messages are at least semi-formal. Jobs in business, engineering, education, health, and many other careers, require people to deliver messages in such a way that others will listen and understand them. When you speak to others on the job, you will want them to listen to what you are saying. A well-organized spoken message always receives more attention than one presented in a haphazard way.

There are some basic organizational patterns you can use.

Enumeration. Enumeration is the process of listing several items in a particular order. When you become a supervisor, you may tell a new worker, "There are six steps in handling this task." Then the new worker will know to listen for six separate, but related, things to do. They will be easier to understand because the listener is expecting them. Using signal words, such as *first, second, third,* and *next,* will also help the listener.

Generalization with Example. Speakers often use generalizations to make a point. Good speakers support their generalizations with examples and evidence. If you work for an insurance company, you won't simply say, "Motor vehicles are the leading cause of accidental deaths in the United States." You will also present evidence: "Of all accidental deaths in 1984, almost half were the result of auto accidents." Evidence in support of generalizations clarifies the message and helps the listener remember the main points. Use signal words such as *for example,* and *for instance.*

Cause and Effect. An effective way of explaining a topic is to discuss it in terms of cause and effect. This pattern leads the listener from the cause of something to the result. This method can also be used in reverse by presenting an effect then considering possible causes. Signal words are *as a result, therefore, accordingly,* and *consequently.*

Comparison and Contrast. Comparison and contrast is another technique for explaining something. An effective way of explaining new concepts is to show how they are similar to concepts already known to the listener. Use words like *however, nevertheless,* and *on the other hand.*

Speaking Standard English

In informal conversations with friends, it's all right to use slang expressions to spice up the conversation. But on the job, in most companies, people are expected to speak standard English. The importance of standard English, especially in job interviews, was discussed in Chapter 5. Because it is *standard,* this form of English is understood wherever English is spoken. By using standard English you reduce the chances of being misunderstood.

Use of Voice

You read earlier that to be a good communicator you will need to use your voice effectively. You have considerable control over the way your voice sounds. By practicing, you can develop a habit of speaking in tones that are pleasant but not artificial. The following paragraphs outline an attractive speaking voice.

Pleasant Pitch. A pleasant voice is not "pitched" too high nor too low. Compared to music, the pitches of voices could range from a tenor flute to a bass drum. Men usually have lower-pitched voices than women. But both men and women can adjust their voices so that they are more pleasing. You may have heard someone whose voice was so highly pitched that you didn't really want to listen to what that person said. Is the pitch of your voice pleasant?

"Relaxed" Sound. A relaxed voice is more attractive than a tense one. A voice sounds relaxed when a medium tone is combined with smoothness.

Most people aren't aware of being affected by a speaker's voice, but a pleasing voice makes every message much more effective.

There is no shakiness in a relaxed voice. When you are tense, you usually speak in a higher voice and your voice may sound shaky.

Medium Volume. The volume, or loudness, of your voice is important. No one likes to strain to hear what is said or ask that the message be repeated. On the other hand, speaking in a very loud voice will cause people to avoid listening to you.

Varied Inflections. You read earlier about the importance of listening for inflections to help you understand spoken messages. As a speaker you can use inflections to make your voice more attractive. You can use inflections for emphasis and interest by placing stress on certain important words and syllables. This helps make your meaning clear. Along with variation of speed and loudness, inflections make a voice sound enthusiastic.

Good Speaking Habits

Along with an attractive voice, it is important to use effective methods of oral, or spoken, communications. A few tips for proper speech are presented here. Try to develop these tips into personal habits that will make you an effective speaker.

Pronunciation. Use correct **pronunciation.** Pronunciation refers to the way a word sounds. Always try to say the sounds of words correctly. For example *girl* is pronounced "gurl," not "goil."

Enunciation. Use correct **enunciation.** To enunciate means to speak each syllable clearly and separately. Many of us squeeze syllables together to make sounds that aren't really words, such as "didja" (for "did you"). Sometimes we drop the last sound of a word. Do you ever say, "The phone's ringin"? Isn't that last word supposed to end with a *g* sound?

If you have bad speaking habits, you may need to force yourself to think about your enunciation. You can develop correct enunciation by practicing. Poor enunciation is often due to laziness or the tendency to speak too fast.

Speed. Don't talk too fast or too slowly. Have you ever heard a person talk so fast that you couldn't understand what he or she was saying? Have you heard anyone talk so slowly that it was boring? A moderate speed that is neither hurried nor drawn out is best. But vary the speed to keep your listener interested. Listen to TV and radio newscasters. The good ones vary their rate of speech.

On the Telephone

A lot of work in the business world is done over the telephone. How effective you are in speaking on the phone can affect your success. This is especially true if you are an office worker.

When you speak on the telephone, your voice becomes even more important than in face-to-face conversations. In face-to-face conversations, facial expressions and body language help get the message across. In phone conversations, the person with whom you are speaking can't see you. In these situations a pleasant voice can have the same effect as a smile or a friendly gesture.

When your phone rings, answer it right away. People who are kept waiting on the phone are frequently not as cooperative as they would be otherwise. When you answer, give the name of your company or department first. Then give your name: "Maddox Company, Ms. Jones speaking."

Ideas about proper phone etiquette do vary, however. It's a good idea to ask your employer how you should answer the phone.

When you speak on the phone, speak clearly and directly into the mouthpiece. Talk loud enough so the other person does not have to strain to hear you. But don't yell! Develop the habit of being courteous and *never interrupt* the other person.

Business by Phone

Without telephones the world of work would probably come to a screeching halt. Workers order supplies, gather information, answer customer questions, and communicate with one another. Developing your confidence and skill in speaking on the telephone will move you closer to your career goal.

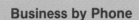

Reading Skills

Reading, like listening, is a mental process of trying to understand a message. Reading with understanding is important in all phases of life. It's a necessity in most careers. In fact, it's rare for anyone to get a job without being able to read. An efficient plan for finding and applying for a job requires reading. You begin by reading the help-wanted ads, then you read the job application forms.

You can improve your understanding by always being aware of *why* you are reading. Asking yourself this question will help you decide *how* you will read something. For example, if you're reading a job application form or a warranty on something you may buy, you read every word. You will probably even reread several sentences to be sure of their meaning.

When you know why you are reading something, you can often save time by **previewing** or **skimming**. Previewing means reading only those parts of a document that outline or summarize its contents. Skimming means reading through something very quickly, picking out the key points.

Previewing

Suppose that you work for an advertising agency. Your boss, Ms. Gordon, is planning a series of magazine ads for a company that manufactures recreational equipment. She has learned that, as we near the turn of the century, many groups are planning national campaigns to remember the early days of our country—Colonial America.

Ms. Gordon asks you to look for information on forms of recreation in Colonial America. You probably won't find any entire books on this topic, but you will find lots of books on recreation and other books on Colonial America.

In this situation you can save yourself a lot of time by previewing. The first thing to check is the title. Does it sound like it might have information on recreation in Colonial America? If not, you may not even want to open the book. If it does, look at the table of contents. Most books list chapter titles, or at least the major topics covered in the book in the table of contents. Many books have an index in

On the job, time is money. You can save a great deal of time by previewing a book's table of contents or index to find out whether or not that book has the information you need.

the back of the book that lists most topics covered, even if they are mentioned only briefly. If what you're looking for isn't listed, then go on to another book. This is previewing.

You may find several books with chapters devoted to your subject. Some may only have part of a chapter on your topic. Other books may show one or two references to your subject in the index. By previewing the table of contents and index in this way, you can find the information you want without reading the whole book.

Skimming

You are skimming when you look up words in the dictionary or read headlines in the newspaper to find articles you want to read. When your time is limited, you may also skim newspaper articles. You may skim a chapter of a book now and then.

When skimming, you will usually be looking for the topic sentence in each paragraph. The topic sentence, usually the first sentence, is the sentence that states the main idea of that paragraph. If the topic sentence is about something you already know, or if it isn't interesting, skip on to the next one. If the topic is interesting, read the whole paragraph. In this way you can read a great deal more of what you want and need to read.

Reading for Meaning

Good readers understand the message sent by the writer. Four activities that will help you better understand the writer's message are listed below.

- Focusing your mind
- Forming pictures
- Forming patterns
- Improving your vocabulary

Focusing Your Mind. Do you use a camera? Some cameras made in recent years focus on the subject automatically. Most cameras, though, must be focused by the photographer—otherwise the picture will be blurred.

None of us has a mind that focuses automatically. We have to do it ourselves, by constant concentration. If we don't force ourselves to concentrate, we get a blurred picture of what we've read. This is why you should be constantly aware of what's on your mind. If your mind wanders from the subject you are reading, you need to refocus.

Forming Pictures. Do you "see" what you're reading? If not, try to form pictures in your mind as you read. The message may describe things, places, situations, people, or actions by certain people. When you picture the message in your mind, it becomes clearer.

Forming Patterns. Try to separate the main ideas from the details. Then, in your mind, outline the writer's organization of ideas. When you can see the relationship of ideas and details, you will have a more complete understanding of the message. The message becomes even more meaningful if you can relate the ideas, or even some details, to your own life. This will also help you remember the message longer.

Improving Your Vocabulary. As we read, we all come across words that we don't know. Many times we can determine the meaning of a new word from the way it's used in a sentence or paragraph. If this doesn't work it is important to find out what the word means. As you know, the best way to check on the meanings of words is to consult a good dictionary.

As you take your place in the world of work, you will encounter words that relate especially to the type of work you do. These words make up something called **jargon**. Jargon is a special word, term, or phrase used to describe something in a particular field. Whatever career field you enter, you will probably have to learn some jargon to read and understand job-related materials.

When you first begin working, you may feel a little embarrassed to ask the meaning of words. But it is better to ask what a word means than to make a serious error in carrying out your work responsibilities.

A conversation overheard in the data processing department of a large firm:

"Jack, I'd like to configure a system of distributive processing here with, say, sixteen micros talking to the mainframe. How much RAM does that new IBM have—the one Dave showed us?"

"512K. The new mini floppies will store 700K on disk. Carmen, do you want to run 9600 baud by transmitting direct or hook up modems?"

"Modems would slow us up a bit. We'll wire direct. What DOS do those micros use?"

"MSDOS."

Most career areas do not have as much jargon as the computer industry. Electrical, medical, and accounting occupations are just a few, however, that have their own vocabularies. Asking questions is the best way to speed up the process of learning your job's jargon.

Make a Decision

Suppose you are in charge of ten workers who take customer orders over the telephone. Each worker enters the ordering information into a computer, then someone in the warehouse uses the information on the computer printout to ship the orders. Several of the telephone workers are making errors, causing customers to receive the wrong merchandise. You need to explain the importance of the workers' being more careful. You can call a group meeting, speak to each worker individually, write a general memo for everyone, or write individual memos to each worker. What's your decision—how will you communicate with these workers? Give reasons for your decision.

Writing Skills

The simplest and fastest way to communicate with someone is to have a conversation. With a telephone we can send or receive messages instantly, even if the other person is thousands of miles away. There are times, though, when writing is a better way to communicate than speaking.

Writing out your message is the best way to organize your thoughts. It gives you a chance to revise your message before sending it. Often, when you see your thoughts in writing, you will think of ways to improve your message. Maybe you can say it in a clearer way or give it more impact.

A written message is an exact record of your message. It's easy to make copies for whoever needs to read it. By filing a copy you have a dated record of when it was written.·

In conversations, we tend to hear what we want to hear and forget the rest. But when you write a message down in black and white, it's all there. It can't be easily ignored. The receiver is more likely to take appropriate action than if he or she had received the same message in a conversation. The impact of a written message also lasts longer since the message can be kept permanently.

There will be many occasions for writing in your personal life. Writing is also an important function on most jobs.

Jill Byers never cared much for writing. When everyone was writing letters in her English classes, Jill did the very minimum to get a passing grade. Besides, she thought, "I'm going to be a horse trainer, and I won't have to do any writing."

Jill did become a horse trainer. Only then did she learn the importance of writing. When she entered her horses in races, she had to write out the information for the racing secretary at Hollywood Park. Every month she wrote statements showing what each horse owner owed for training, horseshoeing, and veterinary charges. On one occasion she had to send a letter to a mail order house in the Midwest to complain about some defective stable supplies and to request replacements. Her activities at horse sales also required a lot of writing.

Jill was quite surprised by the amount of writing she was doing. She wished she had given it more attention in high school. When Jill was back home for a week, she stopped by to see her former English teacher. Jill offered to come and talk with students about the importance of improving their writing skills.

Common Considerations in Writing

There are three common considerations in every kind of writing: the reader, the purpose, and the subject matter.

Know Your Reader. Before you write anything, give some thought to those who will be reading your message. Who are they? Why will they be reading your message? What do they already know about the subject? The answers to these questions, and any others you can think of in each situation, will help you to know the reader better. When you understand the needs of the reader, you can write a more meaningful message.

Before you write any type of business communication, think about the person who will be reading the message. Always keep your audience in mind when writing.

Know Your Purpose. The second thing you will consider as you begin your writing is the purpose of your message. Most writing is done for one of the following reasons.

- Inform
- Request
- Confirm
- Persuade
- Inquire
- Complain

Stop and think about your purpose before you start. Make sure you know why you are writing your message.

Know Your Subject. You will need to know your subject well in order to write about it. On the job you may learn enough about the subject that no further research is necessary. If you are still new on the job, though, you may want to do some reading before you write certain messages. When you know your subject well, you will feel more confident as you write.

Selecting A Writing Style

Some years ago, much of the writing in the business world was formal and stiff. The trend in recent years has been toward more informal business writing. Of course company executives usually set the tone and style of writing for their companies, which means the style will vary from one office to the next. You will probably have an opportunity to read company letters, memos, and reports before writing any. This will give you a chance to see how formal the writing style is where you work.

Most companies today emphasize the direct, clear style of writing. This means writing in a conversational style, using words you would use if you were speaking. When you speak for yourself, say, "I believe. . . ." When you are speaking for another person—Bill, for instance—then you may write either "Bill and I believe. . . ." or simply "We believe. . . ." Try to avoid phrases such as "It is believed. . . ."

Any written message is a reflection of the writer. When your writing is a neat, well-organized message, others see you as a neat, well-organized person.

As you write, keep in mind your main purpose in writing—to communicate something to another person. Select individual words that will make the message clear to the reader. Don't try to impress the reader with your vocabulary as many writers used to, and some still do.

The WATCO company planned major changes in its health insurance coverage for employees. Each branch manager was to notify his or her employees about the change. Each employee was to be told when the new program would be effective.

One manager wrote: "We plan to implement this new program sometime during the timeframe subsequent to March 1 but not extending beyond April 30."

Another manager wrote: "This new program will start in March or April."

Knowing the importance of writing effectively on the job, which manager do you believe is most likely to move up in the company?

Jargon, as we mentioned, serves a purpose. It's a kind of verbal shorthand within a particular career field, and it helps communicate between workers in that field. Jargon presents severe stumbling blocks to communication for people outside the field. Avoid jargon when writing to those not involved in your career field.

The one "best" word that you can use in a written message is the name of the person who will read it. You know the importance of saying others' names in spoken conversations. Writing the name of the person who will receive your written message helps personalize your message. The person reading your message will have a warmer feeling toward you.

Letters, Memos, and Reports

There are many forms of written communication. Which form you use in a particular situation usually depends on the kind of information you are communicating. Sometimes a simple handwritten note is all that's required. In business, most written messages are in the form of letters, memos, or reports.

A Properly Prepared Business Letter

Return Address — WORLD OF WORK COMPUTING
4400 ARGON CIRCLE
Santa Barbara, CA 93105

Date — March 12, 1986

Inside Address — Megabyte Computers, Inc.
1700 Kellogg Boulevard
Wichita, KS 67213

Salutation — Dear Sir:

Body —
After reading about the new Dream Machine computer that you advertised in the March issue of <u>Business World Computing</u>, I would like a price list and specifications on each model. We plan to replace several of our micro-computers, and I would like our Board of Directors to consider the Dream Machine.

Do you have a sales representative on the West Coast? If so, I would appreciate receiving a call from him or her.

Closing — Yours truly,

Signature and Typed Name — Grant Kinsey
President

Reference Initials — GK:sm

Business Letters. Business letters will be your main form of written communication with people outside your own company. You can use letters to inform, request, confirm, persuade, inquire, or complain. An example of a business letter is shown on the opposite page. The form of most business letters includes eight standard parts.

- Return address—the address of the writer of the letter. Most companies have their address printed on their stationery. This printed stationery is called *letterhead*. When you type a business letter on blank paper, you must type the return address at the top of the page.
- Date—the date shows the reader when the letter was written. In doing business it is frequently important to know *when* you wrote a letter. Having the date on the letter is security against a faulty memory.
- Inside address—the name and address of the person who will receive the letter. This same address is typed on the envelope.
- Salutation—the greeting. The most commonly used salutation is "Dear (Mr., Mrs., Miss, Ms.) Smith." If you usually call the person by his or her first name, you may write to Adam Smith as "Dear Adam:" A colon always follows the salutation in a business letter.
- Body—the most important part of the letter— the message.
- Closing—a respectful goodbye. Formal closings for business letters are "Yours very truly," and "Yours truly." Less formal, more friendly closings are "Sincerely," and "Cordially." A comma should follow the closing.
- Signature—the handwritten name of the writer. Sign your name in ink above your typed name. Write both your first and last name—unless you are on a first-name basis with the reader.

Your initials, as writer, and the initials of the typist are called *reference initials*. They are typed two spaces below your typed signature, beginning at the left margin. The writer's initials are always typed first.

Memos. A memo is a written message to someone in your own company. Memos are usually brief and often cover only one topic. An example of a memo is shown below. Much of the important communication that takes place within companies is done in memo form.

Reports. A business report is often written to explain certain things. Usual topics for reports include yearly sales, problems that need attention, results of studies or surveys, and results of special projects. Some reports are "in-house" reports, to be read only by company employees. Others are written for a wider audience.

Some long, complex reports are organized formally with a table of contents, introduction, body, and summary. Others are short, informal reports consisting only of the body—similar to the body of a letter. Before you begin preparing a report, learn whether your company has a preferred way of organizing reports.

A Well-Written Memo

```
              M E M O R A N D U M

Date:      January 6, 1986

To:        George Byerson

From:      Cindy Marshall

Subject:   Reserving parking spaces for staff

As you know, we have fourteen employees, and the company parking lot
will accommodate sixteen cars.  Several of us must make calls during
the day, and when we return to the office, the lot is often full.  It
appears that shoppers in the area are parking in our company lot while
they are at the mall.

I suggest that we have each employee's name painted on a small sign and
placed in front of his or her space.  In addition, we could place a
larger sign at the entrance of the parking lot that says something like
"Byerson and Marshall, Inc., Parking for Employees Only."  Maybe we
should add that other cars will be "TOWED AWAY!"
```

Good Writing

Good writing rarely comes easily—it usually takes a lot of hard work and effort. Because good writing is so difficult to achieve for so many people, those who can write well are usually very successful in the world of work.

How well do you write? Are you satisfied with your writing ability? Do you have any weaknesses? Would you like to be a better writer? You can improve. If you decide that you want to become a good writer, and if you are willing to practice, practice, practice, you can steadily improve your writing skills.

The rules listed below are just a few of the rules good writers try to follow. The first two rules are the most important—you must master these two rules above all others.

1. **Spell all words correctly.** The most obvious errors in any written message are the spelling errors. When these errors appear, the people reading the message usually form a negative opinion of the writer and the writer's message. Look up all the words you are not sure of in the dictionary. If you can't find the word you want in the dictionary, use a word that has essentially the same meaning.

2. **Use correct grammar.** This rule is really several rules rolled into one. It refers to all the rules you've been learning in school. *Write in complete sentences, capitalize proper nouns, separate main clauses with a comma, and make sure the subject and verb agree* ("We *were* the best writers in school," **not** "We *was* the best writers in school."). If you don't already know the rules of grammar, have someone who does check your writing until you know the rules frontwards, backwards, and inside out.

3. **Get started.** In many cases the most difficult part of writing is deciding what to say and how to say it. People use different approaches to overcome this problem. If you are having trouble, make yourself write your ideas down on paper—even if your ideas are rough, crude, and make little sense. Walk away from what you've written for a short time; then come back later and try to improve part of your message. Repeat this process until you build up some momentum.

4. **Get to the point.** Say what you want to say as directly and concisely as possible. Do not begin with "long-winded" introductions; do not wander aimlessly off the point; and do not use unnecessary words. Do not feel that you must fill up several pages, or even one page, to make your writ-

ten message a good one. Keep it short and simple. Be brief. This is especially important in the world of work, where people are busy and have lots of work to do.

5. **Don't try to impress the reader.** Many people try to write long sentences and use fancy words when they aren't necessary. The result is often a message that no one can understand. The most important thing is that you convey your message. Write short, clear sentences and use the most common words. If you concentrate on being clear rather than impressive, your readers will have a much better chance of understanding your message.

6. **Organize your ideas logically.** If you were saying the numbers from 1 to 10, you wouldn't say 6 before 3. When you write a message, present your ideas in the order in which they will make sense to the reader. Sometimes you won't know the most logical order until you write your entire message and reread it. Each paragraph should contain one complete part of your message, and the paragraphs should progress logically from one to the next.

7. **Reread and rewrite what you've written.** Very few people get it right the first time. Almost all good writers rewrite their letters, memos, reports, etc., several times. They read their first attempt as though they were the people who will receive the message. As they read, they ask themselves, "Will she (or he) understand that? Does it make sense? Will she (or he) know exactly what I mean?" Not until all the answers are **Yes** is the written message finished.

The seven rules above are general rules that will guide you in your writing efforts. More help is readily available if you need it. Talk to your teachers and visit the library. Most libraries have several books with lots of specific suggestions and examples for improving your writing skills.

REVIEW YOUR LEARNING

CHAPTER 10

■■■■■■■■■■■■■■■■ CHAPTER SUMMARY

Communication—the process of exchanging information by sending and receiving messages—is an important part of the world of work. You can improve your chances for success by developing your listening, speaking, reading, and writing skills.

There are several strategies for improving your listening skills. They include recognizing your purpose in listening, looking for a plan, giving feedback, taking notes, and distinguishing between fact and opinion. Other strategies are "listening" for more than verbal content, distinguishing between the important and unimportant, asking questions, listening for a conclusion, and using the dictionary. By using these strategies and avoiding the blocks to listening —distractions, emotional blocks, and planning a response—you can become a better listener.

People speak for three reasons—to inform, to persuade, and to entertain. You can use the techniques of enumeration, generalization followed by example, cause and effect, and comparison and contrast to organize your formal speeches. Other tips for becoming an effective speaker include speaking standard English, developing and using an attractive voice, using correct enunciation and pronunciation, and not speaking either too fast or too slowly.

You can improve your reading skills by making sure you know *why* you are reading. Then you can use such techniques as previewing and skimming to save time and find the information you need. Focusing your mind, forming pictures, forming patterns, and improving your vocabulary are four techniques that will help you read for meaning.

There are several advantages to writing messages rather than speaking them. Writing helps you organize your thoughts, it provides a lasting record of your message, and it helps initiate action. Three things to consider before you write anything are your reader, your purpose, and your subject. It's best to write in a friendly, conversational style unless your company executives prefer a more formal style. Your writing will primarily be in the form of letters, memos, and reports.

■■■■■■■■■■■■■■ WORDS YOU SHOULD KNOW

communication
enunciation
feedback
inflection
jargon
previewing
pronunciation
skimming

REVIEW YOUR LEARNING

STUDY QUESTIONS

1. What percent of their waking hours do most people spend communicating? Of that time, what percent is spent listening?
2. What is the difference between hearing and listening?
3. List ten strategies that will help you improve your listening.
4. What are three kinds of blocks to listening?
5. What is the main purpose of most conversations?
6. What four patterns are used to organize formal talks?
7. Why is there less likelihood of misunderstanding when standard English is used?
8. What are four things that make for an attractive speaking voice?
9. Name three good speaking habits you can develop.
10. Asking yourself what question will help you improve your understanding when reading?
11. What are four things that can help you read for meaning?
12. Name at least three advantages of a written message over a spoken message.
13. Name the three common considerations in every kind of writing.
14. Name the six reasons for writing most messages.
15. What are the three most common forms of writing in business?

DISCUSSION TOPICS

1. How do you rate yourself as a listener? What makes listening difficult for you? Do you think you can improve? How?
2. How do you rate yourself as a reader? What makes reading for meaning difficult for you? Do you think you can improve? How?
3. Which of the four primary communication skills do you think is most important in the world of work? Explain.
4. When ordering merchandise from a company several hundred miles away, would you write or call? Why?

SUGGESTED ACTIVITIES

1. Select a product you would like to know more about, then write a letter requesting information about the product.
2. Listen to ten or more TV commercials. Then write down everything you can remember about the products advertised in four of the ads.
3. Ask a worker how communication skills are important on his or her job. Note some specific examples of how this worker uses these skills, then give a two to three minute report to the class.
4. There are hundreds of books written about different aspects of the world of work. Ask your teacher or librarian for suggestions and pick a book to read. Write a short report on what you learned.

Math Skills

In the first ten chapters we've discussed many kinds of skills needed to choose a career, find and apply for a job, and be successful on the job. You may feel that employers expect a lot from their workers, and they do.

In a recent survey employers said that more than anything else new workers needed better math skills. Almost all careers require a good understanding of basic math. Almost all workers must have the ability to calculate simple problems quickly and accurately.

The ability to calculate the answers to math problems is often the reason why certain workers are promoted and others are not. Secretaries and typists, for example, often prepare charts that require dividing the page width and depth by the number of columns and lines. Those who do this quickly and correctly get a lot more work done. This is not forgotten at promotion time.

In this chapter, we will review the basic arithmetic skills you need to be successful on the job. We will also look at a few ways in which you will use these skills in the world of work.

DO YOU KNOW . . .
- how to write the amount $2,025 on a check?
- why "over learning" math skills is helpful?
- how to estimate answers for better accuracy?
- how to use a calculator correctly?

CAN YOU DEFINE . . .
- decimal number?
- difference?
- digits?
- percent?
- product?
- quotient?
- sum?
- whole numbers?

Reviewing Basic Skills

Most of what you are about to read, you have already learned. Use this section as a review of your basic skills and a self-check for weaknesses. If some part of the review gives you trouble, you probably need to get some help from a qualified person. These basic math skills need to be automatic in the world of work.

DeEtta and Jean were friends all through junior high school. They often studied math together, especially when a test was coming up. At home, around the dining room table, both girls were able to do the problems they thought might be on the next test. When test day came, though, DeEtta always scored higher than Jean.

During high school, Jean and DeEtta went their own ways. Then, during their senior year, DeEtta and Jean were both hired for part-time jobs in a fabric store. It was a busy store, and often there were lines of people with yard goods waiting to make their purchases. DeEtta was very quick with her work. She could quickly figure the total cost of $3\frac{1}{3}$ yards at $6.95, for example, then add 6 percent tax. Jean, though, seemed unsure of herself and made a lot of errors. Afraid she might be fired, Jean asked DeEtta, "How can you do all that figuring when there are a dozen people watching and waiting?" Before DeEtta could answer, Jean tossed out another question. "And how were you always able to do so well on your math tests in school?"

After a moment's thought, DeEtta answered. "I think the answer to both of your questions is *over learning.* I never talked about it back in junior high, but I was always afraid the stress of taking a test would confuse me and cause me to do badly. So every night for four or five days, before every test, I would study over and over the things I'd already learned. I called it "over learning," and it helped me understand math so well that nothing interfered with my working out the problems. I think that's why all those customers waiting in line—here on the job—don't bother me either."

Numbers

Our system of numbering is made up of ten basic symbols: 0, 1, 2, 3, 4, 5, 6, 7, 8, and 9. These numbers are called **digits**, and they can be combined to make larger numbers, such as 36, 456, 3,914, and 14,672.

All the numbers above are called **whole numbers** —they are numbers that contain no fractions or decimals. Each digit in each whole number tells *how many* of something. Let's look at the number 36, for example. It is the same as 30 + 6. It is not the same as 63. The *placement* of each digit makes a difference.

The digit on the far right tells us the number of 1s. The next digit left tells us the number of 10s. Thus, in the number 36 we know there are 6 1s and 3 10s.

You sometimes need to know the names of each placement spot for digits. When writing checks for example, you must write numbers in words. To do this you must know the placement names.

Here are some rules that will help you write whole numbers in words.

(1) Translate the number in groups of three digits: millions, thousands, units, and so on.

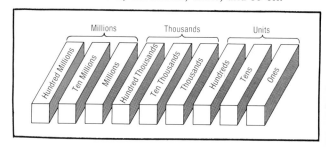

(2) Separate the groups with commas.

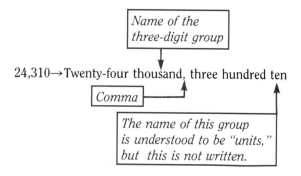

(3) The word *and* is never used when writing whole numbers.

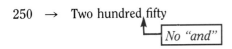

250 → Two hundred fifty

> No "and"

(4) Use hyphens in numbers less than 100 when two words are involved.

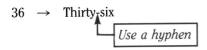

36 → Thirty-six

> Use a hyphen

(5) When a three-digit group consists of all zeros, the name of the group is not written.

2,000,115 → Two million, one hundred fifteen

> No words appear for the thousands group.

Here are some more examples:

67 → Sixty-seven

> Don't forget the hyphen

346 → Three hundred forty-six

> No "and" appears.

4,211 → Four thousand, two hundred eleven

> A comma after "thousand"

24,006 → Twenty-four thousand, six

> No word appears for hundreds

Check Up #1

Write the following whole numbers in words. **DO NOT WRITE IN THIS BOOK. For all practice problems in this book, use a separate sheet of paper.** Check your answers on page 181.

A. 5,010   B. 638   C. 2,007   D. 44,902
E. 308,012   F. 500,264   G. 7,000,015
H. 23,624,983

Addition

Addition is the process of combining numbers to get a total. The total is called the **sum.** Addition is the most basic and most frequently used arithmetic operation. The small symbol (+) called a *plus sign,* indicates addition.

When adding without a calculator, arrange the numbers vertically, in columns. Then use the following procedure.

(1) Count the number of 1s (in the column to the far right.

(2) If the column total is one digit, write it down and go on to the next column to the left.

(3) If the column total is more than one digit, write down only the 1s digit and carry the number of tens or hundreds over to the next column on the left.

(4) Continue this procedure until all columns have been added.

Examples

Tens column *Ones column*

$$\begin{array}{r} 4\,7 \\ +\,2\,1 \\ \hline 6\,8 \end{array}$$ ← The sum is 68

$4 + 2 = 6$ $7 + 1 = 8$

$$\begin{array}{r} 27 \\ +48 \\ \hline 75 \end{array}$$ ← $7 + 8 = 15$, Carry 1

$1 + 2 + 4 = 7$

$$\begin{array}{r} 584 \\ +\ 56 \\ \hline 640 \end{array}$$ ← $4 + 6 = 10$, Carry 1

$1 + 8 + 5 = 14$, Carry 1

$1 + 5 = 6$

Check Up #2

Add these numbers. Remember—DO NOT WRITE IN YOUR BOOK!

```
   36        16        46        58        75
 +45       +38       +29       +69       +49


  417       864       219       765       436
 +266      +916      +784      +544      +988
```

Check your answers on page 181. If you missed more than two, ask your teacher to watch you add a few numbers to determine where you are having difficulty. The most common problems are not understanding how to *carry over* to the next column, or not having memorized the combinations of basic numbers. Check yourself by working these problems as fast as you can. How long does it take you?

Check Up #3

Add these numbers.

```
  2    4    4    5    6    8    7
 +3   +3   +5   +3   +4   +6   +5


  9    3    5    9    7    9    8
 +7   +6   +7   +6   +6   +9   +4
```

If you really know these combinations, you should be able to answer all of them in 15 seconds. Check your answers on page 181. If you missed more than one, or it took more than 25 seconds, you need to practice. You will be able to greatly improve your math skills by practicing these combinations for a few minutes every day for a week.

If the combinations above were easy for you, do the following problems as fast as you can. Check your time.

Check Up #4

Add the numbers below and at the top of the next column.

```
  41       16       71       67       34       19
  26       29       62       91       17       82
  39       71       38       43       28       76
 +62      +46      +14      +22      +63      +48
```

```
  87       79       58       89       78       85
  66       68       95       74       99       97
  47       84       89       98       87       73
 +91      +76      +63      +85      +92      +98
```

Check your answers on page 181. If your answers are all correct and you finished in less than two minutes, you probably have little or no difficulty with addition. If you missed more than one or required more than two minutes to finish, you need practice.

Subtraction

Subtraction is the process of finding the difference between two numbers. The result of subtracting one number from another is called the difference. A short dash, called a *minus sign,* to the left of a problem indicates subtraction. When subtracting without a calculator, arrange the numbers vertically, in columns, with the larger number on top. Then use the following procedure.

(1) Begin with the 1s. If the bottom number is less than the top number, subtract and go to the next column to the left.

(2) If the bottom number is larger than the top number, borrow 10 from the next column to the left. To borrow, make the top number of the next column one less and add 10 to the number from which you are subtracting.

(3) Continue this procedure until all columns have been subtracted.

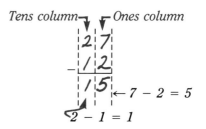

Tens column⏋ ⎾*Ones column*

```
  2 7
- 1 2
  1 5  ← 7 − 2 = 5
  └ 2 − 1 = 1
```

Reduce by one when borrowing

```
    4 1            2 9
    5̸2̸3̸          3̸0̸0̸
  − 1 6 7        −   5 4
  ───────        ───────
    3 5 6̸          2 4 6̸
```

7 won't subtract from 3; borrow 10; 13 − 7 = 6

Check Up #5

Subtract these numbers.

29	38	46	52	47
−15	−21	−36	−23	−29

114	165	258	753	641
− 90	−146	−199	−545	−155

Check your answers on page 181 If you missed more than two, ask your teacher to watch you subtract to determine where you are having difficulty. The most common problems are not understanding how to borrow, or not having memorized the subtraction of basic numbers. Check yourself by working these problems as fast as you can. How long does it take you?

Check Up #6

Subtract these numbers.

8	7	9	16	13	18	14
−2	−5	−5	− 7	− 9	− 9	− 8

12	15	17	13	11	16	17
− 8	− 9	− 8	− 6	− 4	− 8	− 9

If you really know these basic differences, you should be able to answer them all in 20 seconds. Check your answers on page 181. If you missed more than one, or if it took you more than 30 seconds, you need to practice. You can improve your math skills by practicing the subtraction of these basic numbers for a few minutes every day for a week.

If the subtraction of the basic numbers above was easy for you, subtract these numbers as fast as you can. Check your time.

Check Up #7

Subtract these numbers.

86	75	95	115	250	160	500	75
−50	−66	−54	− 85	−165	−145	−155	−48

47	85	66	758	315	130	404	80
−39	−36	−27	−169	−255	− 95	−135	−18

Check your answers on page 181. If your answers are all correct and you finished in less than one minute, you will have no difficulty with subtraction. If you missed more than one or required more than one minute to finish, you need to practice subtraction.

Multiplication

Multiplication is actually a shorthand way of doing addition. For example, you could add 361 + 361 + 361 + 361 + 361 + 361 + 361 and get 2,527. Or you could multiply 361 by 7 and get the same answer. In multiplication, the answer is called the **product**. When multiplying without a calculator, arrange the numbers vertically. Then use the following procedure.

(1) Begin by multiplying the 1s digit of the top number by the 1s digit in the bottom number.
(2) If the product is a one-digit number, write it down. If the product is a two-digit number, write down only the 1s digit—then, after the next multiplication, add the 10s digit of this number to the new product.
(3) Multiply the 10s digit of the top number by the 1s digit of the bottom number.
(4) Continue this procedure until each digit in the top number has been multiplied by the 1s digit of the bottom number.
(5) If multiplying by a two-digit or larger number, multiply each digit of the top number by the 10s digit of the bottom number using the same procedure you used before. The only difference is that in writing down the product you must indent your answer one digit to the left. In other words, the 1s digit of this product is placed under the 10s digit of the first product.
(6) Continue multiplying until all top digits have been multiplied by each digit in the bottom number. Continue indenting each new product one place to the left.
(7) Add all products together to get the final answer.

$$\begin{array}{r} 361 \\ \times\ 7 \\ \hline 2527 \end{array} \qquad \begin{array}{r} ^{14} \\ 526 \\ \times\ 72 \\ \hline 1052 \\ 3682\ \\ \hline 37,872 \end{array}$$

Check Up #8

Multiply the numbers below.

35	41	55	73	96	68	125
× 8	× 6	× 7	× 5	× 4	× 9	× 3

85	37	75	174	213	389	768
×12	×16	×25	× 38	× 47	× 96	× 35

Check your answers on page 181. If you missed more than three, ask your teacher to watch you multiply some numbers to determine where you are having difficulty. Multiplication is more difficult than either addition or subtraction. The most common problem is a less-than-adequate memorization of the multiplication tables that you worked on when you were in grade school. Check yourself on the multiplication tables by multiplying the numbers below as fast as you can. How long does it take you?

Check Up #9

Multiply the numbers below.

5	7	6	4	9	8	3	9	7
×4	×3	×8	×7	×5	×7	×5	×4	×5

6	7	4	9	6	9	3	9	8
×7	×7	×6	×7	×9	×8	×9	×9	×8

If you really know these combinations, you should be able to answer them all in 20 seconds. Check your answers on page 181. If you missed more than two, or if it took you more than 30 seconds, you need to work on the multiplication tables.

If the combinations above were easy for you, multiply these numbers as fast as you can. Check your time.

Check Up #10

Multiply these numbers.

654	395	506	419	725	386	853
× 37	× 24	× 34	× 25	× 36	× 21	× 74

742	905	186	614	372	125	498
× 16	× 37	× 79	× 83	×145	×346	×125

Check your answers on page 181. If your answers are all correct and you finished in less than six minutes, you will have no difficulty with multiplication. If you missed more than two, or if it took you more than ten minutes, you need to practice multiplying.

Division

Division is the reverse process of multiplication. By dividing a number you can separate it into equal parts. The answer to a division problem is called the **quotient**. Suppose you wish to divide 273 into 21 equal parts. To divide 273 by 21 you would use the following procedure.

(1) Place the number to be divided (273, called the *dividend*) inside the division sign and the number by which you will be dividing (21, called the *divisor*) outside the division sign. See below.

(2) Try to find a number that you can multiply by the divisor to get a number that is equal to or slightly less than the dividend. Begin by finding digits on the *left* side of the dividend that form a number equal to or slightly larger than the divisor. For example, 21 goes into 27 one time, so 1 is placed at the top of the division sign over 27. You would then multiply 1 × 21, place this product, 21, under 27 and subtract. Bring down the next number to the right, which is 3, and start the process again.

(3) If the product is equal to the dividend, you have completed the division problem. If the product is less than the dividend, subtract—placing the difference over the divisor as a fraction. This fraction then becomes part of the quotient.

$$21\overline{)273} \quad \begin{array}{r} 13 \\ \underline{21} \\ 63 \\ \underline{} \\ 0 \end{array}$$

$$15\overline{)4605} \quad \begin{array}{r} 307 \\ \underline{45} \\ 10 \\ \underline{0} \\ 105 \\ \underline{105} \\ 0 \end{array}$$

$$36\overline{)72513} \quad \begin{array}{r} 2014 \; 9/36 = \\ \underline{72} \quad 2014\,1/4 \\ 5 \\ 2 \\ 51 \\ \underline{36} \\ 153 \\ \underline{144} \\ 9 \end{array}$$

Check Up #11

Multiply these numbers.

$6\overline{)54}$ $7\overline{)42}$ $9\overline{)108}$ $8\overline{)56}$ $12\overline{)96}$ $13\overline{)273}$

$16\overline{)128}$ $19\overline{)475}$ $24\overline{)264}$ $35\overline{)630}$ $46\overline{)1,430}$ $18\overline{)220}$

Check your answers on page 182. If you missed more than two, ask your teacher to watch you divide some numbers to determine where you are having difficulty. If you missed more than two of these problems, you need to practice division.

Fractions

Fractions are numbers used to describe a part of some standard amount. For example, the shaded area in this rectangle is $\frac{3}{5}$ ("three-fifths") of the total rectangle.

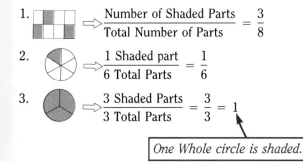

It is especially important that you understand fractions since most calculators cannot work with fractions.

Examples

Write a fraction to describe the shaded part of each of the following.

1. $\Rightarrow \dfrac{\text{Number of Shaded Parts}}{\text{Total Number of Parts}} = \dfrac{3}{8}$

2. $\Rightarrow \dfrac{1 \text{ Shaded part}}{6 \text{ Total Parts}} = \dfrac{1}{6}$

3. $\Rightarrow \dfrac{3 \text{ Shaded Parts}}{3 \text{ Total Parts}} = \dfrac{3}{3} = 1$

One Whole circle is shaded.

4.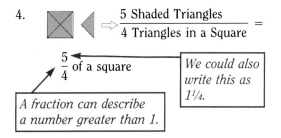

$\Rightarrow \dfrac{5 \text{ Shaded Triangles}}{4 \text{ Triangles in a Square}} =$

$\frac{5}{4}$ of a square

We could also write this as $1\frac{1}{4}$.

A fraction can describe a number greater than 1.

Check Up #12

For each group below, what fraction of the total number of shapes are triangles?

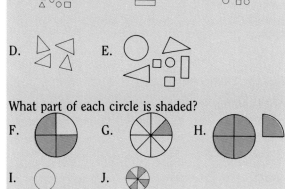

A.   B.   C.

D.   E.

What part of each circle is shaded?

F.   G.   H.

I.   J.

Check your answers on page 182.

On some jobs is it necessary to add, subtract, or multiply fractions. In some cases it may even be necessary to divide fractions. It is much easier, however, to perform these operations if the fraction is first converted to its decimal equivalent. If you are using a calculator, converting to decimals is probably the only way you can do the problem.

To convert a fraction to a decimal number, divide the *numerator* (top number) by the *denominator* (bottom number). For example, to convert ¼ to its decimal equivalent, divide the 1 by 4.

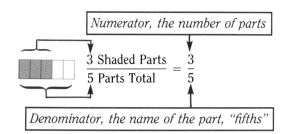

Decimal numbers are very important in the world of work. On many jobs you might use a conversion table to look up the decimal equivalents of common fractions. If you know how to convert fractions to decimals, you will not need to depend on a table.

Make a Decision

You like your job as a sales clerk in a clothing store because you enjoy talking to all the people, and you like clothes. You were never very good at math, though, and you seem to be constantly embarrassing yourself by making mistakes in figuring up tickets. You don't want to take a basic math course or ask someone to tutor you, but you'll quit your job rather than continuing to make so many simple mistakes. What's your decision—a new job without so much math, or relearning some basic arithmetic? Give reasons for your decision.

Decimal Numbers

A **decimal number,** sometimes called a *decimal fraction,* is a fraction or mixed number (whole number and fraction together) whose denominator is a multiple of 10. The decimal number 3.7 is 3 + .7, or $3 + \frac{7}{10}$, or $3\frac{7}{10}$.

You say and write decimal numbers in much the same way you would whole numbers. The decimal number 935.47 can be broken down as follows.

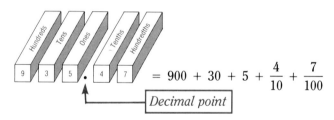

$$= 900 + 30 + 5 + \frac{4}{10} + \frac{7}{100}$$

Decimal point

To find the name in words of any given decimal place, follow the steps below.

Step 1 Write zeros under each digit to the right of the decimal point.

Step 2 Write a 1 directly under the decimal point.

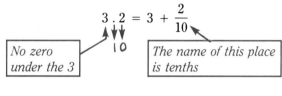

$$3 \,.\, 2 = 3 + \frac{2}{10}$$

No zero under the 3

1 0

The name of this place is tenths

$$15 \,.\, 8\,3 = 15 + \frac{83}{100}$$

1 0 0

The name of this place is hundredths

To read or write a decimal number in words, follow the steps below. Use 15.83 as an example.

Step 1 Write the number to the left of the decimal point as whole number (fifteen).

Step 2 Write *and* for the decimal point.

Step 3 Write the number to the right of the decimal point as a whole number (eighty-three).

Step 4 Write the name of the decimal place of the right end digit (hundredths).

The result is fifteen and eighty-three hundredths.

Decimal Number	Fraction	Write it in words as	You may hear this read as
0.6	$\frac{6}{10}$	"six tenths"	"point six"
0.05	$\frac{5}{100}$	"five hundredths"	"point zero five"
0.32	$\frac{32}{100}$	"thirty-two hundredths"	"point three two"

Examples

1. 3.6 → "three and six tenths"

2. 324.57 → "three hundred twenty-four and fifty-seven hundredths"

The sum of money $324.57 would be written on a check as

"Three hundred twenty-four and - - - - - - $\frac{57}{100}$"

Check Up #13

Write these decimal numbers in words. Check your answers on page 182.

A. 6.7 B. 0.9   C. 15.3 D. 0.05   E. 2.13

F. 8.09 G. 12.44 H. 38.59 I. $201.38 J. $338.97

Adding or Subtracting Decimal Numbers. To add or subtract decimal numbers, first line up the numbers vertically. Make sure you keep the decimal point in the same vertical column. Then add or subtract, the same as you would with whole numbers.

Examples

1. 1.45 + 3.4 = ?

1.45 *Decimal points in line*
+3.40 ◄*Attach zeros needed to fill the columns*
4.85
└*Add as with whole numbers*

2. 13.4 − 7.56 = ?

13.40 *Decimal points in line*
− 7.56 ◄*Attach a zero*
5.84
└*Subtract as with whole numbers*

Check Up #14

Do the following addition and subtraction problems with decimal numbers. Check your answers on page 182.

A. 4.2 + 7.3 =   B. 5.6 + 9.1 =

C. 8.8 + 6.7 =   D. 23 + 5.8 =

E. 15.6 + 3.67 =   F. 5.08 + 67.2 =

G. 7.2 + 0.6 + 1.44 + 3 =

H. 3.8 − 2.6 =   I. $4 − $3.68 =

J. 32.7 − 6.45 =   K. 19.4 − 7.361 =

L. 4.5 − 1.22 + 12.37 + .055 =

M. In August, Yolanda's Ice Cream Shop paid $44.38 for electricity, $32.79 for telephone service, $38.16 for insurance, and $450 for rent. What was her total for these expenses?

N. From a 16-meter length of wire, an electrician cut two pieces 3.86 meters and 8.27 meters long. How much wire was left?

Multiplying Decimal Numbers. To multiply decimal numbers, use the following two-step process.

Step 1 *Multiply* the two numbers as if they were whole numbers. Pay no attention to the decimal points yet.

Step 2 Add the number of decimal places in the two numbers being multiplied. In the product, count from the right the total number of decimal places. Then place the decimal point in the product so that the number of decimal places is equal to the sum of the decimal places in the two numbers being multiplied.

Examples

1. 3.2 × 0.41 = ?

3.2 ◄*3.2 has one decimal place*
×.41 ◄*.41 has two decimal places*
32
128
1312 → 1.312
      └*The answer must have three decimal places*

2. $9.05 \times 4.31 = ?$

$$\begin{array}{r} 9.05 \\ \times 4.31 \\ \hline 905 \\ 2715 \\ 3620 \\ \hline 390055 \end{array}$$

9.05 ◄ *9.05 has two decimal places*
×4.31 ◄ *4.31 has two decimal places*

$390055 \rightarrow 39.0055$

The answer must have four decimal places

Check Up #15

Do the following multiplication problems with decimal numbers. Check your answers on page 182.

$$\begin{array}{ccc} 4.1 & \quad 7.4 & \quad 23.4 \\ \times\ 8 & \quad \times 5.1 & \quad \times\ 9.8 \end{array}$$

$$\begin{array}{ccc} 4.05 & \quad 3.96 & \quad 0.723 \\ \times 0.86 & \quad \times\ 2.3 & \quad \times\ 6.01 \end{array}$$

$3.5 \times 8.7 = \qquad\qquad 0.63 \times 0.02 =$

A. If you earn $6.27 per hour, how much pay should your receive for 38 hours of work?
B. At Dante's Pizza Place, the estimated cost of delivering orders is $.42 per mile. If the delivery van averaged 329.8 miles per day last week, what is the average daily cost of making deliveries?

Dividing Decimal Numbers. Division of decimal numbers is similar to the division of whole numbers. Follow the steps below to divide decimal numbers.

Step 1 Set up the division problem as you would with whole numbers.

69.7 divided by 1.7 = $1.7\overline{)69.7}$

Step 2 Shift the decimal point in the divisor so that it becomes a whole number. Then shift the decimal point in the dividend the same number of decimal places.

$1.7\overline{)69.7} \quad \Leftrightarrow \quad 17.\overline{)697.}$

Shift the decimal point 1 place to the right

Step 3 Place a decimal point in the answer space directly above its new position in the dividend. Then divide as with whole numbers.

$$17\overline{)697.} \qquad \begin{array}{r} 41. \\ 17\overline{)697.} \\ 68 \\ \hline 17 \\ 17 \\ \hline 0 \end{array}$$

Examples

1. $16.38 \div 6.5$

$$\begin{array}{r} 2.52 \\ 6.5\overline{)16.380} \\ 130 \\ \hline 338 \\ 325 \\ \hline 130 \\ 130 \\ \hline 0 \end{array}$$

◄ *Attach an extra zero if necessary*
◄ $65 \times 2 = 130$
◄ $65 \times 5 = 325$

2. $8.91 \div 0.054$

$$\begin{array}{r} 165. \\ 0.054\overline{)8.910} \\ 54 \\ \hline 351 \\ 324 \\ \hline 270 \\ 270 \\ \hline 0 \end{array}$$

◄ *Attach an extra zero*
$54 \times 1 = 54$
$54 \times 6 = 324$
$54 \times 5 = 270$

Check Up #16

Do the following division problems with decimal numbers. Check your answers on page 182.

$0.57 \div 1.9 = \qquad\qquad 3.78 \div 2.8 =$

$1.573 \div 4.84 = \qquad\qquad 9.6 \div 0.016 =$

$0.036 \div 1.2 = \qquad\qquad 6.004 \div 0.2 =$

A. The HMS Corp. paid $253.64 for computer printer paper. If the paper costs $7.46 per box, how many boxes did they buy?
B. Pat averages 4.7 pages per hour when typing budget tables on a word processor. How long will it take her to type 200 pages?

Using a Calculator

Calculators have become essential tools for workers in almost every occupation—from order clerks to engineers, from tellers to bank presidents. If you are to use a calculator correctly in your work, you must be able to do the following.

- Multiply and add one-digit numbers quickly and correctly
- Read and write any whole number, decimal number, or fraction
- Convert fractions to decimal numbers
- Estimate answers and check your work

You may wonder about the importance of estimating an answer before doing a problem. The value of an estimate is in knowing whether an answer is reasonable.

If you were multiplying 3 × 4, you would know that 120 was not a reasonable answer. But if you were multiplying much larger numbers, you might not notice an unreasonable answer. A very good rule—especially when using a calculator—is to never work an arithmetic problem until you know roughly what the answer will be. Use the following "Guess 'n Check" method.

Step 1   Estimate the answer.
Step 2   Work the problem.
Step 3   Check your answer by comparing it with the estimate. If the answer and estimate are far apart, repeat all three steps.

Examples

1.   387   *Estimate: 400 + 1000 = 1400*
   +998
   ‾‾‾‾‾
   1385   *Check: 1385 is roughly equal to 1400. The answer is reasonable.*

2.   87   *Estimate: 100 + 200 = 300*
   +244
   ‾‾‾‾‾
    331   *Check: 331 is roughly equal to 300.*

Here are a few hints to help you use your calculator effectively.

1. Always check the display after you have entered a number and before you have entered the operation to be certain you are using the correct number. If you have made a key-press error, use the "clear entry" key [CE] to remove this last entry. For example, if you wanted to enter 3.8 × 1.2 but you mistakenly entered [3] [.] [8] [×] [.] [1] [2], pressing [CE] will delete the last three key strokes. You can reenter the second number. The first number will remain in the calculator work area. Press the [=] key and the answer will be displayed. [4.56]

2. Always estimate your answer before you do the calculation. In the problem shown in 1, you would estimate that the correct answer is about 4 × 1 or 4. If you had not noticed the key-press error, the calculator would display [0.456]. Your estimate is an immediate warning that something is wrong.

3. Don't worry about leading zeros to the left of the decimal point (as in 0.5 or 0.664) or final zeros after the decimal point (as in 4.70 or 32.500). You need not enter these; the calculator will display all the digits needed.

Number	Enter	Display
0.5	[.] [5]	0.5
0.664	[.] [6] [6] [4]	0.664
4.70	[4] [.] [7]	4.7
32.500	[3] [2] [.] [5]	32.5

4. Express fractions in decimal form. Divide the numerator by the denominator before entering. For example, 4¼ is entered as [4.25], and 5⅔ is entered as [5.6666667].

5. When you solve a problem using a calculator, the display will usually *not* give the answer in a finished form. You must often interpret the answer. For example, if you solve a business problem that has an answer in dollars, the display

[3.2]   means $3.20

[23.462012] means $23.46
            Rounded to the nearest cent

[35.027]   means $35.03
            Rounded to the nearest cent

[14250.2]   means $14,250.20
            No commas are shown in large numbers on a calculator

6. A calculator can operate on only two numbers at a time. You can, however, perform a long and involved string of calculations on more than two numbers without pausing, if you are careful. If the calculation involves only addition and subtraction, the calculator will do them in order as the numbers are entered.

4.1 $\boxed{+}$ .72 $\boxed{+}$ 12.68 $\boxed{-}$ 5.032 $\boxed{=}$ → $\boxed{12.468}$

If the calculation involves only multiplication and division, the calculator will do the operations in order as the numbers are entered.

450 $\boxed{\times}$ .81 $\boxed{\div}$ 4 $\boxed{\times}$ 1.2 $\boxed{=}$ → $\boxed{109.35}$

If the calculation involves a combination of addition, subtraction, multiplication, and division, be very careful. Most, but not all, calculators will do the multiplications and divisions first, working left to right, and the additions afterward.

2 $\boxed{+}$ 3 $\boxed{\times}$ 4 will be calculated as

2 + (3 × 4) or 2 + 12.

Check Up #17

Work these problems using a calculator. Check your answers on page 182.
A. The Candy Shop paid $8,813 for a shipment of 27 storage cases, each one the same model. Find the cost of each case.
B. If weekly sales receipts for the Turner Gas Station are $1,875.37—$3,168.19—and $2,046.82—what income is needed in the fourth week to meet a four-week goal of $10,000?
C. Find the cost of 435.8 gallons of truck fuel at $1.13 per gallon, rounded to the nearest cent.
D. What is Rueben's pay on a construction job if he works 28¾ hours per week for six weeks at an hourly rate of $7.46 per hour?

Working with Percentages

The word *percent* comes from a Latin word meaning *by the hundred* or *for every hundred*. A number expressed as a percent is being compared to some standard or base divided into 100 parts.

For example, suppose you wanted to give 25 percent of your birthday cake to your best friend. This would mean that if the cake were divided into 100 parts, you would give your friend 25 of the parts. A certain percent is a certain part of a whole, using 100 total parts as a basis for comparison.

To write a decimal number or whole number as a percent, multiply it by 100%. This is equivalent to moving the decimal point two places to the *right*.

Examples

$0.60 = 0.60 \times 100\% = 60\%$ or $0.60 = 60.\%$

$0.02 = 0.02 \times 100\% = 2\%$ or $0.02 = 2.\%$

$3.4 = 3.4 \times 100\% = 340\%$ or $3.40 = 340.\%$

To write a fraction as a percent, first write it in decimal form (using your calculator if necessary; then multiply by 100%.

Examples

$\frac{1}{2} = 0.5 \to 0.5 \times 100\% = 50\%$

$\frac{3}{20} \to 3 \boxed{\div} 20 \boxed{=} \to \boxed{0.15}$
$\to 0.15 \times 100\% = 15\%$

$2\frac{3}{8} \to 3 \boxed{\div} 8 \boxed{+} 2 \boxed{=} \to \boxed{2.375}$
$\to 2.375 \times 100\% = 237.5\%$

$\frac{2}{3} \to 2 \boxed{\div} 3 \boxed{=} \to \boxed{0.6666667}$
$\to 0.6666667 \times 100\% = 66.66667\%$ or 66.7%

To find percentages of numbers, it is usually necessary to change the percent to a decimal number. To do this, divide by 100%. This is equivalent to moving the decimal point two places to the *left*.

Examples

14.8% $14.8 \boxed{\div} 100 \boxed{=}$ $\boxed{0.148}$
or $14.8\% = .148$

1.5% $1.5 \boxed{\div} 100 \boxed{=}$ $\boxed{0.015}$
or $01.5\% = .015$

$9\frac{3}{4}\%$ $3 \boxed{\div} 4 \boxed{+} 9 \boxed{\div} 100 \boxed{=} \boxed{0.0975}$
or $09.75 = .0975$
Divide by 100%
Write the fraction as a decimal

Check Up #18

Write each of these numbers as a percent.

0.25	0.06	0.7	2.7
0.98	2.16	0.01	4.75

Write each of these fractions as a percent.

$$\frac{3}{4} \qquad \frac{9}{10} \qquad 2\frac{3}{25} \qquad \frac{7}{8} \qquad \frac{5}{6}$$

Write these percents as decimal numbers.

$$10\% \qquad 6\% \qquad 2.5\% \qquad 6\frac{1}{2}\%$$

$$12\frac{3}{4}\% \qquad 120\% \qquad 200\% \qquad 0.5\%$$

Check your answers on page 182.

Percent Problems

When percent problems appear in on-the-job situations, they do not come neatly packaged with careful instructions, as they do in textbooks. This means that you must be able to first understand the problem. You must then set it up in a mathematical form, and finally, solve it. In this section we will review a few of the basic concepts and typical uses of percent in business.

For example, if you earn $8.74 per hour and you receive a 4% pay raise, by how much will your pay be increased?

First, estimate the answer. 10% of $8 is 80¢. Since 4% is less than half of 10%, the answer will be about half of that, or 40¢.

Second, translate the problem into a math statement.

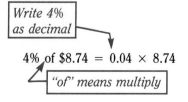

$$4\% \text{ of } \$8.74 = 0.04 \times 8.74$$

Write 4% as decimal

"of" means multiply

Third, do the arithmetic with a calculator.

$$0.04 \ \boxed{\times} \ 8.74 \ \boxed{=} \ \longrightarrow \ \boxed{0.3496}$$

Fourth, round the answer to the nearest cent and check it against your estimate. The pay raise is 35¢ per hour.

Examples

1. Find 73% of 285   *Estimate: 70% of 300 is 210*

$$0.73 \ \boxed{\times} \ 285 \ \boxed{=} \ \longrightarrow \ \boxed{208.05}$$

2. If the sales tax on a purchase is 6½%, what tax would you pay on a camera costing $129.95?

   Estimate: This is a tax of about 6¢ on each dollar, or $6 on $100. The tax will be a bit over $6.

$$6\frac{1}{2}\% \text{ of } 129.95 = 0.065 \ \boxed{\times} \ 129.95 \ \boxed{=} \longrightarrow \boxed{8.44675}$$

The tax would be $8.45.

To improve sales, merchants often sell items at less than their regular price, called the *list* price. The amount of money subtracted from the list price is called a *discount*. The discount is usually given as a percentage of the list price. By subtracting this percent from the list price you arrive at the sale price.

Example

A bicycle regularly priced at $159.75 is advertised for sale at 35% off. What is its sale price?

First, estimate the answer. 35% is about ⅓, and ⅓ of $150 is $50. Subtracting $50 from $150 leaves about $100.

Second, write 35% as a decimal.
$$35 \ \boxed{\div} \ 100 \ \boxed{=} \ \boxed{0.35}$$

Third, figure the discount = 0.35 $\boxed{\times}$ 159.75 $\boxed{=}$ $\longrightarrow$ $\boxed{55.9125}$ or $55.91 and the sale price = $159.75 − 55.91 = $103.84

Salespeople are often paid on the basis of their success at selling. They receive a *commission,* which is a fee they are paid for their work. Commissions are usually figured as a percentage of the salesperson's total sales.

Example

The Happy John Used Car Company pays each salesperson a 4.5% commission on his or her sales. If you were a salesperson for Happy John, what commission would you expect to receive on weekly sales of $7,240.63?

First, estimate the answer. 10% or ⅒ of $7,000 is $700. Since 4.5% is about half of 10%, you should get about half of $700 or $350.

Second, calculate it.
0.045 ☒ 7240.63 🟰 ➡ 325.82835 or 325.83

4.5% ÷ 100% = 0.045

Make a Decision

Suppose you are offered a choice between two sales jobs. Both jobs involve about the same kind of work. One pays a salary of $1,500 a month. The other pays a salary of $800 a month plus a commission of 5 percent of sales. Other salespeople average between $7,500 and $15,000 in sales per month. What's your decision—the straight salary, or the salary and commission. Give reasons for your decision.

In Chapter 18, you will read about the money banks pay on savings accounts and collect on loans. These payments are called *interest.* Interest is usually expressed as a percentage. A bank loan might involve a 15% per year interest payment, while a credit card loan might require 1.75% interest per month.

You will learn more about how interest works in Chapter 18. Here you will do a few practice problems in figuring interest.

$$\text{Interest} = \text{Principal} \times \text{Percent} \times \text{Time}$$

Example

Calculate the interest on a loan of $725 at 14.6% interest repaid over two years.

First, estimate the answer. 14.6% is about ⅐, so the interest will be about ⅐ of $700 or $100 per year, or a total of $200.

Second, calculate:

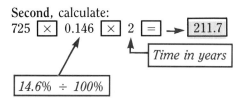

725 ☒ 0.146 ☒ 2 🟰 ➡ 211.7

Time in years

14.6% ÷ 100%

The interest is $211.70

Check Up #19

Do the following problems involving interest. Check your answers on page 182.

A. A VCR unit that sells for $565 is reduced in cost by 20%. What is the new selling price?
B. If Murphy's Ice Cream Store borrows $4,580 at 16½% interest for one year, what interest must they pay?
C. Calculate the commission that a salesperson will receive for selling ten rowing machines at $286.90 each if the company pays a 40% commission.
D. How much will be discounted off a car that has a list price of $8,695 and a discount rate of 18¼?
E. Roberto earns a 9% commission on his weekly sales. What was his commission for a week in which he sold $2,847.65 in merchandise?
F. What is the interest on a loan of $750 at 14½% to be repaid in one year?
G. Figure the interest on a car loan of $5,900 at 16¾% to be repaid in three years.

REVIEW YOUR LEARNING

CHAPTER SUMMARY

Almost all workers must be able to solve basic math problems. Employers say that the ability to use math on the job is an important skill that many employees lack. If you cannot use basic math, you need to learn and practice your skills now.

Addition, subtraction, multiplication, and division are the basic math processes you need to know. You should also understand fractions and decimals, and be able to convert a fraction to a decimal number.

Much of the drudgery of math has been eliminated by the calculator. Still, you must understand basic math to use the calculator correctly. A good habit to develop when using a calculator is estimating your answer before you begin. Estimating will help you eliminate obvious errors. Among the types of problems you should be able to do on the calculator are percent problems, such as figuring discounts and commissions.

WORDS YOU SHOULD KNOW

decimal number
difference
digits
percent
product
quotient
sum
whole number

STUDY QUESTIONS

1. Write the following numbers in words.

76	436	3,511	34,005	999

2. Solve the addition problems below.

27	29	15	28	30
19	31	40	16	41
32	41	19	64	35
+31	+48	+52	+39	+62

3. Solve the subtraction problems below.

887	795	658	418	666
−188	−713	−511	−365	−319

4. Solve the multiplication problems below.

753	518	628	555	425
×354	×687	×674	×789	×698

REVIEW YOUR LEARNING

CHAPTER 11

5. Solve the division problems below.

$68\overline{)3,536}$ $17\overline{)765}$ $58\overline{)2,494}$ $25\overline{)705}$ $85\overline{)1,275}$

6. Write the following decimal numbers in words.

29.6   14.25   8.07   12.10   139.99

7. Solve the following problems with decimal numbers.

$$\begin{array}{ccccc} 15.32 & 13.05 & 28.6 & 14.9 & 4.32\overline{)1.987} \\ +49.07 & -\ 7.29 & \times\ 7.8 & \times 7.01 & \end{array}$$

8. Write the following numbers and fractions as percents.

0.08 $\dfrac{7}{10}$ 2.0 $\dfrac{1}{4}$ $\dfrac{15}{16}$

9. A sign on a dress rack says "30% off all dresses." The price tag on the dress you like is $49.99. How much will this dress cost you? Don't forget the sales tax (use 4% as the sales tax rate).

10. You are selling encyclopedias door-to-door. You get a 25% commission on all sales plus a $10 bonus for every deluxe edition that you sell. During the summer you sold fifteen sets of encyclopedias: twelve of the standard edition, which costs $300; and three of the deluxe edition, which costs $500. How much money did you make?

DISCUSSION TOPICS

1. Have you had to use math in the part-time jobs you've had so far? Were you able to do the necessary math accurately and quickly? Were you able to use a calculator?
2. How do you rate your own math skills? If you feel you need improvement, where will you go for help once you graduate from high school? Discuss the different ways you could improve your skills.

SUGGESTED ACTIVITIES

1. Do a research project to find out how math skills are used in a wide range of occupations. Make a list of twenty-five occupations. Try to include as many different kinds of occupations as possible. Then gather information through interviews and reading to determine the different ways math is used in each occupation. Are there any occupations in which no math is used?
2. As you learned in reading about DeEtta and Jean at the beginning of the chapter, the real math challenge in the world of work is being able to solve problems quickly while people are waiting for you to finish. Act out some work situations in which you must use math. Each person should take a turn at being the worker who must solve the problems. See if the "worker" can solve several problems quickly and accurately under pressure, one after another.

Answers to Check Up Problems

Check Up #1

A. Five thousand, ten   B. Six hundred thirty-eight   C. Two thousand, seven
D. Forty-four thousand, nine hundred two   E. Three hundred eight thousand, twelve
F. Five hundred thousand, two hundred sixty-four   G. Seven million, fifteen
H. Twenty-three million, six hundred twenty-four thousand, nine hundred eighty-three

Check Up #2

81	54	75	127	124
683	1,780	1,003	1,309	1,424

Check Up #3

5	7	9	8	10	14	12
16	9	12	15	13	18	12

Check Up #4

168	162	185	223	142	225
291	307	305	346	356	353

Check Up #5

14	17	10	29	18
24	19	59	208	486

Check Up #6

6	2	4	9	4	9	6
4	6	9	7	7	8	8

Check Up #7

36	9	41	30	85	15	345	27
8	49	39	589	60	35	269	62

Check Up #8

280	246	385	365	384	612	375
1,020	592	1,875	6,612	10,011	37,344	26,880

Check Up #9

20	21	48	28	45	56	15	36	35
42	49	24	63	54	72	27	81	64

Check Up #10

24,198	9,480	17,204	10,475	26,100	8,106	63,122
11,872	33,485	14,694	50,962	53,940	43,250	62,250

Check Up #11

9	6	12	7	8	21
8	25	11	18	$31\frac{2}{23}$	$12\frac{2}{9}$

Check Up #12

A. 4/10 (or 2/5)   B. 1/3   C. 0   D. 4/4 (or 1)   E. 2/7
F. 3/4   G. 1/8   H. 5/4 (or 1 1/4)   I. no parts shaded   J. 4/8 (or 1/2)

Check Up #13

A. six and seven tenths   B. nine tenths   C. fifteen and three tenths   D. five hundredths
E. two and thirteen hundredths   F. eight and nine hundredths   G. twelve and forty-four hundredths
H. thirty-eight and fifty-nine hundredths   I. two hundred one dollars and thirty-eight cents
J. three hundred thirty-eight dollars and ninety-seven cents

Check Up #14

A. 11.5   B. 14.7   C. 15.5   D. 28.8   E. 19.27   F. 72.28   G. 12.24
H. 1.2   I. $0.32   J. 26.25   K. 12.039   L. 15.705   M. $565.33   N. 3.87m

Check Up #15

32.8	37.74	229.32
3.483	9.108	4.34523
30.45	0.0126	

A. $238.26   B. $138.52

Check Up #16

0.3	1.35
0.325	600
0.03	30.02

A. 34   B. 42.553 (or 43) hrs.

Check Up #17

A. $326.41   B. $2,909.62   C. $492.45   D. $1,286.85

Check Up #18

25%	6%	70%	270%	
98%	216%	1%	475%	
75%	90%	212%	87.5%	$83\frac{1}{3}\%$

0.1	0.06	0.025	0.065
0.1275	1.2	2	0.005

Check Up #19

A. $452   B. $755.70   C. $1,147.60   D. $1,586.84
E. $256.29   F. $108.75   G. $2,964.75

Computer Literacy

DO YOU KNOW . . .
- how computers are changing our lives?
- the history of computer technology?
- how a computer works?
- which computer languages are best for certain applications?

CAN YOU DEFINE . . .
- boot?
- chips?
- computer?
- data base?
- data processing?
- disk drive?
- floppy disk?
- hard copy?
- hardware?
- mainframe?
- micro?
- modem?
- program?
- software?

Important inventions often dramatically change the way we live and work. The electric light bulb changed night into day. The internal combustion engine, the airplane, and the telephone brought us all closer together and made things happen much faster.

Today, another invention—the computer—is changing the way we live and work. Computers are eliminating old jobs and creating new ones. Almost everyone now needs to master some level of computer knowledge or skill. Certainly everyone needs to understand what computers can do, how they are used, and how they will continue to change our lives. This understanding is called *computer literacy*.

In this chapter, you will learn about the development of computers and how they've changed our lives. You will also learn about the basic components and operation of computer systems. After reading this chapter, you will have a general understanding of computers that you can take with you into the world of work.

Computers in Everyday Living

Computers have been influencing our lives for several years, perhaps in ways you haven't noticed. At school, in the supermarket, on the telephone, at the bank, everywhere—computers are making an impact on our society.

Computers are powerful tools. They can, and do, improve our quality of life. But they also have the potential to control our lives in many ways. This is why it's important for all of us to understand how a computer works and how it is being used.

Education

One of the first places we notice the presence of a computer is at school. From kindergarten to high school graduation, computers store and process information about us. Our progress in school—grades, test scores, attendance—is computerized in detail. Even before we entered kindergarten, computers played a big part in projecting how many of us would show up for school.

In some schools, student attendance is "encouraged" by a computer. Every evening a computer calls parents of students who have been absent during the day. The computer dials the number and gives a taped message or "speaks" with a computer-generated "voice" when someone answers the phone. If the line is busy, the computer dials again and again until it gets an answer. Absences have dropped in schools where this computer encouragement has been used.

Perhaps an even more important educational use of computers is their use as teaching machines. A student can sit down at a computer and be guided through a learning process by a computer program. The questions get easier or harder, depending on the student's progress. This allows each student to progress at his or her own pace. Some students would rather learn from a computer than a live teacher. They say they don't feel bad when they come up with a wrong answer because the computer isn't "judging" them.

Computers have changed the way students are educated. Computers make good teachers when they are trying to learn certain skills.

Business

Whenever you go into a store to buy something, you are affected by the computer. For example, think about the supermarket where you buy groceries. The lines move faster now because scanners connected to a computer read the prices. Most products are imprinted with a universal product code (UPC). The checker passes the item across the scanner and a computer records your purchase.

The data read by the scanner is stored in the computer and used for several purposes. First, you will receive a printed record of what you bought. You will see not only the prices and the total, but also a description of each item. Next, the computer will list the items you bought and file this list for later use. Finally, the computer will dial the warehouse and order replacement goods for all of the items in short supply.

Another example of how computers affect retail sales is the computer's role in credit card purchases. Many purchases are made with credit cards. This involves checking the number on the credit card with a central computer to be certain the purchase is authorized. The computer checks to assure

Most supermarkets now use scanners that register product information into computers. The computer can actually keep track of how much is being sold, then order more products from the warehouse.

that the card is not stolen, is paid up to date, and that the account provides enough credit to handle the new purchase. If all is in order, permission is given to the store, and the purchase is completed. All of this takes only a few seconds—while your purchase is being packaged!

The banking industry also uses computers extensively. Most people receive their pay by check and pay most of their bills by check. For several years now computers have been processing checks. A scanner reads the special numbers along the bottom edge of the check and deducts the amount of the check from your account.

Automatic teller machines (ATMs) have become popular in recent years. The ATM is a special-purpose computer. We simply tell the computer how much we want to deposit or withdraw, and the transaction is completed.

Health Care

Computers are used to study the causes of diseases and the effectiveness of treatments. Case histories of millions of people have been entered in com- puter files. Scientists study this information to find relationships between possible causes and certain diseases. Computers make this possible because they can sort through huge amounts of information much faster than humans can.

Computerized axial tomography (CAT) uses a scanner to photograph thin sections of the body. The computer assembles images into three-dimensional pictures. Thus, the whole interior of the patient's body can be photographed without the risks that accompany other methods. The information the CAT provides helps in the diagnosis of many kinds of disease.

Doctors sometimes fasten a recording device to the bodies of recovering heart patients. The device is then connected to a telephone so that it can transmit heart activity over the phone to the doctor's office. There, a computer analyzes the information to see if there is an immediate problem. If a problem exists, the doctor is summoned at once by the computer.

Patients in intensive care are often "watched" by a computer. If there is a problem with a vital function, the nearest nurse's station is notified.

Law Enforcement and Government

A police officer in a patrol car is now the first link in a chain of computer-assisted law enforcement activities. Officers needing information call the dispatcher, who can provide computerized information on wanted suspects, stolen cars, and recent crimes—usually within seconds. In some areas, portable computer terminals are installed in the patrol cars.

Judges use computers to issue warrants for arrest. Time is critical since a suspect may be fleeing at the moment the warrant is issued. In the old paper warrant system, it could take up to a week for the warrant to be issued and the information given to law enforcement agencies. Using a computer terminal, the court clerk can issue the warrant and send it to law enforcement agencies within seconds.

Crime labs use computers for fiber analysis. They can "see" tiny fibers found on a person's clothing to determine such things as whether or not a suspect was at the scene of a crime.

Governments at all levels, especially the federal government, could no longer function without computers. Computer storage of vast amounts of information has made it possible for governments to keep track of the growing population. Such information as income tax and social security records for every worker in the country is stored in government computers.

For several years we've had computerized voting machines in many areas. In the future we may vote from our own homes—not just for candidates, but for issues as they are argued in legislatures. This could have a profound effect on our concept of democracy.

On a more exciting "high-tech" level, computers have been essential to our efforts in space. Computers chart the movement of our space vehicles using numbers and formulas that would take months to compute by hand. Computers, in the form of navigation aides, can pilot aircraft from any point on earth to any other point with little or no help from human hands. A new aircraft is so fast and so agile that the flight controls must be corrected more than fifty times each second. These corrections are made by a computer. If left to the human pilot alone, the plane would literally disintegrate.

Communication

Studies have shown that a society's progress can be determined by its ability to communicate within itself and with other societies. Computers affect everyone in this process of communication. Most of the switching of telephone calls and the routing of mail depend on computers.

Now computers are "talking" to one another! This saves a great amount of time. For example, branch offices once had the task of preparing long reports of sales. These reports were then mailed to the main office, where they were typed into the computer for analysis before printing. Today, a branch office computer gives all the needed data directly to the main office computer.

In most cases, computers talk to one another over telephone lines. A device that makes this possible is called a **modem** (MOdulator-DEModulator). To establish contact at the other end, you dial a telephone number—just as you would for a regular call. Then you can send information from your computer to the receiving computer and wait for an answer.

Modems work well for small amounts of information. They can be used through the long-distance telephone network to communicate with almost anyplace in the world. Equipment needs are simple and inexpensive. Of course if you use it very much, your long-distance phone bills might be pretty high.

Computers have played a major role in our exploration of space. Computers easily do the precise calculations necessary to send our astronauts thousands of miles into space and bring them back safely.

The process of using telephone lines to link computers provides access to massive amounts of information. This computerized information, in storage, is called a **data base**. There are a number of very large data bases available over the phone lines, to anyone with a computer. For example, a data base in Lexington, Kentucky holds the racing record of every horse that races in the United States. Other data bases keep copies of articles from thousands of magazines. It's possible to obtain a copy of an article on any subject you can think of, and it's available in minutes. Without access to such a data base, finding certain kinds of information could take a lifetime!

In the Home

The computer has added a new dimension to home entertainment. Perhaps the first and most widespread use of computers in the home was to make available a variety of video games. But computers are now changing our lifestyle in a much larger sense.

Some people never "go" to work anymore. They have computer terminals at home, and they communicate with their workplace computer and co-workers over phone lines. Many jobs can't be done on a computer, but this trend will continue as we move further into the information age.

As we move farther into the information age, this scene will become more and more familiar. More people will do their work at home while communicating with workers and computers in various locations.

Computers also help prevent fires and burglaries. In some newer, planned communities video cameras "watch" the homes while the owners are away. The cameras send signals into the home to set off the burglar alarm or fire alarm when necessary. These alarms are connected to a central computer that alerts the police or fire department. The owner can be dialed at an out-of-town number and notified by recorded message of the problem.

> ### Make a Decision
> You are planning your schedule for the second semester at the local junior college. You have room left for one three-hour elective, and you are considering either an introductory computer programming course or a speech course. Both would be challenging courses, and both would help you when it came time to look for a job. What's your decision—the computer course or the speech course? Give reasons for your decision.

The Development of Computer Technology

Very early in human civilization, someone invented a device for counting and storing information. It was a grooved slab of rock with pebbles in the grooves. The pebbles were moved around to show value and wealth. This device worked well as long as no one bumped the rock, causing the pebbles to fall off. When someone solved this problem by stringing the pebbles on a rod, the abacus was invented.

The abacus was used in Babylonia thousands of years ago to count and do mathematical operations. With improvements it was still being used effectively in the middle of this century. The principle of the abacus served as a basis for almost all mechanical calculating machines for the first five thousand years of business history.

In the seventeenth century, French philosopher and mathematician Blaise Pascal wrote, "I submit to the public a small machine of my invention, by means of which you alone may, without any effort,

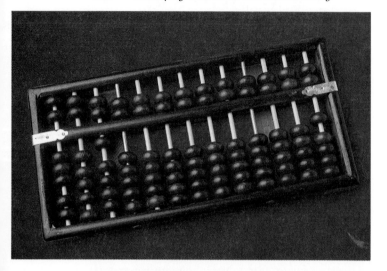

The first counting machine—the abacus—was used in Babylonia thousands of years ago. There is little comparison between the capabilities of the abacus and today's computers.

perform all the operations of arithmetic. And you may be relieved of the work which has often times fatigued your spirit."

Pascal's gear-driven machine sold for about a year's wages. It could only do a few arithmetic functions, and it often jammed and wouldn't work at all. It never caught on.

Three centuries later, the first office calculators sold for two month's wages. They lasted for several years, and could add, subtract, multiply, and divide. Several years after this, the newest calculators sold for a few hour's wages. These new calculators work for years on one battery and can perform advanced math functions.

Early Computers

The development of calculators took thousands of years. The computer, though, is a product of this century. A calculator requires that several human steps be taken to add numbers. Usually steps must be repeated each time numbers need to be added.

A computer, on the other hand, can be programmed to do a series of tasks. Once set in motion, it can perform these tasks without help from humans. It can add numbers, for example, for as long as they are supplied. This capacity does not depend on size. Some true computers are held easily in one hand.

The military needs in World War II brought about the development of the first computers. The speed of battle, particularly in the air, surpassed the ability of the mind to calculate the proper position of guns. Single-purpose computers, operating much faster than the human mind, were developed as a defensive aid.

After the War, engineers began using computers to design new products. Computers became the "brains" for engineers, but they were still too expensive for other business uses.

The Growth of Computer Technology

Most people consider ENIAC (*E*lectronic *N*umerical *I*ntegrator and *C*omputer) to be the first modern, multipurpose computer. ENIAC was designed and built at the University of Pennsylvania in the mid 1940s under the supervision of Presper Eckert, Jr., and John Mauchly. ENIAC worked about one thousand times as fast as the most advanced computers at that time.

Computers such as ENIAC were huge—some as big as a house! The largest, weighing 175 tons, is now on display in the Computer Museum in Boston. These early computers used thousands of vacuum tubes (like old-time radios), which burned out so often that full-time service workers were constantly replacing them. Only a few large businesses —those with a pioneering spirit—used these computers, which are referred to as *Generation I* computers.

In the 1960s a new type of computer was ready. The Generation II computer used transistors instead of vacuum tubes. The new machines were hundreds of times smaller, used much less energy, and were reliable for thousands of hours of operation.

The 1970s saw the development of improved computers with smaller devices that could sit on a desktop. These Generation III computers used a revolutionary part called an *integrated circuit (IC)*. The first ICs contained only a few transistors in a small case. But soon large scale integrated circuits were developed on thin slices of silicon. These integrated circuits on silicon strips were commonly

The first modern computers, such as the ENIAC shown here, were enormous. Although they could do calculations much faster than humans, they broke down frequently and required constant maintenance.

called **chips.** The chips had several different layers of other materials deposited on them. The pattern of these materials caused them to act like thousands of electronic components.

By the middle 1970s the small desktop units began to change. They were no longer just keyboards with access to the big computer—they had intelligence of their own. Now a terminal sitting on a desk could either communicate with the central computer or do computing itself.

In the 1980s the small desktop units had developed into fully capable Generation IV computers on their own. Generation IV computers use very large scale integrated circuits containing thousands of electronic circuits. Each circuit is as complex as a complete computer once was. Some of these computers have become so inexpensive that many people own them for personal use in their home.

As the technology improved and small computers were developed, some new terms were needed to distinguish between large and small computers. The very large computers came to be called **mainframes.** These are the large computers that are placed in special rooms where special conditions can be maintained. Mainframe computers can do a great deal more work than smaller computers. They are usually operated only by highly trained professionals.

The Micro Miracle

Large computer systems can perform millions of math operations per second and store billions of characters of data. Small, personal computers don't run as fast or store as much data, but they are better than the biggest machines of just ten years ago.

Let's examine further these new, little computers. The terms *home computer, personal computer,* and *micro-computer* may have different meanings to some people, but they all refer to the same type of machine. That is, a small computer that can be easily carried in the trunk of a car or placed on a desk. Let's call them **micros.**

A process called *distributive processing* can link a micro with a mainframe computer. This can be done either with a direct cable or over the phone lines. The micro can be a stand-alone computer one minute and an intelligent terminal talking with the mainframe the next minute. Small jobs can be done on the micro under local control. Larger jobs, requiring the sharing of common data, are transmitted to the mainframe.

When micros began appearing in the workplace, few workers felt comfortable with them—especially older workers. Merely sitting down at a computer terminal or micro brought a cold sweat to the brow of some. How did these people become "friendly" with computers?

The answer lies mostly in the miracle of youth. After seeing their young sons and daughters using computers, older workers began to believe that they, too, could learn to use them. Then those youngsters grew up and entered the world of work, unafraid of computers. This has led to the demand that businesses provide their workers with better tools to do their jobs. But it wouldn't have happened had it not been for the micro. It was small enough and inexpensive enough to be played with at home, yet powerful enough to do useful work on the job.

A microcomputer can be a stand-alone computer one minute and an intelligent terminal talking to a mainframe the next minute.

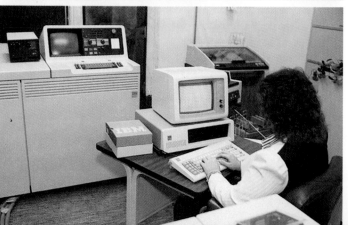

Data Processing

We've discussed how computers have changed our lives and how they were developed. Now it's time to learn what a computer is, how it works, and what it can do.

You've probably had at least one or two opportunities to work with a computer. If someone who had never seen or heard of computers asked you, "What is a computer?", what would you say? How would you answer the question, "What does a computer do?"

A **computer** is an electronic device that stores and processes data. *Data* are facts, small pieces of information, such as dates, numbers, and names. Computers take pieces of data and manipulate and change that data into usable information. This process of changing data into information that people can use is called **data processing**.

Then the answer to the question, "What do computers do?" is—process data. How do they do this? To answer this question you need to know about information systems and how they work.

Information Systems

A complete data processing system can be separated into four functions: input, processing, output, and storage. These four functions were used to process data long before there were computers. In fact, we all use these functions in processing data every day. The brain serves as the processor. Whether we use a computer, a pencil and paper, or simply "do it in our head," the basic functions are the same.

Input. The first step in processing data is to input it, to put it into the system. Input is a recording function. This means that we must record the data in usable form. If we are using a computer, we must record the data in a form that the computer can understand.

Process. In step two, processing, the data is changed to a more useful form. This function is the real heart of the information system. It can be broken down into five functions of its own:

- classifying,
- sorting,
- calculating,
- comparing, and
- summarizing.

You are an information system. You take in data, store it, process it, rework it to your liking, and then output information you can use.

The *classifying* function identifies the data. This makes it easier to process the data further. You are already familiar with the classification function. You classify people every day as men, women, children, family members, friends, and teachers. High school students are classified as freshmen, sophomores, juniors, or seniors.

The *sort* function arranges data by classification. This, too, makes it easier to process data further. Telephone directories sort names alphabetically. Can you imagine finding someone's number if all the numbers were listed at random?

The *calculate* function involves adding, subtracting, multiplying, and dividing. The computer calculates with incredible speed and accuracy. It can use math formulas to solve complicated problems because the formulas are simply combinations of the four basic math functions.

The *compare* function means checking one piece of data against another. Suppose you want to pay your workers $10 an hour for all hours worked up to forty hours. You want to pay $15 an hour for each hour above forty hours. Before you could calculate the worker's pay, you would need to compare the hours worked by each employee with the number 40.

The *summarizing* function often provides information for decision-making. Suppose the president of Lectrik Shavers is concerned about cutting production costs. It would be impossible to determine where costs should be controlled simply by looking

at individual checks. The totals (summaries), however, would show how much is spent in each area of company expense. This information might be the basis for a decision to buy materials from a different supplier or to lay off some workers.

Output. The output function in an information system delivers information to users who need the information for some specific use. Humans output messages in different ways. We speak, or point, or write a letter so that other people know how we have processed the input that has come to us.

Computer output is usually communicated to users in the form of documents or displays. *Documents* are permanent records printed on paper. *Displays* are temporary visualizations, such as those on computer monitors or video screens.

When one computer "talks" to another computer, the output is in the form of *machine-readable* electronic signals that the computer can process. Output can be in any form that delivers information where it is needed in a way that it can be understood.

Storage. The storage function really involves both storing and retrieving information. Storing, of course, simply means placing the information someplace where it can be found later. Retrieving means finding the information and outputting it or processing it as needed.

Records stored in information systems provide the very basis for doing business in the United States and around the world. Major businesses would collapse if their records were destroyed. Records stored in computer files must be kept safe and secure. They need to be protected from fire and other hazards, and secure from those who might profit from stealing information. Copies of records are often kept in another place. The data is protected by allowing access only to those who need to retrieve it.

Computer Systems

A computer system is one kind of information system. A computer system consists of separate, yet carefully-linked, components (pieces). There are four kinds of components.

- Input devices
- Processor
- Output devices
- Secondary storage device

A computer system is similar to a system of stereo components. Each component has a job to do to make the whole system work. As with stereos, some computer systems, particularly micro systems, "package" two or more components as one unit. The components making up a computer system are often called **hardware**.

Input Equipment. The two most frequently used methods of inputing data are keying and reading. Keying inputs data one character at a time,

through a typewriter-like keyboard. This process can produce machine-readable *media* (documents or devices that record data, such as punched cards or magnetic tape).

Until the 1980s, keypunch machines were the most popular devices for keying data. These machines record data by punching holes in paper cards as the operator types on a keyboard. The locations of the holes form a code that can be read into the computer by a card reader.

Newer key-disk or disk drive machines place tiny magnetic signals in specific spots on computer disks. The **disk drive** is the device that receives and operates the disk. You can think of the disk drive as being similar to a tape player.

Key-tape machines place the same kind of signals on tape. Much of this computer tape is just like the cassette tapes you buy at the music store. Sometimes it comes in giant 2400-foot reels.

There are other ways of keying in data. Paper tape is sometimes used. In some new systems you can input data in shorthand form—similar to that used in court reporting. This saves time because it isn't necessary to key in every character of every word.

Another keyboard device, the computer terminal, can be used to input data directly into the computer. This eliminates the need to record on paper or magnetic media. The terminal is replacing other forms of inputing data for many applications.

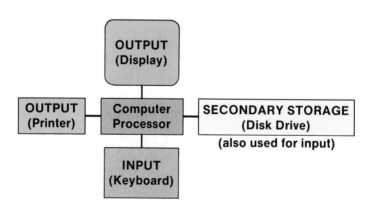

This computer system consists of five components: keyboard, computer, printer, display screen, and disk drive.

Reading is a process of recognizing symbols and inputing data directly into the computer or recording it on magnetic media. One example is the optical character reader (OCR). This device can read typewritten words and numbers—if they are typed in certain type styles—and translate them into electronic signals.

Processing Equipment. The processor is the heart of every computer. It accepts the input and processes the data. The computer processor is made up of two parts: the central processing unit (CPU) and the main memory.

The CPU performs arithmetic and comparison functions in its arithmetic-logic unit (ALU). Another part of the CPU, the control unit, accepts the input and places it in main memory to await actual processing. The control unit also controls the communication between the processor and the other devices in a computer system.

The devices connected to the computer processor are called *peripherals*. Peripheral means around and close to a central object. Peripheral devices are connected to a processor that is the center of the computer system.

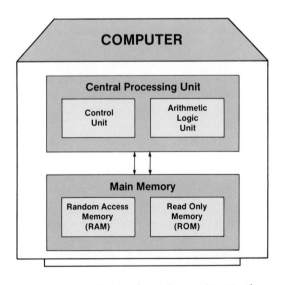

A computer processor is made up of two main parts: the central processing unit (CPU) and the main memory. The CPU performs arithmetic and comparison functions and accepts the input and places it in main memory awaiting processing. The main memory stores both programs and data.

Main memory, or primary memory, consists of Read Only Memory (ROM) and Random Access Memory (RAM). ROM is usually programmed into the machine at the factory. It contains a limited amount of instructions to the computer. You cannot change the content of ROM—it remains there forever.

The greater portion of main memory is RAM. You can store instructions and data in RAM, then tell the computer to process what is in RAM. When you have finished, you can replace the contents of RAM with something new. Whatever is stored in RAM is lost when the machine is turned off.

Computers have different memory capabilities. Mainframes have a lot more storage capacity than micros have. Some micros have more memory than other micros. When people shop for computers, they usually look for a computer with a certain amount of memory. The memory capability for micros is usually measured in Kilos, commonly called *K*, which represents 1,024 characters.

Output Equipment. Several types of output devices are used to transfer information from the computer processor to the computer user. These peripheral devices present information in different forms according to the needs of users. The two most-used types of output are displays and documents.

A display provides output in the form of words, numbers, or graphics (pictures) on some kind of electronic screen. A display is not a permanent record. Most screen displays are on a cathode ray tube (CRT).

Documents are words, numbers, or graphics printed on paper. Unlike displays, they are permanent records. Documents can be produced by the various types of devices listed below.

- Impact printers
- Ink jet printers
- Thermal printers
- Laser printers
- Plotters

Documents are also called **hard copy.** When you hear people talk about hard copy, they are usually talking about a printed version of information also stored on a computer disk.

Storage Equipment. We can store data "off-line" (anyplace not connected to the computer itself) in secondary storage as well as in the computer's main memory. It's less expensive to store data in secondary storage than in main memory. The disadvantage to using secondary storage is that it's much slower to access.

Computer tape and even cards can be used as media for secondary storage. The most common media, however, is the magnetic disk. Data can be stored on the disk, then the disk can be used later to input data by reading the data into the computer's main memory. In other words, the disk can be used for both storage and input.

Mainframe computers use hard disks. These disks are built into the disk drive and may or may not be replaceable.

Floppy disks, also called *diskettes,* are used on smaller systems. Floppy disks are not really "floppy." They are magnetic media in the form of a flat disk encased in paper or plastic. They are called *floppy* in comparison to hard disks, which are not flexible and are much harder.

Floppy disks cannot store as much data as hard disks. They are designed to be loaded and unloaded into a disk drive. Floppy disks are currently made in three sizes: 3½, 5¼, and 8 inches.

Mainframe computers usually store software and data on hard disks. Micros usually use less-expensive floppy disks in the sizes you see on the right.

Software

Fancy machinery won't do anything for anyone without instructions on how it is supposed to act. This is why computers need **programs**. Programs are instructions that tell a computer how to do a certain task or group of related tasks. A program is often called **software**. Software is "soft" in comparison to the equipment, which is hard. There are two basic kinds of software: operating system software and application software.

Operating System Software

Operating system software consists of a set of instructions that causes the components to behave as a system. The operating system software is usually provided by the manufacturer of the machine. The software manages the movement of data to and from peripherals through the computer's main memory.

Operating systems that include instructions for disk drive operations are called *disk operating systems (DOS).* The disk drive loads the DOS into the computer's RAM portion of main memory.

Most computers have an initial set of instructions built into the computer's circuitry. These built-in instructions cause the computer to locate and begin performing the rest of the operating system. The first sequence of instructions the computer reads is called a **boot** procedure. Boot simply means to load an operating system into the computer. This is usually done by placing the disk in the disk drive. It tells the computer what it must do to read the rest of the disk.

When a computer is turned off, the RAM portion of main memory is wiped clean. But the system software must be saved, even when the power is turned off. So it's kept in secondary storage that does not depend on continuous power.

Mainframe computers usually store software on hard disks, sealed in plastic. Micros may use hard disk storage, but they usually use the less expensive floppy disks.

By turning a switch and pushing a button, the computer is transformed from a collection of metal and plastic into an intelligent machine. Once the machine is "up" (operating), it can perform a variety of tasks. Each kind of task, or application, requires its own application software.

Without instructions on what to do, a computer is of no use to anyone. Some of the necessary instructions are built into the computer by the manufacturer. The disk operating system (DOS) instructions and other instructions are on the disk that the user inserts into the disk drive.

Application Software

Mainframe computers use many kinds of application software in business, engineering, education, and other fields. Many of these programs are highly complex, and many are customized to the needs of the users. Our concern here is to understand how application software is used. We will focus on typical application software used in micros.

Application programs, too, are usually stored on disks. Application software may be purchased from the company that made the computer or from other sources. Hundreds of companies and individuals sell programs for micros. You may also write your own programs for your own applications if you have learned how to program computers.

There are many types of software on the market. Among the most popular types for micros are word processing programs. These programs tell the micro how to act like a very efficient typewriter. To print out what you type, you will need to hook up a printer to the micro.

Different word processing programs have different features, but they all let you type your document on the screen. You can then move sentences around until they say exactly what you want. Some of these programs will also check your spelling.

What do you want to do with your computer? You can buy software for just about any application.

When your document is exactly right, you print it out on your printer. You can also store your document so that you can work with it or print another copy at a later time. Writing letters and other documents is two or three times faster on a computer than on an electric typewriter.

The micro that becomes a super typewriter with one piece of application software becomes an entertainment center with another piece of software. You can now play at home many of the games previously found only in arcade centers. By inserting different disks, you can fly to Mars or explore caves inhabited by dragons. You can solve crimes or be eaten by a little screen image, all without leaving the safety of your home. It all depends on the application software you insert.

Although word processing and game playing are by far the most popular kinds of application software for micros, there are dozens of others. Data base management programs allow those without much knowledge of computers to do sophisticated file and data manipulation. Graphics software can make you an artist with the screen being the canvas. Spread sheet software allows manipulation of vast amounts of data for budgeting and money management. With calendar software, you can budget your time in the same way that you budget your money. Electronic mail software lets us write to one another without putting it on paper.

Make a Decision

You've saved about $1,000. You were going to use it as a down payment on a new car, which you need badly, but you've noticed how important computers have become at work. You were thinking about using the money to buy your own personal computer so you can learn about computers at home on your own. What's your decision—a car or a computer? Give reasons for your decision.

Computer Programming

Suppose that you want to use a computer to perform a certain application. There is no software program available that will direct the computer to perform this application. What do you do?

You could hire a programmer. A programmer is a person who prepares a sequence of instructions that enables a computer to perform some special task. These instructions may be written in an electronic code or in a computer language that the computer itself must translate.

If you know how to program computers, you can write the program yourself. An advantage to this is that you will have greater control over how the program works. By writing rather than buying the program, you'll also save money.

Have you ever tried writing a computer program? If so, you know how much a computer depends on software. If not, you may be surprised at how much information goes into a program. A program instructing a computer must cover every detail.

Suppose for a moment that you are a computer, working for your "owner," Miss Jones. Miss Jones wants you to get a certain file (a very basic task). First she must get your attention and identify herself. Then she must tell you what file she needs, where to find it, and how to get into the "filing cabinet." Next, she must tell you where to put the file so that she may look at it.

As a human, of course, you don't have to be told in such detail how to do a simple task. Miss Jones can get your attention with a simple gesture, without saying a word. And you already know who Miss Jones is, where the filing cabinet is, and how to open a cabinet drawer. As humans, we assume so much because of our general knowledge of the world around us. But the computer "knows" nothing, except what it's told. So instructions must be exact and very detailed.

In 1985 there were 443,000 computer programmers. This number is expected to increase by 77 percent by 1995. Programmers must be able to think logically and pay very close attention to detail. If you have these abilities, a career as a computer programmer could be very rewarding.

Lots of people know how to use computers—very few people know how to program them. If you have a logical, analytical mind, you might find a career in computer programming to be both rewarding and challenging.

Machine Language

Computers process data electronically. That is, data is processed through controlling thousands, even millions, of circuits and memory locations. These circuits and memory locations have only two states. They are either "on" or "off." The computer recognizes these two states as either a 1 or 0.

The language of computers, then, is expressed in groups of 1's and 0's. This is called *binary coding*. You have probably studied binary numbers in a math course at some point. Since all computer functions depend on this coding, it is also called *machine language*. This is the only language a computer's basic circuits can understand.

The people who wrote programs for early computers wrote them in machine language—and machine language still produces the most efficient, fastest operating programs. Since writing programs in machine language is a very slow, difficult process, new programming languages were developed.

Programming Languages

Humans prefer to write in human languages. The first uses of human language instructions, instead of binary coding, were assembly languages. The computer converted assembly instructions into machine language with a special program called an *assembler*.

This meant that there were really two levels of coding. The programmer wrote the source code—which was converted by the assembler program into the object code (machine language) recognized by the computer. This made programming somewhat easier, but assembly languages were not too much different from binary coding. Each computer operation required a separate command. There was a need for programs requiring fewer source instructions.

Compiler languages use English-like words and abbreviations. They are known as "high-level" languages. A source code is written, then a special program called a *compiler* converts the source code into the object code. In other words, the computer itself translates the program into machine language. These high-level languages are relatively easy to learn to use. They produce slower running programs, however, and take up more space in memory than does machine language.

Compiler languages have been developed to meet special computing needs. The most frequently used compiler languages are FORTRAN, COBOL, and BASIC.

FORTRAN is an abbreviation of FORmula TRANslator. Introduced in 1957, it was the first important compiler language. It is an efficient way to enter scientific equations and math formulas for processing. FORTRAN is still widely used for math and scientific applications.

Computers, like people, speak different languages. Without a translator (called an *interface* in computer jargon), they cannot "talk" to one another.

COBOL stands for COmmon Business Oriented Language. It was developed for business data processing and was first used in 1960. COBOL uses many common English words and was designed for use on many kinds of computers used in business. It handles very large amounts of input and output.

BASIC is an abbreviation for Beginners All-purpose Symbolic Instruction Code. It was designed to be easy to learn for the non-professional programmer. Most BASIC commands are written in common English. It is the most commonly used language for programming micros.

FORTRAN and COBOL are translated from the source code into the object code using a compiler program. Then the source code is saved in secondary storage. These languages, and others like them, are "recompiled" only when changes are made in the source code.

BASIC works differently. Most computers have BASIC interpreters instead of compilers. This means that each time a program is run, it is interpreted. Because of this, most BASIC programs take much longer to run than programs written in FORTRAN and COBOL.

Special Programming Languages

The compiler languages we have discussed are all procedural languages. That is, you must write instructions out step by step. Other languages are nonprocedural. RPG, standing for Report Program Generator, is a "fill-in-the-blank" language. Special forms are filled in that are translated into instructions to the computer. If, for example, you want output without dollar signs, commas, or leading zeros, all you have to do is fill in a certain code on a form.

Program Development

The actual writing, or "coding," of instruction is program development. This may be done directly on the monitor if you have a micro or a mainframe computer terminal. It can also be done off-line, if you have no computer handy. In this case the program will have to be entered into the computer system as another step.

Program development also includes testing and *debugging*, which is the process of removing errors from the program. You see, programs don't always work the way we think they will. The longer the program, the more likely it is that some sort of error will occur.

One story traces the term *debugging* to the fact that insects used to get lodged in the old Generation I machines. With modern computers, "bugs" are more likely to be syntax or logic errors. Syntax errors are mistakes in writing language code. Logic errors occur when incorrect instructions are given, often because the order of instruction is not correct. Logic errors are the most difficult to find.

The true test of how well programmers do their work is the ease or difficulty experienced by the user. If you have worked with a smooth, easy-to-understand-and-use program, you can be sure an intelligent, hard-working programmer has spent many hours developing and perfecting the program.

REVIEW YOUR LEARNING

■ CHAPTER SUMMARY

Computers are changing the way we live and work. In schools, computers are used to process information about students, take the place of teachers, and even call absent students. Businesses have installed computer systems to help control inventory and speed up lines. Computers are also used in medical research, law enforcement, space exploration, communication industries, and in the home. Almost all aspects of life have been affected by computers.

Computers are products of this century, but the history of devices used for counting and storing information goes back to early civilization and the abacus. ENIAC, developed in the mid 1940s, was the first multipurpose computer. Generation II computers, developed in the 1960s, were smaller and more efficient due to the use of transistors instead of vacuum tubes. The integrated circuit brought about Generation III computers in the 1970s. Soon, small desktop computers that could do all the work of earlier mainframes were being used everywhere.

Computers process data to generate information that people can use. Computer systems are information systems that input, process, output, and store data. Like a stereo system, several pieces of equipment, such as keyboard devices, printers, and central processing units, work together in the computer system to process data.

The instructions the computer needs to do its work are called *programs,* or *software.* The two basic kinds of software are operating system software and application software. Computer programmers write these instructions in computer languages, such as BASIC, COBOL, and FORTRAN. Because of the demanding, logical work involved in writing computer programs, a career in computer programming can be very rewarding.

■ WORDS YOU SHOULD KNOW

boot
chips
computer
data base
data processing
disk drive
floppy disk
hard copy
hardware
mainframe
micro
modem
program
software

REVIEW YOUR LEARNING

CHAPTER 12

STUDY QUESTIONS

1. Name three ways in which computers are used in schools.
2. Name three ways in which computers have improved law enforcement.
3. What device makes it possible for computers to communicate through the telephone lines?
3. What is the basic difference between calculators and computers?
4. What was the major difference between Generation I and Generation II computers?
5. What revolutionary part made the computers of the 1970s superior to those of the 1960s?
6. What is the basic difference between a mainframe computer and a micro computer?
7. Which is most helpful to humans—data or information?
8. What four steps take place in an information system?
9. What are the five functions of processing?
10. What are the two most often used ways of inputing data?
11. What are the two main parts of a computer processor?
12. What are the two kinds of main memory?
13. What are the two kinds of output?
14. In what two places can data be stored?
15. What are the two basic kinds of software?
16. Name at least three kinds of application software.
17. What computer language produces the most efficient programs?

DISCUSSION TOPICS

1. Do you expect computers to change things for the better or for the worse in the next five years? Why?
2. Many schools are making computer courses required for graduation. Do you believe this is a good idea? Why or why not?

SUGGESTED ACTIVITIES

1. For five days, keep a record of your encounters with computers. Write down the location and the use of the computer with each occurrence. At the end of the week compare your list with the lists made by your classmates.
2. Make a class montage of photos representing the historical development of calculating machines and computers. Find as many different photos and drawings as possible. Arrange them with dates to show how the technology has progressed.

CHAPTER THIRTEEN

The Changing Workplace: Our Economic System

Would you try to drive a car if you didn't know the difference between red and green at a stoplight? What if you knew nothing about our highway system, even that in this country everyone is supposed to drive on the right? Without knowing the basic "rules of the road," you would probably have a difficult time getting to where you wanted to go. In fact, there's a good chance that you would *never* get there.

The same is true of your career goals and the need to understand a few basic facts about economics. You will be working within our economic system. To be successful, you will need to know *why* certain things are happening, such as why prices go up and down and why new jobs are created and old ones disappear. You will have a much better chance of reaching your career destination if you know why these things happen—if you know the economic rules of the road.

In this chapter you will learn how our economic system works. You will learn why conditions change so rapidly so that you can prepare yourself for the changes. With a basic understanding of the system you will increase your chances of reaching you ultimate career goal.

DO YOU KNOW . . .
- how our economic system works?
- what resources are necessary to operate a business?
- what factors affect the changes in prices?
- how the government affects our economic system?
- what your role in the economic system will be?

CAN YOU DEFINE . . .
- capital?
- consumer?
- deficit?
- economic system?
- entrepreneur?
- Federal Reserve System?
- free enterprise system?
- Gross National Product (GNP)?
- inflation?
- labor union?
- law of supply and demand?
- marketplace?
- marketing?
- profit?
- unemployment?

Understanding Economic Systems

Every country needs an economic system. What is an economic system? It's everything that goes on in the world of work—all the activities involving money, work, buying, selling, and producing. An **economic system** is a method of producing and distributing goods and services to the people who need and want them.

All economic systems begin with the basic human needs that you read about in Chapter 1. People need food, water, and clothing. They want a comfortable place to live and a car to get them from place to place. After they've satisfied their needs for food and clothing, they want to be educated, entertained, and even spoiled.

Obviously, someone has to produce the food, make the clothes, and build the houses. Someone else must see to it that the food, clothing, and building materials get to the people who want them. It takes lots of people doing lots of work to satisfy the desires of a country's entire population.

All of this activity is what sets an economy in motion. The system may or may not succeed in answering the demands of the people. How successful the system is depends on how well it's managed, which resources are available, and how hard the people work.

Different countries have different ways of organizing people and resources into economic systems. The method used in the United States has proven to be one of the most effective in the world. Our economic system has provided most people with jobs and enough money to buy food, clothing, and shelter. Most people even have enough money left over to buy some of the luxury items and services available in this country. Few countries in the world offer such a high standard of living for so many.

Our economic system is far from perfect, though. Many people cannot find jobs and many do not have enough food to eat or a place to live. The system is constantly changing, making it unpredictable and confusing for many of us. Prices rise and fall. Old jobs disappear, while new ones are being created. Older workers, in their forties and fifties, frequently find that they must start over in entirely new careers.

In the 1970s and in the early part of the 1980s, our economic system went through some of its most dramatic changes. We thought our natural resources would never run out, but now gasoline and heating fuels cost double what they used to. Our automobile and steel industries, which were the most productive in the world, now face stiff competition from foreign manufacturers. Factories are closing all over the country, and thousands of laid-off workers will never be called back to their old jobs.

Our economic system is in a tremendous state of change as you prepare to enter it fulltime. Just as fast as the factories close, computer shops and new high technology companies open their doors. Communication, information processing, and service industries are taking the lead in new economic growth.

No one knows for sure what our economic system will be like ten, fifteen, or twenty years from now. One thing, though, is certain—you will have an impact on what happens to the system. The system will also have an impact on what happens to you and your career.

Although constantly changing, our economy operates on some basic, unchanging principles. In this chapter you will learn about these principles. You will also learn how to prepare yourself for the changes that will occur. By understanding how the system works and by preparing yourself for change, you will increase your chances of achieving your long-range career goal.

Free Enterprise

Our economic system in the United States is known as the *free enterprise system*. You know what the word *free* means; an *enterprise* is an activity, effort, or attempt to accomplish something. Thus, free enterprise means that people are free to attempt whatever activity they choose. A **free enterprise system** is one in which people have the right to make their own economic decisions.

In a free enterprise system such as ours, people can decide what kind of work they want to do and where they want to do it. They can decide whether they want to start their own business or work for someone else. If they want to work at more than one job, that's their choice. In a free enterprise system people also have the right to own property.

Not all economic systems allow people to own property and make their own economic decisions. Socialism and communism, for example, are economic systems in which the government controls

Our economic system is in a constant state of change. It is now in the process of changing from a primarily manufacturing economy to a service and information economy.

almost all economic activity. In these systems the government decides which things will be produced. The government also tells people where they must work and which jobs they must do. In these systems the government often owns all of the property.

In our free enterprise system, which is also known as *capitalism,* people do not have total economic freedom at all times. Our governments—federal, state, and local—are involved in economic matters. The governments do control and regulate many different parts of the economy. For this reason, our economy is not a *true* free enterprise system. It is called a *mixed* system because it does have some of the same government control that other economies have.

No one completely understands what makes our free enterprise system work the way it does. Over 230 million people live in the United States. All of these people have their own personal needs and wants. They are all free to make their own economic decisions. With so many differences and so much freedom, it is not surprising that our system changes so rapidly and confuses so many people.

Economists (scientists who study economic systems) have discovered several basic principles about the free enterprise system in the United States. In this section you will learn about some of these most basic principles.

Make a Decision

In our free enterprise system, you can decide not only *what* you want to do, but *where* you want to do it. Suppose you find that you can get the type of job you want anywhere in the country—and even in a few foreign countries. You know that where you live will be a big factor in determining whether or not you are happy. What's your decision—given your choice, where will you live and work? Give reasons for your decision.

Consumers

The best place to start an explanation of any economic system is with the **consumer**. A consumer is someone who *consumes*—someone who buys and uses goods and services. All of us are consumers.

If consumers wanted square tires for their cars, someone would produce them. Businesses make a profit or fail depending upon their ability to satisfy consumers.

We all use up thousands, even millions of dollars worth of goods (products) and services in our lifetime. Two-thirds of all the goods and services produced are sold to individual consumers.

The needs and wants of consumers play a major role in determining what happens in our economy. If consumers are willing to pay for a certain product, someone will probably provide it. If consumers suddenly change their minds and no longer want that product, the people making it will soon stop.

Regardless of what consumers want, though, they can't buy goods and services unless they have enough money. How much money consumers have determines what and how much they buy. The more money they have, the more they buy. The less money they have, the less they buy.

Few people have as much money as they would like to have. This means that most consumers must be selective in what they buy. They choose the best-made product over the poorly made product. They choose the cheaper product over the more expensive product. They usually choose the things they need over the things they want. Most consumers try to get the most they can in terms of quality and quantity for each of their hard-earned dollars.

Producers

The people who supply the consumers with the goods and services they want are called the *producers*. The producers are free to decide which things they will produce. They are also free to decide how much of each product and service they will produce.

To decide which goods and services and how much of each they will produce, the producers pay attention to the consumers. The producers try to determine what most consumers want and need. When they think they know what the consumers want, they produce it.

Producers organize themselves into separate businesses, or companies. Usually each business concentrates on providing a certain kind of service, or producing a certain kind of product. The local barbershop is a business specializing in the service of cutting people's hair. General Motors is a business that concentrates on producing and selling automobiles and trucks.

Everyone who works is a producer in some way. The owner of the business, the store manager and plant supervisor, and all the employees are producers. If you have a part-time job as a waiter or waitress, for example, you are a producer. You produce a service for the people who come into the restaurant where you work.

Entrepreneurs. The producers who start new businesses are called **entrepreneurs**. These are the people who have ideas about how they can produce a needed product or service for consumers. An entrepreneur can be someone who invents a new product, that he or she believes consumers will want. Or an entrepreneur can be someone like the owner of a new restaurant in your town. This entrepreneur probably believes that he or she can do a better job of preparing and serving food than anyone else in town.

Entrepreneurs are very important in our free enterprise system. In discovering new ideas and responding to the needs of consumers, they help set the economy in motion. They lead the way in creating new products, new services, and new jobs.

In establishing new businesses, entrepreneurs take lots of risks. Usually they must spend a great deal of money to produce the goods or services they believe consumers want. They must hire workers and pay them wages. They must buy tools, equipment, and materials, and pay rent and utility costs. Once they start their businesses, they must pay for these things whether they take in any money or not.

If for some reason the consumers don't buy these goods and services, the entrepreneurs may go out of business. Many go out of business in a short time owing thousands of dollars. You will learn more about how to become an entrepreneur in the next chapter.

Resources. In creating their new businesses, entrepreneurs must bring together many different resources. Probably the most important resource for any business is *labor* (workers). Businesses cannot survive without labor. They need the hard-working, highly-skilled workers who make up our labor force.

Our country has been fortunate in that many people have come here from other lands. These people have brought with them the different skills and know-how from their different countries. As a result, our country's labor force is one of the most productive in the world.

All workers are producers. The ones who are most productive usually receive the most rewards since our system encourages productivity.

Natural resources are also needed to produce many goods and services. Our entire economy uses a tremendous amount of energy, most of which is produced by burning fossil fuels such as oil and coal. Although we must import oil and many other resources, our country has been blessed with a great supply of natural resources.

Another necessary resource for businesses of all kinds is **capital**. Capital is anything, other than land, that is used to produce more wealth. Machines and buildings that can be used for production are called *capital goods*. Money used to pay workers and buy capital goods is also called *capital*. The importance of capital in our free enterprise system is obvious when you remember that our system is also called *capitalism*.

Another resource needed in business is *technology*. Technology includes all the ideas and processes that go together to produce goods and services. You have heard technology in this country referred to as "Yankee ingenuity." This means that we have continually devised faster and more efficient ways to produce goods and services. For a business to survive it must make use of the latest technology.

The Profit Motive

Why do entrepreneurs start new businesses? Why do they risk losing their money? Do they want to produce goods and services just for the purpose of satisfying consumers?

Most entrepreneurs and business owners are in business to make a **profit**. Profit is the amount of money taken in that is more than what was spent. If you pay $10,000 for a car and sell it immediately for $15,000, you have made a profit of $5,000. This is what all businesses are trying to do—make a profit.

Business owners try to produce goods and services that consumers will buy. If consumers buy enough, and the business's expenses are not too great, the business will make a profit. Economists describe the reason for businesses doing business as the *profit motive*.

Businesses continue to operate as long as they can make a profit. Some businesses survive for hundreds of years. Others last only a short time. Several factors, many of which you will read about later, determine whether or not a company will make a profit.

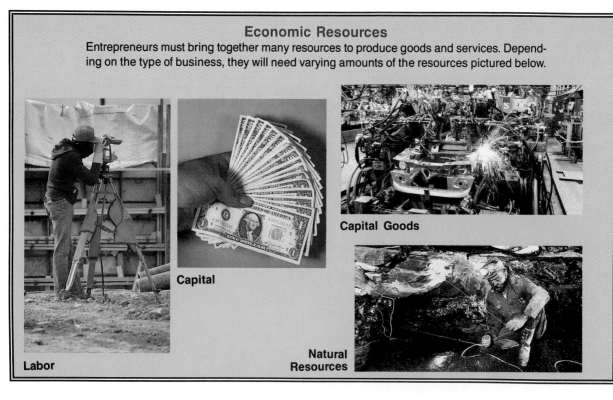

Economic Resources

Entrepreneurs must bring together many resources to produce goods and services. Depending on the type of business, they will need varying amounts of the resources pictured below.

Labor

Capital

Capital Goods

Natural Resources

The Marketplace

To satisfy their needs and wants, consumers must buy the goods and services from the producers. To make a profit and stay in business, the producers must sell the goods and services to the consumers. The place where producers and consumers get together to buy and sell goods and services is called the **marketplace**.

The word *market* and several words made from it, such as *marketplace,* are very important words in our economy. In fact, our free enterprise system is also known as a *market system,* or *free market system.* You will hear and read about the *market* and the *marketplace* frequently when people talk about our economy.

The use of these words comes from the days when the *market,* or *farmer's market,* was a place in the center of town where people would get together to buy, sell, and trade their products. People would set up their individual stands or park their carts in a big, open area where everyone could shop.

The stock*market* is a modern version of the old farmer's market. At certain places in the world, such as the New York Stock Exchange, lots of people gather together in one place to buy and sell. Instead of buying and selling fruits, vegetables, cows, and pigs, however, these people are buying and selling shares in companies.

Consumers and producers do not actually come together in one place as much as they used to. Today, people drive from one store to the next to buy what they need. They also do a lot of their buying and selling by telephone and mail. Although the buying and selling no longer occur in one place, there still is a marketplace. The word *marketplace* is used to describe all of this economic activity, all the buying and selling that goes on all over the world.

Another *market* word that you will hear often is **marketing**. Marketing is the process of getting the goods and services to the consumers who want them. You may remember reading at the beginning of this chapter that an economic system is a "method of producing and *distributing* goods and services." There is no reason to produce goods and services if you have no way to get them to the consumers who will pay for them. Activities such as packaging, shipping, advertising, and selling all go together to make up marketing.

As you just read, the market used to be one small area in a small village. The market or marketplace is now the whole country, or even the entire world. As the marketplace has expanded, so has the importance of marketing. Marketing used to be as simple as carrying your goods a few miles to the village market. Today marketing involves national advertising, trucking goods from California to New York,

The amount of money coming in must be greater than the amount going out, or the business will soon be forced to close. Profit—this is what all companies are trying to accomplish.

The *marketplace* used to be a gathering area in the middle of the village. Today it is wherever buyers and sellers exchange goods or services for money.

and even worldwide distribution. Because the marketplace has expanded, marketing has become more and more important in our free enterprise system.

Prices

In our system of free enterprise, the prices of goods and services are constantly going up and down. Several factors determine how much goods and services cost at any particular time.

Supply and Demand. The amount of goods and services available for sale is called *supply;* the amount of goods or services consumers want to buy is called *demand.* In our economy the relationship between supply and demand has a big effect on the prices of the things we buy. The way in which this relationship affects prices is called the **law of supply and demand.**

The law of supply and demand works as follows. When the supply of a product is greater than the demand, prices go down. When the demand is greater than the supply, prices go up. If the supply

and demand stay the same, the prices will remain unchanged (unless another factor causes a change).

For example, suppose all of your friends wanted to buy a car just like yours, but nobody else had one. If you decided to sell your car, you would be able to sell it at a very high price. In this case the demand would be greater than the supply, so the price would go up.

But suppose a car dealer brought in a shipment of ten thousand cars just like yours before you sold your car. What would this do to your selling price? Obviously you would need to lower your price if you hoped to sell your car. The supply would be greater than the demand, so the price would go down.

Another example of the law of supply and demand is the seasonal price changes in food and clothing. The demand for winter coats is greatest at the start of the winter season. The coat prices are highest at that time. But in February and March, few people want to buy winter coats. Since the demand is less at this time, the prices for winter coats usually go down.

Can you think of other examples of how supply and demand affect prices? In Chapter 16 you will learn how understanding supply and demand can help you become a more effective consumer.

Production Costs. Another key factor in determining price is the producer's costs. The more it costs to make a product or provide a service, the higher the price for the goods and services. Remember the profit motive. To make a profit, businesses must sell their goods and services for more than they cost to produce.

It's because of the profit motive that business people talk so much about *productivity* (high production). They want to produce the greatest amount of goods and services possible at the lowest possible cost. High production and low costs mean lower prices and more sales—which means more profit.

Business people have found that a key factor to being productive is good management. Good managers hire the best workers, organize the work efficiently, and keep up with the latest technological advances. By keeping production costs low to increase profits, good managers are also benefitting consumers.

Competition. Our economy is based on competition between businesses. Those who produce the best goods and services at the lowest prices are generally the most successful. Competition among businesses plays a big part in determining the prices of goods and services.

Consumers benefit from competition among businesses. When two or more companies are producing the same goods or services, both companies must keep prices as low as possible. Each company knows that consumers try to get the best value for their dollar. If the quality is about equal, consumers will buy the lower-priced item. To compete successfully, businesses must keep prices close to or lower than their competitors' prices.

Of course a lack of competition among producers means higher prices. If you produce a new item that everyone wants, and no other company produces this item, you can charge whatever you think consumers will pay. Later you will read how the government prevents businesses from taking unfair advantage of consumers when there is no competition.

Increased competition can cause prices to go down. Business owners know that customers will spend their money wherever they get the best value.

Mary Demski bought a small restaurant in Rossville, a city of 40,000 people. Soon Bill Rogers opened a similar restaurant nearby. When Mary's restaurant began to offer a salad bar, Bill noticed a drop in business. He then added a salad bar plus a Tuesday special. His business increased. Three months later Mary started to offer special prices during the lunch hour. Last month Mary offered Rossville a "first." Her restaurant sponsored a bus to take fans 200 miles to see the Pittsburgh Steelers play. What would you do if you were Bill?

Mary and Bill are not just competing with each other. They are also competing with all the other eating places in Rossville. If any restaurant fails to compete, it will lose customers and go out of business. Who benefits the most from the competition? The hungry consumers in Rossville.

Economic Growth and Change

As mentioned earlier, economists study our free enterprise system, trying to find ways to improve it. In studying the economy, they have found it useful to measure the economy—to see how well it is doing.

Economists call the value of all the goods and services we produce in one year the **Gross National Product (GNP)**. Most economists believe that the Gross National Product is one of the most effective ways of evaluating the economy. You will often read about the GNP in newspaper articles and hear about it on TV when people discuss the productivity of the national economy.

Our economy has grown at a remarkable rate over the years. In 1982 our GNP totaled 3.1 *trillion* dollars. Part of the growth is a result of inflation, which you will read about later. The chart below shows the growth of the GNP in recent years.

Gross National Product (GNP) 1970 to 1982

Trillions of dollars

Source: Chart prepared by U.S. Bureau of the Census.

The sharply rising red line shows the increase in the GNP from 1972 to 1982. The blue line shows how the GNP has not risen so sharply if inflation (see page 214) is taken into account.

There have been times, though, when the economy has not done well. You have probably heard and read about the Great Depression in the 1930s. During this depression our economy was at a near standstill—and millions of people had no money or jobs. There have been other depressions since, but none as severe as this one.

There are many reasons why the economy expands and contracts so frequently. New technologies, the amount of capital available, wars, crop failures, and public confidence in our economic future are some of the factors.

Consider, for example, public confidence. When economic times are good, consumers have jobs and money, and they feel confident about the future. This causes them to spend more of their money. They buy new cars and build new homes. They don't bother to save their money because it seems that there will always be more coming in.

When consumers spend lots of money, businesses start producing more to meet the demand. They hire more workers and build new plants. This creates more jobs and puts more money in the hands of the consumers. The cycle goes on and on —much of it due to public confidence. Unfortunately the cycle works in reverse when public confidence is low.

Income. We all earn income by applying our skills and resources to some productive purpose and being paid for it. When we add up all the 1984 income of individuals and businesses from producing goods and services, the total exceeds $2 trillion. More than 75 percent of this income went to employees in wages and benefits.

The income we receive from all sources is called *personal income.* Among other things, personal income includes wages, interest on savings, and profits if we own shares in businesses. Personal income also includes payments, such as social security or unemployment benefits. The money we have left after paying income taxes is called *disposable income.* This is money we can spend or save in whatever ways we choose.

There is a connection between the skills and the knowledge acquired through education and the income earned later in life. For example, high school graduates earn more than twice the amount earned by those with less than eight years of schooling. College graduates earn about one and a half times the amount earned by high school graduates.

The money businesses have left from their income after paying the costs of doing business is called *gross profit*. These profits are often used for business expansion, for new plants and equipment, or to repay loans. It is from these profits that businesses create new jobs.

When a business does not earn profits, the company must rely on sales of new stock or borrowed money to expand or update its production process. This is difficult because investors' confidence in a business declines when there are no profits—and this makes investment money hard to obtain.

International Trade. When economists and business people talk about *trade,* they are talking about buying and selling, not swapping. *Trade* can refer to any activity in the marketplace, but it is most frequently used to discuss business dealings with other countries.

Trade with other nations is essential to our economic well being. International trade allows us to apply more of our work and resources to activities where we can do a better job than other nations. It also allows other nations to be successful where they can do a better job than we can.

A company can have a production advantage because of the availability of certain raw materials, a favorable climate, lower wages, or more advanced manufacturing processes. Products of our agriculture, aerospace, machine tool, and computer industries are examples of goods that we export (sell to other countries). We export these goods because we have long had superior technology and resources for producing them.

Through international trade we import (buy from other countries) raw materials and foods that are not available in sufficient supply. One obvious example is petroleum—others are tin, chrome, bananas, and coffee.

When the value of our exports is less than the value of our imports, we have a trade **deficit**. A deficit is a shortage. Thus, a trade deficit is a shortage of money that results when we compare the amount spent on imports to the amount received from exports. Huge trade deficits have a negative impact on our economy.

The United States has suffered large trade deficits in recent years. This has been the case, especially, in our trade with Japan.

If we import more goods than we export, we have what is called a *trade deficit*. It is much healthier for our economy if we can sell more than we buy. This is called a *trade surplus*.

Management—Labor

An important factor in our free enterprise system is the bargaining that goes on between labor and management. You've read how entrepreneurs and workers join together to work as producers. Within a company, though, there is often a division, with the owners and top managers on one side and the majority of the employees on the other side. The two sides are called *management* and *labor*.

History. In the early days of industry in the United States, people worked long hours. Men, women—even children—worked twelve hours a day, or more. Working conditions were often dangerous, and workers were paid only enough to buy the bare necessities. If they complained, they were often fired.

Why did employers treat workers like this? Like all employers, they wanted to keep expenses down so they could increase their profits. There were many more workers than there were jobs, so employers could always find someone willing to work for the low wages.

Eventually the workers began to join together to help one another improve their situation. They formed **labor unions.** Labor unions are organizations of workers who join together for the purpose of obtaining higher pay and better working conditions.

The strength and power of the unions grew throughout the first part of this century. As a result, Americans are now paid higher wages than at any time in the country's history. They also work shorter hours and receive more benefits. It is estimated that for every $100 paid in wages, employers pay another $20 in fringe benefits for employees. Much of the credit for obtaining these higher wages and increased benefits belongs to the unions.

In 1950, 30 percent of all workers in the United States belonged to a union. Union membership has dropped, though, and now only about 20 percent of all workers belong to unions. Much of this drop in union membership was caused by the decline in industrial jobs in the past few years. As a result of this drop, the unions do not have quite as much power as they did in the 1950s and 1960s.

Negotiations. As you know, employers are in business to make a profit. An important part of making a profit is keeping expenses low. Since employees' wages are usually an employer's biggest expense, management wants to keep wages from going up and reducing profits.

The unions, on the other hand, want to get the highest possible wages and benefits for all workers. The unions also want management to spend money to improve working conditions.

Obviously, what the unions want is in direct conflict with what management wants. This is why unions and management must get together and settle their differences. They go through a process of give-and-take to arrive at a compromise agreeable to both sides. When an agreement is reached, it is put into writing and called a *labor contract.*

A labor contract is signed by representatives of both labor and management. These contracts usually last for periods of from one to five years. When the contract expires, a new one is negotiated. The labor contract states how much workers will be paid, what fringe benefits workers will receive, and procedures for handling disagreements.

Management wants to keep expenses as low as possible, while labor wants more money, more benefits, and better working conditions. To reach an agreement, representatives from both sides negotiate at the "bargaining table." The net result is usually a union contract.

In negotiations between labor and management, both sides must be willing to give a little. If one side refuses to compromise, agreement is impossible. Sometimes a union may try to force management to give in by going on *strike*. A strike is a refusal by employees to work. It causes a loss in production and, therefore, a loss of profit for the company.

Employees on strike receive no wages from the employer, but they may receive some pay from the union. This money is built up through membership dues.

In some states you must join a union if you want to work for a certain company. When you have no choice but to join a union, the company is said to have a *closed shop*. When you have a choice of joining or not joining a union, the company is said to have an *open shop*.

The Government

In early America our government had little control over business activities. The people involved in business made most of the economic decisions. Even then, though, there was an ongoing debate about how much government should be involved in economic life.

Our economy today is much more complicated, and our governments are much bigger and more involved in the economy. But the debate continues. Depending on which political figures are in power, the government takes a more active or less active role in the economy.

Today our governments employ millions of people. Many of these people are involved in activities that somehow affect the economy. Their involvement can be divided into the four areas described below.

Regulation. People have come to expect the government to pass and enforce laws to regulate business activities. In many different ways, federal, state, and local laws protect consumers and businesses from unfair practices. Some of the more important kinds of laws are listed below.

- **Antitrust**—These laws prevent one or more companies from developing a *monopoly*. Having a monopoly means having complete control of a particular market. A monopoly prevents competition and thus goes against an

Our governments have passed laws that can affect which workers employers hire and how much they pay the workers. Although most people believe these laws are necessary, some people argue that these decisions should be left to the employers.

important principle of free enterprise. The antitrust laws give the government the power to break up companies that have too much control over a market. The government's involvement in the breakup of AT&T in 1984 was an attempt to make the telephone service industry more competitive.

- **Consumer protection**—The government has established agencies and passed laws that require inspection and testing of certain goods and services. You will read much more about these laws in Chapter 16.
- **Fair employment**—Federal and state laws make it illegal for employers to discriminate against job applicants because of race, sex, creed, or age. Laws have also been passed that require employers to maintain safe working conditions and pay a minimum wage.

Public Utilities. There are a few areas in which people have decided that competition would do more harm than good. In the utility service areas, such as electrical power, telephone, and water, local residents do not usually have a choice of companies to buy from. Since there is little or no competition among the utility companies, the government regulates them to prevent them from taking unfair advantage of consumers. Government agencies must approve all raises in rates before new rates can go into effect.

Public Services. Governments provide services, such as defense, protection, education, and transportation, that make up a big part of our economy. Some people argue that private companies could not provide these services. Other people believe that governments should take a less active part in many of these areas. It takes a great deal of tax money to pay for all these services. This tax money is money that consumers could spend on goods and services if they didn't have to pay taxes. Thus, the more services governments provide, the more potential profits they take away from businesses.

A very serious problem has resulted from government's increased role in providing services. The federal government is spending a great deal more money than it is taking in. In 1985, for example, federal spending was expected to exceed income by 222 *billion* dollars.

This 222 billion dollars is called a *budget deficit.* As would be necessary for any business, the government must borrow money when it can't meet expenses. The government must also pay *interest* (see Chapter 19) on the money it borrows. As a result of the deficit, a great deal of the money we pay in taxes (about 12 percent in 1983-1984) goes toward paying interest to banks and other financial institutions.

Many people believe in a *balanced budget,* which means that the government could spend no more money than it takes in. To balance the budget the government would need to either raise taxes or cut spending. The people who argue for a balanced budget believe that the huge deficits are dangerous to the growth and well-being of our economy. Economists have different views on the seriousness of this problem.

Controlling the Economy. You read earlier that our free enterprise system is not a perfect economic system. Many people believe that the system works better if the government helps to control it. It was during the Great Depression of the 1930s, when the economy was doing so poorly, that the federal government began to take a more active part in helping the economy grow and prosper.

The two major problems that occur in our free enterprise system are unemployment and inflation. These are examples of the types of problems that our governments try to solve.

Unemployment refers to the number of workers who want jobs but can't find them. Unemployment is what happens when the economy is going through a depression. Ideally everyone who wanted a job would be able to find one. This ideal condition, called *full employment,* almost never occurs. In recent years unemployment has risen as high as 20 percent in many industrial areas where large factories are closing or cutting back on production. High unemployment rates like this create a serious problem for the entire economic system.

Inflation is an economic condition in which prices rise sharply. During the 1970s, our country suffered through periods of tremendous inflation. Prices were rising at the rate of 10 to 12 percent a year. This is a serious problem since it lessens the value of the dollar. If wages don't go up, people must lower their standard of living.

Governments can do several things to combat these problems. When unemployment is high, they can spend more money, which creates jobs. They can also reduce taxes, which gives consumers more money to spend, which in turn stimulates the economy and creates jobs.

During periods of inflation, governments can do just the opposite—spend less money and raise taxes. The effect is to slow down the economy and stop the increase in prices.

The federal government's use of the **Federal Reserve System** also has a great effect on the economy. The Federal Reserve System is a government agency responsible for controlling our nation's money supply. The money supply is the total of all money in circulation. By changing the monetary policy of the "Fed," as it's often called, the government can lessen the effects of economic ups and downs.

The primary factor in the Fed's monetary policy is interest rates. By raising or lowering interest rates, the Fed affects the amount of money that banks can loan. Generally, the Federal Reserve lowers interest rates and makes money more available when total spending is considered too low. It raises interest rates and makes money less available when total spending is too high.

The Great Depression of the 1930s convinced many people that the government should take action to prevent another collapse. The federal and state governments now conduct many programs for that purpose.

Your Role in the System

You will play several different roles in our economic system. Like everyone else, you will be involved as a consumer who needs and wants certain goods and services. You will also be involved as a producer, either as an entrepreneur or an employee. And finally, you will be involved as a citizen and a voter. In each of these roles you will have to make decisions that will affect your future and the future of our country.

Consumer

You are already affecting our economy as a consumer. When you move away from home and get a full-time job, you'll have even more money to spend. Your impact on the economy will increase as your income and spending increase.

If you are like most consumers, you will not have all the money you want. You will buy those goods and services that you need and want the most. In doing this you will help some businesses make a profit.

If you are a wise consumer, you will help those businesses that provide the best values. If you are not careful with your spending, you may help companies that are not producing quality products stay in business. Part Four of this book will help you learn how to make wise consumer decisions.

Producer

If you have already made a career decision, then you should have a good idea what your role as a producer will be. After reading about our free enterprise system, you should realize more than ever before that you can choose your own role. Whether it's the risk-taking and challenging role of entrepreneurship, or the more secure but potentially less profitable role of employee, you decide.

Whatever type of producer you choose to be, be a productive one. Even if you are an employee with a fixed wage or salary, it's important that you work hard and put in a full day's work. Businesses can't make a profit unless their workers are productive. And you know now what happens if a business fails to make a profit.

Consumer

Producer

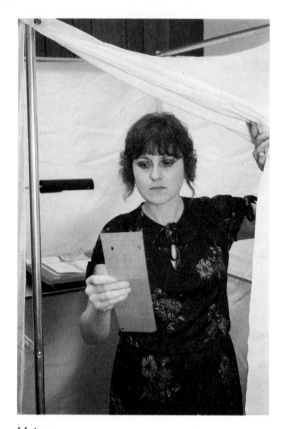

Voter

Each person plays three key roles in our free enterprise system. You will have an impact on the system in each of your three roles.

With the economy changing so rapidly, it's also important that you are able to adapt to change. Do not limit yourself to developing one particular skill that may not be needed someday.

This is where the basic skills that you read about in earlier chapters become important. Employers want to hire workers who have good communication, math, and—more and more—computer skills. They feel they can train workers to do the specific tasks that need to be done in their companies. Employers are not as capable, though, of teaching these basic skills.

You've already done some career research. Continue to read newspapers, magazines, and current books on our economy. Keep up with the changes. By doing this, you will be one of the first to know about new career opportunities. You may be able to take classes or receive training that will qualify you for jobs that few people are qualified to do. Who knows—you might even see a change coming before it happens and turn your idea into a new and prosperous company of your own.

Voter

You've read about the many ways in which governments are involved in our free enterprise system. Many people believe that government should take an even more active role in the economy. These people believe that unemployment and poverty could be eliminated with more government involvement.

Others believe the opposite. They believe our economy would provide a higher standard of living for more people if government would stop interfering with the free enterprise system. They believe that a big, expensive government creates more problems than it solves.

As a voter, you will have countless opportunities to voice your opinion about government's role in our economy. Most candidates have their own definite opinions about economic policy. It is your job as a responsible voter to learn which candidates' opinions are closest to your own.

As you know, our economic system is very complex. Millions of people and countless situations and events affect what happens to the economy. This makes it difficult for most of us to understand the issues. It's important, though, that we all make an effort to understand and vote according to what we believe will be best for ourselves and our country as a whole.

Make a Decision

You are about to vote for U.S. Senator. You've read about the candidates and you know their views. One is a liberal candidate who advocates raising taxes to provide more services for everyone, especially the needy. The other candidate is a conservative candidate who wants to cut back on all federal spending, which could mean lower taxes. What's your decision—do you vote for the liberal, or the conservative? Give reasons for your decision.

REVIEW YOUR LEARNING   CHAPTER 13

CHAPTER SUMMARY

Every country needs an economic system to satisfy the basic needs and wants of its citizens. The economic system used in the United States is called the *free enterprise* system. This system is based on the idea that people should have the freedom to make their own economic decisions. Other key factors at work in our system are the profit motive, competition, and the law of supply and demand.

Briefly, the operation of the system begins with consumers' needs and wants. The producers organize themselves into businesses, started by entrepreneurs, and produce the goods and services that consumers want. The businesses succeed or fail depending on how successful they are at satisfying consumers.

Our economic system is constantly changing. It goes through alternating periods of growth and decline. Some industries die out, and others take their places. Personal and business income, international trade, and bargaining between labor and management are a few of the factors that affect the economy, causing it to change. Those who are able to adapt to the changes are more likely to succeed.

Although our system is a free enterprise system, the governments —federal, state, and local—do have a big impact on the economy. The role of government has increased over the years, and the debate goes on as to how much government involvement is desirable. Government affects the economy in four major areas: regulation, public utilities, social services, and general control of the economy.

You will have three roles in the system: consumer, producer, and voter. The economic system is confusing and difficult to understand, even for economists. But you should do your best to keep up with the changes in our economy. Doing so will increase your chances— and your country's chances—for success.

WORDS YOU SHOULD KNOW

capital
consumer
deficit
economic system
entrepreneur
Federal Reserve System
free enterprise system
Gross National Product (GNP)
inflation
labor union
law of supply and demand
marketplace
marketing
profit
unemployment

REVIEW YOUR LEARNING   CHAPTER 13

STUDY QUESTIONS

1. What is the major difference between free enterprise and an economic system such as socialism?
2. How do the producers decide which goods and services, and how much of each to produce?
3. What are four major resources that entrepreneurs bring together when starting a business?
4. What is the main reason for people to start businesses?
5. Why has marketing become a more important part of our economic system?
6. What are three factors affecting the rise and fall of prices?
7. If the demand for a product goes up, what usually happens to the price of that product?
8. What is one key factor in achieving high productivity?
9. What are five possible reasons why the economy might expand or contract?
10. If you had a personal income of $20,000 and you paid $4,000 in taxes, what would your disposable income be?
11. If U.S. companies exported $200 million worth of products in a given year, while importing $350 million worth of products, would the U.S. have a trade surplus or a trade deficit?
12. What is the difference between an *open shop* and a *closed shop?*
13. In what four basic ways is the government involved in our economy?
14. What two things could the government do to balance the budget?
15. What is the Federal Reserve System's primary method of balancing the economy?

DISCUSSION TOPICS

1. Our economy is constantly changing. How has the economic situation changed in your area during the past two years? What companies have gone out of business? What new companies have started?
2. Our government sometimes charges companies a fee for bringing foreign goods into this country. This is done to help U.S. businesses compete with lower-priced foreign products. The effect of these fees, however, is to raise the price for consumers. Do you believe the government should impose these fees? Explain.

SUGGESTED ACTIVITIES

1. Interview someone who has lived and worked in an economic system other than capitalism. Ask him or her to describe the differences in the two systems. Take notes and report your findings.
2. Take a poll to find out how people feel about the government's role in our economy. Ask five adults if they believe our federal government should be less involved in our economic system. Report your findings to the class.

CHAPTER FOURTEEN

Becoming an Entrepreneur

DO YOU KNOW . . .
- the different types of business organizations?
- where you can get money to start a new business?
- how to set up a business?
- how to keep your business profitable?

CAN YOU DEFINE . . .
- corporation?
- franchise?
- inventory?
- net profit?
- operating expense?
- partnership?
- profit ratio?
- revenue?
- sole proprietorship?

In Chapter 13 you read about the important role entrepreneurs play in our economy. There are about 14 million businesses in the United States—all of them started by entrepreneurs. With their new ideas and their willingness to take risks, entrepreneurs create the businesses that give millions of Americans a place to work.

There are both advantages and disadvantages to being an entrepreneur. All entrepreneurs have the satisfaction of being their own boss, and many earn lots of money. On the other hand, entrepreneurs must take great financial risks and they must work long, hard hours to keep their businesses profitable. Almost two out of every three new businesses go "out of business" within four years of their beginning.

In this chapter you will get a better idea of what it's like to be an entrepreneur. You will learn about the importance of planning and the many different ways you could go about starting your own business. You will also learn about the record keeping and financial planning that must take place once you've got your business started. After completing this chapter you will probably have a much better idea of whether or not you would like to operate your own business someday.

Although many entrepreneurs end up in debt, some become extremely wealthy. This lady started a cosmetics company that has made her rich and famous.

Planning a Business

What is the most important factor in determining the success or failure of a new business? One expert answered this question by saying, "They've got to have a plan—they've got to know where they're going." He was talking, of course, about entrepreneurs.

If you become an entrepreneur, *you* will be the one who plans the business. This will require knowledge and motivation. The same expert mentioned above also said that "starting a business is not a 9 to 5 job, 5 days a week—it's 24 hours, 365 days a year." If you enjoy the work and receive satisfaction from it, those factors will be your motivation to do the necessary work and planning.

Making Decisions

You shouldn't start a business unless it involves work that you like and know something about. For example, if you are a good welder and like the work, that may be a good business for you.

Before you make a decision, consider several things. First of all, look at what you want the business to do for you. Think about the following questions.

- Will I have time for this business?
- What will be the start-up cost?
- How much competition will I have?
- Will sales be great enough to make a profit?
- Can I find competent employees to help me?
- Should I do it alone or have partners?
- Will this business keep me away from my friends and family?
- What growth potential does the business have?
- Will the business give me the status I want?
- What will be my interest in this business after five, ten, or fifteen years?

Your answers to these questions will help you decide whether or not you should go into business for yourself. The questions will also suggest more questions about your own location, business idea, and expectations. The more questions you can answer before you begin your business, the better. Re-

---

Make a Decision

You are good at what you do, and everyone says you have a real knack for getting along with people. The idea of starting your own business has crossed your mind several times. You have some money saved up—probably enough to get someone else to loan you the rest of what you'd need. But you would have to give up your job and the steady, reliable income that it provides. You like your job alright, but you know you will never do more than just get by. With your own business you'd have a chance to really get ahead. What's your decision—do you take a chance with your own business, or play it safe at your present job? Give reasons for your decision.

Many new businesses fail before they ever get started. Why? In most cases, failure is due to a lack of planning—many entrepreneurs rush into their new business without thinking—or planning.

member what you've been reading throughout this book—planning is the key to success. Good planning, more than any other factor, will contribute to a successful new business.

Look at Jane's reasons for starting her own business. Do you think she made good decisions?

Jane graduated from the cosmetology program at the Vocational Technical Institute. During the five years since then she has worked at the Vogue Shop. She likes her boss but has always wanted to have her own shop. She thinks she can earn more money operating a shop in her home. Having her own business would also give her the freedom to plan her own schedule. She would then have time to take care of her kindergarten-age daughter. There seem to be lots of advantages to starting a business.

Jane and her husband live in a large, old house close to the business district. Several apartments are located only a block away. Jane thinks the location is good. Most of her regular customers have said they would be willing to drive to the new location. The house has enough interior space for the shop and a large driveway for parking. Jane's husband approves of the idea and can remodel the interior space for the shop.

Jane and her husband have decided to borrow the money they need to remodel and to start the new business.

Gathering Information

Vocational programs often include courses in entrepreneurship. In these programs you can gain knowledge and experience with the products or service that you would be offering in your business. You would study business trends that may affect your business. You would learn to analyze a geographical area to estimate the number of customers or clients and the competition that you can expect.

An important part of entrepreneurship is learning what types of assistance you will need and can expect to find from experts. For example, you will probably need an accountant. An accountant can help you devise a bookkeeping system. An accountant can also make sure you file the required forms, such as the many different tax and insurance forms.

You will almost certainly need to borrow money. A banker can give you financial advice and information on obtaining loans. An insurance agent can help you choose the kinds and amounts of insurance you will need for your business operation.

In many cases you can get free information from knowledgeable people. Many of the people who work in the same business or industry as you will answer your questions. For example, the salespeople who would be supplying you with materials can be valuable sources of information.

There are several other sources of information. Contact the small business institute at the nearest university. The local Chamber of Commerce and the public library are also good sources of information. You will, of course, want to contact state

Small Business Administration

If and when you decide to start your own business, you will want all the help you can get. A great place to start your information hunt is with the United States Small Business Administration. This agency is in the business of helping new businesses get started. SBA makes business loans, provides expert counseling and advice, and prints a large number of informative pamphlets and brochures on topics such as

- The ABCs of Borrowing
- Should You Lease or Buy Equipment?
- How to Get Started with a Small Business Computer
- Managing Employee Benefits
- Delegating Work and Responsibility
- Reducing Shoplifting Loss

These are just a few of the many publications available. For more information contact your local SBA office or write to the Small Business Administration, 1441 L Street NW, Washington, D.C. 20416.

and federal agencies to make sure you fulfill all your licensing requirements.

A good beginning source of information is the Small Business Administration. You can contact the national office in Washington, D.C. or the regional office closest to you. The SBA will send you lots of information about various problems and questions related to starting a new business.

Types of Ownership

One of the planning decisions to be made is the choice of legal ownership. There are three basic kinds of ownership. A business may be operated as a sole proprietorship, partnership, or corporation.

Small businesses usually start as **sole proprietorships.** This means that the business is completely owned by one person. About 75 percent of all businesses in this country are sole proprietorships.

In a sole proprietorship business, the owner keeps all the profit. This is the major advantage to this type of ownership. The major disadvantage is that the owner has complete financial responsibility. If the business loses money, the one owner must pay all the debts.

A **partnership** is a business owned by two or more persons. These people pool their money, time, skill, and knowledge to operate the business. They share both the profits and the risks.

Partnership agreements should be prepared by an attorney who knows the state and federal laws. Operating a business with a partner can be beneficial, but a poor or dissatisfied partner is a great disadvantage. The partnership agreement should cover all phases of decision-making, responsibility, division of profits, and the means for ending the partnership if that becomes advisable.

A **corporation** is a business owned by a number of people who buy shares in the business. These people are called *stockholders.* The stockholders vote to elect a board of directors, which is responsible for making general policies and hiring people to manage the business. Stockholders share the profits, which are called *dividends.*

Forming a corporation protects the personal savings of the owners. Any legal judgment against the corporation is limited to the value of the business. Corporations may pay a lower tax rate than sole proprietorships and partnerships. They may also find it easier to borrow money to expand the business. Strict legal requirements must be followed to form a corporation.

Frank studied plastics technology at King City Area Vocational School. After graduation he was employed by the City Plastic Container Company. He became very skilled in design and fabrication.

After work Frank enjoyed his hobby of building small, fiberglass boats. He used his garage as a workshop. The boats were of high quality, and many of Frank's friends bought them. In fact, so many people wanted boats that Frank started a small factory in a barn. He worked evenings and weekends to fill orders for the boats.

The business increased rapidly, and soon Frank had more orders than he could fill. His wife, Lisa, and his friends urged him to devote all of his time to his boat business, which he decided to do. Lisa, an accountant, managed all the financial records. With the help of Lisa, his friends, and some of his suppliers, Frank established the King City Boat Company. To raise the money he needed to expand the business, Frank incorporated the business and sold stock. In five years the business employed about twenty people and had over $500,000 in sales. Frank, Lisa, and all the stockholders were very pleased with the success of the new business. Frank and Lisa became quite wealthy.

Business Permits

All businesses must meet city, county, state, and federal operating requirements. Tax numbers, permits, and licenses are needed. Jane, whom you read about earlier, will need a state license to operate her beauty shop. Both Frank and Jane need city permits as well as tax numbers, building permits to remodel or build, and zoning approval. All requests for permits should be approved before setting up the business. Even entrepreneurs, such as inventors, artists, and consultants, who work out of their own homes, usually need business tax numbers and sometimes licenses.

Choosing a Location

If the entrepreneur needs to work outside the home, the choice of a business location may be essential for success. This is especially true of retail businesses and businesses that provide services, such as laundromats, beauty shops, and car washes. The convenience of the customers is of major importance. If the location is wrong—if it's too far from most customers or in an undesirable area—people will go somewhere else. Careful research is needed before a decision is made. For each potential site the following factors should be considered.

- The type of business area
- The condition of streets and buildings in the area
- The cost of renting or buying property
- The location of competition
- The area residents—how many and their potential as customers

Jane's business is called a *sole proprietorship* because she owns the entire business herself. She gets to keep all the profits, but she also gets to do all the work and take all the risks.

S am started working in a pizza restaurant when he was a sophomore in high school. He is now assistant manager of the Quincy Street Pizza. He knows that pizza restaurants have been very successful, and he wants to start his own business in a neighboring town. He has found three possible locations in that town.

Site one is in a mall on the south side of the city. The mall has a small theatre, a deli, and a recreation business. The space is adequate, and the rent is $1,000 a month, including utilities. The nearest fast food establishment is one-half mile away. Most of the area is residential, and there's a state university within walking distance.

Site two is an unused service station just south of the business district. This location has thirty parking places and all utilities needed for the pizza restaurant. It is fifteen blocks from the university and ten blocks from two other pizza restaurants. The area is a combined residential and small business area. The building will require remodeling, but the rent with a six-month lease is only $300 per month.

Site three is on a highway at the north side of the city. Seven fast food establishments are within one-half mile. The building is new, with thirty parking places, and was recently used as a pizza restaurant that failed. It is still equipped, ready for use, and rent is $500 per month.

Sam made his decision. The rent for site one was more than he could pay. Site two would be expensive to remodel, but the rent would be low for six months. Besides it was the most desirable location. More people lived in the area, and traffic past the location was heavier than at site three.

Location is a major factor in determining the success or failure of a new business. Careful planning includes a thorough search and analysis of all possible sites.

Setting Up a Franchise Business

A **franchise** is the legal right to sell a company's goods and services in a particular area. In recent years franchise businesses, especially in the food service industry, have grown rapidly. A number of entrepreneurs who started food service businesses and sold franchises have become very wealthy.

When you buy a franchise, you buy an established business concept and the right to operate the business. Your local business becomes a member of the parent company's chain of franchises. The parent company gives you use of the name, advertising, training, and other services.

There are about two thousand different chains of franchise businesses in operation in the United States. These businesses offer nation-wide service and account for about 35 percent of all retail sales in this country.

There is usually less risk involved in opening a franchise than in opening a totally new, individual business. You would probably receive training and consultation, thus reducing the risk of failure. Your franchise would also identify with a national name (such as Pizza Hut or McDonald's), which usually means more customers and easier-to-obtain loans.

Still, you must be cautious—there are some disadvantages. The expense of buying the franchise and continuing the operation will take a huge bite out of the profits. The franchise contracts are complex, and it is sometimes difficult to meet all the requirements imposed by the company. Increases in the fees can drive many people out of the business. Another disadvantage is that you get little personal recognition as a franchise owner.

Buying an Existing Business

If your interest is in owning a retail or wholesale business, you may find it easier and safer to buy an existing business than to start a new one. There are several advantages to buying a business.

You can sometimes buy at a low price from someone who is retiring. Depending on how eager the person is to sell, you may be able to finance the purchase with the owner at a low interest rate.

If the business has a good customer base and has been successful, you gain from the store's past advertising and name recognition. Often, employees remain with the business and provide valuable assistance. You can also avoid costly start-up expenses, and you can sometimes benefit from an existing lease that was signed when rents were lower.

There are also some disadvantages to buying an existing business. You may find the business is in a declining or changing area. It may be that new competition is entering the area. The business may be making only marginal profit and have little potential. Equipment may be old and in need of replacement.

A disadvantage that is difficult to check, and yet is most important, is the business' public image. You don't want to buy a business that has a reputation for poor service or poor quality products.

You may have to wait a long time for the right opportunity. Buying a thriving business from a retiring owner is, however, often the safest way to get started.

Tom Combs studied auto body repair in a high school vocational class. After graduation he worked in the Kimmons Body Shop and attended the university at night. After six years of experience Tom had become a skilled auto body mechanic. He had also earned a degree in automotive technology.

Mr. Kimmons had established the auto body business thirty-five years ago and was now planning to retire. He was proud of his highly successful business, and if at all possible, he wanted it to continue under his name.

Tom was offered a number of good positions, but he liked Mr. Kimmons' offer best. Mr. Kimmons agreed to sell Tom the business and finance the debt. Tom would pay the debt over a ten-year period.

Tom was pleased to get this "once in a lifetime" opportunity to buy a well-established business under such favorable terms.

One of the safest ways to go into business for yourself is to buy an existing business from someone who is ready to retire. If the business has been profitable for many years, you have a head start on success.

Financing a New Business

Getting money to start a new business is a major problem for entrepreneurs. This is especially true during a tight economy with high interest rates. The potential owner of a new business has only a few sources of capital available.

Before setting out to get a loan, determine the financial requirements of starting and operating the business. Include detailed plans and expectations for the new business. You will also want to include information about yourself and a statement of your total financial need.

The business description should clearly and precisely present the following information.

- Description of the products or services you will offer
- Operation plan, including location, size, and lease for the business site
- Financial plan, including start-up capital, expected profit and sales, and loan payment plans
- Personnel plan, including needed staff, salaries, benefit plan, and retirement plans
- Competition, including the number of competitors and their strengths and weaknesses
- Timetable and schedule for starting the business

The amount of information included in your business description will depend on the size of the loan you are seeking. The larger the loan, the more information you will need.

The third item above, the financial plan, is necessary to determine your financial need. This type of plan will help the lending company better understand your actual needs. Your financial plan should include the following.

- Start-up expenses for the first few months. This will include remodeling, equipment, supplies, and advertising expenses
- Operating expenses to cover the months the business is becoming established and may operate at a loss
- Total expenses for the first few months of operation

> There's an old saying, "You've got to spend money to make money." Most entrepreneurs must convince bankers, friends, and relatives to invest in their idea for a new business. A well-developed financial plan helps to convince potential investors.

When you apply for a loan, you will have to supply personal information. The credit businesses, banks, and loan companies use standard forms to list personal information. These forms usually ask for the following.

- Your education and experience in the business you want to start
- Your credit rating
- Your assets (cash and property) and liabilities (money you owe)
- Your collateral (security—see Chapter 19 for more information)

It can take a great deal of money to start a new business. Where will you get this money? There are several possible sources.

- Your own savings—the best source of capital. Unless you put some of your own money into the business, it will be difficult to convince others to share the risk.
- Banks and credit unions
- Small Business Administration
- Family and friends—a good source of loans with low interest rates
- Suppliers and distributors
- Leasing companies

Obtaining a loan from a bank or savings and loan agency is difficult. These institutions prefer making loans to businesses that are already established since there is less risk with these businesses. Once you achieve success as an entrepreneur, though, getting financial help becomes much easier.

Since most loan agencies hesitate to finance start-up businesses, entrepreneurs usually risk most of their own money. If you borrow money from a friend or family member, do so in a legal way. The statement of the loan should be written in legal form. The terms should be clearly stated. This will help prevent financial matters from getting in the way of a friendship.

The more of your own money you can put into your new business, the less finance expense you will have. Saving to start a business may take several years. You can find more information on money matters in Chapters 17, 18, and 19.

Operating a Business

In the manufacturing business, a primary goal is to produce a salable product. The cost and quality of the product are of prime importance. The cost must be competitive and the quality acceptable, or the product will not sell.

Manufacturing requires a much greater investment than some other types of businesses. Special machines, which can be very expensive, are often needed. It may be necessary to keep large quantities of raw materials in stock.

Service businesses, such as restaurants, motels, and trucking firms, do not sell goods—they provide a service. Operating costs for these businesses include salaries, equipment, rent, utilities, and buildings. Operating expenses vary and depend on the type of business.

In the retail business, everything centers on selling goods, such as groceries, shoes, and clothing. A big part of the retailer's expense goes toward buying the inventory. The **inventory** is the total amount of goods *in stock* (available at that time).

An important part of being a successful retailer is keeping the inventory large enough to serve the customers, without making it too large. Since the retailer must buy the inventory, a large inventory costs a great deal of money. On the other hand, the retailer can lose a customer if the customer can't find what he or she wants. A balance between sales and inventory is needed for a profitable operation.

The use of modern, computerized bookkeeping makes inventory control much more efficient. Many small retail businesses do not need a lot of special equipment, though. Les Mason, for example, controls his inventory on a daily basis and needs little equipment to operate his business.

Entrepreneurs who start their own retail businesses must invest a great deal of money in inventory. They try to keep the inventory at a minimum without disappointing their customers.

L es Mason, a community college student, needed summer work. Since he was studying selling, he decided to get some practical experience. First, he bought a used concession trailer at an auction for $600. After spending $400 for paint and equipment for the trailer, it was ready to use. He found it was easy to pull with his jeep.

Les paid the city $400 for a concession license to sell food in the city park, and he spent $100 for insurance. Expenses for his trailer, equipment, license, and insurance totaled $1,500. He called this "start-up" expense. Les's operating expenses include the cost of supplies and gasoline for the jeep.

The Pittsfield Ice Cream Company agreed to sell Les soft drinks at 40¢ per can, ice cream bars at $30 per hundred in containers packed with dry ice, and cakes at $3 per dozen. Les decided on a 100 percent markup, so he will charge 60¢ for ice cream bars, 50¢ for cakes, and 80¢ for a canned soft drink.

The first day Les sold 100 ice cream bars, 90 cakes, and 100 soft drinks. Sales totaled $185. Expenses were $92.50 for ice cream bars, cakes, and drinks—plus the cost of napkins, straws, and gasoline for the jeep.

Les thought he was beginning a successful business. He knew his prices were comparable with other concessions in the park. Besides, he could move his trailer to places more convenient for his customers if necessary.

He knew he had spent $1,500 and had expenses every day. When would he begin to make a profit? To find out, he made a break-even chart for his costs and his sales. Based on present sales and operating expenses, he made estimates for twelve weeks, working seven days each week. That would mean a total of eighty-four days, so he estimated sales at $15,540. He had start-up costs of $1,500, plus operating expenses of $8,590. The estimated net profit would be $5,450.

Setting Prices

The prices Les charged were decided in part by customer demand and competition. Les knew if his prices were not comparable with those at other concessions, people would not buy from him. They would either not buy at all or buy where things cost less. In some situations, though, an industry may have a monopoly and charge whatever the buyer will pay.

The selling price of a product is determined by (1) the cost of the goods to be sold, (2) the total operating expenses, including start-up costs, (3) the amount of customer demand, (4) the competition, and (5) the percent of profit desired. The cost of goods is the actual cost the business owner must pay the supplier. Some suppliers may give discounts to owners who buy in large quantities.

Keeping Financial Records

Keeping accurate business records is a legal requirement. It is also essential to making a profit. Every business owner keeps records of all transactions. These records must be kept for daily, monthly, and annual reports. The size and type of business will determine the extent of records needed, but every business needs the following records.

- **Revenues**—Revenue is the money taken in from sales. Records of sales and services must be recorded each day in a ledger. Cash register receipts and sales slips are used as records of revenue. These records give the owner a base to determine if the break-even point is being reached.
- **Expenses**—records in several accounts, including purchases, utilities, rent, salaries, depreciation, taxes, and all other expenses.
- **Business reports**—special forms for reporting sales taxes, payroll tax, and income tax. Reports on worker's compensation and unemployment insurance must also be sent to government agencies on the local, state, and federal levels.

Planning Your Bookkeeping. Bookkeeping systems should be established before the business is in operation. A beginning entrepreneur should become familiar with bookkeeping procedures. A course in bookkeeping and computer operation will be helpful. Assistance from an accountant may be needed to select and set up a bookkeeping system.

Using Sales Slips. Sales slips provide a good way to record sales. They can also be used for inventory control. Sales slips are numbered and printed to make two or more carbon copies. Most of the slips have places to write the following information.

- Date of sale and salesperson's number
- Name, address, and telephone number of customer
- The quantity, stock number, and name of item sold
- Unit price, amount of sale, sales tax, and total amount charged the customer
- The warranty information

Businesses offering credit or credit card sales may also use a sales slip for that information.

Entrepreneurs can't tell how much money they are making—or losing—unless they keep accurate financial records. They must either learn some basic accounting or get help from an accountant.

Business Checking Accounts. Sales slips are useful in recording revenues and managing inventory, but an expense record is of equal importance. A business checkbook is usually used for this purpose. It provides a record of income from the daily deposits of sales receipts. It also provides a record of expenses if all bills are paid by check. The records from your checking account will help you decide if your business is profitable. Chapter 18 provides additional information on the use of payroll checks and checking accounts.

J ane started her hair styling business in January. Her business was so good that she was considering hiring someone to help. At the end of the first year, revenues were $15,600. Expenses were $2,000. Her profit before paying taxes for the year was $13,600.

Jane decided to make some changes in the second year. Many customers wanted to schedule appointments after 5:00 P.M. Jane saw that she needed to keep the shop open later in the evening so she decided to hire a part-time stylist. Jane also made a study of charges made by other shops. She found that most of them charged 15 percent more than she did. To be competitive she raised her prices only 10 percent.

Now that the business was started, Jane decided to reduce the advertising cost. She would keep the ad in the Yellow Pages, but reduce her advertising in the local paper to one ad per week.

In December Jane found her profits were up. She had already recovered the cost of starting her new business.

Keeping Your Business Profitable

Making money is the major goal of any business owner. Without adequate profit, the business will fail. Profit is the financial reward for the work, investment, and risk involved in entrepreneurship.

As an entrepreneur, you will encounter certain terms that deal with figuring profits and losses. Two of these terms are **net profit** and **operating expenses**. Net profit is the amount of money remaining after all expenses are paid from revenues. Operating expenses include all the expenses that must be paid to keep the business going.

ANY SMALL BUSINESS, INC.
Condensed Hypothetical Income Statement
For year ending December 31, 1985

Item	Amount	Ratio Percent
Total sales	$773,888	
Less returns, allowances, and cash discounts	14,872	
Net sales	$759,016	100.00
Cost of goods sold	589,392	77.65
Total profit on sales	$169,624	22.35
Selling expenses	66,916	8.81
Administrative expenses	28,010	3.69
General expenses	50,030	6.59
Financial expenses	5,248	0.69
Total expenses	150,204	19.73
Operating profit	19,420	2.56
Extraordinary expenses	1,200	0.16
Net profit before taxes	18,220	2.37
Federal, state, and local taxes	19,542	2.57
Net profit after taxes	−$1,322	−1.71

Most new businesses lose money during the first year or two of operation. Entrepreneurs must have enough money and patience to keep the business operating until it begins to show a profit.

Jane's net profit was calculated by deducting all operating expenses from total revenues. Her salary, FICA, and income taxes are to be deducted from her net profit.

To prepare a profit and loss statement, Jane would want to figure her **profit ratio**. A profit ratio is a comparison of the net profit to total revenues. The profit ratio is expressed as a percentage. This percentage is determined by dividing the net profit by the total revenue.

$$\text{Profit Ratio} = \frac{\text{First Year}}{\$15,600} = 87\% = \frac{\text{Second Year}}{\$25,600} = 57\%$$

This profit ratio is used to compare profits and expenses from year to year.

During the second year, Jane had salary expenses that reduced her profit ratio. Comparing the revenues, expenses, and profits for the two years, the revenues increased by $10,000, but the profits increased by only $1,237. The decrease in the profit ratio indicates that the profits did not increase with the revenue increase. To business people, this is often a sign that expenses should be cut. The second year profit was only 9 percent greater than for the first year. Jane decided the 9 percent increase was about as high as could be expected with her small business.

With some financial help, careful planning, lots of hard work, and a little luck, a young entrepreneur may soon have a successful business. The independence and personal satisfaction is usually as valuable as the financial rewards.

REVIEW YOUR LEARNING   CHAPTER 14

CHAPTER SUMMARY

People who start new businesses are called *entrepreneurs*. Entrepreneurs have new ideas, a desire to be their own boss, and a willingness to take risks. The rewards of being a successful entrepreneur are money, independence, and the satisfaction of doing something well.

The most important factor in becoming a successful entrepreneur is planning. There are several things to do before starting the business. You need to gather all the information available and decide on the type of ownership you'll have—sole proprietorship, partnership, or corporation. Choosing a location is also an important step in planning a new business, especially for retail businesses. Buying a franchise business or an existing business usually involves less risk. Regardless of how you start your business, you will need to develop a financial plan in order to finance the business.

Your primary concerns in operating a business will depend on the type of business you have—manufacturing, service, or retail sales, for example. You will need to keep your prices competitive. You also need to keep extensive financial records if your business is to be profitable. Unless you have accounting experience, you will probably want to obtain bookkeeping advice and assistance from an accountant.

WORDS YOU SHOULD KNOW

corporation
franchise
inventory
net profit
operating expense
partnership
profit ration
revenue
sole proprietorship

STUDY QUESTIONS

1. About how many businesses are there in the United States?
2. What is the rate of failure within four years of opening for new businesses?
3. List nine traits that contribute to successful entrepreneurship.
4. What are four advantages to being a successful entrepreneur?
5. What is the major disadvantage to being an entrepreneur?
6. What is the most important factor in determining whether or not an entrepreneur will be successful?
7. Name at least five possible sources of information for someone starting their own business.

REVIEW YOUR LEARNING

8. What are the three types of business ownership?
9. What are three advantages to a corporation type of ownership?
10. What are four factors that should be considered in choosing a business location?
11. What are four advantages to owning a franchise business?
12. What three pieces of information should you include in your financial plan when applying for a loan?
13. What is the retail business owner's major problem regarding to inventory?
14. What five factors determine the selling price of a product?
15. What would your profit ratio be if your new business had sales of $250,000 and a profit of $45,000?

DISCUSSION TOPICS

1. Do you know anyone who, in your opinion, could be a successful entrepreneur? Tell why you selected that person.
2. Do you know anyone who has started a business that failed? Why did the business fail? Could that person have done anything differently to make the business a success?

SUGGESTED ACTIVITIES

1. Imagine that your class is going to open a shoe store in your city. Scout around for possible locations. Identify two, three, or four sites, depending on how many are available. Obtain information on rents, inspect the facilities, and analyze the potential markets surrounding each location. Each person should then pick what he or she believes is the best location and give reasons why.
2. Outline a plan to start a new business that will give you employment during the three summer months. Use the information in this chapter as a guide.
3. Interview an entrepreneur, preferably a small business owner in your community. Ask the questions below and any others you can think of. Report back to your class on what you learned about entrepreneurship.
   - Why did you start your business?
   - What was the biggest obstacle you had to overcome?
   - Did you need help from other people, such as accountants and bankers?
   - What is the biggest problem you have in running your business from day to day?
   - What advice would you give someone about to start a new business?

CHAPTER FIFTEEN

Leadership in the World of Work

The world of work needs leaders—many leaders. Without leadership, workers are unproductive and resources are wasted. Without leadership, problems remain unsolved and millions of dollars are lost.

Good leaders are needed to organize, motivate, and provide direction. Leaders at all levels—company presidents, division managers, department supervisors—are necessary if workers are to achieve their maximum potential. Good leaders provide that extra push or pull that's needed to reach peak efficiency and excellence. Good leaders help people make decisions and then follow a plan of action.

You can be one of these leaders. You are entering the world of work at a time of change and innovation. New businesses are starting. People are learning how to do jobs that no one has ever done before. It's a time for experimentation and learning. Those who seize the opportunity to learn and work now will move into leadership roles for the young workers to follow.

In Chapter 7 you learned about the things you must do to receive promotions. Many of the same qualities are needed for leadership. Here you will learn about some of the skills a person needs to be a good leader. You will learn how to conduct meetings, which leaders must often do. And perhaps most important, you will learn to think of yourself as the successful leader you can be.

What Makes a Leader?

Some people believe that leadership ability is inherited. They believe that only a small number of people are born with a gift for leadership. All other people are destined to be followers.

Certain people do have greater natural leadership ability than others. But many who are not "born" leaders can and do learn to be good leaders. Many leaders who end up being successful make lots of mistakes in their first leadership roles. They learn from their mistakes and gradually become more and more effective as leaders. Hard work and intelligence are probably more important than inherited traits when it comes to making great leaders.

Authority

Many people believe that authority makes a leader. In every organization—whether it's a business, government, school, or social organization—there is a system of authority. In the past especially, leaders used their position of authority to control those under them. All orders came "from the top." These leaders paid little attention to whether the workers approved or disapproved of the orders they were given.

Today authority is much less effective than it used to be as a leadership tool. The concept of teamwork at all levels of operation is becoming a more common practice. The key to success with this approach is increased worker participation in decision-making. Groups of workers take on more leadership responsibility. The good leader guides and assists workers rather than passing out unchallenged orders.

No longer is authority itself enough to make people follow a leader. Do you know anyone who tries to use his or her authority to make others do things a certain way? Does this approach work?

Qualities

If not authority, then what do the good leaders have that makes others follow them? What characteristics do good leaders have? What qualities do leaders have that make them leaders instead of followers?

Most effective leaders are mentally alert, vigorous, and energetic. They are very enthusiastic and have positive attitudes. Studies also show that they have the ability to make quick and accurate decisions.

A list of personal traits possessed by effective leaders might include such qualities as intelligence, imagination, honesty, integrity, knowledge, and good health. No one knows for sure what makes a leader a leader. These are just some traits that many successful leaders seem to have.

It's difficult to say what qualities are necessary for leadership since there are so many different kinds of leaders. Leaders seem to come from all kinds of backgrounds and possess a wide range of qualities.

One of the benefits of leadership is the increased sense of accomplishment. A leader's success is multiplied by the number of people in the organization.

Other people of their time were thought to be smarter, and have more electrifying personalities, but these men were among the greatest leaders our country has known. No one knows for sure what makes someone a leader rather than a follower.

There is no one best way to lead. Different leaders have different styles—what works for one may not work for another. Some lead quietly, preferring to lead by example. Others are more vocal, constantly giving pep talks and encouragement. Some leaders get involved in every part of the job, others prefer to delegate authority and stay in the background until they are needed.

You have probably noticed that some people who are not leaders seem to have more leadership ability than some people who *are* leaders. Why do you think this happens?

Some people simply don't want to be leaders. It's their choice, and this is perfectly all right. Only in critical situations, when there is no one else to lead, would we want these people to step forward and take charge.

Other people have the ability and desire but lack the self-confidence they need to take charge. Many of these people don't give themselves enough credit. They don't think themselves worthy of leadership. Are you one of these people?

Your Image

How do people become leaders? Why are some selected for leadership roles, while others are not? A lot has to do with the images that people project and the images they have of themselves.

Make a Decision

You belong to a group of workers who are choosing someone to represent them in some negotiations with the company owners. You are trying to decide between two people—an intelligent, knowledgeable person who seems quiet and insecure, and a very confident, forceful person, who probably doesn't understand the issues as well as the other person. You want to vote for the one who is more likely to be successful in leading your group. What's your decision—the more knowledgeable, meeker person, or the less knowledgeable, but more forceful person? Give reasons for your decision.

Your image is how others see you. If most people have a favorable impression of you, you have a good image. If you appear to be intelligent, honest, well-organized, respected by others, and someone who gets things done, people will see you as a potential leader. They will trust you and award you with leadership opportunities.

Some students are recognized early for their athletic performance. Others are identified with artistic or academic excellence. Still others are noted for their outstanding personalities, which make them instantly popular wherever they go. As a result of their superior accomplishments, these students often become well known and are given leadership roles. To maintain a leadership image, though, these students need qualities other than the talents that won them recognition.

Leaders have positive self-concepts. They are self-motivated—they don't need someone else to push them along. They are also knowledgeable in all the areas related to the organization they are leading.

It is possible to overcome a negative self-concept. You can learn to like yourself and develop self-confidence. Psychologists tell people who lack confidence that they should participate in activities at which they can excel. "Find something you're good at and do it," they say.

When he was a junior in high school, Harry was very shy and self-conscious. He was the tallest person in school but too slow-moving to play basketball. Other students teased him about his height and his lack of speed. Harry thought his hair was ugly and that his ears and nose were too big. His self-concept was low, and he felt his chances for success were limited.

One day his English teacher had Harry write a report on the life of Abraham Lincoln. Harry discovered that President Lincoln had many of the same problems Harry had. Harry read that Lincoln was a very homely man who had had many disappointments. Despite his physical defects and lowly beginnings, Lincoln became one of the most famous men in American history.

The story of Lincoln inspired Harry. Perhaps he, too, could overcome his homely appearance and low self-esteem. So he set goals to improve his appearance. He had his hair cut by a cosmetologist so that his hair covered the top of his ears. He thought he looked better. Then he joined the debate club to improve his communication skills. Next he joined VICA and that motivated him to work even harder on his self-improvement goals. It was hard to participate in club meetings, but it became easier each time he spoke before the group.

In his senior year, Harry was elected treasurer for his VICA club. Harry felt that his image had changed as he worked hard for his club and school.

Learning Leadership Skills

Preparing for leadership is a very important part of your education. You can start learning how to be a leader early in your school years. You can continue learning on through high school and through your entire adult life. By studying and practicing leadership skills, you can learn to be a good leader.

The best way to learn leadership skills is to take part in activities with others. An important part of good leadership is cooperation. If you don't know how already, you must learn to cooperate.

Vocational education clubs, such as the Vocational Industrial Club of America and the Future Homemakers of America, provide lots of opportunities to build confidence. Club members work on projects in areas for which they have an interest and a talent. Other clubs, such as the Circle K Clubs of Kiwanis International, concentrate on developing good self-concepts and high self-esteem.

Participation in school organizations is an ideal way to develop your leadership skills and have some fun at the same time. Wouldn't one of these groups have some people and activities that would interest you?

Communication Skills

Because they are so important to success, a whole chapter of this book, Chapter 10, is devoted to communication skills. As important as communication skills—listening, speaking, reading, and writing—are to the average worker, they are even more important for leaders. Almost all successful leaders are outstanding communicators. As an example, world leader and fortieth president of the United States, Ronald Reagan, is often referred to as "The Great Communicator."

The communication skills of listening and reading are important because they are learning skills. Leaders usually must know many things—they can never stop learning. Two good ways to learn are to listen to others and to read.

Writing is also an important skill for most leaders. In the business world leaders write lots of memos and reports describing their ideas and plans to workers and investors. The success of the company can depend on how clearly and persuasively the leader writes these messages.

The ability to use correct English and speak fluently is essential to leadership. Many leaders must make formal speeches from time to time, and almost all leaders must be skilled at **extemporane-** ous speaking. Extemporaneous means spontaneous and unprepared.

For their formal speeches, leaders carefully write out and practice what they are going to say. In conducting meetings, though, they do not have an opportunity to prepare and practice. They must be able to react quickly to what other people are saying. Speaking effectively in these situations is a very valuable skill. If you are like most people, you get nervous, even scared, at the idea of speaking in front of a group of people. You can overcome this fear with desire and hard work. The following suggestions may help.

- If you have any grammatical weaknesses, learn and practice proper grammar.
- Do lots of writing. Concentrate on saying what you want to say as clearly and precisely as possible.
- Work at increasing your vocabulary. It also helps to learn famous quotations and funny stories to fit different occasions.
- Use a tape recorder to evaluate and improve your speech delivery.
- If possible, videotape your speeches in private to improve your facial expressions and gestures.
- Get suggestions from teachers and friends.
- Look for opportunities to speak in public.
- Practice, practice, practice.

Don't expect to become one of the world's great speakers in just a few weeks. It takes time and effort.

The only way to conquer your fear is to force yourself to speak in front of others. Many of the world's most successful business and political leaders had to struggle to overcome this fear.

The time and effort you put into developing communication skills will increase your chances for successful leadership. Chapter 10 provides more information on how to develop these skills.

Almost everyone has a fear of speaking before large audiences. Not all leaders must give formal speeches, but all leaders do need to speak clearly and effectively.

You, as a Leader

Right now you may have no desire to be a leader. If not, why should you concern yourself with developing leadership skills? Maybe you don't think you'll be a leader.

There are lots of leadership roles, though, in our economy, and not just at the very top. Big companies have different departments, each of which needs a leader. And the departments are divided into divisions, and the divisions into segments, and so on. There can be hundreds or even thousands of leaders between the top leader and newly hired workers.

Many people are forced into leadership positions in adult life. Workers who had no intention of leading others often accept promotions into management and leadership positions. Someday you may fill one of these leadership positions.

Use the following checklist to examine your leadership qualities. Each statement that accurately describes you indicates a positive attitude and leadership qualities.

- I enjoy working with all people.
- I respect the rights of others.
- I enjoy helping other people in need.
- I try to never embarrass other people.
- I try to avoid arguments and making other people angry.
- I never take unfair advantage of others.
- I try to avoid becoming angry.
- I try not to show off my knowledge.
- I am dependable and responsible.
- I am friendly to all and smile often.
- I am a good listener.
- I admit my mistakes.
- I try to remember other people's names.

- I try not to talk loudly, swear, or participate in horseplay.
- I dress neatly and appropriately for the occasion.
- I do my best at home, in school, and at work.
- I have enthusiasm and a sense of humor.
- I congratulate others for high achievement.
- I make good, quick decisions.
- I try to profit from constructive criticism.
- I practice on improving my grammar, speech, and voice.
- I strive to develop positive attitudes.
- I accept honors and awards graciously.
- I try not to brag about achievements.
- I hold no ethnic prejudices.
- I try not to be sarcastic and arrogant.
- I am courteous, polite, and sincere.
- I follow the golden rule ("Do unto others as you would have others do unto you.").
- I am slow to criticize others.
- I accept assignments cheerfully from supervisors.
- I obey all local, state, and national laws.

Remember, these statements are for your self-evaluation. Try to think most often about those you do *not* practice. Your goal is to be able to answer, "Yes, I do that," after reading each statement. If you can do this, you will probably be an effective leader someday.

Reluctant Leaders

Some people have all the leadership qualities, but have no desire to be leaders. One such person was the legendary Roman leader, Cinncinatus. Cinncinatus preferred farming to leadership and when Roman leaders sent word to Cinncinatus that Rome was being threatened by hostile tribes, the messengers found Cinncinatus plowing his fields. With his country in danger, Cinncinatus quickly took charge of the Roman forces and led them to victory against the enemy. As the conquering hero, Cinncinatus could have been the leader of Rome. Instead, he chose to return to his fields and his plowing.

Over a thousand years later another leader and hero, George Washington, was the called the *American Cinncinatus,* because he led his country only as long as he thought his country needed him. Cinncinatus and George Washington were both reluctant leaders, but great leaders.

Conducting Meetings

Leaders are frequently responsible for conducting meetings. This is an important responsibility. Meetings are usually held to make business decisions and plans for the future. How the meetings are conducted has a lot to do with whether or not the meeting results in good decisions and plans.

Conducting a meeting is not as simple as it might sound. The leader must give everyone a chance to speak, but still reach some conclusions. The leader must keep the meeting on track so the purposes of the meeting can be accomplished. In this section you will learn some skills that will help you conduct productive meetings.

Parliamentary Procedure

Long ago, members of democratic gatherings found that they needed rules for group discussions. Without rules, some people did all the talking, while others never got to speak. Gradually people developed rules that helped keep meetings running fairly and smoothly.

Some of the first crude rules were used in England's Parliament (England's version of our Congress) in 1580. These rules were revised and published in 1583. As more and more people began using the rules, they became known as **parliamentary procedure**.

Parliamentary procedure is a democratic method of conducting meetings. It is as important today as it ever was. Today's leaders may not follow the rules as strictly as leaders used to, but the principles are still there. It is through these principles that leaders can give everyone an opportunity to express their opinions, and then reach a majority decision.

Parliamentary procedure is based on the following principles.

- During a debate, group members must be fair and polite.
- Any member of the group may debate under the established rules.
- The majority (group with the most votes) decides the issues.
- The minority (group with the least votes) is free to express its opinion.
- Minority members must go along with the decision made by the majority.

Everyone who belongs to a club or organization should learn parliamentary procedure. Knowing parliamentary rules can help you become a leader in your school and at work. Many of today's local, state, and national leaders are still using the parliamentary skills they learned in school clubs and organizations.

Parliamentary Terms

Listed below are some terms commonly used in meetings conducted by the rules of parliamentary procedure. You will need to know the meanings of these terms if you wish to participate in any meetings using the procedure.

Not all of the terms or rules used in parliamentary procedure are listed here. If you are elected to office or want to learn more about parliamentary procedure, study *Robert's Rules of Order Newly Revised* (1970, Scott, Foresman, and Co., Glenview, IL.).

Acclamation: A method of voting Yes without a ballot. Used in the election of officers.

Adjourn: A motion to close the meeting.

Agenda: List of items to be covered in a meeting.

Amend: To change a motion by another motion.

Assembly: The gathering of eligible members at a meeting.

"Aye": Formal word for Yes. *Aye* is pronounced ī.

Ballot: A written vote, usually made in secret.

Chair or Chairperson: The person who is in charge of the meeting.

Convene: The act of getting together for the meeting; to call a meeting to order.

Debate: A discussion in which members present arguments for opposite sides of an issue.

Debatable: A motion that may be discussed by the members.

Gavel: A hammer-like mallet used by the chairperson to bring the meeting to order.

(to) Have the Floor: Permission to speak to the group.

Majority: A number greater than one-half of all the votes cast by the voting members.

Meeting: The length of time a group remains together without adjournment.

Minority: A number less than one-half of the voting members at a meeting.

School organizations do not usually conduct local meetings according to the strictest interpretation of parliamentary rules. To participate in many national meetings, however, you would want to be familiar with the rules of parliamentary procedure.

Minutes: The written record of what is said and done during a meeting. The secretary keeps and reads the minutes.

Motion: A formal proposal for action.

"Nay": Formal word for No.

New Business: Topic brought before the group for the first time.

"Point of Order": A statement made (without permission) by a member to question a ruling or to enforce the regular rules.

"Call to Question": Statement made by a member when that member believes it is time to vote on a motion.

Quorum: The minimum number of members that must be present at a meeting for the group to conduct official business.

Recess: A short intermission.

"Second": A statement made by a member who approves of a motion made by another member of the group. At least one member must second a motion before that motion can be discussed.

Standing Vote: A voting method in which members stand up to signify "Yes" or "No" on the motion.

Table the Question: A motion to postpone making a decision on a motion being discussed.

Unfinished Business: Topic brought before the members for at least the second time.

Voting: An expression of preference or opinion by eligible members of a group.

Withdraw a Motion: A request by a member who made a motion to cancel the motion. This request must be made before the motion has a second or a vote.

Planning a Meeting

The president of an organization or club is usually responsible for planning meetings. Careful planning is very important. It will keep the meetings interesting and productive. This will keep attendance high and help to build a spirit of cooperation and pride within the group.

Several people besides the president have definite duties concerning meetings. Committee chairpersons are responsible for having reports ready for the meeting. There may be an arrangement committee which would be responsible for obtaining a meeting room and any needed equipment. This committee might also be responsible for refreshments.

No business can be officially conducted unless a quorum is present. The number of members making up a quorum is usually a majority. The number can vary, however, depending on the organization's bylaws (rules).

Many school clubs and organizations, such as the Future Farmers of America and the Future Homemakers of America, have established procedures for conducting their meetings. The order of business below is a common procedure for meetings.

- Call to order
- Reading and approval of the minutes
- Treasurer's report
- Officers' reports
- Standing (permanent) committee reports
- Special committee reports
- Unfinished business
- New business
- Announcements
- Adjournment

If the order of business for your group has not been agreed upon, you might try the one listed above.

If you have never attended a meeting conducted according to the rules of parliamentary procedure, now is your chance. The following passages represent an imaginary meeting of a local Vocational Industrial Club of America. See if this meeting is conducted in the way you thought a properly conducted meeting would be. The meeting begins as the club president taps his gavel and says

"The meeting of the Pittsburg VICA Club will come to order. The Secretary will now read the minutes of our last meeting."

The Secretary then reads the minutes. When the secretary finishes, the president says

"Are there any corrections to the minutes?"

If no corrections are needed, the president says

"The minutes stand approved as read."

If someone points out a mistake, the minutes are corrected. Once all corrections have been made, the president would then go on to say

"We will hear the Treasurer's report".

The Treasurer then reports on the receipts, expenses, and the account balance. After the Treasurer's report is approved, the President says

"The next order of business is officers' reports."

After these reports are given, the President says

"The next order of business is to hear reports from the standing committees."

At this point the standing committees give their reports. Standing committees might include committees for membership, finance, and operations. After all the standing committees have reported, the president would say

"Next we will hear reports from the special committees."

All special committees would now give their reports. Special committees are committees created for a short time to handle upcoming events, such as Christmas parties and group picnics. After all the special committees have reported, the president would say

"Is there any unfinished business to be considered today?" (pause) *"If there is no unfinished business, the meeting is now open for new business."*

Making a Motion. It's at this point in the meeting that anyone wanting the club or organization to take some action stands up and makes a motion. Any member can make a motion to introduce a new item of business. For example, John Smith rises and addresses the chair.

"Mr. President."

The president recognizes John by calling his name. Then John says

"I move that the club buy a new ceremonial emblem before the state contest in April."

Carol Wallis, a club member who agrees with John's idea says

"I second the motion."

The president will then say

"It has been moved and seconded that the club buy a new ceremonial emblem before the state contest in April. Is there any discussion?"

At this point the members may discuss the motion. Each member who has something to say will stand, address the chair (the president), be recognized by the chair, and then state his or her opinion. If no one seconds the motion, the motion is *not* discussed or voted on.

Amending a Motion. It often happens that during the discussion of a motion someone will want to change the motion. For example, suppose Juana Mendoza thinks that in addition to a new emblem, the club needs new flags. Juana would stand and say

"Mr. President"

Once the president recognized her, Juana would say

"I wish to amend the motion by adding the words 'and new ceremonial flags' after the words 'new ceremonial emblem'."

In most cases a speaker must be recognized by the chairperson before speaking. This rule prevents meetings from becoming chaotic as everyone tries to talk at once.

If someone seconded Juana's motion, the president would say

"It has been moved and seconded that the pending motion be amended to say that the club should buy a new ceremonial emblem and ceremonial flags before the state contest in April. Is there any discussion?"

As before, the members would discuss the motion. When the time for discussion was over, or when no one had anything to say, the president would call for a vote on the amendment.

"All in favor of the amendment to the motion signify by saying 'aye'. (Pause) All opposed to the amendment signify by saying 'no'."

The president would count the votes and announce that the amendment passed or was defeated. At this point the president would either resume discussion or call for a vote on the original motion.

Tabling a Motion. It may be that someone will want to postpone voting on a motion. If so, that member will move to table the motion. For example, Bill Brown, the VICA treasurer, might be recognized and say

"We do not have money now to purchase the flags and emblem. I move that the pending motion to buy ceremonial flags and emblem be tabled."

A motion to table a pending motion may not be debated or amended. If it is seconded, it goes directly to a vote. If the motion is seconded, the president would say

"All in favor of tabling the motion say 'aye'. (pause) *All opposed to the motion say 'no'."*

If the tabling motion carries, further action on the motion is postponed until the next meeting. If the tabling motion is defeated, either discussion resumes or a vote is taken.

After all new business and any announcements have been taken care of, the president will usually ask for a motion to adjourn. After a motion to adjourn and a second to the motion, the president will then say

"All those in favor say 'aye'. (pause) *Opposed say 'no'.* (pause) *I declare this meeting adjourned."*

If the club members wish to adjourn before completing all business, someone must make a motion. The motion must be seconded and a vote taken without discussing or amending. A majority vote is required.

Motions

As you read about the VICA meeting, you learned that

- business is introduced at a meeting through the use of motions.
- a motion is a proposal made by a member requesting some action by the group. At most meetings any member may make a motion.
- after a motion is made, it must receive a second from another member before it can be discussed by the members.
- Before a member can make a motion, he or she must stand and be recognized by the chair.

Only one main motion at a time can be discussed by the group. Secondary motions to amend a main motion must be voted on before the main motion comes to a vote.

Only the most basic kinds of motions were included in the imaginary VICA meeting. There are many additional kinds of motions. Reading about these will help you participate more fully in future meetings.

A motion to *reconsider* allows the results of a vote to be put aside. The motion in question is discussed and voted on again later. Only a member who voted with the majority can move to reconsider. For a reconsider vote to pass, it must be seconded and receive a majority vote.

A motion to *postpone*, either indefinitely or for a definite time, stops consideration of a motion. A motion to postpone cannot be made when someone has the floor. It must have a second, it is debatable, and it requires a majority vote.

An indefinite postponement can be reconsidered only if the majority votes to do so. A postponement to a definite time can only be amended according to the amount of time. A definite postponement is debatable only in regard to the reasons for postponement.

The motion to *refer to a committee* is used to send a business matter to a committee for study and recommendation.

The motion to *limit* or *extend debate* is used to set the amount of time allowed for the debate of a motion. This type of motion requires a two-thirds vote of those present. The person making this motion cannot interrupt while someone else has the floor. The motion must be seconded, is not debatable, and cannot be reconsidered. The time limit may be amended.

The motion to *lay on the table* is used to delay action until a more favorable time or until more facts are available. This motion must be seconded and cannot be debated, amended, or reconsidered. It can be taken from the table later in the same meeting or during the next meeting. The question cannot be considered at a special meeting unless members are notified in advance. If the business is not taken up at one of these three possible times, the question dies.

The motion to *appeal* is used by a member to question a decision of the chair. The appeal is stated immediately after the chair's decision and is in order even if someone else has the floor. A motion to appeal must have a second. A majority vote in the negative is required to reverse the chair's decision.

A member makes a *point of order* motion when he or she thinks someone else has violated a rule. To make this motion the person says "I rise to a point of order." A point of order does not require a second and is not debatable or amendable. The motion is decided by the chair, often on the advice of the parliamentarian (expert on rules), and no vote is taken. Before making a point of order, a member

If someone does or says something contrary to the rules, you may "rise to a point of order." Make sure you are right before you do this.

should carefully consider its importance. It can be a source of disruption to the meeting if made without good reason.

The motion to request a *division of a question* is sometimes used when there are two or more ideas in one motion. The ideas can then be considered and voted on separately. This motion cannot interrupt a speaker or be reconsidered. It requires a second and is amendable, but is not debatable. A majority vote decides.

The motion for *division of assembly* is made if there is doubt about the vote count. In a small group a show of hands may be adequate for voting. In larger groups a standing vote counted by appointed members is required.

The member making the division-of-assembly motion may interrupt. No second is needed, and the motion is not debatable, amendable, or able to be reconsidered. The motion is decided by the chair who may request another vote.

A *question of privilege* is used to call attention to physical problems or distractions in the meeting room. As an example, this motion might be stated by saying, "I rise to a point of personal privilege. This is a cold room. Can someone turn up the heat?" Such a motion requires no second and is not debatable or amendable. It does not require a vote —the chair makes a ruling on the question.

The motion to *suspend the rules* is used to propose a deviation from the standard rules of procedure. This motion may be used to consider a question out of its proper order on the agenda. The motion must have a second, but it cannot interrupt a speaker or be reconsidered, debated, or amended. A two-thirds vote is required to pass the motion.

An *objection-to-consider* motion is used to prevent consideration of a motion when a member does not want the motion to come before the assembly. The objection can interrupt a speaker and does not need a second. A two-thirds vote is needed to carry the motion.

The motion to *withdraw a motion* permits the person making the motion to remove it from the floor. This is done when discussion and debate show that there is no need for the motion. It is not debatable, amendable, and only a negative vote can be reconsidered. It cannot interrupt a speaker and requires a second. The decision to withdraw the motion is made by the chair when there is no objection from the meeting.

The *request for parliamentary inquiry* is a motion directed to the chair by a member who wants more information on a parliamentary question. The motion is decided by the chair and no vote is required. It is not seconded, debatable, or amendable. It can interrupt a speaker but not be reconsidered.

Election of Officers

The democratic process requires leaders to be nominated and elected by the members of the club or organization. Nominations are made from the floor by the members, by a committee, or by ballot.

In many clubs, new officers are nominated by a committee. The members of the committee are either appointed by the president or elected by the members. The committee should be given enough time to make selections and contact persons to be nominated. Some clubs instruct the nominating committee to select two persons for each office. Other clubs require that the nominating committee choose only one person for each office.

On the date set for the election, the president asks for a report from the chairperson of the nominating committee. An imaginary election day might go as follows.

The chairperson lists the nominations:

"For President, Shirley Davis; for Vice-President, Tim Beal; for Secretary, Kay Wells; and for Treasurer, Kim Spears."

(Officers for other offices may also be a part of the list.)

After the committee report, the president says

"For the office of President, Shirley Davis has been nominated by the Committee. Are there further nominations for President?"

Usually, if a committee made the list of nominations, there will be no further nominations. If none are made, the chair will ask again for nominations for President. If none, then the chair will say

"Are there further nominations for President? (pause) Without objection (pause) nominations are closed."

The chair will repeat this procedure for each office, saying the position and the name of the person nominated by the committee, asking twice for further nominations, and declaring nominations for that office closed. After nominations are closed, a majority vote is required to reopen.

When only one person is nominated for each office, that person is unofficially elected. But it still must be done officially. A member of the nominating committee may stand and say

"I move that we accept the nominations of the Nominating Committee and elect the new officers by acclamation."

Make a Decision

You have been nominated as an officer in a club you belong to at school. As an officer in the club you would have to spend a couple of hours after school two nights a week helping to organize and plan club activities. This after-school time is time you usually spend with your friends at a local hangout. You've always wanted to be one of the club's leaders, but you enjoy the time with your friends. What's your decision—accept the nomination, or turn it down? Give reasons for your decision.

Many of today's business and political leaders served as officers in their school organizations. There may be no better way to train for future leadership responsibilities.

REVIEW YOUR LEARNING

CHAPTER SUMMARY

The world of work needs many good leaders, especially now, as our economy is going through a period of great change. Authority itself no longer makes a leader. Leaders must earn the respect and the support of those who follow them by being mentally alert, positive, and good decision-makers. Leaders must also be intelligent, honest, knowledgeable, and in good health. You can make yourself into a leader with hard work and desire. Participation in school clubs, such as the Vocational Industrial Club of America and the Future Home-makers of America, will help you build self-confidence and develop leadership skills. The communication skills—reading, writing, listening, and speaking—are especially important skills for leaders.

Leaders in school clubs and in the world of work must frequently conduct meetings. It is very important that the meetings go smoothly and that all business is accomplished. This is why leaders must plan their meetings and know the basic rules of parliamentary procedure. Leaders must know the proper order of business, the meanings of the various motions, and the rules stating when members can and cannot make certain motions.

WORDS YOU SHOULD KNOW

chairperson
extemporaneous
minutes
motion
parliamentary procedure
point of order
quorum

STUDY QUESTIONS

1. Is authority more or less effective than it used to be as a leadership tool?
2. List at least five qualities most leaders have.
3. Give at least two reasons why the people who would make the best leaders do not always have the leadership positions.
4. How can membership in a school club help you develop your leadership skills?
5. Why are the communication skills of listening and reading important skills for leaders?
6. List eight things you can do to improve your speaking skills.
7. Why were the rules of parliamentary procedure developed?

REVIEW YOUR LEARNING   CHAPTER 15

8. What book is recommended for learning more about parliamentary procedure?
9. What is usually the first order of business after the leader calls the meeting to order?
10. What must occur before a motion can be discussed and considered?

DISCUSSION TOPICS

1. Have you ever wished that you could be a leader of a club or group? Have you ever tried to become a leader? If not, why not? Do you think you could ever be a good leader? Why or why not?
2. Think of some leaders—class, club, church, athletic teams— with which you have been associated. Do any of these leaders stand out as being especially effective? What made the best leader(s) superior to the others?
3. Do you think that the best leaders are born with leadership qualities, or do these leaders develop their skills through desire and hard work?

SUGGESTED ACTIVITIES

1. Watch a national political leader's appearance on TV. Analyze the leader's style and other characteristics that are considered important to leadership. Make notes during the appearance and write a report on your observations.
2. Look over your student body to identify a student who is a leader. List this person's personal traits that appear to be important. List any traits or characteristics this person lacks. Summarize your findings in one page or less.

BECOMING A WISE CONSUMER

PART FOUR

Unless you hit it rich, you will never quite have all the money you want. There will always be another bill to pay or something new that you need to buy. You'll work long and hard for what will seem like a lot of money. You will probably be surprised at how quickly that money disappears when you start writing the monthly checks for rent, insurance, automobile payments, and all the rest.

The five chapters in this section will help you get the most for your money. You will learn how to spend your money wisely on everything from hamburgers to car insurance. You will learn how to budget your expenses and save some money for unexpected bills. You will also learn how to handle your money through a checking account and how to decide whether or not you should buy on credit. Reading this section carefully will not help you get rich quick, but it will help you enjoy the full benefit of your hard-earned money.

You, the Consumer

You read earlier that people have basic human needs. All people must have food, water, and shelter to survive. You also read that few people are satisfied with the necessities—most people also want the luxuries that make life enjoyable.

If you are like most people, you will buy the things you need and want. When you do this buying, you are a *consumer*—a person who uses goods and services. Whether you knew it or not, you've been a consumer ever since you made your first purchase in the super market or department store.

As a consumer, you want to get the most value possible for your money. This chapter will help you do this by making you more aware of why and where you spend your money. In this chapter, you will also learn how to inspect goods for quality and how to avoid some of the more common methods people use to cheat consumers. After reading this chapter, you should be better able to get the most for your money when you buy goods and services.

Influences on Buying

In our society we have many chances to spend our money. With so many goods and services available, how do we decide which ones to buy? We must buy food, clothing, and shelter—but which food, and which pieces of clothing from the thousands that are available?

Many factors will affect your buying choices in the years to come. Being aware of these factors will help you get the most for your money. Understanding how, and by whom, you are influenced will help you become a wise consumer.

Your Income

Of course your income, more than any other factor, will influence your buying. You can't spend more than you earn, not for long anyway. If you have a high-paying job, you will be able to buy most of the things you want. If you have a low-income job, you will have to be more careful how you spend your money.

Your Work

The type of work you do will also affect your buying. If, for example, you do a lot of physical work, you will have a greater appetite than someone who sits at a desk all day. This means that you will probably eat more than an office worker and will, therefore, spend more money on food. The office worker, on the other hand, might be expected to dress in a certain way. The office worker would buy more expensive clothes than, say, a construction worker who does more physical labor.

Your Interests

What are your interests? What do you like to do in your leisure time? Whatever your interests may be, they will greatly affect your buying.

If you are interested in sports, you will probably buy such things as golf clubs, tennis racquets, and tickets to ballgames. If you like to travel, you will spend a good share of your money on gasoline or plane tickets. But if your idea of a good time is making and repairing things, you might buy lots of tools and equipment for a home workshop.

Your Environment

The climate and customs of the place where you live will affect your buying. If you live in Northern Maine, for example, you will spend money on heavy coats, snow tires, and heating bills. If you live in Southern California, you won't spend much pro-

Since she spends most of her day sitting behind a desk, this young woman spends a good deal of her money on sports equipment.

tecting yourself from the cold weather. What things would people in Southern California buy that people in Maine probably wouldn't buy?

Your Group

Do you have a certain group of close friends? If so, the people in your group will probably affect your buying. For example, if an important member of your group buys a new-style coat, you may want to buy a similar coat. Can you remember when you bought something just because a friend had one?

The people in your group are your *peers,* and the influence that your peers have on you is called *peer pressure.* Don't let peer pressure make your decisions for you. Ask yourself, "Do I buy things because *I* want them, or because I want to be part of the group?" Don't try to keep up with the group, especially if you have less money than most of your friends.

You probably don't realize how much of your buying is influenced by your friends. What things have you purchased lately just because someone you know bought one?

Advertising

Another big influence on your buying is advertising. Advertising is so much a part of our lives that most of us don't realize how much it affects us. Television, radio, billboards, newspapers, magazines—advertising is everywhere.

Advertising can help you be a wiser consumer. For example, you can find out about new and better products through advertising. You can also find the best buys when you pay attention to advertisements. Comparing prices advertised in a local newspaper, for example, can save you time and money.

Advertising can help you be a better consumer, but it can also cost you money. Most companies raise their prices to pay for their advertising costs. This means that heavily advertised products usually cost more than similar products that are not widely advertised. Don't buy a product just because you have heard of it. In many cases the less familar **brand names** (company names) offer products of equal quality.

Advertising can also cost you money if you don't think carefully about the advertised message. Advertising companies spend billions of dollars to study human behavior and to hire talented writers, artists, and salespeople. Their goal in doing these things is to convince you to buy a certain product. They use methods such as those described below to cleverly persuade you to buy their products.

Association. A favorite method of advertisers is to link a product with a popular idea or person. For example, most people think rodeos are lively and exciting. If an advertiser wants people to think a certain car is exciting to drive, the ads may show a cowhand driving this car through a rodeo.

Another example of association is the ad in which a well-known person is shown using a product. When people see the ad, they link the popularity of this famous person with the product. This will cause some people to buy the product. If the great linebacker, Bill Block, uses Kool Shave Cream, so will lots of other people.

Snob Appeal. Most of us like to believe that we are as good as or better than other people. For this reason, advertisers sometimes suggest that eating or drinking certain products will raise us above the crowd. We are told that we will be more popular, respected, or admired if we use this product.

Advertisers are competing for your attention constantly. They use every possible means to make you like and buy their products. Use the ads to gather information.

Group Appeal. As you read earlier, most people like to belong to a group. If everyone else uses a product, we think it must be good. We are told that more people take a certain cold medicine than any other brand. We see a large group of people, all drinking the same soft drink. Many of us will try the cold medicine or soft drink because we want to do what others do.

Responsible Buying

One meaning of *responsible* is the ability to choose between right and wrong. Thus, *responsible buying* is the ability to make the right buying choices. The more you know about such things as supply and demand, planned spending, and mail order buying, the better your chances of making the best buying decisions.

Supply and Demand

You read about the law of supply and demand in Chapter 13. You will remember that when the supply of a product is greater than the demand, prices go down. When the demand is greater than the supply, prices go up.

The law of supply and demand affects consumers every day. Prices are constantly rising and falling as a result of its effect. The recent series of events in the sale of personal computers is a typical example. When the first personal computers were manufactured, more people wanted computers than there were computers available. The prices were very high. But as more and more computers were manufactured, the supply increased, demand was satisfied, and prices went down.

A few days before Christmas these trees sell for over $20. How much do you think they'll be worth on December 26? The law of supply and demand causes prices to rise and fall constantly.

Try to think of other examples of how supply and demand affect prices. Have you noticed prices going up and down on a particular item in your area? It's important to understand and be aware of the law of supply and demand. This understanding can help you become a more effective consumer.

Long-Range Buying Plans

You will be able to pay less for many of the things you buy if you make a long-range buying plan. To make such a plan work, you will need to save a little money each payday for things you will buy in the future. You can then buy each item at the best possible buying time—when the prices are lowest.

The first step in long-range planning is to **inventory**, make a list, of the items you now have. In your inventory, note the condition of each item. This will help you determine how long the items will last and when they will need to be replaced.

The second step is to determine what you will need to buy during the upcoming year. For example, after doing your clothing inventory, consider your needs for school, work, sports, and "dress-up" clothes—as well as clothes for different seasons. If the clothes you already have won't meet these needs, you can plan to buy the clothes you do need.

Wise consumers use this type of two-step process to make long-range buying plans. By using such a plan they avoid being without a necessary item at a time when the item is priced high. Long-range planning ensures that these people buy what they want when they want it.

If you inventory what you have and decide when you will need new items, you can buy them at the lowest possible price. If you know you will need a new swimming suit next summer, you should buy it when the prices are marked down at the end of the preceding summer.

Make a Decision

The battery in your car is dead. You learn that you can buy a well-known, brand-name battery for $100, with a five-year warranty. You can buy another battery with a three-year warranty for $50. The salesperson hasn't had much experience selling batteries, but he thinks the cheaper battery is a good one. What's your decision—do you buy the $100 battery, or the $50 battery? Give reasons for your decision.

Shopping for Value

After completing your inventory and doing long-range planning, you are ready to do your shopping. A wise consumer knows the following things about shopping.

- How to judge quality
- Which items receive heavy use and need to be of better quality
- What makes one item wear longer than another
- What the difference in cost should be for different levels of quality

Think about how you will use your purchase. Will you use it every day or just two or three times a month? Is it something that will get worn from use (like shoes), or will it only be "looked-at" (like a wall poster)? Is it something you will use for months or years, or will you use it just this week? Your answers to these questions will help you know which items need to be of better quality.

Checking Quality. Usually the most important factor in shopping for value is judging the quality of products. It is especially important that purchases you will use often or for a long time should be of good quality. You can determine quality by checking what the product is made of and how it is made. For example,

- tightly woven cloth usually wears longer than open weaves.
- leather usually wears longer than plastic.
- heavy, thick plastic lasts longer than light-weight plastic.
- stainless steel outlasts aluminum.

For most purchases you will want to take the time to check quality. This is especially important when you will be using the product for a long time. In looking at the sleeves of these two sweaters, can you tell which sweater is the higher quality sweater?

A list such as this could go on and on. There's a great deal to learn about various materials and the quality of those materials. If you know someone who uses a product similar to the one you want to buy, ask that person about its quality.

How an item is made also affects how long it will last. The seams in clothing should be made with small and even stitches. Check the strength of all fasteners. Rough edges usually mean the item was made quickly, and maybe poorly. From experience, you will learn what makes one item last longer than another. Learn from both your good and bad purchases.

Price and Quality. Usually things of better quality cost more than things of lesser quality. This is not always true, though. The price of an item is not always a good guide to its quality. Sometimes a less expensive product is just as good as a costlier one.

There are several reasons why items of the same quality would have different prices. One reason is supply and demand, which you read about earlier. If one item is in demand when another is not, the item in demand will cost more, regardless of quality.

Different prices for equal quality also result from the different quantities companies buy. Large companies buy in large amounts. When they do this, they can buy at a low price. A small company buying smaller amounts has to pay a higher price.

Thus, the small company must charge its customers more for the same item.

Lee paid $55 for some brown Neet-Fit boots at Monroe's Shoe Store in downtown Whiteville. He had worn Neet-Fit shoes before and knew they were a good brand. The next day, Lee and his friend Pat were at the Bigtown Discount Store. Lee saw brown Neet-Fit boots exactly like his, except the price was $45. Lee was angry. He felt cheated.

Pat tried to explain that Monroe's had to charge more. They bought only a few pairs of each size and style, so they didn't get the quantity discount that Bigtown received. Pat explained that Monroe's paid higher rent because their store was downtown. Bigtown was outside the city limits. Also, Monroe's paid salespeople to measure Lee's feet, get the right size for him, and make sure that the boots fit him. At Bigtown Lee would have to get the boots from the shelf and check the fit without help. No wonder he paid more at Monroe's.

Another reason for different prices for the same quality has to do with brand names. Many people buy well-known brands thinking these brands are of better quality. Sometimes they are of better quality, sometimes they're not.

Many products sold under unknown brands are identical to the higher-priced, well-known brands. For example, household appliances made by a large company are sometimes sold to smaller companies, who then put their own brand name on the appliances. Food canning companies do this, too. The same food is canned, then different labels are put on the cans. The smart shopper learns it is possible to get the same, high-quality items a lot cheaper under an unknown brand.

Can you see how much there is to know about price and quality? If you feel you need help in making wise purchases, you might check some consumer magazines. These magazines offer much information on the quality of products.

Buying by Mail

Being a wise consumer is harder than ever when you shop by mail. When you shop by mail, you must depend on the advertisement for your information because you cannot actually see what you are buying.

Most of us shop by mail now and then. We like to send in for things we want, especially if they seem to be bargains. Here are some tips to help you buy wisely through the mail.

- Have a good reason for shopping by mail. Is the item something you can't find locally? Is the price lower by mail? When you shop by mail, you don't see the item you are buying before ordering, and it takes time and postage to order.
- Read the catalog or advertisement carefully. What sizes does the product come in? What colors are available? What is it made of? Is it ready to use? Does it have to be put together?
- Print your order carefully. Give your name, address, and zip code. Copy the item number, color, and size that you want.
- Never send cash. Send a check for the exact amount and keep the cancelled check as a receipt. If you don't have a checking account, send a bank check or money order.
- Record your order. List the date, the company's name and address, the item, cost, and number of the check or money order. Keep this information for your records.
- If you don't receive your order within thirty days, write to the company. Ask what has happened to your order.
- If you receive your order and don't like it, send it to the company's customer service department. Attach a letter to the package telling what is wrong with the item. Be sure to insure the package and keep the receipt.

Large mail-order companies depend on repeat orders. They try to correct all errors and please customers. A few smaller companies, however, may not be so careful about correcting errors. Later in this chapter you will read about reporting consumer problems.

Selling prices for similar items may not be the same in all stores. These same boots may cost more or less at another store. Quality, supply and demand, service, and business expense affect the selling price.

Before you buy by mail make sure you have a good reason for doing so. You can't inspect and compare items you receive through the mail until you've already purchased them.

Make a Decision

You have decided that you are going to buy a new stereo system. A local store has some top-rated systems, but all the prices seem too high. A mail order catalog lists some of the same systems at lower prices, but you are worried about buying a system that would be shipped almost all the way across the country. You have heard that a new discount stereo shop will be opening in your neighborhood in three months, so you could wait and see what the new store has to offer. What's your decision—buy locally now, buy through the mail, or wait and hope for a better deal? Give reasons for your decision.

Types of Fraud

Most business people believe that honesty and quality products and services lead to a successful business. These people usually give the best-possible service and produce the best-possible products.

Some business people, however, try to cheat their customers. This practice of trying to trick or cheat consumers is known as **consumer fraud**. Being aware of some of the more common types of fraud will help you detect dishonest business people.

Auto Service and Repair

Millions of people must frequently have their cars and trucks serviced and repaired. With so many customers needing their services, some people in the car repair business see a great chance to use fraud.

Fraud occurs when a mechanic replaces parts that do not need replacing. It also occurs when the labor cost is *padded*. This means that the customer is charged for work that wasn't done at all or for more hours than were actually worked.

Here is what happened in one large U.S. city. After many people had complained about a transmission repair shop, the state attorney general sent agents to investigate. The agents put a defective part in a new car so that the car wouldn't run properly. The agents then asked the transmission repair shop to fix their car. As expected, the shop owners had an entirely new transmission put into the car at a cost of several hundred dollars. As a result, the shop owners were arrested, and the shop was closed. The people who had complained about the shop were able to file lawsuits to get back their money.

Service-station owners and their employees have also been caught replacing parts that work fine. One trick is for the employee to remove the air filter from the engine and replace it with a used, dirty filter. The car owner is then told that a new filter is badly needed. The same trick is used to sell car batteries and other parts.

Many types of fraud can occur when you have your car serviced or repaired. The best way to avoid this type of fraud is to find a reliable mechanic and become a regular customer.

When you're a long way from home, it's a good idea to have someone stay close to your car. Most people are honest, but it doesn't hurt to play it safe.

Sometimes service people actually do real damage to a car. Some of these tricks have been called the *fifty-percenters*. The owner and the employee split the profit in half, "fifty-fifty." They do this most often when the drivers are from out of state and seem to know little about cars.

Some service-station owners have been known to mix regular gasoline with premium and sell this at the premium price. This practice gives the station a higher profit. Another tactic is to install a less-expensive oil in place of a better oil. The owner doesn't notice, and again the station owner makes a higher profit.

It is important to protect yourself against dishonest automobile service and repair people, especially if you do not know much about cars. The following suggestions will help you avoid fraud.

- **Be a regular customer**—Try to become a regular customer at one service station rather than going to different stations. The people at that station will get to know you. Once they know who you are these people will probably give you better service than they would a stranger. They will be less likely to take advantage of you.

- **Keep it serviced**—To avoid breakdowns on the road, keep your car serviced. It is very important to have tires, batteries, hoses, and belts checked often. Have your car checked and serviced before long trips. A great many incidents of auto fraud occur when people are away from home.

- **Don't leave**—Be careful when you stop at unfamiliar service stations. Don't leave your car. Watch the attendant while the car is being serviced.

- **Watch closely**—When you stop for gasoline, watch closely if the attendant starts to do something unexpected, such as take off the air filter. Also be careful if the attendant checks the battery with a tester or inspects other parts of the car without your asking. Don't be talked into buying parts for your car if the attendant does one of the things mentioned above.

- **Use a reliable place**—For major repairs and tune-ups, take your car to a place with a good service department.

- **Discuss the work**—Discuss the list of things you want done to your car before signing the work order. Don't let extra work be done until you understand the problem and know the cost. Most owners and mechanics are honest, but it's a good idea to show your interest in the work being done.

- **Use praise**—Everyone likes to be told they are doing a good job. A little praise and courtesy for the people who service your car may help you get the best service.

Bargains and Contests

Sometimes consumers are cheated by retail stores. Some consumers are cheated without knowing it.

One frequently used trick is called *bait and switch*. An advertised bargain "baits" people to get them into the store. When they get to the store, though, they find that the store is out of the bargain item. The salesperson then suggests a similar item that is much more expensive. By using this trick the store doesn't lose money on its "sale." The store also makes money from many of the extra customers who came in for the bargain.

The *contest winner* is another trick used to cheat the consumers. It works like this. You are called on the telephone and asked a simple question anyone could answer. After you answer the question, you are told you are a winner. Your "prize" is a discount on one of the store's products. Unless the discount is really a big one, the prize may not be a prize at all. You may end up paying what the item is actually worth. In such a case the store tries to make you think you are a winner when you are not.

Sometimes salespeople try to sell customers an item priced higher than the one advertised. Don't buy the higher priced item unless you are sure that's what you want.

Door-to-Door Sales

Some door-to-door salespeople are dishonest. One of the oldest door-to-door frauds is the phony magazine subscription. You should be suspicious if you are told any of the following.

- "I'm working my way through college."
- "I'm selling for a charity group."
- "I'm earning points for a promotion."

Not all door-to-door magazine salespeople are dishonest, but be careful.

Encyclopedia salespeople have also been known to trick consumers. The salesperson might offer you a big discount on the new edition if you let the company use your name to promote the books. To accept this offer you are asked to pay $50 down on the books you will get. Many times the salesperson and your $50 are never seen again.

Door-to-door salespeople must, however, register with local officials, and in many cities buy permits. If a door-to-door salesperson seems dishonest to you, ask to see identification or a city permit. If you have any questions about salespeople or their companies, call your local police station. Someone there may be able to help you.

Be careful about buying from door-to-door salespeople. Many have good products at reasonable prices, but many others do not.

Used Cars

If you want to buy a car, you will probably check the newspaper want ads. You will find "for sale by owner" ads. Be careful of these ads. The sellers are sometimes part-time salespeople. They may give false reasons for selling their cars at low prices. It is usually better to buy from a dealer who will give you a guarantee.

Home Inspections

Beware of people who come to your home, unasked, offering free inspections. Some of these people will check your roof, furnace, or insulation, and then tell you that repairs are badly needed. Some pest-control companies also do a free, unasked-for inspection—then tell you that you have termites.

The wise homeowner questions free inspections, especially by people from another city. Deal with a local business. Check on these inspectors as you would door-to-door salespeople.

Social Clubs

Lonely people are often cheated by social clubs, such as *lonely hearts clubs.* These clubs charge very high fees and take advantage of people. Computer dating is another so-called service that may include fraud.

Lawsuits have been brought against some dance studios by people who felt they had been cheated. The studio gave two or three free lessons. Then the people were talked into signing up for more lessons. Before they knew it, these people had signed contracts costing them several hundred dollars.

Job and Educational Opportunities

Young people sometimes learn about fraud when they try to get jobs or more education. High school and college graduates must be careful about offers to sell insurance, go into their own business, or get extra education.

To attract students, correspondence schools often make false promises. Sometimes they are dishonest about the real chances for jobs.

Beware of high school diplomas and college degrees offered by non-accredited (not officially approved) schools. Unless the school is accredited, the diploma or degree is worthless.

While she was in the work-experience program during her senior year, Dorothy worked in a legal office. Last month Dorothy graduated from high school, and she is now employed full-time in the legal office.

Recently Dorothy received a letter from an out-of-state school urging her to study law by correspondence. When she finished the course, the letter said, she would get an immediate promotion.

Dorothy showed the letter to Mrs. Lynn, her supervisor. Mrs. Lynn said schools and businesses sometimes get lists of graduates. These graduates are then contacted about job and educational opportunities. In many cases these schools and businesses make false promises.

Mrs. Lynn also said that the school writing to Dorothy was non-accredited, and that graduating from the school would not help Dorothy earn a promotion. Mrs. Lynn suggested that Dorothy consider the local community college. Not only did the community college cost less, credits earned there could eventually help Dorothy advance on her job.

Foods

Did you ever buy a can of peaches that contained more juice than peaches? How can you tell if a can has the food in it that it's supposed to have? The answer to that question is "Read the label."

The law requires the contents of food packages to be listed on the labels. The law also says that the ingredients should be listed in order of amount. The ingredient making up the biggest part of the product must be listed first, then the ingredient making up the second biggest part, and so on.

Nutritional information on food packages is voluntary—it is not required by law. But if the food contains added nutrition (or is advertised as having it) the label must say that.

Fats and cholesterol are listed on the label to help consumers on special diets. Artificial flavoring must be listed on the label. The word *imitation*

Foods in health food stores and other speciality shops usually cost more than the same foods would cost in a supermarket. Read the labels and compare.

Get in the habit of reading food labels. You can learn a lot about what you are eating and you'll probably become a smarter shopper.

must be used when the food doesn't come from natural sources. For example, a lemon pie made without real lemons must say "imitation lemon flavor" on the label. It also must compare well with the taste of real lemons.

In one large city, inspectors found that hamburger had been mixed with horsemeat, which is much cheaper than hamburger. Before being stopped, the dealers made a lot of money by tricking buyers. Some meat processors have also been caught adding a soybean product to ground meat. Under the labeling laws, soybeans should have been listed as an ingredient.

Government agencies frequently file lawsuits against people for selling impure food. In many cases, careless work, not fraud, caused such foods as candies and peanut butter to become impure.

Another kind of food fraud has to do with the sale of *natural* foods. Our laws do not give a definition of natural foods, but natural foods should definitely not have artificial or imitation ingredients.

Natural foods should not have preservatives (chemicals added to prevent spoilage). Nor should they have added coloring or be grown with commercial fertilizers or sprays. Yet some laboratories have tested so-called natural foods and found bits of insect sprays—just as most foods do.

It is often hard to tell natural foods just by looking at them or tasting them. Check the labels carefully. If necessary, ask the store owner or product supplier questions.

Drugs

In watching old movies on television, you have probably seen traveling medicine shows. Around the turn of the century in this country, fast-talking salespeople made great claims about the curing powers of their medicines. Most people in rural areas and small towns enjoyed the show's music and entertainment. A few were tricked when they bought the medicine.

Sometimes the medicine consisted of herbs mixed with alcohol. The alcohol made the user think the medicine was helpful. In some cases people were poisoned by the drugs. These drugs were mixed by people with no knowledge of chemistry.

This salesman is probably telling his audience that the content of that bottle can cure every illness known. Today government agencies protect consumers against false claims.

Traveling medicine shows no longer exist, but today many drugs are advertised on radio, television, and in newspapers. Some of these drugs are made by companies whose claims have been proven false.

Government agencies have a great deal of control over what the drug companies do and sell. Some of these companies have been forced to change their advertisements. Some commercials no longer say that a certain product is a cure. Instead, the commercials say the product will make the user feel or look better. Companies must pay large fines if they don't obey orders to stop false product claims.

Rosa's consumer education class was studying fraud in advertising. One evening she heard a TV commercial that sounded like a fraud. Fast Action aspirin was being advertised as "twice as strong as Ease aspirin."

The following day Rosa found both brands of aspirin at a discount drug store. She was surprised when she read the list of ingredients on each label. Each Fast Action tablet contained ten grains of aspirin, while Ease tablets had only five grains each.

Rosa decided that not all commercials that sound dishonest, really were. She realized the importance of reading labels on food and drugs.

Health Care

Many people are uncertain about whether or not they are getting the best health care possible for their money. They don't know how to judge either the ability or the honesty of doctors. In an emergency, they want medical help immediately—they don't take the time to carefully select a doctor. They simply go to whoever is available.

Fraud in health care is hard to identify and prove. How can you prove that some expensive tests or treatments were not needed and were done only so the doctor could collect a fee? Some tests and treatments are done to be on the "safe side."

Most surgery that's done is necessary. The real value of some operations, however, is doubtful. It's often hard to know which tests and treatments are needed, and which aren't.

Some hospitals and nursing homes have been charged with fraud. Sometimes the fraud occurs when the patient is charged for medicine or services that he or she never received. In some cases false charges for doctors' visits have been discovered. The following suggestions will help you protect yourself from health care fraud.

- Ask your doctor's advice before taking any drugs.
- Know the usual costs for health care in your area.
- Choose a doctor carefully. The local hospital has a list of doctors on its staff. Ask your friends and family members to make suggestions. Learn as much as you can about the doctor you select.
- Select a hospital before you need one. Don't wait until there is an emergency. The hospital should be accredited (approved by the state health department). Find out if it is a teaching hospital. Such hospitals usually have more doctors on their staffs.
- When possible, discuss costs before entering a hospital. Compare rates.
- If health insurance pays your bill, check to see if the charges are correct. If they're not, sooner or later the insurance company will have to raise its rates.
- Do not rush into surgery or tests. Find out the reasons and the risks. A good doctor usually tells you these things without being asked.

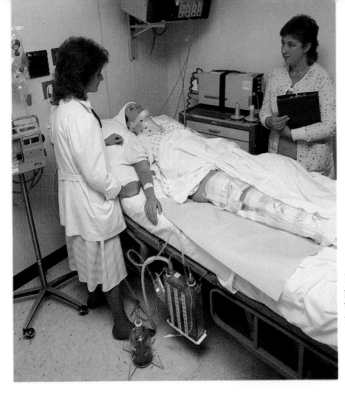

Health care has become too expensive for most people. Avoid the tendency to treat the health care situation different from other consumer situations. Check your bills, ask questions, and don't be intimidated.

- Before any surgery, get an opinion from another doctor. A good doctor won't object if you consult someone else.
- To get the most help from a visit to a doctor, make a list of what you want to ask. Don't be afraid to ask questions. If you don't understand the doctor's answer, ask for more explanation. Remember—the doctor is working for you.

Protecting Consumers' Rights

With special laws and agencies, the federal government helps protect your consumer rights, and the rights of all consumers. Three important consumer agencies are the

- Food and Drug Administration (FDA),
- Federal Trade Commission (FTC), and
- Consumer Product Safety Commission.

Many private citizens have also joined together to form consumer groups that fight for consumer rights.

Food and Drug Administration

The **Food and Drug Administration (FDA)** is a federal agency that regulates the production and sale of foods and drugs. FDA technicians do tests and experiments on new drugs and medical devices to make sure that they are safe. FDA inspectors visit such places as bakeries and canneries to make sure that these businesses are not selling spoiled or damaged products. The FDA also sets standards and does tests to make sure that products meet the standards.

The FDA also checks product labels. The Fair Packaging and Labeling Act makes it illegal to put misleading information on a label. The label must not give the consumer the wrong idea about what's in the product or what the product can do. The FDA can take action against false and misleading labeling on the products regulated by the FDA.

The federal law requires that certain products carry labels that describe the contents and possible effects of using these products. Government agencies such as the FDA enforce the law.

Federal Trade Commission

The **Federal Trade Commission (FTC)** is a federal agency that administers several laws ensuring fair trade. The FTC prevents unfair competition and enforces rules that define unfair or deceptive acts in various industries. Consumers are most familiar with the FTC's requirement that companies place care labels and product **warranties** on their products. A warranty is a written guarantee of a product's quality and the manufacturer's promise to repair and replace defective parts.

The FTC also enforces laws that control advertising. This is done to make sure that consumers know what to expect. Like the FDA, much of the FTC's authority in this area comes from the Fair Packaging and Labeling Act.

The description of products needs to be clearly stated in all advertising. For example, a clothing manufacturer can't advertise a shirt as being wash-and-wear unless it actually is.

The FTC requires cloth manufacturers to put labels with instructions for care on all their products.

These labels give directions for proper washing or dry cleaning of that item. If you're buying material to sew, the care labels are tied to the bolts of fabric. A colored triangle on the bolt has a code number. When you buy the fabric, the salesperson can use the code to tell you how to clean that material. Knowing how to care for your clothing will save you money.

Consumer Product Safety Commission

In 1972 Congress passed a law to protect consumers from equipment that could harm the user. This law, which is part of the Consumer Product Safety Act, tries to do several things.

- Protect people from injuries caused by consumer products
- Help consumers judge the safety of products
- Encourage companies to develop products that meet safety standards.

As part of this law, the Consumer Product Safety Commission was formed. Like the FDA and FTC, the Consumer Product Safety Commission is a government agency. It determines the safety standards for products, then makes sure that the products meet those standards. This commission can take a product off the market if the product is dangerous to the user.

Consumer Groups

Consumer groups work at local, state, and national levels. These groups are aware of consumer rights. They check complaints and tell the public about them. They *lobby* (try to influence lawmakers) for the passage of laws that protect consumers.

Lobbyists work in many ways. They study the issues and publish their findings. Then they mail their findings to the lawmakers and the people who live in the lawmakers' districts. Concerned people then write to their lawmakers asking them to vote for the consumer laws. The lobbyists also talk to lawmakers and try to get their message publicized through newspapers, TV, and radio coverage.

The efforts of consumer groups have resulted in several laws that help consumers. For example, consumer groups helped bring about several highway safety laws. Under these laws, manufacturers must recall (take back) cars with faulty parts and replace or repair those parts.

Tires are also recalled when they do not pass highway tests. The people who sell tires must list each buyer's name and address with the type and serial number of the tires. If that type and number of tire is found unsafe, the buyer is notified.

Without the present consumer laws, few (if any) products would be repaired or replaced. All consumers should be grateful for the work these groups have done.

Reporting Fraud

Government agencies and consumer groups work hard to prevent fraud, but they need your help. You should realize that fraud can happen to anyone. It is everyone's responsibility to report fraud.

If you feel you've been cheated, call or visit the company. Give all the facts. Then give the company a chance to settle your claim.

If you have a problem with an out-of-town company, write to the company. The company's name and address is usually printed somewhere on the product or its package. If not, ask for help at the public library.

Writing a Complaint Letter

If you paid for a product that is faulty in some way, let the company know about it. If you can't find the company's address on a package or label, check the Standard & Poor's *Register of Corporations, Directors, and Executives* at your local library. Write directly to the president of the company if you can find a listing of the president's name.

Dear Consumer Action:

Last week I bought a shirt at Smith's. During the first washing, the shirt shrank and raveled. As I had washed it according to instructions, I was very angry.

When I returned to Smith's and asked for a refund, they said the giving me one would be against store policy. I then asked for the name of the manufacturer, and the manager would not tell me.

Can you help?

Sincerely,

Jerry Meyer

Jerry Meyer

In your letter, you should tell exactly what is wrong. Give the date and place of purchase. Include the name and model number of the product. If your problem is an order you paid for but haven't received, send the number of your check or money order. Be sure to keep a copy of your letter.

When you order an expensive item by mail, make a photocopy of the order. If you are sending payment, lay the check or money order beside the order form on the photocopy machine. You will then have a record of your order and payment. If you need to write about a problem, make another copy of this record to send with your letter of complaint.

Keep complete records of everything you buy, and never give these records to anyone. Keep ads, receipts, checks, money orders, and dates. If someone else must see these records, make photocopies. There are photocopy machines in shopping centers and libraries.

Better Business Bureau. If a company doesn't help you with your complaint after a reasonable length of time, ask the local **Better Business Bureau** for help. The Better Business Bureau is a private agency that tries to improve local business services. The Bureau tries to eliminate false adver-

tising and to settle consumer complaints. Better Business Bureaus also provide consumers with useful information through radio and TV announcements and newspaper articles.

You can usually find a telephone number for the Better Business Bureau in the Yellow Pages. If you suspect fraud, give the Bureau a call.

Other Sources of Help. You may get help on consumer problems by writing to a radio or TV station in your area. These stations often have employees who work on consumer problems. Some newspapers also offer this service. In your letter, tell what you have done to try to solve the problem—and keep a copy of your letter.

In some areas the local police department handles cases of fraud. If you feel you have been cheated, talk to your local police. Even if they don't handle problems like yours, they can tell you who does.

In many states the attorney general checks into cases of fraud. If you cannot get help in your area, write to your attorney general. You may find the address under "Government—State" in the Yellow Pages. You may also find a toll-free number for reporting fraud.

REVIEW YOUR LEARNING CHAPTER 16

◼ CHAPTER SUMMARY

As a consumer you will buy many things. Which things you buy will be affected by your income, the work you do, your interests, your environment, the group to which you belong, and advertising.

If you practice responsible buying, you will get the most for your money. To do this you must understand that the prices of the goods and services that you buy will be affected by supply and demand. You will also need a long-range buying plan to get the most for your money. Such a plan involves making an inventory of what you have and determining your primary needs. You can then buy when prices are lowest.

Be alert to any type of consumer fraud. Lobby groups, the FDA, and the FTC help prevent fraud. If you have questions, check with the Better Business Bureau in your area. You can also ask for help from your local police, newspaper, radio, or TV consumer-problem departments.

◼ WORDS YOU SHOULD KNOW

Better Business Bureau
brand names
consumer fraud
Federal Trade Commission (FTC)
Food and Drug Administration (FDA)
inventory
warranty

◼ STUDY QUESTIONS

1. What are six factors that will influence your buying?
2. What is the main goal of advertising companies?
3. What are two ways that advertising can help you become a wise consumer?
4. What are two ways that advertising can cost you money?
5. Name three methods that advertisers use to persuade people to buy certain products.
6. If half of the Florida orange crop freezes this year, will the price of oranges go up or down next year?
7. What are the two steps in a long-range buying plan?
8. What is usually the most important factor in shopping for value?

REVIEW YOUR LEARNING

9. Give three possible reasons why one product might cost more than a similar product.
10. You should have a good reason for buying by mail. Give two possible reasons.
11. Name three government agencies that work to protect consumers.
12. Name at least five things you can do to protect yourself from dishonest auto services.
13. How can you tell which ingredients make up the biggest part of a packaged food product?
14. What is the first thing you should do if you feel you've been cheated by a local company? If this doesn't work, what should you do next?

DISCUSSION TOPICS

1. What are some of the specific influences on your personal buying habits?
2. In what ways have peer groups influenced your buying?
3. What long-range planning should you do before buying a winter jacket?

SUGGESTED ACTIVITIES

1. Make an inventory of your clothing. Beside each item, write its approximate cost if you were to buy it today. Total these amounts to find the value of your clothing. At your present income, how long would it take to save enough money to replace your clothing?
2. Check the price of your favorite brand of toothpaste at a discount store, a grocery store, and a convenience store. Be sure the weight is the same each time. Is the price the same in the three places? Can you explain this?
3. From newspapers and magazines, clip examples of the methods used by advertisers to convince people to buy certain products. Use poster board to mount each clipping with the name of the advertising method as explained in this chapter.

Managing Your Money

DO YOU KNOW . . .
- why you are often "broke"?
- how to make and "stick to" a budget?
- where you can get help with your money problems?

CAN YOU DEFINE . . .
- budget?
- financial responsibility?
- money management?

Do you have enough money to buy all the things you would like to have? Do you go to the movies as often as you'd like? If your answer is "no," you may feel better knowing you aren't alone. Very few people have all the money they want.

You may have noticed, though, that some of your friends have more cash than you do. This may be true even though some of them don't earn as much money as you. Why do you think these people have money whenever they need it?

It could be that some of your friends have learned how to manage their money. Learning **money management** (using money wisely) isn't easy, however. It's sort of like learning to drive a car—you get better with practice.

In this chapter you will learn how to manage your money You will learn how to set up and stick to a budget. You will also learn how to anticipate and deal with changes in your financial situation. This type of good money management will help you get the most out of your money.

Planned Spending

To be successful in managing your money you must accept responsibility. You need to set your own goals and make a plan that will help you meet your goals. This process is called *planned spending.* The actual plan that you use to manage your money is called a **budget**. To practice planned spending you must know how to make and keep a budget.

Making a Budget

You might think that while you are in school you don't need to make a budget. But even if you have very little money and few expenses, you can benefit from making a budget. You can gain valuable budgeting experience that will help you later in life. Making a budget will also help you avoid wasting your money.

To plan a budget you must have several pieces of information. You must know what your goals are. This is where decision-making becomes important. You also need estimates of your expected expenses and income.

The first step in preparing a budget is to make a list of all your goals. Include things you want to do and to buy. If the list is very long, underline the

The first step in making a budget is to list your goals.

things that are most important to you. Copy these items on another sheet of paper.

Put the first list in your personal file for safe keeping. Someday you will enjoy looking at this list. Your goals may be the same in the future, or you may have new interests and goals. It will be interesting to see how many goals you achieve.

Now look at your second list. Cross out anything on this list that you really don't need. You must first take care of your needs. After you have budgeted money for your needs, you can plan to spend for things that you simply want.

Group your needs. You can group them under such headings as food, housing, education, and clothing. Keep a record of the amount you spend under each heading each day. Your budget sheet may look like the one at the top of the next page.

After one week of recording your expenses, see if you spent more or less than you earned. Your income, whether daily, weekly, or monthly, will not always equal expenses. Emergencies do come up. Your savings must get you through these periods.

Your expenses will probably not be exactly the same each week. Your first week may have been more or less expensive than what your average week will be. This is why it's a good idea to have a monthly, rather than a weekly, budget.

To estimate your monthly income, multiply your weekly income by four. To estimate your monthly expenses, multiply the expenses under each heading on your budget sheet by four. Add in any monthly expenses such as car payments or credit card bills. You may even have to make some new headings on your budget sheet. Your monthly record sheet may look like the one in the second column on the next page.

After making a weekly and monthly budget, you should be able to make a yearly budget. Your yearly budget would contain all the same information as your monthly budget, but for each month of the year. Remember to add in big expenses such as a down payment for a car and insurance premiums that you pay only once or twice a year. You may need to use your savings to pay for these things.

Does it look as though you will have enough money for everything? Few people have enough money to buy all the things they want. You may have to cut back your spending in certain areas. You may need to cut your expenses under clothing or recreation, for example. A budget is something

Date	Gifts or Contributions	Food	Housing	Education	Clothing	Savings	Trans-portation	Medical Care	Recreation	Insurance
1/6	$	$ —	$	$	$	$	$	$	$	$ 2.00	$
1/7		3.00						5.00			
1/8		.50			10.00						
1/9	2.00	1.50									
1/10		1.50				5.00					
1/11		.50								11.00	
1/12		4.00						1.50			
Total	2.00	11.00			10.00	5.00	6.50			13.00	

A record of your weekly expenses might look something like this. Do you spend more or less than the person who filled out this chart?

you keep working and reworking until it "fits" you. Do not expect your expenses and income to balance the first time you plan a budget. They'll come closer to balancing as time passes.

Budgeting Hints

Making and using a budget is hard, especially at first. But if you can stick to it, your budget will be an excellent tool for managing your money. It will show you where you spend too much. It will help you match your expenses to your income.
Here are some tips that will help you stick to your budget and keep it working well.

- Keep it simple. The easier your budget is to use, the easier it will be to stick to it.
- Be realistic. If your income is less than your complete list of expenses, your budget will show that. Don't try to spend money you don't have.
- Keep day-to-day records. It's easy to forget what you spend unless you record your daily expenses.
- Keep your budget, incoming bills, receipts, and cancelled checks, all in one place. This will help you organize your budgeting efforts.
- Choose a definite time to pay bills and review your budget.

Monthly Budget

Income, set-asides, and expenses	Amount per month
Total Income	$_____
Set-asides:	
Emergencies and future goals	$_____
Seasonal expenses	_____
Insurance	_____
Debt payments	_____
Regular monthly expenses:	
Rent or mortgage payment . . . $_____	
Utilities . . . . _____	
Installment payments . . . . _____	
Other . . . . _____	
Total	_____
Day-to-day expenses:	
Food and beverages . . . . $_____	
Household operation	
and maintenance . . . . _____	
Education . . . . _____	
Clothing . . . . _____	
Savings . . . . _____	
Transportation . . . . _____	
Medical care . . . . _____	
Recreation . . . . _____	
Gifts and contributions . . . . . _____	
Total	_____
Total set-asides and expenses	$_____

Doing a detailed, monthly budget will show you where your money is going. If your set-asides and expenses total more than your income, you need to revise your budget.

You don't spend much money on yourself for extras, but you have gotten in the habit of buying a couple doughnuts for coffee break in the morning and a 40¢ candy bar in the afternoon. You figure that by doing without these snacks you could save over $200 a year— enough money to buy several things you want. What's your decision—a few small pleasures daily, or one or two large, lasting purchases at the end of the year? Give reasons for your decision.

Dealing with Changes and Problems

Managing your money is not something you do once or twice, then it's over. As you grow older and move into the adult world, you will have more income and more expenses. Even if you don't take on new expenses, many of your present costs will probably go up. You must constantly be alert to changes in your financial situation and in the economy as a whole.

Financial Responsibility

Responsibility where money is concerned is called financial responsibility. Some people have more financial responsibility than others. While you are in school, for example, you probably earn only a small amount of money from an allowance or part-time job. This means that you can be responsible for only a small part of your expenses.

But when you get a full-time job, you will probably help pay more of the household expenses. You will take on greater financial responsibility. If you move away from home, you will have even greater financial responsibility.

If you get married, you have a different level of responsibility. When a husband and wife both work, they often share all the financial responsibilities. Or, you may be the only one in your family with a job. You would then be entirely responsible for yourself and others. Food, clothing, car payments, and medical bills are just some of the expenses included at this level of financial responsibility.

You can see that different people have different levels of financial responsibility. You probably know that the responsibilities usually grow as you get older. But many young people have them, too. To understand better some of the problems of young consumers, let's look at a few case studies.

Do you have any idea how much it costs to feed, clothe, and provide a home for this family? Do you suppose these children realize that someday they may have as much financial responsibility as their parents now have?

Joe Thompson is eighteen years old and a senior at East High School. He has two brothers and three younger sisters. Even though Joe's mother and father shop wisely, it's hard to meet the expenses of a large family living in Waynesville, a city with a population of 125,000.

Last summer Joe decided he would help the family by going to work. His father is a sales representative for the Johnson Supply Company. Joe's father gets a salary and commissions. Joe thought he, too, might like sales work, so he got a job selling aluminum cooking utensils in the seven-county area around Waynesville.

Traveling from town to town to sell utensils meant that Joe would have to buy a car. He also needed expense money until he made some sales. Joe's father co-signed a bank loan for $1500. The car cost $1200, leaving $300 for travel expenses.

Joe worked very hard during June, July, and August. His earnings were high, but so were his expenses. He was unable to repay the loan completely. Now he works evenings and Saturdays so he can make payments on his loan. He even plans to work full-time during Christmas vacation.

Joe has more financial responsibilities than most of his friends. He is determined to pay for his car. This would prove that he can manage his money—and it would show that he is trustworthy.

After graduation from high school, Joe hopes to work as a salesperson. From this experience with a loan, he has learned a lot about managing money.

Marta Lu is seventeen years old and a junior at Washington High School. She lives with her father, two brothers, and a sister. Her mother died three years ago.

Marta's father is a carpenter. Bad weather and strikes have kept him unemployed for much of the last three years. The family has had to cut back on its spending several times.

Marta has been given a small allowance for school supplies and clothing, but she must earn money for luxuries and recreation. She has been working at the public library and saving some of her money for the last two years. Marta knows the family's financial picture is not too bright at this time. She realizes that she will be responsible for herself after finishing high school.

Marta has studied available occupations and has found television repair very interesting. Her friend Jane has an older sister who owns a television repair service. Marta enjoys visiting her shop and watching Jane's sister work.

Marta discussed her goals with the school counselor, with her father, and with friends. She then decided to take the television repair course at the community college after graduating from high school. The cost of this course is $900.

Marta has been saving one-fourth of the money she earns. She works two hours each day after school and three hours on Saturdays. She is paid minimum wage. Marta expects to have the $900 saved before graduation. Do you think this is a realistic goal?

H elen Lane has always wanted to be a bookkeeper. Her family encouraged her to take bookkeeping courses at the Northern Area Vocational School.

To be closer to the school, Helen needed to leave the farm where she had lived all her life. At first she was nervous. But she was determined to accept this new responsibility.

Helen rented a furnished apartment five blocks from the school. She chose this apartment because there was a shopping center nearby. She wanted to live near the school and a shopping center because she didn't have a car. The shopping center had a bank, several stores, and a supermarket. The apartment was furnished with just about everything she would need.

Helen's family had encouraged independence, so managing on her own wasn't too difficult for Helen. She was glad she had studied consumer education in high school. The units on budgeting in her business courses also proved to be helpful.

Helen's family sent her an allowance each month, and Helen managed this money wisely. She always had enough to pay the rent and buy the groceries. Sometimes she was even able to entertain friends from her class and cook special dishes for them.

After four months of living on her own, Helen felt she had learned a lot. She was able to keep accounts and manage a budget. She knew about buying food and clothing and caring for the apartment. She had become a wise consumer.

Helen's family was very proud of her. She had proved that she could handle financial responsibility.

L ori Sharp had known Stanley Woodward since grade school. They started dating two years ago. It was taken for granted they would be married someday.

Last fall Lori and Stanley were seniors at Jackson High. They were both taking the distributive education class. Lori worked at Bradley's, a children's clothing store, and she made good wages while learning sales skills. Since Stanley had worked several summers in a grocery store, he first applied at the grocery store. He was hired as a trainee who would work in all areas of the store.

Rather than wait until after graduation, Lori and Stanley decided to get married in December. Both had saved some money. If they both worked, they thought they could

support themselves and still finish their senior year. Neither of them was interested in going to college. Stanley hoped to become a manager someday. Mr. Kyser, the store manager, promised Stanley full-time work after he graduated. Lori was happy in sales, and she and Stanley agreed retailing would be a good career.

They were married during the Christmas holidays. Their families knew this young couple would have to budget carefully, so the Sharps asked Stanley and Lori to live with them until they completed high school. The Sharps and the newlyweds reached a financial agreement. Stanley and Lori would take over certain jobs around the home. They also would pay one-third of the cost of running the household.

The arrangement worked very well in this case. Lori and Stanley were, for the most part, independent. Both were working and taking their places in the adult world. They were also completing their last year of high school. Lori and Stanley were able to handle their responsibilities at home, at work, and at school. Their success was due, in part, to their own maturity. But they also gave credit to their distributive education class. It was a good introduction to the adult world.

Felipe and Maria Luna had been married six years. They had liked living in their apartment because it was close to the factory where Felipe worked and the hospital where Maria was a nurse. But since Armando, their two-year-old son, needed more room to play, they began saving for a down payment on a small house.

Six months ago they found a small, three-bedroom home. Because it was an older house, it cost less than most of the houses they had seen. Felipe and Maria thought their savings would cover the down payment. With Felipe's latest pay raise they were sure they could meet the payments each month.

Felipe and Maria studied their budget. Then they talked with a lady at the First National Bank. She asked about their finances and suggested they spend no more than $350 per month on house payments. She gave them a list of things to look for when checking the house.

According to this checklist, the house Felipe and Maria found was perfect for them. Both the inside and outside were in good condition. The house also had a good location for their needs. The school was only five blocks away. The neighborhood seemed quiet, and there were only a few busy streets. Most of the houses on the block were well cared for and were owned by young families.

The Lunas thought the house met their needs so they called the bank. A bank employee looked at the house and decided the bank would lend the money for it. The loan was approved.

The Lunas have now lived in their new house for four months. They like it more than ever, but the $310 monthly payments have not been easy to make. Felipe and Maria have had to give up some things to make the payments. They spent less on recreation, watched TV instead of going to the movies, and ate out less. They also saved money by joining a car pool instead of driving to work by themselves. They felt that buying a home was worth these changes in their lifestyle.

Felipe and Maria were wise money managers. First, they saved enough money to make a good down payment. Second, they chose a house within their price range. Third, they planned their spending to meet the goal of paying for their house. They had been very responsible in the purchase of their first home, which is extremely important when "starting out."

In each of the five case studies you just read, someone accepted financial responsibility.

- Joe's first plan wasn't successful, but he then acted in a responsible way. When he borrowed money, he agreed to repay it, and he did.
- Marta planned her career with the advice of adults and friends. Then she made a savings plan to meet her goal.
- Helen set a goal and then worked toward it. She studied, managed her money, and lived in an apartment so she could meet her goal.
- Lori and Stanley received help from her parents. But they still had more responsibilities than most young people. Since they planned ahead, Lori and Stanley were able to accept their responsibilities.
- The Lunas' goal was a major purchase, a house. They knew this purchase would affect their lives for many years. Therefore, they spent a lot of time planning for it. They made use of their own knowledge as well as professional advice. These efforts paid off because now they are satisfied with their purchase.

Inflation

Added financial responsibilities are not the only reasons for reviewing your spending. You may need to change your budget from time to time because of higher prices. You probably don't remember a time when a cola or a candy bar cost ten cents, or a nickel. Today both cost much more, and they will probably cost even more in a few years.

As you know from reading Chapter 13, when prices are constantly rising, we have an economic condition known as *inflation*. In a time of inflation workers want higher wages, and they buy more with credit. This causes general prices and the cost of credit to go up even higher. Thus, inflation causes more inflation. It is sometimes very difficult to break this cycle.

During inflation, as prices go up, your dollar buys less. It loses some of its value. It's still a dollar, but it takes more and more dollars to buy the same things.

Although hard to believe, inflation can help some people. People who borrowed money before the inflation started can repay their loans with dollars that are worth less. Obviously this is to the advantage of those who borrowed money.

But the people who saved their money are hurt by inflation. The dollars that they put in the bank years ago are worth much less when they withdraw them from their savings. Matt was a typical victim of inflation.

When this man was the age of the teenager at the next pump, gasoline cost about 20¢ a gallon. Today it costs about a dollar more. Because of inflation, everything, not just gasoline, is more expensive today than it was fifty years ago — or even ten years ago.

M att loved music. For Matt, listening to a good album through his headphones was one of life's greatest pleasures.

When he was fourteen, Matt started to save for a good stereo system. He read magazine articles and checked local shops trying to decide on the system he wanted. Finally, he decided on a system in the $400 price range.

For three years Matt put all of his extra earnings into his stereo fund. He thought that he would be able to buy the system he wanted right after graduation. He figured the money he got as gifts plus his savings would be a little more than $400.

Then he started shopping in earnest for the particular stereo he wanted. Matt was amazed to find that the type of system that had cost $400 three years ago was now closer to $600. It would be a while longer before he could pay for his dream. His money just didn't buy as much as it would have three years ago.

Inflation is a very difficult problem. Even the experts disagree about the best way to stop it. Until inflation is stopped, we must learn to live with it. This means learning to review and adjust your budget from time to time.

Getting Help

Most people could manage their money better than they do. If you're having trouble managing your money, try to find out why. Did you have to pay any large, unexpected bills? These bills are often the major cause of money management problems.

Sometimes people find themselves in economic trouble because of the way they respond to problems. For example, Anita felt angry when she broke up with her boyfriend, so she went on a buying spree. She did the same thing when her boss criticized her work last week. If she isn't in debt already, Anita soon will be.

Here is another example. Loren is shy and has no close friends. He tries to buy friends by taking them to expensive restaurants. He also buys costly sports equipment that he lets others use. Loren owes a lot of money. Chances are that his poor money management will continue. Loren is sure that no one could like him for himself. His low self-esteem leads to economic problems.

Neither Anita nor Loren sees the cause of their trouble. Do you sometimes act as they acted? If you want to avoid these problems and improve your money management, help is available.

School

Many high schools have consumer education courses. In these classes, students learn the best ways to buy and use goods and services. Other courses, such as social studies courses, often include a unit on consumer education. Many high schools and community colleges also offer adult education classes that help people learn money management.

Don't forget that your teachers can help you with your problems. Most teachers in agriculture, business, homemaking, and industrial arts have studied consumer education. Your school counselor is another possible source of help.

Newspapers and Magazines

You can find a great deal of information about money matters in newspapers and magazines. Most newspapers print daily or weekly columns by writers who are experts on handling money. Several magazines, such as *Business Week, Forbes,* and *Fortune,* are devoted entirely to financial matters. Your parents, teachers, and librarians can direct you to the most helpful articles.

Government Agencies

Many government agencies publish free or inexpensive booklets that will help you get the most for your money. These booklets are available at federal and county offices and in many local libraries. County agricultural agents and extension services also provide consumer information for individuals and groups.

Banks

Many banks employ people to give free financial information to customers. Information is given on savings plans and bank loans. As a public service, some banks sponsor courses, called *seminars,* in money management. The seminars may be at the bank in the evening or on Saturday, but more often they're held at a high school or college. If you have money problems, ask at your bank if such a seminar is planned.

Lawyers

Sometimes money problems require professional help. A lawyer should be consulted when a legal opinion is needed. This is necessary when making contracts, selling property, and collecting money. You can find more information on legal help in Chapter 21.

Other Sources

Check the Yellow Pages of your phone book. Look under the name of your city or town. You may find agencies that can help you. In some areas, for example, a Department of Family Services may be able to assist you.

Banks are in the money business. If you have a money problem, someone at your local bank could probably give you some advice on how to solve your problem.

REVIEW YOUR LEARNING   CHAPTER 17

████████████████████████ CHAPTER SUMMARY

To get the most for your money, you must plan your spending. The actual plan that you use is called a *budget*. To make a budget work, make a list of your goals, group your needs, record your expenses, and estimate your earnings. Then work hard at sticking to your budget, while constantly reviewing your budget to allow for changing financial responsibilities, income, and inflation.

As your financial responsibilities increase and you continue to budget your money, you will improve your money management skills. If you do need help, plenty is available. School courses, newspaper and magazine articles, government agencies, lawyers, and banks are just a few of the places you can turn to for help.

████████████████████████ WORDS YOU SHOULD KNOW

budget
financial responsibility
money management

████████████████████████ STUDY QUESTIONS

1. What is the advantage of using good money management?
2. What are two reasons why you should plan a budget while you are still in school?
3. What information must you have when planning a budget?
4. List at least five headings for needs that you might find in a typical budget.
5. What are five hints that will keep your budget working well?
6. What two major factors make it necessary to constantly review and change your budget?
7. Where can you get help in managing your money? Give at least four sources of help.

REVIEW YOUR LEARNING

DISCUSSION TOPICS

1. Why will your financial responsibilities grow as you get older?
2. Why do you think that so many people spend much more than they can afford?
3. How has inflation affected you?

SUGGESTED ACTIVITIES

1. Write a short paper describing your financial responsibilities. If you have no responsibilities, describe those of someone you know.
2. Imagine you and your friends are discussing budgets. Your friend thinks making a budget is just too much trouble. Try to convince your friend that a budget will really help. Explain why it is worth the time and trouble. Also tell why it's important to keep within the estimated budget.
3. Make a daily record of all your expenses for one week. Use this record to plan a budget for yourself for one month. Try to follow this budget. At the end of the month, revise the budget wherever necessary. Continue to follow your budget.
4. Find out what money management services are available in your community. Check the following:
   - banks
   - county-extension services
   - credit unions
   - finance companies
   - savings and loans

   Give a report to your class. Show any booklets or folders that you received. Describe the savings plans available and the instruction or classes offered.

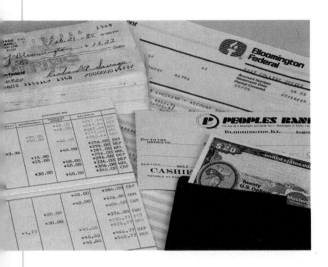

Bank Services: Savings and Checking

You may not realize it, but a bank is a business much like any other business. Just as grocery stores, insurance companies, and hardware stores are in business to make a profit, so are banks. What makes banks seem so different is that the products they handle are money and credit, not groceries and hardware.

Banks provide many services. They manage personal checking accounts for thousands of customers at a time. They help people save their money. Banks also loan money to people who want to buy expensive things such as cars and houses.

In this chapter you will learn about the many different ways that banks can help you handle your money. You will also learn how to do such things as write and endorse checks and balance your checkbook. In the next chapter, Chapter 19, you will learn more about the different kinds of credit that banks provide for their customers.

DO YOU KNOW . . .
- what services banks offer?
- the advantages of having a checking account?
- how to endorse and write checks?
- how to balance a checking account?

CAN YOU DEFINE . . .
- balance?
- bank statement?
- cancelled check?
- deposit insurance?
- endorse?
- interest?
- interest rate?
- overdrawn?

Saving Your Money

Most people who want to save money put their money in a bank. There are several reasons why people save at banks. Here you will read about these reasons and the different savings plans that banks offer.

Banks are Safe

You probably won't spend all the money you make as soon as you get paid. After paying your bills and buying what you need, you will probably have some money left over.

Where will you keep your extra money? In your room perhaps, or in your car? Do you think these are safe places to keep money? What would happen if there was a fire at your house or someone broke into your car?

The safest place for your money is usually in a bank. Banks keep the money in huge vaults, and they hire guards to watch the bank. Banks take many other precautions to make sure that the deposits are neither lost nor stolen.

The federal and state governments also do many things to guarantee the safety of money deposited in banks. For example, government agencies require that banks be *chartered* (receive official permission to operate). These government agencies also regulate the operations of banks. In these ways the government makes sure that only qualified, responsible people are allowed to manage banks.

Many banks provide additional protection for your money by taking out **deposit insurance**. Deposit insurance is a guarantee to replace bank deposits up to $100,000 should the money somehow be lost. About 97 percent of all banks in the U.S. carry deposit insurance.

Suppose you deposited your money in an insured bank, and then the bank made some bad investments and went out of business. You would not lose all of your money. The Federal Deposit Insurance Corporation (FDIC) would pay you the amount of money lost up to $100,000. If you had more than one account, each account would be insured up to $100,000.

Most savings institutions, such as credit unions and savings and loan associations, also have deposit insurance. In deciding where you will keep your money, consider how the bank or savings firm insures its deposits.

Banks Pay Interest

Another advantage to putting your savings into a bank is **interest**. Interest is money that banks pay you in return for letting them keep your money for you. Interest makes it possible for your savings to grow, even if you don't add more of your own money to the account.

Interest is calculated as a percent of the money you deposit. For example, if you deposit $100 at 5 percent interest, the bank will pay you $5 in interest at the end of the year (5% of $100 = $5). The next year the bank will pay you 5 percent of $105.

This enormous vault is just one of several reasons why your money is safe in a bank. Even if the money were stolen, all deposits are insured by the FDIC up to $100,000.

How much interest the bank pays you depends on the interest rate, how much money you deposit, and how often the interest is calculated. The **interest rate** is the percentage that the bank uses to figure your interest. The interest rate could be 5, 5½, 6¾, or 8 percent. It could be any percentage the bank chooses to pay, within government regulations.

You can see that the higher the interest rate, the more money you will make. Suppose you have $100 that you want to save. If you deposit your money in a bank paying 5 percent interest, you will make $5 in one year. If, however, you deposit your money in a bank paying 8 percent, you will make $8 in one year. In this case you wouldn't need to be a financial genius to know where to deposit your money.

How much interest you make also depends on the amount of money you deposit. Suppose your bank pays a 5 percent interest rate, and you deposit $100. At the end of one year you will have made $5 in interest. But if you had deposited $500 at the same interest rate, you would have made $25 (5% of $500 = $25). The more money you deposit, the more money you will earn in interest, regardless of the interest rate.

Another factor in determining your interest earnings is the frequency at which your interest is calculated. For all of the examples above, the interest was calculated once a year at the end of the year. Interest calculated in this way is called *simple interest*.

For some savings accounts banks calculate interest *quarterly* (every three months) or even daily. When the interest is figured daily, it is said to be *compounded daily*. When it is figured quarterly, it is said to be *compounded quarterly*. The more often the bank calculates the interest, the faster your money grows.

Obviously, you would prefer to have your interest figured daily. You should realize, though, that

This graph shows how just a small difference in the interest rate can make a big difference in how fast your savings grow. The red bar shows how much money you would have in twenty years if you deposited $1,000 at 5 percent. The yellow bar shows how much you would have if you deposited the same amount for the same time, but at 8 percent instead of 5.

banks have different plans for saving money. Even if the bank has a plan that pays daily interest, it may not be the best plan for you.

Savings Plans

You may wonder how much money, if any, you should save. Some experts say that to handle emergencies you should have from three- to six-months' pay in a savings account. You, however, are the only person who knows how much you can and should save.

Banks offer their customers many different plans for saving money. Three of the more commonly used savings plans are explained in this section. In addition to these plans you can put your money in money market funds and treasury notes.

Which savings plan is best for you will probably depend on how much money you have and when you might need to withdraw it. Discuss your situation with someone at the bank. That person will help you pick the best savings plan for your needs.

As you know from reading about interest, you will want to get the highest interest rate possible. You will also want to have your interest calculated as frequently as possible. You may prefer, however, to take less interest so that you can withdraw money as you need it.

Savings Accounts. For most people starting out in the world of work, a savings account is the best way to save. You don't need a lot of money to open a savings account. A few dollars will probably be enough to get you started.

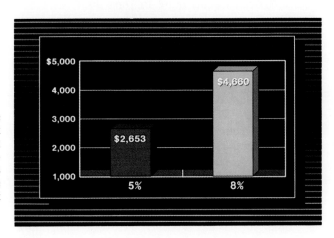

Another advantage to savings accounts is that you can withdraw your money at any time without a penalty. You will read later that you can't do this with some savings plans.

Savings accounts give you flexibility with your savings. If you need a large amount of money to make a big purchase, you can take it out of your savings account at any time. If an emergency comes up that you can't handle with your day-to-day cash, you can use your savings.

Most savings accounts pay between 5 and 6 percent interest. When you open the account, the bank will give you a *passbook* (savings book) to keep track of how much you have in the account. The interest will be paid once at the end of the year. The interest won't be as high as with some other accounts, but you will be able to withdraw and use your savings whenever you need it.

Certificates of Deposit. Another way to save your money is to buy a *certificate of deposit (CD)*. A certificate of deposit is a piece of paper that says that the bank will pay you back your money, plus interest, on a certain day.

You can buy a CD for different lengths of time—six months, one year, and two years, for example. Usually the longer the time period, the higher the interest rate. Interest rates on CDs are often several percentage points higher than they are on savings accounts.

You usually need a large amount of money to buy a CD. It may be $500, $1,000, $2,000, or more. You will need to ask at your bank to find out the minimum amount you need. Usually, the more you invest, the higher the interest rate.

You can see that there are some disadvantages to CDs. One is that you need to have a certain amount of money to buy one. Another disadvantage is that you can't withdraw your money as quickly and easily as you can from a savings account. Some banks require a thirty-day notice. In most cases there is a penalty for withdrawing your money before the payment date. The penalty is usually the loss of some or all of your interest.

If you have a large amount of money that you won't need for a long time, you may want to buy a CD. Talk to someone at the bank about the different amounts, time periods, and interest rates. If you will need to use your savings from time-to-time, you should probably keep your money in a savings account.

Savings Bonds. Another way to save is by buying U.S. Savings Bonds. You can buy these bonds at your bank. Because they are issued by the U.S. government, savings bonds are one of the safest ways to save money.

You can buy savings bonds in different amounts: $25, $37.50, $50, $100, up to $5000. In ten years the bond will be worth at least twice the amount you paid for it. For example, if you buy a $25 bond in 1986, you can cash it in for $50 in 1996. In fact, the bond that you buy for $25 will have a *face value* of $50. This means that $50, not $25, will be printed on the bond.

You must keep savings bonds for at least six months, but you can cash them in any time after that. Of course, you will not receive the face value if you cash them in early. You are guaranteed to at least double your money if you hold the bond for the full ten years. You could receive more than this amount, depending on changes in the interest rates while you hold the bonds.

Talk to someone at the bank about your situation. The bank representative will recommend the one or two savings plans that best meet your needs.

Lots of people like to save their money by buying U.S. Savings Bonds. Buying bonds is a sure, safe way to save, and it also helps finance government activities. You can buy savings bonds in several different denominations at your local bank.

There are several advantages to U.S. Savings Bonds.

- You need not have a large amount of money, as you do with CDs, to start saving.
- You can earn a higher interest rate than you can with a standard savings account.
- You are helping support your government since the money you use to buy the bond goes to the government treasury.
- As previously mentioned, bonds are one of the safest ways to save.

Make a Decision

Lucky you! You won $1,000 in a drawing at the local supermarket. There are several things you'd like to buy, but your parents insist that you save the money at least for a while. At the bank, you learn of different savings plans—but basically it comes down to putting the money away for a year or two at a high interest rate, or keeping the money available at a lower interest rate. What's your decision—high interest and untouchable, or lower interest and available? Give reasons for your decision.

Your Personal Checking Account

Most people have a personal checking account at a bank near their home or place of work. People use their checking account to pay most of their bills and most of their major purchases. In this section you will learn about the many different types of checking accounts—why people use them, and how you can open your own account.

Checks versus Cash

There are many advantages to using checks instead of cash. In fact, it would be very difficult to keep our economy going without checks.

If you paid all of your bills with cash instead of checks, you would need to have large supplies of cash at all times. Keeping lots of money in your home is not, however, a good idea. Nor is it a good idea to carry a large sum of cash around with you or send it through the mail. In all cases, using checks is a much safer way to pay.

Another reason for using checks is that you receive **cancelled checks** (checks that have been cashed). At the end of a certain period, usually each month, your bank will send you your cancelled checks. These checks serve as receipts, proving that

There are many advantages to paying with checks rather than cash. Checks are safer and more convenient. They also help you keep track of where your money goes.

you paid your bill. They also help you with your budgeting and bookkeeping.

A third advantage of checks over cash is that checks save time for everyone. For example, without checks, companies would need to pay their employees with cash. For the employees this would mean standing in line to receive their pay. They would also need to sign a payroll book to show that they had received their money. All of this would take a great deal of time.

Types of Checking Accounts

There are many different kinds of checking accounts. As with savings accounts, you must find the checking account that best meets your needs. You may need to "shop around" to find the bank that offers the best checking account for you.

Interest-Paying Accounts. More and more banks are offering checking accounts that pay interest. These accounts work much like the savings accounts that you read about earlier. The amount of interest you receive depends on how much money you keep in your account.

You will probably find that most banks in your area offer similar interest-paying accounts. One type will allow you to write as many checks a month as you want. As long as you keep a certain minimum amount, say $100, in the account, the bank will pay you a little over 5 percent interest. If your **balance** (amount of money) drops below the minimum, the interest payments stop.

At the same bank you can probably open an account that will pay a higher interest, maybe 8 or 9 percent. The minimum balance for this account will probably be much higher, maybe $1,000 to $2,500. With this account you will be allowed to write only a few checks a month.

When you are starting out in the world of work, you will probably not have a large surplus of money. You will need most of your money to pay your bills. In this case you would probably need the type of account that pays a lower interest but allows you to write as many checks as you want. Later, as the balance in your account grows, you may be able to open an account that pays a higher interest.

Individual or Joint Accounts. Depending on your situation, you may want to open either an individual or a joint checking account. An individual account is just what you would expect—an account for one person. If you have an individual account, you are the only person who can write checks on your account.

A joint checking account is one in which two or more people can use the same account. Each person involved can deposit money and write checks. Husbands and wives often share a joint checking account.

Some banks require that you be at least eighteen years old to open a checking account. These banks may, however, let you open a joint account with a parent or guardian.

Service Charges. Banks usually charge monthly fees for providing the service of managing checking accounts. The fees charged for these services are called *service charges*. Most banks calculate service charges in several different ways, depending on the type of account.

With many checking accounts, the amount of the service charge depends on the balance in your account. The bank may use either a minimum balance or an average balance to calculate your service

Choosing a Bank

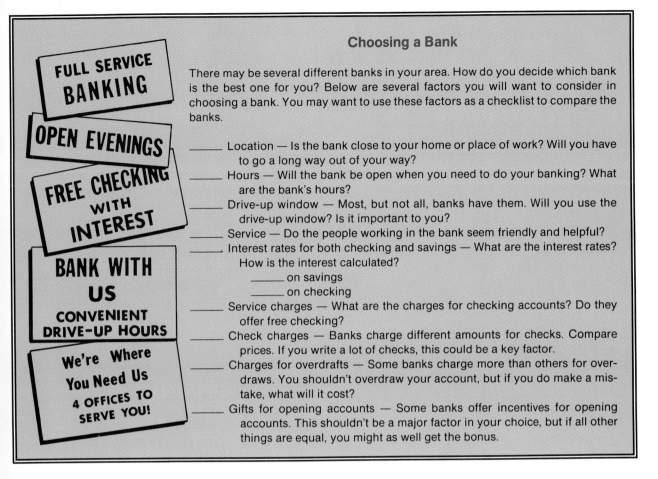

There may be several different banks in your area. How do you decide which bank is the best one for you? Below are several factors you will want to consider in choosing a bank. You may want to use these factors as a checklist to compare the banks.

_____ Location — Is the bank close to your home or place of work? Will you have to go a long way out of your way?

_____ Hours — Will the bank be open when you need to do your banking? What are the bank's hours?

_____ Drive-up window — Most, but not all, banks have them. Will you use the drive-up window? Is it important to you?

_____ Service — Do the people working in the bank seem friendly and helpful?

_____ Interest rates for both checking and savings — What are the interest rates? How is the interest calculated?

     _____ on savings

     _____ on checking

_____ Service charges — What are the charges for checking accounts? Do they offer free checking?

_____ Check charges — Banks charge different amounts for checks. Compare prices. If you write a lot of checks, this could be a key factor.

_____ Charges for overdrafts — Some banks charge more than others for overdraws. You shouldn't overdraw your account, but if you do make a mistake, what will it cost?

_____ Gifts for opening accounts — Some banks offer incentives for opening accounts. This shouldn't be a major factor in your choice, but if all other things are equal, you might as well get the bonus.

charge. For example, you could have a checking account that requires no service charge as long as you have at least $250 in the account. If your balance drops below $250, you must pay a $3 service charge.

Some banks offer special checking accounts for people who write only a few checks a month. The service charge for these special accounts is based on the number of checks you write. The cost may be 15¢ to 25¢ per check. If you write lots of checks, this type of service charge would be more expensive than the typical monthly charge. If you write only two or three checks, though, this type of account would save you money.

Many banks offer special checking accounts from time to time. They may have discounts for senior citizens or recent high school graduates. In some cases a bank may even offer free checking. Since banks offer so many different accounts, talk to people at several banks to find the best checking account for your needs.

Opening an Account

Opening a checking account is easy. Visit the bank of your choice and introduce yourself to a bank employee. Ask to talk with the person in charge of new checking accounts. Someone will interview you and help you decide which type of account is best for you.

You will need to sign a signature card when you open an account. Write your name on this card in the same way that you will write your name on your checks. The bank can then compare the signatures on your checks with the signature on the card. In this way the bank can prevent other people from forging (copying) your name in order to get money from your account.

When you open a checking account, the bank will give you an account number. This number will be written on your signature card. You will use the number each time you add money to your account or write a check.

The bank will let you choose from the various styles of checks available. They will then have your name, address, and your telephone number printed on the checks you choose. The bank will probably give you a few temporary checks to use until your personal checks are ready.

You won't have to pay for your checks when you open the account, but you will be charged for them later. The cost is minimal, usually 2¢ or 3¢ a check, but the prices can vary from bank to bank. Choosing a special style of check and having extra personal information printed on your checks can raise the price. You might want to compare the check costs at a couple of banks in your area.

Writing Checks

As soon as you open an account and receive your checks, you can begin writing checks on the account. If you have never written a check, don't worry—it's easy. There are just a few things you need to do to make sure that no one alters your check. You also want to make sure that everyone can read your check clearly.

When you write a check, make sure you write clearly. Write all checks in ink. This will make it more difficult for someone else to change your checks for their benefit.

Write the check number in the upper right-hand corner if it is not already printed there. Be sure to date each check.

After *Pay to the Order of,* write the name of the person or company to whom the check is to be paid. Then fill in the amount of the check in figures. Notice below, on Bill's check to the garage, that this figure is $13.50.

On the next line write the amount in words with the cents shown as a fraction of a dollar. For example, on Bill's check the amount is *Thirteen and* $^{50}/_{100}$. If you're writing a check for an even dollar amount show no cents as $^{xx}/_{100}$ or $^{00}/_{100}$.

Draw a line from the fraction to the word *Dollars*. This will prevent anyone from changing the amount of the check. After the word *Memo,* jot down the purpose of the check. Then sign your name exactly as it is on your signature card. When you finish writing the check, look it over carefully to make sure everything is correct.

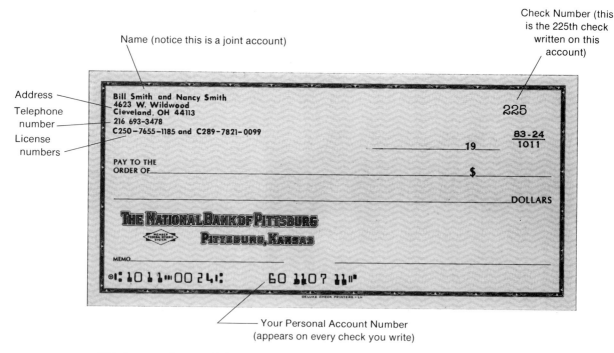

This is a typical personal check. Notice what pieces of information Mr. and Mrs. Smith have chosen to have printed on this check. Many businesses want to know your driver's license number when you write a check so the Smiths had theirs printed on the checks.

Bill Smith and Nancy Smith
4623 W. Wildwood
Cleveland, OH 44113
216 693-3478
C250-7655-1185 and C289-7821-0099

225

2-1 19 85 83-24/1011

PAY TO THE ORDER OF *Speed Service Storage* $ 13.50

Thirteen and 50/100 ———— DOLLARS

THE NATIONAL BANK OF PITTSBURG
PITTSBURG, KANSAS

MEMO *car parts*   *Bill Smith*

⑈1011⑈0024⑈   60 1107 11⑈

Bill used check 225 to pay for new parts for his car. Bill always writes in the purpose of the check next to *Memo* because the notes come in handy when Bill does his income tax.

Making Deposits

Each time you put money in your checking account you will fill out a deposit slip. Most deposit slips look much like the two shown on the next page. The bank will put several deposit slips, with your name and account number on them, in the back of each book of personal checks. The bank will also have blank deposit slips available at the bank. You can use these slips by filling in your name and number.

When you fill out a deposit slip, write in the amount of cash, if any, you are depositing. *Cash* includes both *currency* (paper money) and *silver* or *coin* (quarters, dimes, nickels, pennies). Write the amount of currency and silver you are depositing next to the correct words.

You can also deposit checks that have been written to you. If you deposit these checks, write the amount of each check on the lines labelled *checks*. Each check should be listed separately.

Before you can deposit a check written to you, you must **endorse** it. This means that you must write your name on the back of the check. When you do this, you are transferring your rights to the check to someone else—in this case, the bank. The bank then adds the amount of the check to your account.

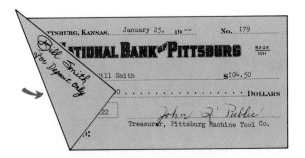

You cannot cash or deposit a check written to you until you endorse it. If you plan to deposit the checks in your account, and you must mail or endorse the check before reaching the bank, write "For deposit only" on the check.

Bill made two deposits for the same amount on the same day. The deposit slips are identical in every way but one. Can you see the difference? Bill took the slip on top from the back of his checkbook; he got the bottom slip from the bank teller.

If you deposit checks by mail, you should write *for deposit only* above or below your signature on the back of the check. You should also write *for deposit only* if you endorse the check before you get to the bank, when there is a chance you could lose the check. Writing *for deposit only* prevents anyone from using your check for their own purposes.

After filling in the cash and checks you want to deposit, add up the total amount. You will need to write the total on the slip. Some slips also require your signature.

When making a deposit, you will often want to keep some cash. If so, fill in the amount you want to keep where it says *Less Cash Received* on the slip. Then subtract this amount from the total and write the difference on the line labelled *Net Deposit.*

After endorsing your checks and filling in the slip, give your cash, checks, and the slip to the bank teller. The teller will give back a duplicate slip or another slip that shows how much you deposited. It is very important that you keep this bank slip. It is your proof that you deposited the money. If the bank makes an error, you can use the slip to prove that you made the deposit.

Making Withdrawals

You can, of course, withdraw cash from your checking account. You can do this by writing a check to yourself or to "Cash."

It is a good idea to wait until you are at the bank to write a check to cash. If you lose a check written to *cash,* anyone can cash it.

On her way to work this morning, Sharon drove past one of her favorite stores, the Flower Basket. In front of the shop was a hanging basket that Sharon thought her mother would love. Sharon thought to herself that she would stop on her way home and buy the basket for her mother.

During her lunch hour Sharon counted the money in her wallet. There wasn't enough to buy the basket so she wrote a $10 check to cash. She'd get the money at the bank's drive-in window after work.

That evening at the bank Sharon opened her wallet to take out the check. It wasn't there. She was sure she had put the check in her wallet. She looked everywhere, but there was no check to be found.

Sharon knew that anyone who found the check could cash it. She had learned a valuable lesson the hard way. She knew she would always wait until she was at the bank to write a check to cash.

Keeping Track of Your Account

You probably know that you can't write checks for more money than you have in your account. If you do this, your account will become **overdrawn**. In other words, you would have *drawn* from your account an amount *over* your balance. Since banks charge a fee (usually $10-$20) for each overdrawn check, you want to avoid overdrawing your account.

Keeping track of how much money you have in your account at all times will help you avoid overdrawing your account. Your bank will help you keep track by including a check register in each box of checks they send you. A check register is a small pad that fits in your checkbook and is used to record your checks and deposits. It's important to get in the habit of filling out your check register as you write checks and make deposits.

Notice on this page how Bill filled out his register. He opened his checking account with $94.50 from his first paycheck. This $94.50 was the first entry in his register at the top of the *Balance* column.

In the first column, Bill listed the number of the first check he wrote. The number was 101. In the second column he wrote the date. Under *Description of Transaction,* Bill wrote the name of the business (Speed Service Garage) to which he wrote that check.

In the next column, Bill wrote the amount ($13.50) of the check. Bill would have put a *T* in the next column if the check had been needed for tax records. His account had a service charge of 20¢ per check, so he wrote that amount in the next column. Of course he skipped *Deposit/Credit* since he was writing a check, not making a deposit. Then, in the last column, he wrote the total of the check plus the fee ($13.50 + .20 = $13.70).

The next step was to subtract this amount from the balance. He then wrote the new balance ($80.80) on the tinted line. Finally, back in the third column he noted that the check had been written to pay for car parts.

You can see that Bill has continued to keep track of his account. Chances are he will not overdraw his account.

Whenever you write a check or make a deposit, record it in your register. If you do this, the correct balance will always be shown in the tinted space. You will always know if you have enough money to write another check.

Make a Decision

You just got a part-time job at Sam's Sandwich Shop. Most weeks your take-home pay is going to be right around $100. You drive your own car and buy lots of your own meals, so you do need a fair amount of cash. You had thought about opening a checking account. What's your decision—cash your paychecks each week, or deposit most of the money in a checking account? Give reasons for your decision.

NUMBER	DATE 1–25	DESCRIPTION OF TRANSACTION	PAYMENT/DEBIT (−)	√ T	FEE (IF ANY) (−)	DEPOSIT/CREDIT (+)	BALANCE 94 50
101	2-1	Speed Service Garage car parts on 1–25	13 50		.20		13 70 / 80 80
102	2-4	Cash	25 00		.20		25 20 / 55 60
	2-15	Deposit				80 00	80 00 / 135 60
103	2-25	Jones Store jacket	42 75		.20		42 95 / 92 65
104	2-25	Music Town record	5 98		20		6 18 / 86 47

RECORD ALL CHARGES OR CREDITS THAT AFFECT YOUR ACCOUNT

If you use your register to keep track of your checking account, as Bill has done, you will always know exactly how much money you have in your account.

Balancing Your Checkbook

You read earlier that banks return cancelled checks on a regular schedule, usually once a month. Along with these checks, the bank will send you your deposit slips and a **bank statement**. This statement is a record of your account during that certain time period. The statement lists all the deposits, cancelled checks, and charges that were handled during that time. The statement also tells you what your balance is at the end of this period.

When you get your statement and cancelled checks, you should *balance your checkbook*. This is the process of making sure that the checks, deposits, and balance in your check register agree with those shown on your bank statement. You need to balance your checkbook to make sure your register is correct and that the bank hasn't made any mistakes. Do this as soon as possible after receiving your statement. If there are any errors in your statement, notify the bank.

You will find instructions on how to balance your checkbook on the back of your statement. When you are finished, the balance in your checkbook should match the ending balance shown on your statement. In the box on the opposite page you can see how Joe balanced his checkbook.

Special Checks and Money Orders

In certain cases you will want to use special checks and money orders to make payments. There will be times when you won't be able to use your personal checks. This section explains some of the common uses of checks other than personal checks.

Cashier's Checks

Some people write personal checks without the money to back them up. When this happens, the business that took the check does not get its money. This is why all businesses are very careful about whose personal checks they accept—especially when the check is for a large amount. Some businesses simply refuse to take any personal checks at all.

Can you read this bank statement? How much did Bill have in his account at the beginning of the month? At the end? How much was his service charge?

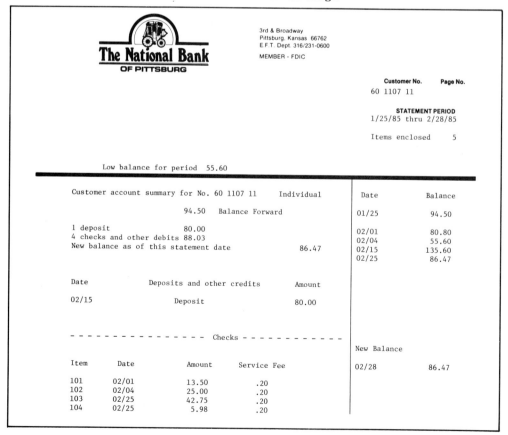

HOW TO BALANCE YOUR ACCOUNT

1. SUBTRACT FROM YOUR CHECK REGISTER ANY SERVICE CHARGES POSTED ON THIS STATEMENT.

2. PLACE A CHECK MARK (✔) BESIDE EACH ITEM IN YOUR CHECKBOOK FOR EACH TRANSACTION LISTED ON THE FRONT OF THIS STATEMENT.

3. CHECK OFF DEPOSITS SHOWN ON THE STATEMENT AGAINST THOSE SHOWN ON YOUR CHECKBOOK.

4. COMPLETE THE FORM AT THE RIGHT.

5. THE FINAL "BALANCE" IN THE FORM TO THE RIGHT SHOULD AGREE WITH YOUR CHECKBOOK BALANCE. IF IT DOES NOT, READ "HINTS FOR FINDING DIFFERENCES" BELOW.

HINTS FOR FINDING DIFFERENCES

RECHECK ALL ADDITIONS AND SUBTRACTIONS OR CORRECTIONS.

VERIFY THE CARRY-OVER BALANCE FROM PAGE TO PAGE IN YOUR REGISTER.

MAKE SURE YOU HAVE SUBTRACTED THE SERVICE CHARGES FROM YOUR REGISTER BALANCE.

IF NO ERRORS IN YOUR CHECKING ACCOUNT ARE REPORTED WITHIN 10 DAYS YOUR ACCOUNT WILL BE CONSIDERED CORRECT. IF YOU HAVE ANY QUESTIONS PLEASE CALL 791-6222.

1. STATEMENT ENDING BALANCE (Transfer amount from other side, includes monthly earnings)	632	57
2. ADD: DEPOSITS MADE SINCE ENDING DATE ON STATEMENT.	150	00
3. SUB TOTAL (LINE 1 PLUS LINE 2)		
CHECKS NOT LISTED ON THIS OR PRIOR STATEMENTS	782	57

DATE	AMOUNT	
10/2	12	32
10/2	15	19
10/6	7	09
10/7	14	16
10/8	51	97

4. TOTAL CHECKS NOT LISTED ⟶	100	73
SUBTRACT TOTAL CHECKS NOT LISTED FROM SUBTOTAL ABOVE.		
5. (LINE 3 LESS LINE 4) BALANCE $	681	84

THIS SHOULD AGREE WITH YOUR CHECKBOOK BALANCE   *yes*

If you must pay someone who won't take your personal check, you may want to get a cashier's check at your bank. A cashier's check is a check written by a bank employee, and guaranteed by the bank to be a good check.

To get a cashier's check, you pay the bank the amount of the check plus a small fee. A bank employee will then write out the check to the person or business you want to pay.

Traveler's Checks

Traveling with large amounts of money is not very safe. It's too easy to lose the money or have it stolen. This is why many people use traveler's checks when they are away from home. You can buy traveler's checks at a bank, a savings and loan association, or at a credit union. You can usually buy $10, $20, $50, or $100 checks. The cost of these checks is quite low.

When you buy traveler's checks, you sign your name on each check. Then, when you use a check, you sign it again. The signatures must be identical before the check will be accepted in place of cash.

If you lose traveler's checks, go to the nearest bank. The bank will help you stop payment on the lost checks and will issue you new checks. This is what makes traveler's checks a safe way to handle your money.

Money Orders

The major use of money orders is to buy and pay through the mail. Sending a money order is a safe way to mail money. You can buy money orders at banks, U.S. Post Offices, and at some supermarkets and department stores.

When you buy a money order, you will write your name and address on the order. You will also write in the name and address of the person or business to receive the money. The purpose of the money order should also be included to make a complete record of the payment on the order.

You will be charged a fee for the money order. The amount of the fee will depend on the amount of the money order. The larger the money order, the higher the fee.

REVIEW YOUR LEARNING   CHAPTER 18

CHAPTER SUMMARY

One of the many services that banks provide is the management of savings plans. Most people keep their savings in banks because banks are the safest and most convenient places to keep their money. Another reason for saving at a bank is interest. Banks offer many different ways, such as savings accounts, CDs, and U.S. Savings Bonds, to save money, all of which pay interest.

Another vital service provided by banks is the management of personal checking accounts. You can choose from several different kinds of accounts, many of which now pay interest. If you have your own checking account, you will use your check register to keep track of your balance at all times so that you do not overdraw your account. In some cases you may choose to use special checks and payment methods, such as cashier's checks, traveler's checks, and money orders.

WORDS YOU SHOULD KNOW

balance
bank statement
cancelled check
deposit insurance
endorse
interest
interest rate
overdrawn

STUDY QUESTIONS

1. What does the Federal Deposit Insurance Corporation do?
2. What three factors determine how much interest you can earn on money you deposit in a bank?
3. What is an advantage of putting your money in a savings account rather than buying a CD that pays higher interest?
4. What are three advantages to using checks instead of cash?
5. What factor usually determines the interest rate for checking accounts?
6. What are two factors that can raise the price of personal checks?
7. When should you write "for deposit only" on the back of a check? Why should you do this?
8. What is the purpose of a check register?

REVIEW YOUR LEARNING CHAPTER 18

9. Why is it important to balance your checkbook as soon as you receive your bank statement?
10. List three special ways to make payments when you cannot use cash or a personal check.

DISCUSSION TOPICS

1. Do you feel that it's hard for people to save money? Why?
2. What percentage of a person's paycheck should that person save?

SUGGESTED ACTIVITIES

1. Rank the following according to what you believe is the best method for taking money on a vacation. Write 1 before the best choice, 2 before the second best choice, and so on.
   _____ low-denomination bills (one's, five's, and ten's)
   _____ personal checks
   _____ traveler's checks
   _____ cashier's checks
   Discuss your reasons for ranking these methods as you did.
2. Cut out newspaper advertisements of savings plans offered by banks, savings and loan associations, credit unions, and private investment firms. Compare the amounts required for each interest rate. Answer the following questions.
   • Which savings plan pays the highest rate for the lowest minimum balance?
   • How does the rate of interest compare with the length of time the money must remain on deposit for each plan?
   • Which agencies advertise insurance for savings? Does this make a difference in the interest rate?

Using Credit

Have you ever started to pay for something and then been asked by the person behind the counter, "Will that be cash or charge?" In the newspaper or on television, have you seen or heard phrases like the ones below?

- "No money down"
- "Easy financing"
- "Buy now, pay later"
- "Your credit is always good"

You have probably noticed that you can often buy and use expensive items *before* you pay for them. Many businesses seem to make it easy for you to buy on credit, or to "charge it."

Do you know what credit is? Do you know what it means to "charge it?" If you have your own car or motorcycle, you've probably already had some experiences with credit. If you haven't used credit yet, you almost certainly will.

In this chapter you will find out what credit is and how you can use it. You will also learn about the different types of credit and how to figure the costs of credit. You will learn about both the advantages and disadvantages. You will then be able to get the greatest benefit possible from credit buying.

What Is Credit?

Credit is a method of buying that involves trust. When you buy on credit, a business *trusts* you to pay later for a product, service, or money that they give you today. The business accepts your promise that you will make regular payments until you have paid all that you owe.

The advantage of using credit is probably obvious. When you buy on credit, you get to use a product even if you don't have enough money to pay for it. You don't have to wait until you save the full amount. This is especially helpful when you need something that is very expensive, such as a car or house.

When you promise to pay back a loan, do you keep your promise? You won't be able to use credit unless businesses can trust you to pay what you owe.

J im loved baseball—it was his favorite sport. He never missed his favorite team, the Yankees, when they played on TV, and now he was especially excited because the Yankees would be playing in the World Series.

Then it happened. Just two days before the series was to start, Jim's TV went completely blank. He took his set to a local TV shop to see if he could get it fixed. He almost fainted when the store owner told him that the set needed a new picture tube, and that the picture tube would cost $200. The owner told Jim that he might as well spend a little more and buy a new set.

All Jim could think about was the World Series being only two days away. He only had about $50 in his savings and that wasn't close to what he would need to buy a new TV.

When Jim said that he didn't have enough money either to fix his old set or buy a new one, the store manager said he could buy a new one on credit. Jim couldn't believe it. As long as his credit rating was good and he could pay a little money now, he could actually have a new TV the next day—just in time for the series. Jim couldn't have been happier.

There is, however, an important disadvantage to using credit. Do you know what that disadvantage is?

There are advantages to using credit, but there is also one major disadvantage — it costs money. When you buy on credit, you almost always pay more.

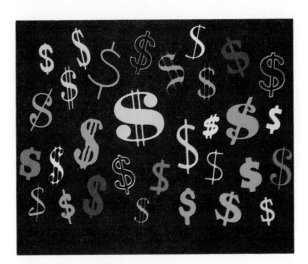

When you buy something on credit, it almost always costs more. You pay more than you would if you paid the full price at the time of the purchase. In fact, the more expensive the item and the longer you take to pay, the greater your total cost.

S ally was excited when she found just the right sofa for her new unfurnished apartment. The only problem was the cost—$450. Sally had the money. In fact, she had exactly $459.24 in her savings account. But she didn't want to spend her entire savings on the sofa. That would leave her with no money to take care of any unexpected bills. It looked as though she would have to find a cheaper sofa or wait until she saved some more money.

When Sally said she couldn't afford the sofa right now, Ron, the salesman who had shown Sally the sofa, told Sally about the store's credit plan. Ron said that if Sally could pay just $45 now, she could have the sofa delivered tomorrow. She could take up to three years to pay. This sounded great to Sally, and she said OK. It wasn't until much later that Sally learned about the cost of credit. She figured up how much the sofa had really cost her. Instead of $450, Sally ended up paying $540. Sally realized that she could have saved $90 by paying for the sofa in cash.

Who Offers Credit?

Most businesses, especially those that sell expensive items, let their customers buy on credit. Department stores, furniture stores, and clothing stores are just a few of the businesses that offer their customers credit.

These businesses know that most people do not have large sums of money to pay for expensive purchases all at once. If they want to sell their products, these businesses must trust their customers to pay a little at a time until the product is completely paid for.

Banks are another type of business that offers credit. Banks are a little different since the product they provide on credit is money. When you need a very large amount of money, the bank will *credit* your account with the money you need. You will then pay back the money in monthly payments. This is one type of credit.

Who Uses Credit?

Almost everyone uses credit at one time or another. When you borrow a dollar from a friend, you are using credit. You are also using credit when you agree to make monthly payments for several years to pay for a car. Few people go through life without using these sorts of credit at least once or twice.

Even large companies and governments use credit. Most companies must borrow money to operate their businesses from day to day. The government usually needs to spend more than it collects in taxes. Both companies and governments borrow lots of money from banks to meet these needs.

Not just anyone can use credit, though. Only people, businesses and governments, who have proven that they can be trusted to make their payments, are given credit. Most banks and businesses that offer credit will trust someone until that person gives them a reason not to be trusted. As long as you keep your promise to pay, you will be trusted with credit.

It is not difficult to find businesses that sell their products on credit. You can buy almost anything with a down payment and a promise to pay later.

Should You Use Credit?

Before you buy something on credit, you should weigh the advantages against the disadvantages. Ask yourself if you need to have the product right away. Will it be worth the extra cost of buying on credit to have this item now, instead of later? Could you do without it until you save enough to pay the full price at the time of purchase?

Remember—it is almost always cheaper to pay the full price at the time of purchase. The longer you take to pay, the more you end up paying. If at all possible, pay cash. If you must use credit, make sure you can handle the payments. Make sure the extra cost is worth the advantage of having the product right away.

W endy cashed her paycheck and felt great! She decided to buy that new ski jacket that she'd been wanting. Before she could do that, though, she had to pay her bills.

On her way home Wendy paid the water and phone bills. Then she stopped at the realtor's office and paid her rent. After a quick sandwich, she drove to Cox Sport Center to make the payment on her small motorboat. While she was there, she planned to buy the ski jacket on credit.

While Wendy was looking at the jackets, Mr. Cox reminded her that she hadn't made last month's payment on her boat. Then Wendy remembered. Last month, after paying bills and credit charges, she had barely had enough money to buy food. She hadn't been able to make the boat payment. Mr. Cox had given her one month to get payments up to date. If she didn't, Mr. Cox was going to take back the boat. No need for a ski jacket if she didn't have a boat!

So Wendy made the two monthly payments plus an extra interest charge. She counted her money. It looked as if she would have to buy only what she really needed this month. There couldn't be any more credit buying until she paid for what she already had. She had a good credit rating now—she didn't want to lose it.

Many people lose control of their credit buying. They buy more and more things on credit until they reach a point where they cannot afford to make all their monthly payments. Make sure that your credit payments are no more than you can afford.

Do you know how much credit you can afford each month? You can easily find out if you have a budget. Subtract your total expenses from your income, then divide by two. One-half the money you have left after paying your regular bills is the most you should spend on credit payments. The other half should be kept for savings and emergencies.

If you do not have a budget, use your check register to estimate your total expenses. Subtract the amount you spend in the average month from your monthly income, then divide by two.

Credit payments are usually made each month. Since they usually continue for many months, you must consider special expenses when determining how much you can afford.

First, be sure your monthly income will be the same for a year or more. Then make a list of your special payments, such as tuition, insurance, vacation, and taxes. Find the total of these special payments, then divide that by twelve. Add this amount to your monthly expenses to estimate your average monthly expenses. Subtract this amount from your monthly income, then divide by two. This answer will be a more accurate guide to how much you can afford in monthly credit payments.

Make a Decision

You are going to buy a used car for $3,000. You have $2,500 in a savings account that pays 5½ percent. If you put down $500, the bank will loan you $2,500 at 12 percent interest. You were thinking you might use your entire savings, and just borrow $500. Of course you could pay anything between $500 and $2,500 and borrow the rest. What's your decision—keep your savings and borrow most of the money, use your entire savings and borrow just a little, or something in between? Give reasons for your decision.

Without careful planning and accurate bookkeeping, you can accumulate more credit payments than you can handle. Don't get in over your head. Make sure you can make the payments before you buy on credit.

Types of Credit

There are many different kinds of credit. Some kinds are so commonly used that we don't even think of them as credit. Reading about the different kinds of credit will help you decide how you will want to use credit.

Credit Cards

More and more people are using **credit cards** all the time. Credit cards are cards that allow you to use a certain amount of credit. With some credit cards you can buy almost anything.

There are many different kinds of credit cards. You can use some of the better known cards, such as American Express, VISA, and MasterCard, all across the country. You can buy many different kinds of products from many different businesses with these cards.

Of course, a business does not have to accept a credit card. Some businesses do not accept any credit cards; others accept only certain kinds. Ask before making a purchase whether or not that place of business will accept your card.

Many large companies issue their own credit cards for their customers. Many of the oil companies, for example, have credit cards that you can use at any of the service stations selling that company's gasoline. You can only use this type of card to buy gasoline and other products at these certain stations.

Many people have several different kinds of credit cards. They might have a gasoline credit card for buying their favorite brand of gasoline. They might have a credit card at their favorite local department stores where they buy many different things. They might also have one of the nationally known cards that they use for meals and motel expenses when they travel.

When you pay a bill with a credit card, it seems at the time as though you don't really have to pay for what you get. Don't overspend because you've got a credit card. You'll receive a bill soon enough.

Some credit card companies require you to pay a fee in order to receive and use their card. Most companies will send you a monthly statement showing how much you owe. Depending on the company, you will be expected to pay all or part of what you owe each month.

Try not to lose your credit cards. Someone else might use your card, charging goods and services that you would have to pay for. If you do lose a credit card, notify the company as soon as possible.

Charge Accounts

Many local businesses that do not issue their own credit cards, do offer **charge accounts**. Charge accounts work just like credit cards, but without the cards. A charge account is the privilege of being able to buy on credit. When people say they "charged it," they mean that they bought something on credit.

Businesses that offer charge accounts keep individual records for each customer who has an account. These records show the amount of each purchase and each payment. Many businesses send each charge account customer a statement at the end of the month.

Each business has its own payment policy for its charge accounts. Some businesses require that you pay the full amount at the end of each month. Others let you carry your balance over into the next month. Find out how you will be expected to pay for each charge account that you have.

Remember—the faster you pay off what you owe, the less money you will end up paying. Most companies will give you up to thirty days to pay your full amount before they begin adding credit costs.

Installment Plans

Many businesses will let you buy on an **installment plan**. An installment plan is a form of credit in which you agree to make regular payments while using the product. You don't own the product until you have paid the full purchase price. You do get to use the product, though.

People usually use installment plans to buy expensive products. Most businesses require a **down payment** at the time of purchase. A down payment is a certain percentage, usually 10 or 20 percent, of the total price.

When you buy on the installment plan, you must make your payments on time. If you fall behind in your payments, the company may **repossess** the product. This means that the company will take the product back. In such a case you would *not* get your money back.

Loans

A **loan** is another form of credit. You probably know what a loan is. A loan is something, usually money, that someone gives you with the understanding that you will give it back. When someone loans you money, you agree to pay it back.

Most people need cash loans from time to time. Very few people have enough money to pay for expensive items such as cars and houses. When they want to buy these things, most people go to a bank or savings and loan company to borrow the money. You can also borrow money from credit companies and loan companies.

Don't borrow money from just anybody — you might end up paying excessively high interest rates. Go to a local bank or well-established lending institution if you need a loan.

Applying for Credit

After deciding that you need a certain type of credit, you must apply for the credit. This is true for credit cards, charge accounts, loans—all kinds of credit. In each case, the company offering you credit will want to find out certain things about you.

You will fill out an application form, listing your name, address, place of employment, length of time at present job, and much more. From this information, the company will try to determine how long you usually stay at one job. The company is also interested in whether or not you move a lot. Companies have found that the people who stay at one job and residence for long periods of time are the best credit risks.

Credit Rating

The company will also check with the local credit bureau to find out your credit history. The credit bureau is an agency that keeps track of how people pay their bills.

Most businesses in a community belong to a credit bureau. Each business reports the names of people who are receiving credit to the bureau. These businesses inform the bureau about which people are paying on time and which people have failed to make their payments.

With the information it receives, the credit bureau can give each person a **credit rating**. A credit rating is an estimate of how likely a person is to pay his or her bills on time. A person who always pays on time gets a good credit rating. Someone who is always late or who fails completely to make payments gets a poor credit rating.

You can see how important it is to maintain a good credit rating. When you apply for credit, the company will check with the credit bureau. If the bureau's records show that you have a poor credit rating, the company may decide not to give you credit. This could mean that you would have to do without the product you wanted to buy.

When you pay bills on time, you build up a good credit rating. By continuing to pay on time, you will keep this rating. With a good credit rating you will probably not be denied credit.

If a company does refuse you credit, the company should tell you which credit bureau gave you a poor credit rating. You may go to that credit bureau and ask about your records. If you feel there's a mistake or misleading information, you may add your version of the facts to your file. If you do this within thirty days of being denied credit, there is usually no charge.

Credit Contracts

When you buy on credit and take out loans, you will almost always be asked to sign a contract. When you sign a contract, you agree to everything that the contract says. This is why it is very important that you read and understand every word of a contract before signing it.

Most credit contracts will include statements about the following items.

- Purchase price or amount borrowed
- Interest and extra charges in dollars
- Down payment
- Trade-in allowance
- Insurance charges or other special charges
- Total amount due
- Amount of each payment
- Number of payments
- Date each payment is due

Be sure all the information is correct before you sign the contract. Ask questions about anything you don't understand. By signing, you are saying that the contract is accurate. Be sure to get a copy of the contract for your own records.

In many cases the contract for use of a credit card is the application form. Contracts for other types of credit may be more detailed application forms. Once you sign these forms, though, they are as legally binding as any contract.

Some contracts, such as home mortgages, are very long and detailed. You should probably have a lawyer read such a contract to make sure everything is in order. You will read more about contracts in Chapter 21.

Remember—the costs of your credit are explained in the contract. Read the contract very carefully. Make sure you understand how much and when you must pay.

You will be in a hurry to complete the business and enjoy your purchase, but force yourself to read the credit contract before you sign it. Don't hesitate to ask questions.

Credit Costs

As you read earlier, you almost always have to pay for the privilege of buying on credit. How much you pay will depend on the following factors.

- Credit policy of the company giving you credit
- Amount of money you owe
- Length of time you take to pay back the full amount

You will find that banks and credit agencies charge different rates for credit. It is usually a good idea to shop for credit when you can. Try to get the credit at the lowest possible cost to fit your purpose.

In some cases your credit rating and whether or not you have any **collateral** will also affect how much you pay. Collateral is something you own of value that you promise to give up if you can't make your payments. Collateral is most often asked for by banks as security that you will pay back the money you owe.

Each company will have its own rules and regulations regarding credit payments. In most cases the costs will be based on a certain interest rate. Make sure each time you buy on credit that you understand how charges will be calculated. This section will help you understand credit charges.

Interest

In Chapter 18 you read about the interest that banks pay you. The interest that you are charged for credit works much the same way. Interest rates sometimes seem confusing. If you don't understand the credit charges, ask questions until you do. A good lending agency will be willing to explain all charges.

Two methods businesses use to calculate interest are explained below.

Simple Interest. Simple interest is explained in Chapter 18. Some credit charges are figured by using simple interest. When this method is used, you will pay one "lump" sum after a certain period of time. This lump sum will include the amount you owe plus the interest. For example, a 12 percent interest rate on $100 for a year would mean $12 in interest. You would owe $112 after one year.

Sometimes you can repay what you owe before the set time. If you can do this, it is to your advantage. The shorter the time period, the less interest you pay. For example, if you paid off the $100 mentioned above in six months instead of a year, you would pay only $6 in interest.

The Costs of Credit

Credit can cost you a great deal of money. The more you owe and the longer you take to pay, the more credit costs.

Suppose you wanted to borrow $40,000 to buy a house. The best interest rate you could find was 13 percent. In comparing how much the interest would cost you over different time periods, you found you could save a great deal of money by making a little bit higher monthly payment and paying the loan off in only fifteen years, instead of thirty. You found that a thirty-year loan would cost you $68,194.80 *more* than a fifteen-year loan. The credit cost for a thirty-year loan would be almost $120,000 — enough to buy three more houses!

Monthly Payments	Number of Years	Total Paid	Amount of Interest
$506.10	15	$ 91,098.00	$ 51,098.00
$468.63	20	$112,471.20	$ 72,471.20
$442.48	30	$159,292.80	$119,292.80

Interest on Unpaid Balance. Interest is also figured monthly on the unpaid balance. This type of interest is often called a **finance charge**. Each payment includes money paid toward the amount owed plus the finance charge. The finance charge is a percent of the unpaid balance, as stated in the credit contract.

Here is an example of how interest on unpaid balance works. Josh wanted to buy a bicycle that cost $200. Payments of $20 plus 1.8 percent interest on the unpaid balance were due each month. Josh divided $200 by $20 and knew he would need to make ten payments. Because the interest was on the unpaid balance, the amount to be paid would be less each month. Josh made the following calculations:

$$\begin{array}{r} \$200 \\ \times \ \underline{.018} \\ 1600 \\ \underline{200} \\ \$3.600 \end{array}$$

Interest on $200.00 at 1.8% is $3.60. The first payment is $20.00 + $3.60 = $23.60

$$\begin{array}{r} \$180 \\ \times \ \underline{.018} \\ 1440 \\ \underline{180} \\ \$3.240 \end{array}$$

Interest on $180.00 at 1.8% is $3.24. The second payment would be $20.00 + $3.24 = $23.24

Each month, Josh subtracted the payment of $20 and calculated the interest on the unpaid balance. He figured out that the total interest paid was $19.80.

Although Josh figured that his interest charge would change slightly from month to month, he made payments of $21.98 every month. Can you see why this happened? What do you get if you add the total interest—$19.80—to $200, and then divide by ten?

Most banks and companies offering credit figure the total cost of what you owe, including the interest charges. They then divide the total by the number of payments. Using this method allows the customer to pay equal amounts each month, which is much easier than paying a different amount each month.

Buying a Used Car

Your first car will most likely be a used one. Good used cars are available, but they are hard to find. You will probably need a loan. Here are some suggestions for buying your first car and getting a loan.

1. Decide how much money you can spend for a car.
2. Check the *Blue Book* for used car prices. You can get one of these books from someone at your local bank.
3. Look for the best loan rates you can find to buy a car. These rates do vary from bank to bank. Do some shopping.
4. Start looking for the car you want.
5. Compare prices of comparable models at reputable car dealers. You can usually buy cheaper from an individual, but be careful. You probably won't get a guarantee.
6. When you find a car you think you want, visually inspect both the inside and outside. If you know someone who is a mechanic or autobody repair person, ask that person to look the car over.
7. Be sure the care is licensed and insured before taking it for a test drive.
8. If you have a doubt about its mechanical condition after the test drive, have a good mechanic check the car.
9. If the dealer guarantees the car, be sure the guarantee is written on the contract.
10. Examine the purchase contract with your loan officer. Be sure you can make the monthly payments on the loan.
11. Sign the contract after you have decided everything is in accurate form.

Calculating Your Costs

You can calculate the cost of credit in dollars and cents. The contract will usually give the cost as a percentage rate. You should, however, figure the actual dollar cost of the credit.

1. Multiply the amount of the monthly payment by the number of months.
2. Add the down payment, if there is one.
3. Subtract the cash price of the purchase from the total of #1 and #2. In the case of a loan, subtract the amount of money you are borrowing from this total.

The answer you get in #3 is the dollar cost for using credit.

Mac bought a guitar that cost $310. He made a down payment of $35. That left a balance due of $275. He agreed to make eighteen monthly payments of $17.50. The dollar cost of credit can be shown as:

Eighteen monthly payments at $17.50 each ...	$315.00
Add down payment when purchased	+ 35.00
Total cost of guitar on credit	350.00
Subtract cash price of guitar	−310.00
Dollar cost of using credit	$ 40.00

Hidden Costs. In many cases there are "hidden" costs in using credit. For example, when you buy gasoline with credit, it costs the company money to keep a record of what you owe and to mail you a bill. This added expense causes the company to raise the price of its gasoline. This is why people who pay cash often receive a discount at service stations offering credit cards.

When stores offer credit, they often have costs in addition to the bookkeeping and billing costs mentioned above. Some customers don't pay their bills, which takes away from the store owner's profit. To make up for this loss, the store owner may raise the prices. This is why stores that sell on a cash-only basis can sometimes sell at lower prices than a store that offers credit.

Other Costs. Before using credit, figure out the real cost. In some cases there are extra charges that increase the total cost.

One example of extra charges is the charge for late payments. Different companies have different policies regarding the amount of late charges and when you must pay them.

Another type of extra charge is credit life insurance. Depending on how much you owe, the company may require you to have life insurance. This insurance is used to pay the full amount of what you owe if you die. Make sure you know how much you are paying for insurance—you may be able to buy it cheaper somewhere else.

Make a Decision

Once you are eighteen years old, you can apply for almost any credit card you want. As you know, there are several advantages to having your own credit cards. There are no major disadvantages as long as you exercise good judgment and pay what you owe on time. Credit cards can, however, lead to serious problems for those unable to control their spending. What's your decision—will you apply for credit cards, or continue to use cash? Give reasons for your decision.

REVIEW YOUR LEARNING

CHAPTER 19

CHAPTER SUMMARY

Almost everyone, including governments and large companies, uses credit. The main advantage to buying on credit is that you get to use right away something that you can pay for later. The main disadvantage to buying on credit is that you almost always pay more than the actual purchase price or loan amount. In fact, the more you owe and the longer you take to pay, the greater your overall cost.

There are several different types of credit: credit cards, charge accounts, installment plans, and cash loans. Whichever type you use, you will need to apply for credit. During the application process, the credit company will gather and check a great deal of information about you, especially your credit rating. Companies will not let you buy on credit if they find that you cannot be trusted to make your payments.

To get the most for your money, you must understand how credit charges are figured. Learn to calculate the actual cost in dollars of any loan or credit purchase. Learn, too, to recognize any hidden or special charges that increase your overall costs.

WORDS YOU SHOULD KNOW

charge account
collateral
credit
credit cards
credit rating
down payment
finance charge
installment plan
loan
repossess

STUDY QUESTIONS

1. What is the major advantage to using credit?
2. What is the major disadvantage to using credit?
3. Why do businesses offer credit?
4. Who *cannot* use credit?
5. What is a good guideline for determining the maximum amount of your income that you should spend on credit payments?
6. Why do companies want to know how long you've worked at your present job when you apply for credit?

REVIEW YOUR LEARNING

7. What three factors determine the cost of credit?
8. What are two common methods used by businesses to calculate interest on credit?
9. How much would your credit cost be if you owed $350 for a year at 18 percent?
10. By using what three steps can you calculate the cost of credit?
11. If you bought a stereo system for $360, and you agreed to make monthly payments of $35 a month for a year, what would be your credit cost?
12. What are two examples of extra charges that increase the cost of credit?

DISCUSSION TOPICS

1. People often buy on credit, and therefore pay more, even though they have enough money to pay cash. Why do people do this? Can you think of a situation in which you would do this?
2. Does credit encourage people to live beyond their means? Explain.
3. Should teenagers be allowed to use their parents' credit cards? Discuss.

SUGGESTED ACTIVITIES

1. Do a comparison of the different rates and charges involved with different credit plans in your area. Each student can be responsible for gathering information on three or four local businesses that offer credit. Someone should also inquire at two or three local banks. How do the different plans compare? Are there any differences?
2. Make a list of all the ways you now use credit. Add to that list the ways you plan to use credit during the next five years. Write one paragraph explaining the advantages of using credit. Add another paragraph telling how you will use credit wisely. After your teacher corrects the papers, discuss them in class.

Buying Insurance

Imagine that you have just paid $12,000 for a new car. You drive the car out of the lot, turn the corner, and hit a parked truck. The entire front end of your new car is demolished. Where will you get the thousands of dollars you will need to fix it, if it can be fixed?

Imagine that you have married and started a family. You are the main wage earner since your spouse is unable to work and must stay home with the children. It takes every penny you earn to pay all the bills. Then one day at work you fall from a high platform and severely injure your back and legs. The doctor says you will be unable to work for a least a year, possibly longer. How will your family manage without your income, especially now that you will have lots of medical bills?

You can't do anything to guarantee that you will never be involved in a serious accident. You can, though, do something to help yourself pay for the tremendous financial costs of such accidents. You can do what almost everyone does—buy insurance.

In this chapter you will find out what insurance is and how it works. You will learn about the many different kinds of insurance. You will also learn how to buy enough insurance to meet your needs, without buying too much.

DO YOU KNOW . . .
- why people buy insurance?
- what different types of insurance are available?
- how to go about choosing the best insurance policies for your needs?

CAN YOU DEFINE . . .
- beneficiary?
- cash value?
- deductible?
- face value?
- group insurance?
- insurance?
- liability?
- policy?
- premium?

Understanding Insurance

Insurance is a financial precaution against injury, loss, or damage. It is a way of protecting ourselves against enormous bills that we could never pay without help. When people buy insurance, they pay a little bit of money at regular intervals. They do this to guarantee that they will receive a large sum of money later, when they need it.

People buy most of their insurance from insurance companies. There are many different kinds of insurance companies in our country. Some specialize in selling one or two types of insurance; others sell all kinds.

Insurance companies are in business to sell insurance **policies**. An insurance policy is a contract between a person, called a *policyholder,* and an insurance company. People buy insurance policies to protect themselves against loss, damage, or injury.

An insurance policy states how much the insurance company will pay if a certain thing (auto accident, death, fire) occurs. The insurance policy usually states certain conditions under which this event must happen. For example, people are not entitled to payments from their fire insurance policy if they set their own house on fire. This is just one simple example of the conditions stated in most insurance policies.

In talking about the conditions written in policies, insurance people say, "You are *covered* for that," or "You don't have *coverage* for this." *Covered* and *coverage* are words insurance people use to talk about what is included in an insurance policy.

If the insurance agent says you are covered, that means you have insurance for that particular loss, damage, or injury. Two policies may be very similar, but one may *cover* more kinds of loss, injury, or damage. Or two policies may cover exactly the same things, but one may have *more coverage.* This means that one policy pays more if the policyholder has a claim.

If the event specified in the policy does occur, and it occurs under the conditions of the policy, the company pays the policyholder a certain amount of money. This amount is often called the *benefit* or *cash benefit.* In the case of life insurance, which you will read about later, the insurance company pays the benefit to a **beneficiary.** A beneficiary is someone named by a policyholder to receive payments from the insurance company. Most husbands and wives name each other as their beneficiaries on their life insurance policies.

Insurance policies are legal agreements that state very specific terms and conditions. You should read your policies carefully to know exactly what protection is and is not included.

SECTION 1. THE CONTRACT

1.1 LIFE INSURANCE BENEFIT

The Northwestern Mutual Life Insurance Company will pay a benefit on the death of the Insured. Subject to the terms and conditions of the policy:

- payment will be made after proof of the death of the Insured is received at the Home Office;
- payment will be made to the beneficiary or other payee under Sections 8 and 9; and
- the amount of the benefit will be the Basic Amount shown on page 3, plus the Extra Life Protection then in force.

1.2 EXTRA LIFE PROTECTION

Description. Extra Life Protection consists of one year term insurance and paid-up additions. At first, it is all one year term insurance. Each dividend is used to purchase paid-up additions. These additions reduce the amount of one year term insurance until Extra Life Protection is all paid-up additions. After that, dividends

net annual premium will be based on the Commissioners 1958 Standard Ordinary Mortality Table with an annual effective interest rate of 4½%. The increase will be based on the Insured's attained age. It will be payable for the remaining premium period.

1.3 REDUCTION OF EXISTING PROTECTION BY OWNER

When the Owner surrenders any paid-up additions or directs that dividends be used other than for paid-up additions:

- any one year term insurance in force will terminate;
- any remaining guaranteed period of Extra Life Protection will terminate; and
- the amount of Extra Life Protection will be the amount of any paid-up additions remaining in force.

1.4 ENTIRE CONTRACT; CHANGES

This policy with the attached application is the entire contract

In addition to the amount and the conditions for payment by the insurance company, the policy also states the amount of the **premium**. The premium is the money that the policyholder agrees to pay to the insurance company at regular periods. Premiums are usually paid monthly, twice a year, four times a year, or yearly. If the policyholder fails to pay a premium on time, the policy is usually no longer in effect.

You can buy insurance policies for different amounts. For example, you can insure your life for as little as $1,000, or for more than $1,000,000. It's your decision based on what you can afford and how much money you think your beneficiary will need. You should know, of course, that the greater the coverage, the greater the premium. Insurance is just like anything else—the more you buy, the more it costs.

When an accident, death, or loss occurs, the policyholder reports it to the insurance company. Reporting a loss to collect payment is called *making a claim*. After you make a claim, the insurance company often investigates to find out what happened and why it happened. The company will then decide if your claim meets the policy conditions, and if so, how much money you should receive.

One of the first things you should do after an accident is notify your insurance agent. The sooner you make your claim, the sooner the insurance company can pay for the damage.

In buying some insurance policies, you will be asked to specify the amount of the **deductible**. A **deductible** is the amount of money the policyholder must pay before making a claim. If you wreck your car, for example, and your insurance policy says you have a $100 deductible, you must pay the first $100 of damages. The insurance company will then pay the rest. You might have a $100 deductible, $200 deductible, or no deductible at all. The higher the deductible, the lower your premium will be.

People buy insurance policies for all kinds of protection against loss. The most common kinds of insurance are for life, property, and health. It is in these areas that people suffer the greatest financial trouble when something bad happens. Of course the money from the policy does not make up for the death or serious injury of a loved one. The insurance does, however, help people make it through extremely difficult financial times.

Besides life, property, and health, do you know of any kinds of losses for which people buy insurance? In many cases it depends on the person. Many farmers have hail insurance. Homeowners buy title insurance. Banks buy deposit insurance. Some people buy insurance for special, one-time events. A company in England, Lloyds of London, is famous for writing insurance policies against all sorts of unusual losses.

You have probably just encountered many new words. Insurance has a language all its own. You will realize this even more when you read your first insurance policy. If you've read one already, you know that these contracts can be very difficult to understand. You are not alone—most people have just as much trouble.

It is very important, though, that you learn some basic insurance terms and try to understand your insurance policies. A lot of money will be at stake. You want to be sure you have the right protection. You also want to be sure that you do everything necessary to keep the policy in force.

Your insurance agent is your best resource in insurance matters. Find an agent you know and trust. You will then be sure that you are getting good advice. If you don't know any insurance agents, go to the most well-known companies. If a company has been in business for a long time, chances are it has been providing good service to its policyholders.

Do you know anyone who sells insurance? You will feel more secure if you buy your insurance from someone you know and trust.

Automobile Insurance

The first kind of insurance many people buy is automobile insurance. If you own your own car, you probably bought an insurance policy. If you have a car but no policy, get one soon. With the rising costs of cars and car repairs, no car of any value at all should be without insurance.

Types of Coverage

When you buy a standard automobile insurance policy, you are usually buying several different kinds of coverage. Each type of coverage insures your car and you for a different kind of loss, damage, or injury. Insurance companies will give you some choices about which types of coverage you want in your particular policy.

Liability. The most important part of any automobile insurance policy is the liability coverage. Liability means responsibility. Liability insurance covers your responsibility to others. If you cause an accident—if you are at fault—you are responsible for any injury, loss, or damage that other people receive due to your mistake. Your liability insurance would pay the other peoples expenses.

Liability insurance can be divided into two types —bodily injury and property damage. You should have both. In fact, many states require that you have both types of liability insurance.

Mike, Jean, and Tom were on their way to a party. They were all in a good mood and ready for a good time. Tom, who was in the back seat, was telling a funny story about something that had happened that day at school. Mike, who was driving, became so absorbed in the story that he momentarily forgot about what he was doing and turned to look at Tom. At just about that same instant, Tom yelled "Watch Out!" It was too late. Mike had let his car drift over the center line and he had hit an oncoming car. Mike, Jean, and Tom were OK, but the driver of the other car appeared to be seriously injured. The ambulance arrived quickly and sped off with the other driver.

In an accident such as this, everyone's first concern is for the safety and well-being of those who are injured. The next concern is for the costs of the accident. Who will pay for the damages? Who will pay for the hospital costs? If someone is injured for life, who will pay for all the hardships that person will have to endure as a result of the accident?

The laws for liability vary from state to state, but in most states, Mike would have to pay the repair costs for the other person's car, as well as his own. Mike would also be liable for the other person's medical expenses. If the injury was serious, the other person might even sue Mike for a lot of money. Unless Mike has liability insurance, Tom's funny story could result in Mike's being in debt for a long time to come.

No one has to tell you that automobiles can be very dangerous. Everyone who drives a car runs the risk of causing serious injuries to other people. When accidents do happen, people suffering permanent disabilities often file lawsuits for large sums of money against the person responsible for the accident. Very few people have enough money to pay these sums of money. That is why most people buy liability insurance.

If *you* are injured or *your car* is damaged in an accident caused by someone else, that person's liability insurance should pay for your injury or damage. You should not use your own insurance to pay for expenses that someone else has created.

You might think that it doesn't make any difference whether your insurance company or the other person's pays the expenses—as long as you don't have to pay it. But don't look at it this way. There are several reasons why it's to your advantage that the other person's company pays.

First, if you have a deductible, you would have to pay it before your company would pay the remaining costs. Whatever the deductible, however small,

that is money you shouldn't have to pay. Second, insurance companies keep track of driving records and the claims made by their policyholders. The more violations and claims a person has, the higher that person's premiums will be. This means that by filing a claim for an accident that wasn't your fault, you may be adding to the cost of your future premiums.

Uninsured Motorist. Although almost everyone has liability insurance, some people don't. You could be injured and your car damaged in an accident caused by a driver without liability insurance. Insurance companies have special coverages for just such an event.

You can buy two kinds of uninsured motorist insurance. One kind insures you for bodily injury. Your medical expenses are paid if you are injured and someone else was at fault. Some states require people to have a certain amount of this coverage.

The other kind of uninsured motorist insurance covers property damage. This coverage pays for repairs on your car if the responsible person cannot pay. If you have collision coverage (see next page), you probably won't need much property coverage for uninsured motorists. Some states do require this coverage for people who do not have collision coverage.

If you cause an accident that results in a serious injury, you could be responsible for an extremely large financial payment. Liability insurance is a must if you drive a car.

One day while Ken was waiting for the traffic light to change, a pickup truck hit the side of his van. When he saw the damage, he knew repairs would cost a lot. But the accident wasn't his fault, so he thought the other driver would pay repair costs.

The police soon arrived on the scene. While writing the report, the police officer asked the other driver for the name of his insurance company. Ken was shocked to hear the driver of the pickup say that he didn't have any insurance. The officer told the driver that state law required liability coverage. Legal action would be brought against him. The officer also told the pickup driver that he would be responsible for the cost of repairing Ken's van.

Ken never heard from the other driver again, and he never received any money. He had to take care of the costs himself even though the accident was not his fault. Ken was glad he had bought property damage coverage for uninsured motorists.

Collision. If you have a new car or a valuable older car, you will certainly want your automobile insurance policy to include collision coverage. Collision covers you for the costs of damage to your car. Whether the accident is your fault or someone else's, collision coverage pays to repair or replace your car.

You read earlier in this chapter about deductibles. The amount of the deductible is an important factor with collision coverage. The greater the deductible, the cheaper your premiums. You need to think, though, about how much money you could afford in case there's an accident. If you won't have $100 in your savings, you may want a smaller deductible, or no deductible at all.

Not everyone needs collision insurance. Your car may be old and worth very little. In this case the cost of your insurance might be more than the value of your car. You would be wise not to buy any collision coverage for such a car.

Comprehensive. Comprehensive automobile insurance covers most kinds of damage other than that caused by collisions. Damages due to fire, lightning, wind, flood, and hail are covered. Your comprehensive coverage may also include losses due to glass breakage, theft, vandalism, and falling objects. As with collision insurance, there may be a deductible with your comprehensive insurance.

What Will It Cost?

Automobile insurance can be very expensive. Obviously you don't want to pay any more than you have to. Still, you want to be sure you have enough insurance to cover any losses, damage, or injuries you might have.

Costs for automobile insurance vary considerably. Some people pay much more than others for the same coverage. Insurance companies take several factors into account in determining how much your premiums will be. Understanding these factors may help you get the coverage you need and want for the lowest possible cost.

If you owned both of these cars, would you buy the same amount of collision insurance for both? As your car gets older and becomes less valuable, you may want to save some money by cutting back on your collision coverage.

Driving Record. The most important factor in determining the amount of your premiums is your driving record. In fact, if you have a history of violations and accidents, you may not be able to get any insurance at all. In some states—those that require liability insurance—that means you can't drive.

Insurance companies also base their rates on the number of claims. If you are involved in several accidents and make several claims, your rates will go up. Insurance companies usually go back three years in checking your records. Driving safely is the surest way to save money on insurance premiums.

The Company. Rates vary from company to company. Some companies are very selective about which people they sell automobile insurance to. They do not sell policies to drivers with bad driving records. Because they are selective, they have fewer claims. This means that they can charge lower rates. If you have a good driving record, you may be able to get a cheaper rate at a selective company.

Age. Insurance companies have found that male drivers under the age of twenty-five file more automobile claims than any other group. Since these people have more accidents, they pay a higher rate for insurance. You'll find that when you get older, your rates will go down.

Where You Live. Everything else being the same —same car, same driving record, same company— your premiums will vary from place to place. Urban areas have a higher rate of accidents than rural areas. For this reason, the premiums are higher in cities. Some cities have more accidents than others. If you move, your rates may go up or down.

Other Factors. There are some additional factors in determining rates. Some companies give special discounts for students who have high grades in school. People who have taken driver education classes sometimes get lower rates than those who haven't. Ask your insurance agent about any special factors that might affect your rate.

Other Vehicles. Vehicles other than cars, such as motorcycles or motorboats, should also be insured. The same kinds of coverage are usually available. The same factors—number of claims, age, company, and location—will determine the rates.

A report card with all *A*s could mean lower insurance premiums. Many insurance companies have special rates for people who they believe are less likely to have accidents.

Make a Decision

The premium will soon be due on your car insurance. Since you're a little short of cash, you're looking for a way to cut costs. Your insurance agent tells you that you can lower your premium $40 every six months ($80 a year) by raising your deductible from $50 to $200. An unexpected repair bill around $150 would be difficult, but you think you might take a chance. What's your decision—high deductible and low premium, or low deductible and higher premium? Give reasons for your answer.

Whose Fault Was It?

You can tell from reading about the different types of coverages that it's important to find out who was at fault in any automobile accident. Most people believe that the person who caused the accident should pay for the damages.

There are usually disagreements about who was at fault in an automobile accident. Someone other than the people involved must decide which driver, if either, caused the accident. This is why the police should be called to the scene of an accident. The police officer will frequently make a decision as to who was at fault. If the police officer cannot tell who was at fault, the case may go to court.

You will also want to notify your insurance company if you are involved in an accident. The insurance company wants to protect their interests. They may have to pay a large amount of money—they want to make sure that the accident is handled properly and all the evidence is gathered.

Reaching a legal decision about who caused an accident can be a time-consuming, costly process. Legal expenses for insurance lawsuits cost over two billion dollars each year. This means that about one dollar out of every three paid in premiums goes toward these expenses.

In addition to being expensive, lawsuits lead to delays in settling claims. In many large cities, the courts are very busy with these cases.

To reduce these delays and costs, some states have passed *no-fault* automobile insurance laws. These laws say that insurance companies must pay for their own policyholder's damages, regardless of who is at fault. With this type of system, there are no guilty parties. All victims are paid by their own insurance companies. This type of law reduces the number of lawsuits.

Health Insurance

Now, while you are young and healthy, you probably don't think much about hospitals and doctors. As you get older, though, you will become concerned about health and health care. If you have a family to support, you will need lots of medical attention for your young children. All this medical care can cost a great deal of money.

Your parents or guardians are probably taking care of your health care costs at the present time. They almost certainly have a health insurance policy for this purpose. Very few people have enough money to pay for the extremely high costs of hospital service, should they need it. A long hospital stay can be a financial disaster.

A routine visit to the family doctor can cost $30 or $40. Room and board in a hospital for one day is usually over $100. Charges for even the less complicated, more commonplace surgeries can be hundreds or even thousands of dollars. Health insurance is the method that almost all people use to pay for these medical expenses.

Who Pays for Health Insurance?

For most people there is no decision about whether or not they want health insurance—they do. The decisions to be made are where they will get the insurance and how much they will get. Depending on their job and family situation, people get their insurance from different places.

If you are involved in an accident, it's important that you call a police officer. The officer will collect information to determine who, if anyone, was at fault.

Adam and a group of his friends from work liked to play football. On Saturdays they often met in the city park, divided into teams, and had a great game.

About a month ago things changed. Adam made a fast tackle and then didn't get up. Adam's friends had to call an ambulance to take Adam to the hospital.

Adam was told he would be kept in the hospital in a body cast for several weeks. Adam wondered how he could pay for several weeks in a hospital. He knew it would cost several thousand dollars. Adam had decided not to enroll in the group medical plan at work. He thought young people didn't need health insurance.

Group Plans. Most people today get their health insurance through a **group insurance** plan at work. Group insurance is a method of buying insurance in which a group of people go together to buy a policy. The main advantage to group insurance is that the insurance company can offer better rates to a large group of people than it can to a single individual. Another advantage to group plans is that the employer usually pays part or all, of the premium for each employee. As a result of these advantages, employees can obtain much more coverage for much less money.

When you belong to a group insurance plan at work, you have less say in the kinds and amounts of coverage you get than you would if you bought the policy yourself. If you belong to the group plan, you must go along with what your company and most of the employees want. In most cases, though, the group plan will offer the kinds and amounts of coverage you want. Getting more insurance for less money is usually far more important than having the exact policy you want.

If you belong to a group plan, your employer will either pay your premium for you or deduct a certain amount from each of your paychecks. This amount is usually considerably less than you, yourself, would have to pay for the same coverage. As explained, you pay less because you belong to the group and because your employer is contributing money for you.

In most plans, employees can add their spouse and children to the policy. This means that more money will be deducted from the employee's paychecks. Plans differ as to how much extra it costs to add family members. In most cases it is much cheaper to insure family members through a group plan at work than by buying individual policies.

The most economical way to buy health insurance is usually through a group plan at work. The personnel officer or your employer will probably explain the major features of the group plan to you shortly after you begin working for the company.

When you check into the high costs of health care and health insurance, you will better appreciate the value of a group plan at work. Not all employers provide group health insurance for their employees. The group plans offered by some companies are much better than those offered by other companies. Some include dental and eye care, for example, although most do not. If you are deciding between two or more job offers with similar pay, the health insurance plans should be an important factor in your decision.

Buying Your Own Policy. If you don't have a job or you work for a company without group health insurance, you will need to buy your own health insurance. Since some insurance companies specialize in health insurance, make sure you talk to these companies before you buy a policy.

When you buy your own policy, you will have several decisions to make. First you will need to decide what types of coverage you want. You will read about the different kinds of health coverage later in this chapter.

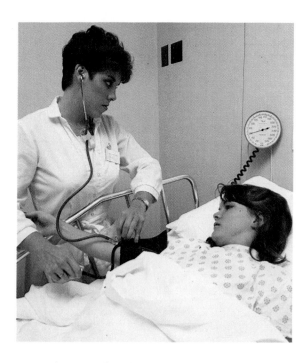

Do you have any idea what a hospital stay of just three or four days can cost? Only the wealthiest people can afford to be without health insurance.

Next you will decide how much insurance you want and can afford. The policies can be written with different limits. You might want up to $50,000 of hospital insurance, while someone else would want only $25,000. By now, you know enough about insurance to know that the more insurance you buy, the higher your premiums.

Types of Coverage

Most health insurance policies, like automobile policies, divide the insurance into several kinds of coverage. Different companies will have different ways of explaining and organizing the coverages. The following descriptions will help you understand the general areas of health insurance coverage.

Hospital-Surgical. Hospital-surgical coverage includes hospital and surgery costs. Room and board in the hospital, drugs, x-rays, use of an operating room, and the surgeon's fees are some common expenses paid for by this coverage. There is usually not a deductible. Many plans pay 80 percent of the total expense, though there is usually a maximum amount that the policy will pay. Check to see what percent the policy pays and what the limit is for any policy you are considering.

Medical. The medical coverage for most policies includes non-hospital expenses. Visits to the doctor's office, x-rays, drugs, and many other expenses are usually covered. Most plans call for a deductible of $100 or more. This means that you pay the first $100 of expenses, and the insurance company pays the remaining expenses for that calendar year. Each year you would pay the deductible before the insurance company began paying.

Most medical coverages pay 80 percent, not 100 percent of the total expense. Don't expect to find a policy that pays 100 percent of the expenses.

Major Medical. Many policies include a major medical coverage. This type of coverage pays for heavy expenses resulting from long-term illnesses or injuries. Major medical covers expenses above a certain amount. It usually involves a deductible and pays 80 percent of the total.

Disability. Disability coverage provides money for people unable to work. This money takes the place of the worker's regular paychecks. The amount of the regular payments could be equal to, or a percentage of, the employee's regular pay.

Disability coverage is often broken down into two kinds: short-term and long-term disability. Short-term pays for just a few months; long-term can pay for a full lifetime. Many group policies include short-term disability in the overall coverage, but charge an additional amount for long-term disability. In many other plans, both short- and long-term disability coverage cost extra.

Life Insurance

Just as you don't think much about hospitals and doctors while you are young and healthy, you probably don't think much about dying. Few young people do—it seems so far away and it can be painful to think about. Painful or not, though, you should think about your death long enough to decide whether or not you want to buy life insurance.

Life insurance is a way of leaving money to people you care about when you die. You probably won't want these people to pay your burial expenses or any debts you might have. At the very least you will want to make sure there is money available for these expenses.

The chances are good that as you grow older, you will marry and raise a family. You will probably help to support your family. If you die, the family may have a difficult time paying bills and buying food without your income. Life insurance can provide enough money for your family to continue its usual lifestyle after you've gone.

If you are young and single, life insurance is not as important to you now as it will be later. The best time to buy life insurance, though, is when you are young. The rate of death for young people is much lower than for older people. This means that young people pay less in premiums.

Another advantage to buying life insurance now is that your health is probably at its peak. You will probably have to have a physical exam when you buy life insurance. If you have a serious medical problem, the insurance company will consider you a high risk. This will mean very high premiums or perhaps no life insurance at all. If you buy the insurance now, while your health is good, you avoid the possible high costs or refusal that might result later.

A third advantage to buying while you're young is that you probably will have more extra money before you get married and have children. You can more easily afford to pay the premiums now, when you are single. Buying life insurance at an early age, before your need is so great, is a way of getting a head start.

When you buy life insurance, you can buy as much as you like. You could buy a $1,000 policy or a $100,000 policy. The size of the policy would depend on how much your family would need and how much you could afford. Obviously the premiums for a $100,000 policy are much higher than those for a $1,000 policy.

Armstrong World Industries, Inc.

Chances are you will someday be providing for a family of your own. Life insurance is one way to make sure your children will be taken care of if something happens to you unexpectedly.

Types of Life Insurance

People have different life insurance needs. As a result, life insurance companies have developed many different kinds of policies. The type of policy that's best for you at one point in your life may not be the best type for you at another time.

Two important terms to understand when discussing life insurance are **face value** and **cash value**. The amount of protection stated on the policy is the face value. This is the amount of money the beneficiary is paid if the insured person dies. All policies have a face value, which is also called the *death benefit*.

Make a Decision

You've read that the best time to buy life insurance is when you are young. Since you are working and saving a little money every week, you could afford to buy a policy now. You don't have a family yet, but you probably will someday. A close friend, who happens to sell life insurance, has just asked you to buy a policy. What's your decision—do you buy life insurance while you are young and single, or will you wait until you have a greater need for it? Give reasons for your answer.

Some policies can be converted into cash by the policyholder. The amount of money a policyholder receives by ending coverage is the cash value. Not all life insurance policies have cash value.

Term Insurance. Term insurance is insurance that covers the insured person for a set period of time. This time period could be five, ten, twenty years, or more. If the insured person dies during that time, the beneficiary is paid the face value of the policy. When the term ends, so does the protection.

Term insurance is the most inexpensive kind of life insurance when the insured person is young. The disadvantage to term insurance is that it has no cash value.

The cost of term insurance is largely determined by the age of the person insured. The premiums go up as the insured person gets older. Usually the insured person may renew the policy at the end of the term, but the premium will almost certainly be higher.

When you buy term insurance, you should find out whether or not it's *convertible*. Convertible means that the term insurance can be changed to *whole life* insurance (see next page). The advantage to this is that you don't have to take a physical

Before you buy life insurance, discuss the pros and cons of whole life insurance and term insurance with your insurance agent. Your financial and personal situation will determine which type of life insurance is best for you.

exam to buy a whole life policy. This can be very important if you wait until you are older and your health is more questionable.

Whole Life Insurance. Like term insurance, whole life insurance pays a face value to the beneficiary when the insured person dies. Whole life is also called *ordinary* or *straight* life insurance.

Whole life differs from term insurance in several important ways. First, whole life coverage does not end after a certain period of time, as does term insurance. Whole life coverage continues for the insured person's "whole life," or until the policyholder stops making payments.

A second difference is that the premiums for term insurance go up as the insured person gets older. This usually means that term insurance is less expensive in the early years, but more expensive later. Whole life premiums stay constant throughout the policy.

The third and most important difference between term insurance and whole life insurance is that whole life builds up cash value. When you buy term insurance, your premiums pay for the death benefit, and nothing more. If you don't die during the term of the insurance, you get no money back. If you buy a whole life policy, though, your premiums buy more than the death benefit—they also buy cash value.

People use their cash value in different ways. Some people wait until they are older, then use the money from their policy as retirement income. They can take the money in one lump sum or in monthly installments. Others "cash in" their policy to obtain the money they need for an emergency. When you cash in a policy, you lose the death benefit of the policy. With most policies you must pay premiums for at least two or three years before the policy has any cash value.

One special kind of whole life insurance is called *limited-pay life.* With this type of policy the policyholder pays higher premiums, but pays them for a shorter period of time, usually from ten to thirty years. People who have enough money to pay the high premiums often prefer this type of policy.

Other Life Insurance. There are many kinds of life insurance in addition to the basic term and whole life policies. There are endowment policies that provide a fixed amount on a certain date. There are group life policies that often allow employees to buy life insurance at a lower cost than they would be able to individually. There are also many variations of the basic term and whole policies you read about earlier.

How Much Life Insurance?

It's not always easy to know how much life insurance you should have. You must consider several factors. Your financial responsibilities and your income are the major considerations. Before you buy life insurance, ask yourself the following questions.

- How much money do I want to leave my beneficiaries if I die this year? Do I need more insurance to provide for them in the way I want to?
- What are my retirement plans? Will I need income from an insurance policy?
- How much can I afford to pay for insurance? How much life insurance will my employer provide?
- Do I want just the death benefit, or do I want to build up some cash value?

After answering the questions above, you will have a better idea of what you need from an insurance program. When you know what you need, talk to an experienced insurance agent. Try to balance the amount of insurance you want with what you can afford.

Don't be afraid to ask questions. Make sure you know how much both the premium and the benefit will be. You should also know such things as how long you will make payments and when you can cash in your policy.

From time to time, you should analyze your insurance situation. Ask yourself if anything has changed since you bought your policy. If the answer is yes, you may need more or less insurance.

Property Insurance

Property insurance is insurance you buy to protect yourself against damage to your personal property. When you buy personal property insurance, you also buy liability coverage for injuries that occur to other people on your property.

When you read about automobile insurance, you were reading about personal property insurance. Your automobile is your personal property. Automobile insurance is explained separately because it will probably be the first piece of personal property that you need to insure. A few other types of personal property insurance are explained here.

Renter's Insurance

When you first move away from home, you will probably rent rather than buy a place to live. If you have many valuable personal possessions, consider buying renter's insurance. Renter's insurance is property insurance renters buy to protect against loss or damage to their possessions.

While he was in high school, George saved enough from his part-time job to buy an expensive stereo. Then he bought as many records as possible. He received an electric typewriter and several more albums as graduation gifts.

Last fall George and his friend, Mario, both began working for the Homes Construction Co. They rented a mobile home near the job site. George moved his stereo equipment, typewriter, and kitchen items into the new place. Mario moved in only a small amount of clothing.

George had learned in high school that renters need property insurance. He figured that his clothing and all the things he owned were worth over $2,000 so he insured his personal property against fire, storm, and theft.

A few months later George was glad he had bought the insurance policy. While he was home one weekend, the mobile home burned to the ground. Mario was able to get their clothing out of the closet, but that was all. George used the insurance payment to replace his household goods, stereo, and typewriter.

Try estimating the value of the personal property you see in this apartment above. What do you think it would cost to replace the furniture, stereo, TV, fireplace, carpet, plants, and all the rest? Renter's insurance is often a good idea if you have lots of personal property.

The owner of the building where you rent will have insurance on the property. That insurance will not pay to replace the personal belongings of the renters. If you have several expensive items, such as a stereo and TV, and lots of furniture, check into the cost of insuring these items. Estimate how much it would cost to replace everything in your apartment. A small monthly premium compared to the total replacement cost might be a bargain.

Homeowner's Insurance

If you save enough money and someday buy your own home, you will want to buy insurance to protect your home against damage or loss. You can do this by buying a homeowner's policy. If you borrow money from a bank or savings and loan association, you will probably have to buy homeowner's insurance. The people loaning you the money want to make sure that their investment is protected against fire, storm, and other possible damages.

When people buy homeowner's insurance, they usually buy a policy that pays enough to replace the home. For example, if you bought a house that would cost $50,000 to build, you would probably buy at least a $50,000 homeowner's policy. If the costs of building a home went up, you would want to buy more insurance.

Most homeowner's policies include several kinds of coverage. In addition to replacement costs, personal property within the house, liability, and medical payments are often parts of the policy. If you own some exceptionally valuable items, list each individual item on your policy.

My Personal Property

Make an inventory of your personal property. Then ask an insurance agent how much it would cost to insure your property. When you think of all the things that could happen — fire, theft, storm — property insurance could be a smart purchase.

Item	When bought	Purchase price
Television set		
Stereo		
Radio		
Tape recorder		
Camera		
Sports equipment		
Musical instruments		
Jewelry		
Stamp collection		
Coin collection		
Silverware		
Watch		
Typewriter		
Calculator		
Guns		
Bicycle		
Motorcyle		
Boat and motor		
Mower		
Power tools		
Clothing		

REVIEW YOUR LEARNING

CHAPTER SUMMARY

Most people buy insurance policies to protect themselves against the tremendous financial cost of accidents and death. A general understanding of what insurance is and how it works will help you buy the kinds and amounts of insurance you need, without buying too much.

The major types of automobile insurance are liability, uninsured motorist, collision, and comprehensive. How much these coverages cost you will depend on such factors as your driving record, the company from which you buy, your age, and where you live.

Most people buy health insurance through a group plan at work. The major types of health coverage are hospital-surgical, medical, major medical, and disability. The high costs of hospital and general health care make health insurance necessary for most people.

Life insurance is a way of leaving money to people whom you care about when you die. The major types of life insurance are term insurance and whole life. Term insurance does *not* build up cash value—whole life does.

You can buy insurance to protect personal property other than your car. Many renters with lots of valuable personal property buy renter's insurance. Home owners almost always buy insurance to protect the large investments they have in their homes.

WORDS YOU SHOULD KNOW

beneficiary
cash value
deductible
face value
group insurance
insurance
liability
policy
premium

STUDY QUESTIONS

1. Why do most people buy insurance?
2. What happens to the policy if a policyholder fails to pay the premiums?
3. How does changing the deductible on your automobile insurance policy from $100 to $250 affect the amount of your premiums?
4. Who is usually your best resource person when you have questions about insurance?
5. List the four major types of automobile coverage.
6. Of the four types of automobile coverage, which is the most important?

REVIEW YOUR LEARNING CHAPTER 20

7. Give two reasons why you should not use your own insurance to pay for damages to your car when someone else was at fault.
8. What are the two types of uninsured motorist coverage?
9. If you trade in an old car for a brand new car, would you buy more or less collision coverage?
10. Name four causes of damages covered by comprehensive automobile insurance.
11. List five factors that affect the amount of the premiums you would pay for automobile insurance.
12. Why should a police officer always be called to the scene of an accident?
13. Where do most people buy their health insurance today?
14. What are four major types of health insurance coverage?
15. Why do people buy life insurance?
16. What are three advantages to buying life insurance while you are young?
17. What are the two major types of life insurance?
18. Which type of life insurance builds up cash value?
19. What factor determines whether or not you should buy renter's insurance?
20. What factor determines how much homeowner's insurance homeowners buy?

DISCUSSION TOPICS

1. You have just had an accident while riding in a friend's car. The car is damaged, and your ankle is hurt. You have no insurance, but your friend has liability insurance. How can this situation be resolved?
2. What is your opinion of no-fault insurance?
3. What kind of life insurance—term or whole life—will you buy? Why?

SUGGESTED ACTIVITIES

1. Make a class file of insurance advertisements. Sources include newspapers, magazines, and mail received by students, their families, and teachers. Classify the advertisements under automobile, other property, life, and health. Compare the types of coverages and their costs.
2. Use library reference materials to prepare a short report on no-fault insurance. Include reasons why your state does or does not have this method of settling claims.

PART FIVE

MEETING YOUR ADULT RESPONSIBILITIES

Up until now, someone else has probably been responsible for you. Someone else has probably talked to unhappy business people, police officers, and judges, if and when you had legal problems. Someone else has probably signed your contracts, thereby taking on the legal responsibility of fulfilling those contracts. Someone else has probably paid most of the expense involved in providing you with a place to sleep and something to eat.

As you know, this will all change soon, and you will become more responsible for yourself. This last section in the book provides you with some basic information you need to meet your adult responsibilities as a tax-paying citizen. You will also learn how to go about choosing and setting up a place of your own, in case you decide to move away from home. You will find all of this information helpful as you take on more and more adult responsibilities.

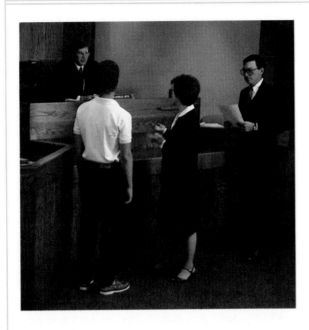

Handling Legal Matters

For people to live together and get along, they must have some rules. Without rules there are no guidelines to follow when problems occur.

You are probably very familiar with rules—most families have their own rules. Parents make rules to protect their children's health and safety. Family members agree on rules for doing chores around the house. As you grow older, you will probably have more and more say in your family's rules.

Laws are rules, not for a family, but for a city, state, or country. Laws are rules that our governments enforce through the courts and other government agencies. You've heard people say "It's against the law." This means that to do that certain act is to break the rules established by the people of our country or by the residents of a certain community.

The purpose of having laws is to protect the safety and rights of all people. Laws make sure that all people are treated fairly. Our laws prevent strong and powerful people from taking advantage of weaker, less powerful people.

In this chapter you will learn some basic facts about the law and how it affects you. As you become more responsible for your own actions, you will have more dealings with the law.

The Legal System

The word *legal* refers to anything having to do with the law. In our country the **legal system** is the combination of laws, processes, and people that go together to protect our rights and safety. Elected officials, judges, the courts, lawyers, and police officers are all part of the legal system.

As a citizen, you have a legal responsibility to know and obey the federal, state, and local laws. Once you reach voting age, you will also have a voice in making these laws. Don't forget that most of the people in the world do not have this right. You should exercise your right to vote so that you can improve the laws.

Levels of the Law

Laws are made at three levels: federal, state, and local. At all levels the laws are written and voted on by elected officials. Our system of government has set up some guidelines by which the laws can be passed and enforced.

The United States Constitution. The Constitution is the highest law of the land. It tells how the federal government is to be organized and lists some basic laws and freedoms. The Constitution also gives Congress the power to pass new laws when we need them. Any new laws passed must not conflict with the Constitution.

State Constitutions. Each state has its own constitution. Most of the state constitutions are patterned after the United States Constitution. Laws differ from state to state, however. One state may have laws that have not been passed in another state.

Most states do have uniform (of the same type) *commercial laws.* These are the laws dealing with sales and contracts. Because commercial laws are similar in all states, people living in one state can do business with people in another state. Agencies of the federal government also help to regulate business between states.

Local Laws. County and city laws are called *ordinances.* County and city officials are elected and have the power to pass ordinances that apply only to people living in that country or city. No local ordinance may conflict with state or federal laws.

Types of Laws

There are two major classifications of laws: public law and private law. *Public laws* are laws that regulate the relationships between individuals and the government. Public law includes constitutional, international, administrative, and criminal law. *Private laws,* also called *civil laws,* are the laws that regulate the relationships among people. Private laws control such things as contracts, real estate dealings, and personal injuries.

Our federal and state laws are made by the people we elect to the United States Congress and to our state legislatures. With this democratic system every citizen has a voice in making our laws.

Our legal system involves many people doing many different kinds of jobs. They are all working to protect our safety and legal rights.

You probably have heard more about criminal law than you have about civil law. Criminal law is usually more exciting and dramatic. Much more court activity and lawyer time is spent, however, on civil law cases.

When a case goes to trial, the person accused of wrongdoing is the **defendant**. The person who takes the case to court is the **plaintiff**. In the case below Mr. Brown felt that going to court was the only answer for him.

C ity Construction Company (the defendant) owed M. K. Brown (the plaintiff) $2,500 for plumbing work. The company refused to pay the bill so Mr. Brown hired a lawyer to help him collect. When the lawyer was unable to persuade City Construction to pay Mr. Brown, he advised Mr. Brown to file a lawsuit. Mr. Brown filed a suit and won his case. He was awarded the $2,500 plus court costs.

Contracts

Of course you know that it is against the law to drive your car ninety miles an hour down the wrong side of the road. You also know that you cannot steal, or do violent harm to someone without suffering the penalties for breaking these laws. You are probably not, however, as familiar with the civil laws. This section will help you learn about contracts, which will be such an important part of your dealings with civil law.

Contracts are legal agreements between two or more people. The legal term for a person who enters into a contract is **party**. Each party in a contract agrees to do or pay something in return for something from the other party, or parties. As you become more independent, you will become involved in many contracts.

It is important that you understand how contracts work. You must know your rights and responsibilities concerning contracts. Contracts contain many legal terms that are difficult to understand. The most important terms are explained in this chapter.

What kinds of contracts will you be involved with? You've already read brief discussions of credit contracts, insurance policies (a type of contract), and union contracts. You will enter into contracts when you buy things and when you agree to do work for a certain amount of money. For example, a professional actor may agree to perform a stage play at a certain time and place. The theatre company agrees to pay him a certain amount of money for acting in the play. Both the actor and theatre company agree and sign a contract.

Contracts may be informal (spoken) or formal (written). Informal contracts are made when you buy clothing at the local store. The store agrees to turn over a shirt to you, and you promise to pay some money. No papers are signed. You also enter into an informal contract when you have your shoes repaired or your clothing cleaned.

Spoken agreements are legally enforceable only when they deal with goods priced at low amounts. For example, a contract for building materials may be informal if the price is less than $500. A contract for buying an expensive piece of property must, however, be a formal agreement. Help from a lawyer may be needed in drawing up this type of contract.

When you enter into a contract, you want the contract to be *binding*. A binding contract is one that is legally valid and cannot be broken. Five elements are essential if a contract is to be binding. Each of these essential elements for a binding contract is explained here.

Mutual Agreement

In every contract one party offers something, and another party accepts it. Mutual agreement takes place when both parties are in complete agreement on the terms of the contract. This means that both parties understand and are willing to enter into the agreement. A contract is not valid unless the parties freely agree.

Some contracts must be very carefully worded to protect the legal rights of the people entering into the contract. Before you sign an important contract that you don't understand, have a lawyer read the contract for you.

Mr. Jones, a farmer, had fifty riding horses for sale. The horses were priced from $300 to $600. Mr. Jones told Mr. Smith that he would sell him a horse for $300. Mr. Smith thought he could take any one of the horses for $300.

Mr. Jones' offer was not clearly stated, and Mr. Smith did not understand it. As a result, there was no legal contract to sell a certain horse.

To be considered legal and binding, a contract must be clear and definite. Both parties must understand completely what the other party is offering to sell, pay, or do.

Competent Parties

According to civil law, **competent parties** are people who are responsible for their actions. No contract is binding and valid unless the parties involved are competent parties.

Competent parties are those who are able to understand their rights and obligations. These people can be considered responsible for what they do. Various state laws define who is competent to make contracts. Certain persons are prevented by law from making enforceable contracts.

People who don't have the ability to understand the contract may be declared incompetent in a court of law. They may be mentally handicapped, or they may have been mentally unfit when the contract was made. Contracts made with such persons are not enforceable. People who have been drinking heavily and people who are declared temporarily insane are examples of people who can be considered incompetent parties.

Other people considered legally incompetent are *minors*. A minor is someone who is not yet old enough to receive certain legal rights and responsibilities. In most states, for most laws, anyone under the age of eighteen is considered a minor. The legal definitions for who is and who is not a minor vary considerably. Even in the same state a nineteen-year-old might be considered a minor with regard to one law, but not another.

Contracts made by minors can be voided (broken) by the minor. If an adult makes a legal contract with a minor, though, the adult must carry out his or her part of the contract. Only minors may void the contracts on the basis of the competent party requirement.

Although minors may cancel many kinds of contracts, they *must* honor others. When minors agree to pay for necessities, such as food, clothing, shelter, and medical attention, they must honor the contracts. Minors cannot use the excuse of being minors to avoid necessary obligations. If, however, the item in question is not a necessity, the contract can be voided.

R achel, a fifteen-year-old, bought an expensive leather jacket from a local clothing store. Since Rachel's family had already bought her several jackets, she didn't really need the leather jacket. Rachel's parents refused to pay for the leather jacket. Rachel had no choice but to return the jacket. The store was forced to accept the jacket and refund the full amount of the purchase. Since Rachel did not need the jacket for protective clothing, she was able to void the contract as a minor.

Because of problems with voidable contracts, store owners often ask parents to **countersign** contracts involving minors. To countersign means to sign a contract in support of someone else. If someone else countersigns a contract with you, that person is agreeing to make your obligation good if you fail to do so. Knowing that minors are not always considered competent parties, you can see why business people often want parents to countersign agreements made by their children.

Other contract problems are caused by minors who do not tell the truth about their ages. In such cases, the purchase price and money for damages can usually be collected from the minor. Most store owners protect themselves from these problems by asking for identification.

Being a minor does not necessarily prevent you from entering into a binding contract. In many cases you can have a parent or guardian countersign a contract.

Legal Purpose

The purpose of a contract must be legal for the contract to be binding. The agreement must be lawful. No agreement that is illegal or harmful to public health is a binding contract. Such agreements are not enforceable.

Agreements dealing with gambling or betting are illegal in most states. Suppose gambling is illegal in your state, but you made a bet with someone anyway—and won. If that person refused to pay you, you couldn't take legal action to collect the money. Your agreement wasn't binding. You might be able, however, to take legal action to collect your winnings if you lived in a state where gambling was legal.

Obviously a contract to steal or commit murder would not be binding. You may not be aware, though, of some other types of unlawful acts that can void a contract. For example, in many cities and states, people who do certain kinds of work must be licensed. Contracts involving people without the necessary licenses are not valid.

T om Woods built a small house for his family. He had no trouble doing the carpentry work, but he knew nothing about electrical work. Tom's neighbor, Joe Johnson, had done some electrical repair work on his own house, so Tom asked Joe to help him.

Joe agreed to furnish the materials and wire the house for $1,000. Joe wrote a contract stating what he would do and how much payment he would receive. Then he and Tom signed it.

When Joe went to buy the electrical material, he told the dealer about his contract with Tom. The electrical dealer advised Joe not to buy the materials. The city wouldn't provide service to Tom's house until the job was approved by an inspector. The dealer said that the inspector wouldn't approve work done by an unlicensed electrician. Since Joe did not have a license, Tom and Joe's contract did not have a legal purpose. The contract could be voided.

Consideration

For a contract to be binding, something, such as money or property, must be exchanged between the parties. One party may agree to do something, while the other party agrees to give the first party something in return. Whatever one party gives the other in return for the promise is known as **consideration**.

For example, Mr. South agreed to let the electrical company run an electrical line across part of his farm. In return, the company gave him $1 as consideration when he signed the contract. Although Mr. South did not really want any money, the $1 consideration was necessary to make the contract legal.

Consideration is not always in the form of money. It can be services, goods, or a promise to not do something one has the legal right to do.

Legal Form

The law requires that certain contracts be in writing. Among those that must be in writing are the following.

- installment contracts
- contracts to buy or sell real estate, including buildings, land, trees, and mineral rights

These people signed a contract granting permission for their pictures to be printed in this textbook. Although they didn't ask to be paid, they received a $1 consideration to make the contract binding.

- contracts to pay the debt of another person if that person doesn't pay it
- contracts to sell personal property valued at over $500 (the amount varies in different states)
- contracts not to be carried out until one year from the date of signing

Written contracts must be in proper legal form. This means that the contract must contain certain pieces of information. To be legal and binding, a written contract must contain the following.

- the date and place of the agreement
- the names and addresses of the parties entering into the agreement
- a statement of the purpose of the contract
- a statement of the amount of money, goods, or services given in consideration of the agreement
- the signatures of both parties or their legal agents
- signatures of witnesses when required by law

Don't be embarrassed about asking questions or asking for advice when it comes time to read and sign a contract. Most people, other than those with legal training, have trouble understanding the language used in formal contracts.

Make a Decision

Just as you are about to sign a contract to buy a color TV on the installment plan, you realize that the contract says nothing about a warranty. You ask the owner about this, and she says that the warranties are handled separately from the contract. You don't want to imply that the owner is dishonest, but you think the warranty should be mentioned in the contract. What's your decision—do you go ahead and sign, or do you postpone signing until you've checked this out with someone you know and trust? Give reasons for your decision.

- Read the contract carefully before signing. Be sure the terms and amounts of money are accurate.
- If part of the contract is in small print, be sure to read that part. If you don't understand, ask someone to explain. Be sure you understand everything before you sign.
- Always keep a copy of the signed contract for yourself. The copy should be signed by both parties. Keep your copy in a safe place.

You may not want to sign a contract until you've had a lawyer examine it. This is your right, so feel free to have a lawyer check any contract. Complex contracts that involve large amounts of money should be prepared by a lawyer.

A contract is defective if it lacks any of the five elements mentioned above. Under certain conditions, either party may break a defective contract. One or both parties may have been pressured to enter the agreement under threats of violence. The terms of the contract may have been fraudulent, or a mistake may have been made. In any of these cases, the contract can be voided.

Before You Sign

Many people have trouble understanding contracts. Sometimes fraud is involved. If you are going to sign a contract, be extremely careful. In the next column are some suggestions for making sure that in signing the contract you are agreeing only to what you want to agree to.

If someone forces you to sign a contract, the contract can be broken. Both parties must enter into the contract willingly for the contract to be binding.

Criminal Law

Criminal law is one of several kinds of public law. Criminal laws are passed to protect your safety and legal rights. These laws are the basis for punishing people who commit crimes.

In our legal system a person is considered innocent until proven guilty. This protects innocent people.

Criminal laws differ from state to state. The maximum and minimum punishments also vary from state to state.

Two groups of people—those considered mentally incompetent and minors—are treated differently than other people who break the law. Mentally incompetent people cannot tell right from wrong. If there is any doubt about someone's mental abilities, an expert will examine the person. The expert will then state whether or not the person is mentally competent. If experts decide that someone being charged with a crime is mentally incompetent, that person will not have to go to trial.

As you know, minors are not legally responsible for their actions in the same way that adults are. When minors are charged with a crime, their cases are usually tried in a special court called *juvenile court.* A juvenile court is a court that handles only those cases involving minors.

The laws do not call for the same punishments for minors as for adults. Punishments are less severe for minors—they don't include death or life imprisonment. In a few special cases, though, a judge may order that a minor be tried as an adult. This can happen when the crime is very serious.

Types of Crimes

A serious crime is called a **felony.** Felonies include such crimes as murder, rape, armed robbery, and arson (setting fires). Felonies may be punished by fines, prison terms, and even death in some states.

Less serious crimes are called **misdemeanors.** Misdemeanors include petty theft (stealing something of minimal value), traffic violations, and disturbing the peace. Punishments for misdemeanors are usually fines, short jail terms, and community service. Misdemeanors often result in an evaluation period, called *probation.* During this period the guilty party is given an opportunity to show that he or she will not commit further crimes.

Corporate crimes (crimes that take place in businesses) are sometimes called *white-collar crimes.* These crimes include forgery and fraud. Forgery is the dishonest changing of forms and records. Fraud was discussed in Chapter 16.

Being Arrested

If you are ever stopped by the police, what will you do? Suppose you decide to jog home after getting off work at 11:30 p.m. You're four blocks from home when you are stopped by two officers. Don't panic! The officers will ask you for identification, and they may ask other questions. Answer as completely as possible. You may ask, "Am I under arrest?" or "Why are you arresting me?"

If you are under arrest, don't resist in any way. You could be charged with resisting arrest. Tell the police that you will have nothing to say until you see a lawyer. You have the right to remain silent.

If you are stopped by a police officer, do not cause trouble for the officer. Answer questions as politely as possible and cooperate in every way. You can only make matters worse by arguing and resisting.

The officer has the right to search for concealed weapons. A legal paper called a *search warrant* permits a police officer to search your home. Police officers cannot obtain search warrants whenever they want. They must convince a judge that there is good cause to expect that stolen goods or unlawful possessions, such as drugs or gambling equipment, will be found.

Booking. If you are arrested, the police officer will take you to a police station to be *booked*. Being booked means having formal charges filed against you.

The time and place of the arrest may affect the procedure. If you are arrested after midnight, you may not be booked right away. You would probably be kept in jail until morning. Formal charges will come later.

Legal experts advise people to remain silent after they are arrested. Don't discuss your case with others in the jail. Don't sign any forms except the list of personal belongings taken from you, such as your money, papers, jewelry, and clothing. These things will be placed in the police safe until you are released.

Anyone arrested must be charged with a crime or be released. If formal charges are made, the court will set **bail**. Bail is money deposited with the court so that an accused person can be freed from jail until the trial. The amount of bail varies with the crime.

Bail money is held by the court until the case is over. If the accused person does not appear at the trial, the money is not returned.

If you have no money for bail, you may contact a bail bondsman. For a fee, the bondsman will give you money to pay your bail. The fee, which is set by law, is often 10 percent of the amount borrowed. The bail money is returned to the bondsman when the case is over.

Court. Some people choose to defend themselves in court, but this is usually not a good idea. If you are like most people, you do not know enough about the law to defend yourself properly. If at all possible, hire a lawyer. The lawyer will gather all the facts about the case and then advise you to plead either *guilty* or *not guilty*. If you plead *not guilty*, you will have a trial.

In our court system, every effort is made to protect the innocent. If you are arrested, you will be given a fair chance to prove your innocence. Few innocent people are ever punished for crimes.

Using Legal Services

Almost everyone needs a lawyer's help from time to time. A lawyer can do the following things for you.

- Examine contracts before you buy real estate
- Write your will (a plan to divide your property after your death)
- Determine whether or not a will is valid
- Handle cases of divorce and child custody
- Help you collect debts
- Write or examine a lease for the use of land or property
- Defend you if you are arrested

Many lawyers specialize in one kind of law. Some lawyers specialize in criminal cases; others specialize in civil cases. You should think about the type of case you have when seeking legal help. If you need help with a contract, a small firm or legal clinic can help you. For a serious criminal case, you should put a great deal of attention into finding a lawyer.

You can find a lawyer in several ways. Your friends or family members can sometimes suggest

The best way to find a lawyer who can help you is to talk to friends and people you know who have had experience with lawyers. One of your friends or relatives can probably recommend a very competent lawyer.

a lawyer they know. If you are in a new area, look in the Yellow Pages of the telephone directory. You may find a toll-free number for a state legal association. When you call this number, be ready to describe the service you need. You will then be told the names of lawyers in your area who might help with your problem.

You can also use the Yellow Pages to find the names and phone numbers of lawyers in your area. You might call several firms and ask about fees. With this method, though, you won't learn much about the experience or legal ability of the lawyers you call.

Legal services are expensive. Be sure you know the lawyer's fees before requesting services. Legal clinics are the least expensive.

If you have no money to hire a lawyer, you can still receive help. In criminal cases the court appoints a *public defender* if the defendant is unable to pay for a lawyer. A public defender is a lawyer paid by the government to give legal help to those who cannot pay. In civil cases people with low incomes may also qualify for free legal help.

Make a Decision

You have gotten yourself into some minor trouble with the law. A police officer suggests that you get a lawyer. You know you are guilty, and you have already decided to plead guilty. You think you can handle the problem yourself, without a lawyer, and save yourself some money. At best, the lawyer might get you off with a smaller fine. What's your decision—defend yourself, or hire a lawyer? Give reasons for your decision.

James Young was employed by City Electric, a company located about six miles from James' home. There was no bus service and little chance to ride with other workers. So James decided he needed a good car, but he couldn't afford to spend much for it. After looking over his budget for next year, he felt he could pay no more than $800.

James looked at several cars and finally found a clean-looking one at Jack's Quality Cars. The price was lower than others of the same make, style, and age. Jack said he had just bought the car from a boy who needed the money to start college. He urged James to drive the car around the block.

The car started easily and everything seemed okay except that the transmission slipped slightly. James wished the car could be checked by his friend Roger who was a master mechanic at Westside Motors. But it was Saturday afternoon, and the service department at Westside Motors was closed.

When James returned to Jack's Quality Cars, Jack said another customer had wanted to see the car while James was gone. But the contract was ready for James to sign if he wanted the car. The contract required $100 as a down payment and eighteen additional payments of $60 each. These payments included credit charges and insurance. James knew he should be cautious, but it was hard to pass up what looked like a good deal. So he signed the contract and paid the $100 down payment.

On Monday James drove to work, and the car ran smoothly. But trouble started on the way home. The car seemed to lose power when he tried to pass a truck. Something smelled hot. Then there was a grinding sound in the transmission. The car lost all power, and James was forced to pull onto the side of the highway.

James called Roger and asked him to drive out to look at the car. It didn't take Roger long to find the trouble. The transmission was burned out. So the car was towed to the garage. Roger estimated it would cost $325 to replace the transmission.

James called Jack, the used-car dealer, to tell him of the car's problem. Jack just said that at the low cost of the car, he shouldn't expect any guarantee on the transmission.

James didn't have $325 to replace the transmission. In desperation, he called his father for advice. His dad suggested that he take the contract to Mr. Walker, a lawyer.

When Mr. Walker read the contract, he knew that James hadn't read it carefully. The sentence "This vehicle sold as is" had been typed on the contract. James had signed it, and the seller was released from any responsibility.

By signing a contract containing such a clause, James lost his rights as a buyer. He had given up his right to expect any warranty on the car. He was stuck with a $325 repair job and eighteen payments. A total of $1080 had to be paid. James was twenty-one years old, so the contract wasn't voidable on the basis of age. James had learned a good lesson. Unfortunately the lesson was an expensive one.

REVIEW YOUR LEARNING

CHAPTER SUMMARY

Our laws are the rules that our society has decided we need to protect the safety and rights of all people. As citizens we all have a legal responsibility to know and obey all the laws, both public and private.

Everyone enters into contracts. There are many different kinds of contracts, but to be legal and binding a contract must have five essential elements. These essentials are mutual agreement, competent parties, legal purpose, consideration, and legal form. Read and understand every part of a contract before you sign it. If you are confused or uncertain, have a lawyer examine the contract for you.

Criminal law is the type of public law with which people are most familiar. Crimes are divided into two major types—felonies and misdemeanors. If you are arrested, remain quiet until you speak with your lawyer. Your lawyer will gather the facts of the case and advise you on the best way to proceed. If you cannot afford a lawyer, you can be represented by a public defender.

WORDS YOU SHOULD KNOW

bail
competent parties
consideration
contract
countersign
defendant
felony
legal system
misdemeanor
party
plantiff

STUDY QUESTIONS

1. What are the three levels at which our laws are made?
2. What are the two major types of laws?
3. What is the difference between a formal and informal contract?
4. When is an informal contract enforceable?
5. What are the five essential elements of a binding contract?
6. Name two groups of people who may not be held to the terms of a contract.
7. A store wants to protect itself against voidable contracts made by minors. How can it do this?

REVIEW YOUR LEARNING   CHAPTER 21

8. Why do many contracts call for one party paying another $1?
9. Name five kinds of contracts that must be in writing to be binding.
10. A friend is planning to sign a contract. What three suggestions would you give to this person?
11. What are the two major types of crimes?
12. Why is it not a good idea to defend yourself?

DISCUSSION TOPICS

1. Some people feel that criminals who have committed very serious crimes should be executed for what they've done. What do you think?
2. Do you know of any law that was changed by the federal, state, or local government? Why was the change made?

SUGGESTED ACTIVITIES

Act out the situation on p. 334 to show proper behavior of the person being questioned by two police officers.

Paying Taxes

You are going to earn a lot of money in your lifetime. At the very least, you will probably make close to $1,000,000. There's a very good chance that you will make much, much more.

Most of the money you earn will be yours to spend as you please. Most of it will be yours, but not all. Do you know what happens to the part of your earnings that isn't yours to spend?

The answer is taxes. Taxes are the payments people must make to maintain their government and provide government services. Most people pay between 20 and 24 percent of their income in taxes. That means that if you make a million dollars in your lifetime, you will pay between $200,000 and $250,000 in taxes. Some people have pointed out that the average person works the first four months of every year—January through April—just to pay taxes.

You can see that a lot of your hard work and time will go toward tax payments. This being the case, you will surely want to know all there is to know about taxes. This chapter will help you learn about your taxpayer responsibilities and how the tax system works.

Understanding Taxes

Our tax system and the ways in which governments spend tax money are very involved, complex subjects. This section of the chapter will get you started toward a good understanding of taxes. Listed below are the general areas you will learn about.

- Who collects taxes
- How taxes are spent
- Your tax responsibility
- What makes a good tax system
- Types of taxes

Governments Levy and Collect Taxes

All governments must have some kind of tax system. It costs money to run a government, and the tax system is the government's way of obtaining this money.

In our country there are several levels of government: federal, state, and local. Since the government at each level needs money to operate, each government must **levy** (require people to pay) taxes. Some of the taxes you pay go to the federal government, other taxes go to the state government, and still others go to your local government.

At the federal level, Congress has the power to levy and collect taxes. Congress was given this power by the Constitution of the United States, in Section 8, Article I.

"The Congress shall have the power to lay and collect Taxes, Duties, Imposts, and Excises, to pay the Debts and provide for the Common Defense and general Welfare of the United States: but all Duties, Imposts, and Excises shall be uniform throughout the United States."

This article in the Constitution gave Congress the authority it needed to establish The Department of the Treasury. One branch of the Treasury Department is the **Internal Revenue Service**, commonly referred to as the **IRS**. The IRS is the federal agency responsible for collecting taxes. Congress passes the laws that say what kinds of taxes will be

Levels of Government

You will pay taxes to support three levels of government. All three need money to continue providing public services.

Federal

State

Local (County, Municipal, Township)

levied, who must pay, and how much. The IRS then enforces these laws and collects the taxes. All the tax money collected goes into the U.S. Treasury.

Each state and local government has its own version of the IRS. Although much smaller and less complex, these state and local agencies have authority to levy and collect taxes from their citizens. The money then goes into the state or local treasury.

How Tax Dollars Are Spent

The federal, state, and local governments collect taxes because they need money to maintain the government. It costs money to run any government. It costs a lot of money to run a government as large as your state government, and even more to maintain the federal government. In 1983 and 1984, for example, our federal government collected over 600 *billion* dollars in taxes. Even with this tremendous amount of money, the government still had much less than it needed to pay all of its bills.

Why do governments need so much money? A big part of the expense goes toward paying the salaries of government employees. The President of the United States, the governor of your state, the legislators, the judges—all these people are government employees. About 5,000,000 people, including civilians and military personnel, work for the federal government alone. All of these people must be paid, and the money to pay them must come from taxes.

In addition to the salaries of the government workers, taxes must provide the money to pay the cost of all the facilities and equipment government workers need to do their jobs. Office buildings must be built, and these buildings must have light, heat, telephones, and all the other necessities. The armed services must spend tremendous amounts of money to buy airplanes, ships, weapons, uniforms, and countless other items. Because it needs so much,

the federal government spends millions of dollars just for small, inexpensive items, such as pencils, paper, screwdrivers, and hammers.

What is the result of spending all this money? The results are many. In exchange for the tax dollars you pay to the federal, state, and local governments, these governments provide you with valuable services. It would be impossible for you to go about your normal routine were it not for the things that governments do for you.

Probably the most important services governments provide are protection and enforcement of the law. The armed services have stationed military personnel all over the world to maintain our national defense. The Federal Bureau of Investigation, the National Guard, your state police force, and your local police force all work to make life safe for everyone. Judges, prison guards, and lawyers then work to see that criminals are punished.

Governments also use our tax dollars to build airports, interstate highways, bridges, dams, canals, state roads, city streets, and sidewalks. All of these are needed to help us get from place to place. It takes a great deal of money to pay for the workers and materials needed to build and maintain these facilities from year to year.

Governments spend your tax dollars on education and research, too. Governments pay for the buildings, teachers, and books that make "free" public education possible. Governments also pay to maintain libraries and research centers that promote learning and new technology. A great deal of medical research and all the work that has gone into our exploration of space have been paid for with tax dollars.

Make a Decision

Once again you find yourself in the voting booth. This time you're voting on a tax referendum. Voting *yes* means you are in favor of paying higher property taxes next year so that your community can build a new school building. Voting *no* means you're against paying higher taxes for a new school building. What's your decision—*yes* or *no*? Give reasons for your decision.

Some people complain about having to pay taxes, but few people would want to give up the protection and services provided by their tax dollars.

You are probably beginning to see what governments do with the tax money they collect. It would be impossible to list all the services either fully or partially provided by governments using your tax money. Just a few more of the many services are listed below.

- **Health services**—hospitals, community and public health centers, Medicare programs, health inspections
- **Welfare**—payments and help for the needy
- **Social services**—payments to veterans, legal services, social security, employment services, and protective agencies, such as Children and Family Services and the Department of Rehabilitation
- **Protective agencies**—environmental and conservation departments
- **Postal services**—deliver the mail
- **Fire departments**—protect against fire

Your Tax Responsibility

It is the responsibility of every able citizen to pay his or her fair share of taxes. Since we all share in the benefits of taxes (the protection and services you just read about), it's only fair that we all contribute. Later in this chapter you will learn about the different types of taxes and how you go about fulfilling your responsibilities.

Although few people would want to give up the services provided by taxes, few people enjoy paying taxes. Some people have a serious problem accepting their responsibility for paying taxes. There are several reasons for this.

Very few people have all the money they need and want. Many people like to keep all of their money for themselves. There is a tendency to say, "Let someone else pay for that. I worked hard for my money, and I don't want to give it away."

People are also reluctant to pay their taxes because they often disagree with the way the government spends their tax money. They feel that the government spends tax money for things that aren't necessary, or for things that they personally don't need.

Unmarried men and women without children, for example, may not feel that they should have to pay taxes that pay for public education. Many people feel that it's wrong to spend so much money on space exploration and military weapons when people are hungry and homeless. Other people feel that it's wrong for the government to take tax dollars from hard working people and give it to people who don't have jobs, no matter how needy they may be. In other words, people have many different opinions—sometimes very strong opinions—about how tax money should be spent.

There is another reason why people sometimes complain about their taxpayer responsibilities. Some people feel they are paying more than their fair share of the taxes. They think that wealthy people have ways to avoid paying taxes. They also believe that others simply don't pay their taxes and aren't penalized. The idea that those more able to pay are not paying at all makes it difficult for many people to live up to their responsibilities.

There is one answer to all of these reasons people have for avoiding their responsibility to pay taxes. The answer is—to vote in all public elections. In fact, voting is another responsibility you will have as a taxpayer. It will be your duty as a taxpayer to vote and express your opinion about how the tax laws should be written and the dollars spent.

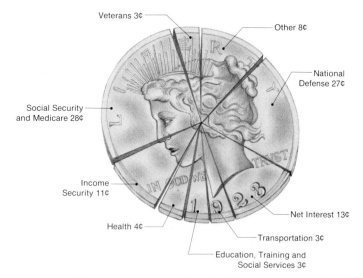

Veterans 3¢
Other 8¢
National Defense 27¢
Social Security and Medicare 28¢
Income Security 11¢
Net Interest 13¢
Health 4¢
Transportation 3¢
Education, Training and Social Services 3¢

The chart above shows how the federal government divided each tax dollar in 1984. Social security payments (including Medicare) and national defense take by far the biggest chunks of our tax dollar.

In 1984 our federal government spent 227.4 *billion* dollars for national defense. Many people believe part of this money should be spent for other purposes. As a voter, you will have a say in how your tax dollars are spent.

The United States Congress, your state legislature, and your local city council pass the laws and ordinances that determine what taxes you must pay. The legislators and council members who vote on these tax laws are all elected to their positions. It is your responsibility to know each political candidate's opinions and to vote for the candidate that will represent your beliefs. In this way you will have just as much say on how taxes are collected and spent as will any other American citizen.

Learning about the candidates and voting for the candidate of your choice does not guarantee that the tax system will be managed the way you want it. In our system of government, the majority rules. You may not always hold the majority opinion. Fulfilling your responsibility as an informed voter will, however, give you a great deal of satisfaction. You will know that you did your part to see that everyone paid a fair share and that your money is being spent wisely.

A Good Tax System

Governments have tried using all sorts of tax systems to obtain the money they need. Because people feel strongly about how much they must pay and how their money is spent, it has been difficult to develop a system that satisfies everyone. If you are going to exercise your responsibilities as a taxpayer, you will need to have some basic ideas about what you believe makes a good tax system. There are some basic principles that most people believe should be part of every tax system.

- **Fairness**—Almost everyone believes that taxes should be fair and just. Everyone should have to pay his or her fair share of the taxes. No one who is able to pay should be allowed to avoid paying.
- **Simplicity**—The tax system should not be so complicated that most people can't understand it. This is a criticism many people make of our present system. If you believe the system should be simpler, it's your responsibility to vote for a legislator who believes as you do.
- **Convenience**—Taxes should be levied at a convenient time, when most people are able to pay.
- **Stability**—People need to know how much they will have to pay so they can plan ahead to make their payments. This means that the tax laws cannot be constantly changing, demanding payments that people weren't expecting.
- **Flexibility**—At certain times, during a war for example, governments need more money than during other times. The government should have the ability to adjust the tax system to bring in more or less income, as needed.
- **Minimal Payment**—Many people believe taxes should be kept at the absolute minimum. They

Knowledgeable voters, who know the issues and candidates, help shape our tax laws. If you are unhappy with our tax system, vote for a candidate who feels as you do.

Types of Taxes

There are many different kinds of taxes. You are probably already familiar with some of them. If you bought something at the grocery store or ate in a restaurant this week, you paid some taxes. If you have a part-time job, your employer probably takes some money for taxes out of your paycheck.

You may never have to pay some of the special kinds of taxes. In your lifetime, though, you will pay several different taxes, some to the federal, some to the state, and some to the local governments. In some cases you will make your payments yourself directly to the government. In other cases employers and business people will take your money and then turn it over to the government.

As the tax needs of the government and the ability of the people to pay taxes change, so do the tax laws. This section will explain in general the most common types of taxes. If you need the most current, detailed information, contact the closest IRS or state revenue office.

believe that governments should reduce spending so they don't need as much money. This sounds good to taxpayers, but the problem is deciding which government services to reduce or eliminate.

- **Expanded Payment**—Many people believe just the opposite of those who would minimize taxes. These people would have everyone pay the maximum amount they can afford so that governments can provide more service and help for those who need it most. These people believe that a strong, central government can accomplish a great deal for the country as a whole. To accomplish these things, the government needs more tax dollars.

What you've just read are but a few of the many ideas that people and governments have about what makes a good tax system. Several of the ideas are directly opposed to each other. You must decide what you feel is important. You can then vote for candidates who will represent your ideas when it comes time to develop and change the tax laws.

The first type of tax that most people pay is sales tax. Business people must turn over the money you pay in sales tax to the state and local governments.

Income Tax. Income tax is just what you would expect it to be—a tax on income. Income tax is figured as a percentage of the money you make in a given year. Your employer will deduct money from your paychecks to pay your income tax for you.

By April 15 of each year you must have filed an income tax return for the previous year. This return shows how much you earned, your deductions, and any other relevant information about your tax situation. On the basis of this tax return and how much money has been deducted from your pay, you will either pay additional money or receive a refund from the government. Later in this chapter, you will learn how to file an income tax return.

The federal government and most state governments levy an income tax. There are also approximately four thousand cities in the U.S. that levy income taxes. Corporations, as well as individuals, must pay income taxes.

Personal income tax is by far the federal government's biggest source of income. For example, in 1983 the government collected about 600 billion dollars in taxes. About 290 billion, almost half, came from personal income tax.

State Income Tax

As of 1984, all states but Alaska, Florida, Nevada, South Dakota, Texas, Washington, and Wyoming levied a state tax on personal income. Listed below are the tax rates for each of the other 43 states. Even though these rates may have changed, this chart will give you an idea of the ways that states charge income tax.

STATE	INDIVIDUAL RATES
Alabama	From 2% on 1st $1,000 to 5% on income over $6,000
Arizona	From 2% on 1st $1,017 to 8% on income over $6,102
Arkansas	From 1% on 1st $2,999 to 7% on income over $25,000
California	From 1% on 1st $4,620 to 11% on income over $25,430
Colorado	From 2.5% on 1st $1,415 to 8% on $14,153 or more; 2% surtax on intangible income over $15,000
Connecticut	7% on capital gains, on dividends and interest, 6% on income between $50,000 and $59,999; 13% on income over $100,000
Delaware	From 1.4% on 1st $1,000 to 13.5% on income over $50,000
Dist. of Col.	From 2% on 1st $1,000 to 11% on income over $25,000
Georgia	From 1% on 1st $1,000 to 6% on income over $10,000
Hawaii	From 2.25% on 1st $1,000 to 11% on income over $61,000
Idaho	From 2% on 1st $1,000 to 7.5% on income over $5,000; each person (husband and wife filing jointly are deemed one person) filing return pays additional $10
Illinois	3% on net income
Indiana	3% of adjusted gross income
Iowa	From 0.5% on 1st $1,023 to 13% on income over $76,725
Kansas	From 2% on 1st $2,000 to 9% on income over $25,000
Kentucky	From 2% on 1st $3,000 to 6% on income over $8,000
Louisiana	From 2% on 1st $10,000 to 6% on income over $50,000
Maine	From 1% on 1st $2,000 to 10% on income over $25,000
Maryland	From 2% on 1st $1,000 to 5% on income over $3,000
Massachusetts	Interest, dividends, net capital gains, 10%; earned and business income, 5%; additional surtax, 7.5%

STATE	INDIVIDUAL RATES
Michigan	All taxable income, 6.1%
Minnesota	From 1.6% on 1st $672 to 16% on income over $36,925
Mississippi	From $5,000, 3%; over $10,000, 5%
Missouri	From 1.5% on 1st $1,000 to 6% on income over $9,000
Montana	From 2% on 1st $1,200 to 11% on income over $42,000
Nebraska	19% of federal income tax liability
New Hampshire	5% on income from interest and dividends
New Jersey	2% on 1st $20,000; 3.5% on income over $50,000
New Mexico	0.7% on 1st $2,000 to 7.8% on income over $100,000
New York	From 2% on 1st $1,000 to 14% on income over $23,000
North Carolina	From 3% on 1st $2,000 to 7% on income over $10,000
North Dakota	From 2% on 1st $3,000 to 9% on income over $50,000
Ohio	From 0.95% on 1st $5,000 to 9.5% on income over $100,000
Oklahoma	From 0.5% on 1st $2,000 to 6% on income over $15,000
Oregon	From 4.2% on 1st $500 to 10.8% on income over $5,000
Pennsylvania	2.35% on all taxable income
Rhode Island	24.9% of federal income tax liability
South Carolina	From 2% on 1st $2,000 to 7% on income over $10,000
Tennessee	On dividends and interest, 6%; on dividends from corporations having 75% of property taxable in state, 4%
Utah	From 2.25% on 1st $1,500 to 7.75% on excess over $7,500
Vermont	26% of federal income tax liability
Virginia	From 2% on 1st $3,000 to 5.75% on income over $12,000
West Virginia	From 2.1% on 1st $2,000 to 13% on excess over $60,000 + 12% surtax
Wisconsin	From 3.4% on 1st $3,900 to 10% on income over $51,600

Income tax is a *progressive* tax. A progressive tax is one in which the tax rate goes up as the taxable income goes up. There are currently fourteen levels, or *brackets,* as they are often called. Someone who earned $50,000, for example, pays 12 percent on income from $3,400 to $4,400, but pays 42 percent on income over $41,500.

We use a progressive tax because most people believe that those who are more able to pay should pay more. The wealthiest people pay up to 50 percent of their income in federal taxes, while people with the lowest income pay a much lower rate. Most states also have progressive income taxes. The state rates are usually much lower, though, than those for federal taxes.

Social Security Taxes. Social security taxes are federal taxes that people pay while they are working so that they can receive monthly checks after they quit working. Like income tax, social security tax is based on income. Almost every worker in the United States participates in the social security program.

An entire chapter, Chapter 23, is devoted to social security. If you want to read about the many programs that are financed by your social security taxes, you should read Chapter 23. Here you will read about the tax itself and how it is calculated and paid.

Your employer will deduct social security taxes from your paycheck. This deduction is separate from your income tax deduction. Your check stubs will show your social security deduction as an *F.I.C.A.* deduction. *F.I.C.A.* stands for *Federal Insurance Contribution Act.*

The F.I.C.A. deduction is calculated as a percent of your earnings. The rate changes from year to year according to the current social security laws. In 1985 the rate was 7.05 percent. In the years 1986-87 the rate will be 7.15 percent; in 1988-89 it will be 7.51 percent; and in 1990, and years after, it will be 7.65.

As of 1985, the maximum amount of earnings that can be taxed is $39,600. This means that if you earn $50,000 a year, you only pay social security tax on the first $39,600. This maximum amount will go up as earning levels go up in the future.

Many people don't realize that their employer matches their tax contributions to social security. For example, if in one certain week in 1985 you earned $100, your employer would deduct $7.05 for F.I.C.A. ($100 × .0705 = $7.05). Your employer would set aside another $7.05, making your total contribution $14.10. Your employer is responsible for sending this money to the IRS.

Sales Tax. You are probably more familiar with sales tax than any of the other kinds of taxes. Sales tax is the tax paid on goods and services that people buy. Almost every state levies sales tax. Many local governments also levy sales tax.

Sales tax is calculated as a percentage of the sales price. For example, if your bill at the hardware store comes to $50 and the rate for sales tax in your state is 5 percent, the sales clerk will add $2.50 ($50 × .05 = $2.50) to your bill. This brings your total to $52.50.

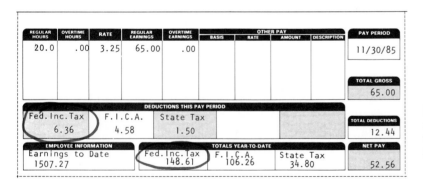

If you have a part-time job, you have probably already had your first encounter with income tax. The good news is that you will probably get some of your money back.

The sales tax rates vary from state to state. Some states charge as little as 2 percent, others charge over 7 percent. In most states the rate is between 4 and 6 percent.

The rate you are actually charged is usually higher than the state rate. It is common for your city or municipal government to add 1 or 2 percent sales tax to the state rate. If, for example, your state has a 4 percent rate and your city adds 1 percent, the store owner will add 5 percent to your bill.

Many states have different sales tax rates for different kinds of goods and services. Food and drug items, for example, are not taxed at all, or taxed at a lower rate, in many states. In some states packaged food, such as you buy in the grocery store, is *not* taxed—but prepared food, which you get in a restaurant, is taxed at the regular rate.

If you need to know the sales tax rates for your area, contact both your state and local revenue agencies. Although store owners charge and collect sales tax as one payment, it is usually two separate taxes—one state, one local.

Property Taxes. Property taxes are taxes levied on the value of property. *Property* usually means land and buildings. Business equipment and inventory, and even stocks and bonds, are sometimes considered property. Only those people who own property have to pay property tax.

Like sales taxes, property taxes are levied by the state and local governments. In some states the money needed to maintain the public schools is primarily property tax money. Property taxes are also used to pay for police and fire departments, street repair, and other state and local services.

State Sales Tax Rates

Since states frequently change their state sales tax rates, the rates given below may no longer be in effect. The chart will give you an idea, however, of the many different ways that states charge sales tax.

As of 1984 the sales tax rates in individual states are as follows:

(No Tax)	3%	4%	5%	6%	7½%
Alaska	Colorado	Alabama	Arizona	Minnesota	Connecticut
Delaware	Georgia	Arkansas	Florida	Mississippi	
Montana	Kansas	Hawaii	Illinois	New Jersey	
New Hampshire	North Carolina	Idaho	Indiana	Pennsylvania	
Oregon	Oklahoma	Iowa	Kentucky	Rhode Island	
	Virginia	Louisiana	Maine	Dist. of Col.	
	Wyoming	Michigan	Maryland		
		Nebraska	Massachusetts	**6½%**	
	3.75%	New York	Ohio	Washington	
	New Mexico	North Dakota	South Carolina		
		South Dakota	West Virginia		
		Vermont	Wisconsin		
		4⅛%	**5½%**		
		Missouri	Tennessee		
		4¾%	**5¾%**		
		California	Nevada		
		4⅝%			
		Utah			

If you are like many people, your first encounter with property taxes won't occur until you buy your first house. A **tax assessor** will *assess* your home and the land upon which it's built. To assess property is to estimate its value. A tax assessor is someone who estimates the value of property for the purpose of levying taxes.

Your property tax will be a certain percentage of the assessed value. The local government, usually the county government, will use the assessor's estimated value to calculate your tax.

Let's say, for example, that your property was assessed at $50,000, and the property tax rate was 5 percent. Your yearly tax bill would be $2500. You would receive a bill that you would have to pay by a certain time. Many people add their taxes to their monthly mortgage payments so that they don't have to pay one large sum all at once.

Estimating the value of property is a difficult task. Many people believe that their property is assessed too high, causing them to pay more taxes. If you believe your property has been overvalued, you can appeal your assessment. Your local government will have a process for filing such an appeal.

Other Taxes. Most of the taxes you pay in your lifetime will consist of those types you've just read about: income, social security, sales tax, and property tax. There are a great many other taxes that you may or may not pay at one time or another. Brief explanations of these taxes are provided below.

- **Excise tax**—This is a federal or state tax on certain goods and services, such as liquor, tobacco, and gasoline, produced within this country. The manufacturers and distributors of the products pay the excise tax. Since they usually add the amount of the tax to the selling price, the consumer indirectly pays the tax.
- **Estate (Inheritance) tax**—This is a tax on the value of the money and property a person leaves behind after dying. The federal government and almost all states levy estate taxes. The tax rate for estate tax is progressive, like income tax, and ranges from 18 percent up to 50 percent.
- **Gift tax**—This is a tax on gifts to individuals that exceed a certain value. This tax prevents

older people from giving all their money to their heirs before they die as a way to avoid estate taxes.
- **Licenses**—The licenses you buy that allow you to do certain things, such as drive a car and go fishing or hunting, are also a form of tax. The money you pay for license plates or license stickers for your car is money the state uses to maintain the state roads and highways.

When you buy license plates for your car, you pay much more than what the plates cost to make. The fee for obtaining license plates is really a tax that pays for construction and maintenance of the state highways.

Filing Income Tax Returns

In our country everyone is responsible for figuring and paying his or her own federal income taxes. This is done by **filing** an income tax **return.** An income tax return is a formal statement of a person's income and taxes. Filing is the process of turning in (usually by mail) the completed return to the IRS.

Unless you live in one of the few states that does not levy an income tax, you will have to file a state income tax return as well as a federal return. The laws for filing state returns are usually similar to the laws for filing federal returns. State returns are filed at the same time as the federal returns.

In this section you will read some general information about filing income tax returns. This information will help you understand how you go about filing your return. The tax returns themselves will give you more detailed instructions. You can also get assistance from the IRS office in your area and your state's revenue office.

Should You File and When?

What determines whether or not you need to file an income tax return? The answer depends on your particular situation. Usually, if you earn any money, you should probably file a return. Even if you are not required by law to do so, filing a return could be to your advantage.

The IRS has very specific guidelines as to who must file a return. Whether or not you are required to file depends on several factors. The most important factor is how much money you earn.

In general, if you earn $3,300 or more in a calendar year (January 1 to December 31), you must file a return. The $3,300 amount was in effect in 1985. The IRS does change this minimum from time to time.

If you earn $3,300 in a calendar year, you must file your return no later than April 15 of the following year. For example, if you earned $4,000 in 1985, you would have to file your income tax return for *1985* on or before April 15 of *1986.*

The IRS will penalize you for filing your return after April 15. The penalty is usually a late charge based on how late your payment is and how much tax you owe the IRS. The IRS will give you more time to file your return in certain cases.

Even if you earn less than $3,300, you may want to file a return. Your employer deducted federal, and probably state, income tax from each paycheck. It may be that the total amount deducted was more than what you owe. You cannot get your money back, though, unless you file a return.

How to File

Filing an income tax return can be a quick and easy process, or a long and difficult one. It depends on how much money you made, how you made your money, and many other factors. When you are just starting out in the world of work, your income tax returns are usually pretty simple to do.

Each January, employers are required to send each employee a **W-2 Form**. A W-2 Form is a statement of how much money was earned and how much was deducted for taxes during the preceding year. If you worked for more than one employer during that year, you should receive a W-2 Form from each employer. Employers must send a W-2 to every employee, even if the employee worked only one day during the year.

Employers deduct money from their employees' checks on the basis of the employees' **W-4 Forms**. A W-4 Form is a legal statement allowing an employer to deduct pay from an employee's check. If you have a job now, you filled out and signed a W-4 when you started. The information that you supplied on the W-4 told the employer how much to deduct from your checks.

Ask any person in the world of work what April 15 brings to mind and the answer will probably be "income tax." Filing your return after April 15 usually means paying a penalty charge.

| Form **W-4** (Rev. January 1984) | Department of the Treasury—Internal Revenue Service **Employee's Withholding Allowance Certificate** | OMB No. 1545-0010 |

1 Type or print your full name
Carol Annette Wallis

2 Your social security number
987-65-4321

Home address (number and street or rural route)
201 East Third Street

City or town, State, and ZIP code
Plaintown, Kansas   66762

3 Marital Status
[X] Single   [ ] Married
[ ] Married, but withhold at higher Single rate
Note: If married, but legally separated, or spouse is a nonresident alien, check the Single box.

4 Total number of allowances you are claiming (from line F of the worksheet on page 2)   2

5 Additional amount, if any, you want deducted from each pay . . . . $

6 I claim exemption from withholding because (see instructions and check boxes below that apply):
a [ ] Last year I did not owe any Federal income tax and had a right to a full refund of **ALL** income tax withheld, **AND**
b [ ] This year I do not expect to owe any Federal income tax and expect to have a right to a full refund of **ALL** income tax withheld. If both a and b apply, enter the year effective and "EXEMPT" here . . . ▶   Year
c If you entered "EXEMPT" on line 6b, are you a full-time student? . . . .   [ ]Yes [ ]No

Under penalties of perjury, I certify that I am entitled to the number of withholding allowances claimed on this certificate, or if claiming exemption from withholding, that I am entitled to claim the exempt status.
Employee's signature ▶ *Carol A. Wallis*   Date ▶ *June 4* , 19 *84*

7 Employer's name and address (**Employer: Complete 7, 8, and 9 only if sending to IRS**)   **8** Office code   **9** Employer identification number

One of the first things you will be asked to do when you start a new job will be to fill out a W-4 Form such as you see above. This form gives your employer the authority and the information he or she needs to deduct federal income tax from your paycheck.

1 Control Number		OMB No. 1545-0008	
2 Employer's Name, Address, and ZIP Code	**3** Employer's Identification Number 743-2126-48	**4** Employer's State Number 51-0174610
Jackson Manufacturing Co. Plaintown, KS 66762	**5** Stat. Employee [ ] Deceased [ ] Legal Rep. [ ] 942 Emp. [ ] Subtotal [ ] Void [ ]	
	6 Allocated Tips	**7** Advance EIC Payment
8 Employee's Social Security Number 987-65-4321	**9** Federal Income Tax Withheld $122.40	**10** Wages, Tips, Other Compensation $1600.00	**11** Social Security Tax Withheld $112.80
12 Employee's Name, Address, and ZIP Code	**13** Social Security Wages $1600.00	**14** Social Security Tips
	16	
	17 State Income Tax $32.00	**18** State Wages, Tips, Etc.	**19** Name of State
	20 Local Income Tax	**21** Local Wages, Tips, Etc.	**22** Name of Locality

Form W-2 Wage and Tax Statement 1984
36-2515832 APP. 4/84

Copy B To be filed with employee's FEDERAL tax return
This information is being furnished to the Internal Revenue Service

Department of the Treasury
Internal Revenue Service

In January you will receive a W-2 Form like this one from every employer you worked for during the preceding year. The W-2 Form tells you how much you paid in federal and state income taxes.

In most cases the IRS will send you an income tax return to fill out. The IRS has three different forms: the 1040EZ, the 1040A, and the 1040. The 1040EZ is the easiest form to fill out. If you can use it, you should.

If you do not receive a form in the mail, you can write or call the nearest IRS office and ask for the form you need. For a number to call, look under United States Government, Internal Revenue, in your local phone book or the phone book for the nearest large city. You may also get tax forms at your local library.

How do you know which form to ask for? Before you can decide, you must first know the meanings of three important income tax terms: *exemption, dependent,* and *deduction.*

An **exemption** is a set amount of money that is not taxed. The IRS lets you set aside $1,000 (in 1985) for each of several possible exemptions. You are allowed an exemption for yourself. Under certain conditions you are also allowed exemptions for your spouse, blindness, deafness, and each dependent.

A **dependent** is a person who is supported by a taxpayer. If you live at home and your parents pay most of your bills, you are a dependent. Your parents will list you as a dependent on their tax form. Since each dependent qualifies as one exemption, you parents would be able to subtract $1,000 from their income because you are their dependent.

A **deduction** is a personal expense that can be subtracted from income before figuring tax. The IRS will let you subtract certain expenses, such as some medical costs, business expenses, real estate taxes, and interest on home mortgages from your income. There are far too many deductions to list here. You will need to read your tax form booklet to learn about all the possible deductions.

Now that you understand these terms, you can probably determine which tax return you should file. Remember—Form 1040EZ is the easiest to file. You can look at a sample 1040EZ on the next page.

You can probably file Form 1040EZ if you

- are single,
- do not claim exemptions for age or blindness,
- have no dependents, and
- earned less than $50,000 during the year.

There are some additional requirements for using the 1040EZ, but they will probably not apply to you. Most people can use the 1040EZ at least in their first few years of filing tax returns.

If you get married and start to raise a family, you will need to use Form 1040A or Form 1040. Most people who do not *itemize* (list) their deductions, use Form 1040A. The IRS has looked at the deductions claimed by thousands of people to determine a standard deduction. The people who use 1040A are given the standard deduction for people in their filing category.

People who believe they have more deductions than the average, use Form 1040 and itemize their deductions. If their deductions add up to more than the standard deduction, they can subtract the higher total. These people must be able, though, to prove that they paid each expense listed as a deduction. They must keep receipts, cancelled checks, and any other legal records necessary to prove their deduction amounts are correct.

If you are not sure how to go about filing your return, don't worry. There is plenty of help available. There are instructions for every form and additional booklets and instructions for every part of the filing procedure.

Toll-free numbers are listed under the IRS in the phone book. By calling these numbers you can talk to someone who can answer your questions.

You can also hire an accountant to do your tax return for you. Millions of people do this every year. For not too high a fee, you can have a professional handle your taxes. You can find companies that specialize in tax matters under *Taxes* in the Yellow Pages of your phone book.

Make a Decision

Several friends have told you that for only $35 they had their taxes done for them by an accountant. They say you are silly for doing your own taxes. At first glance, the form does look pretty complicated, but you think that if you take your time you can figure it out— maybe. What's your decision—do your own taxes or have someone else do them for you? Give reasons for your answer.

Department of the Treasury - Internal Revenue Service

Form 1040EZ Income Tax Return for Single filers with no dependents (0)

1984

OMB No. 1545-0675

Name & address

Use the IRS mailing label. If you don't have one, please print:

Please print your numbers like this.

1234567890

CAROL A. WALLIS

Print your name above (first, initial, last)

201 EAST THIRD STREET

Present home address (number and street)

PLAINTOWN, KS 66762

City, town, or post office, State, and ZIP code

Social security number

987 65 4321

Presidential Election Campaign Fund
Check box if you want $1 of your tax to go to this fund. ▶

	Dollars	Cents

Figure your tax

1 Total wages, salaries, and tips. This should be shown in Box 10 of your W-2 form(s). (Attach your W-2 form(s).) **1** — 1,600.00

2 Interest income of $400 or less. If the total is more than $400, you cannot use Form 1040EZ. **2**

Attach Copy B of Form(s) W-2 here

3 Add line 1 and line 2. This is your **adjusted gross income.** **3** — 1,600.00

4 Allowable part of your charitable contributions. Complete the worksheet on page 21 of the instruction booklet. Do not enter more than $75. **4**

5 Subtract line 4 from line 3. **5** — 1,600.00

6 Amount of your personal exemption. **6** — 1,000.00

7 Subtract line 6 from line 5. This is your **taxable income.** **7** — 600.00

8 Enter your Federal income tax withheld. This should be shown in Box 9 of your W-2 form(s). **8** — 122.40

9 Use the **single** column in the tax table on pages 31-36 of the instruction booklet to find the **tax** on your taxable income on line 7. Enter the amount of tax. **9** — 0

Refund or amount you owe

Attach tax payment here

10 If line 8 is larger than line 9, subtract line 9 from line 8. Enter the **amount of your refund.** **10** — 122.40

11 If line 9 is larger than line 8, subtract line 8 from line 9. Enter the **amount you owe.** Attach check or money order for the full amount, payable to "Internal Revenue Service." **11**

Sign your return

I have read this return. **Under penalties of perjury, I declare that to the best of my knowledge and belief, the return is true, correct, and complete.**

Your signature *Carol A. Wallis* Date 3-25-85

For Privacy Act and Paperwork Reduction Act Notice, see page 41.

The easy-to-read instructions for filling out Form 1040EZ are on the back. You can see at a quick glance that this form is probably not too difficult to complete. You will probably be able to use 1040EZ for at least the first few years that you file a tax return.

REVIEW YOUR LEARNING

CHAPTER SUMMARY

Since all levels of government—federal, state, and local—levy several different types of taxes, you will pay a great deal of money in taxes during your lifetime. These governments need your tax dollars to maintain government operations and to provide needed services. National defense, law enforcement, transportation, and social services for individuals are services that we've come to expect. People who disagree with the ways in which taxes are collected and spent can voice their opinions by voting for legislators sympathetic to their beliefs.

There are many different kinds of taxes; income, social security, sales tax, and property taxes are the major kinds. The federal government, and most state governments, levy an income tax. Social security taxes are taxes that people pay while they are working so they can receive payments during their retirement. Most states levy a sales tax, which is a percentage of the goods and services people buy. Local and state governments also levy property taxes on the assessed value of property. Some additional kinds of taxes are excise taxes, gift taxes, estate taxes, and licenses.

Every citizen is responsible for paying his or her own income tax. A federal income tax return, showing the amount of tax owed for the previous calendar year, must be filed by April 15. During your first years in the world of work, you will probably be able to file Form 1040EZ, which is fairly simple to complete.

WORDS YOU SHOULD KNOW

assessor
deduction
dependent
exemption
filing
Internal Revenue Service (IRS)
levy
return
taxes
W-2 Form
W-4 Form

STUDY QUESTIONS

1. What percent of their income do most people pay in taxes?
2. Why is it essential for governments to have a tax system?
3. What agency of the federal government is responsible for collecting taxes?
4. List at least ten services we receive in return for paying taxes.
5. What can you do if you disagree with the way our tax dollars are collected or spent?

REVIEW YOUR LEARNING

6. List five principles generally thought necessary for a tax system to be a good one.
7. List eight different types of taxes.
8. What is the official cut-off date for filing income tax returns?
9. Why do we have a progressive income tax?
10. How is the social security deduction on your paycheck labeled?
11. What was the rate of social security tax in 1985?
12. If your employer deducts $140 from your checks for social security, how much is paid into social security in your name?
13. For what two types of items is sales tax frequently *not* levied?
14. What tax provides most of the money for public education?
15. If you owned a home assessed at $100,000, and the property tax rate in your county was 4 percent, how much property tax would you have to pay on your home?
16. Why might you want to file an income tax return even if you made less than $3,300?
17. What form must you receive from your employer before you can prepare your tax return?
18. List four examples of personal expenses you can deduct from your income before figuring your income tax.
19. Name the three types of federal income tax returns.
20. What is the simplest federal income tax return to fill out?

DISCUSSION TOPICS

1. Is progressive taxation fair? Why or why not?
2. Some people believe that taxes need to be lowered. What do you think? Give reasons for your decision.

SUGGESTED ACTIVITIES

1. For one week, list all the taxes paid by you and your family members. Include all purchases: clothing, food, transportation, entertainment, and bills (telephone, electricity, gas, and water). What was the total amount of taxes paid? Do you think this is a fair amount to pay? Why or why not? Discuss this in class.
2. Write to the IRS Forms Distribution Center for your state. You can get the address from your teacher. Ask for Publication 21, *Understanding Taxes*, for the current year. Then do the following activities.

- Get tax information for your first job.
- Learn where to get tax forms and how to file.
- Use the tax tables to find what amounts are due at different income levels.
- Find out how to get a tax refund.
- Complete Form 1040EZ, and Form 1040.
- Learn about career opportunities with the IRS.

CHAPTER TWENTY-THREE

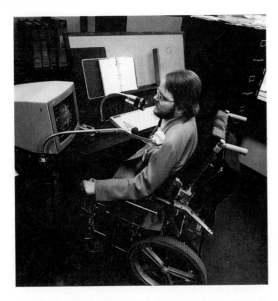

Social Security Services

Most American pioneers were farmers. Families lived together on the farm, and younger members of the family usually took care of their older relatives who were unable to support themselves.

But America gradually changed from an agricultural to an industrial society. As people left the farms to work in the cities, many family members and friends were separated. Then, when economic problems developed in the industrial cities, there was no one to help. Many people were unable to save enough money to support themselves during retirement.

The Great Depression of the 1930s made matters much worse. More people than ever before lost their jobs and were unable to find work. During the depression many people came to believe that the government should do something to help the needy.

In 1935 Congress passed the Social Security Act. This act outlined a national social security plan that would do several things. It would provide money to help people who were temporarily out of work. It would also set aside funds for retired people, workers who were unable to work, and the families of workers needing assistance.

Today the social security system is supporting millions of people. In this chapter you will learn how the system works and what kind of benefits are available.

DO YOU KNOW . . .
- how the social security system works?
- who pays for social security?
- what kinds of social security benefits are available?
- how a social security card can be useful?

CAN YOU DEFINE . . .
- benefits?
- disability?
- Medicare?
- unemployment insurance?
- work credits?
- worker's compensation?

How It Works

The basic idea of the social security program is simple. During their working years, people make social security payments to the government, which holds the money while the people are working. When they can no longer work, they receive **benefits**. Benefits are payments made to individuals who are eligible. If a worker dies, the worker's spouse or children receive the money.

The social security program has been changed several times since 1935, and each time more workers have been included in the program. The percentage of pay that goes toward social security contributions has increased, but cost-of-living adjustments have meant higher payments for those receiving benefits. The number of years a person must work to qualify for benefits has also changed.

Nine out of every ten workers participate in the social security program. Chances are you will, too, if you aren't already.

Contributions

Unless you are self-employed, your employer will deduct social security payments from your paycheck. The amount of the deduction will be listed under *FICA* on your check stub. Your employer will pay an equal amount. If you're self-employed, you will pay about two times the employee rate. Chapter 22 has a more detailed explanation of how FICA deductions are calculated.

As long as you have earnings covered by the social security law, you will continue to make payments. You will make these payments regardless of your age. You will make them even if you are receiving social security benefits.

Eligibility for Benefits

The law is very precise in stating who is eligible for social security benefits and who is not. The law also states clearly how much benefit a person is entitled to.

The amount of a benefit depends primarily on the number of **work credits** you have. Work credits are measurements of how much time you have worked. For each three months of work you receive one quarter of credit. Four quarters, or twelve months, represents a full work credit.

Having enough work credit, though, means only that you qualify for minimum benefits. It doesn't determine the full amount of your benefit. This amount will usually depend on your average earnings covered by social security.

The type of benefit involved also affects the amount of benefit. You will learn more about this in the next section.

Social security payments go to many people other than retirees. For example, social security helps support many families who have lost one of the family's wage earners.

The basic requirement for receiving social security benefits is that you work. Depending upon the type of benefits you are claiming, you must accumulate a certain number of work credits to be eligible.

Types of Benefits

Chances are that when you think about social security you think mostly about older people and retirement. That's not the whole story, though. Several different kinds of benefits are paid by the social security system. Young people, as well as older people, receive these benefits.

Disability Benefits

One type of social security benefit is paid for disability. Disability is the physical or mental condition that prevents someone from working. A worker who has a disability is called a *disabled worker.*

Social security laws are very exact about who is and who is not a disabled worker. A disabled worker is one who will be (or has been) unable to work due to a mental or physical condition for at least twelve months. Someone who is expected to die as a result of such a condition is also considered to be a disabled worker.

Several factors determine how much benefit a disabled worker receives. Age and work credits are the two most important factors. The type of disability involved can also be a factor.

If you become disabled before age twenty-four, you need credit for one and one-half years of work in the three years before you become disabled to receive benefits. If you're between twenty-four and thirty-one, you must have credit for half the time between your twenty-first birthday and the time you become disabled.

If you become disabled at thirty-one or later, you generally need credit for at least five years of work out of the ten years ending when you become disabled. You may need additional credit, depending on your age and the date your disability starts.

If you are disabled by blindness, you need not meet the requirement of recent work. You do need, however, one quarter of work credit for each year since you turned twenty-one. This credit is counted up to the year you become blind. A minimum of six quarters of credit is needed.

Disability benefits can be very important to workers and their families. These benefits may be the family's only source of income while the wage earner is disabled.

Work Credits for Disability

The years of work credit needed for disability checks depends on your age when you become disabled:

- *Before 24*—You need credit for 1½ years of work in the 3-year period ending when your disability starts.
- *24 through 31*—You need credit for having worked half the time between 21 and the time you become disabled.
- *31 and older*—You need the amount of credit shown in the following chart.

Born after 1929, become disabled at age	Years of work credit you need
31 through 42	5
44	5½
46	6
48	6½
50	7
52	7½
53	7¾
54	8
55	8¼
56	8½
58	9
60	9½
62 or older	10

Survivor Benefits

Another very important part of social security is the plan for *survivor benefits*. Survivor benefits are payments made to the family of a worker who has died. These payments can be very important to the family of a parent who has died unexpectedly.

A twenty-nine-year-old father of two small children, both under five, was killed in an accident in 1985. He had maximum earnings covered by social security each year. As a result, his widow and children received almost $1,232 per month in social security checks. This was about $14,784 per year at 1985 benefit rates. By the time the oldest child reaches eighteen, this family probably will have received at least $200,000. It's likely that the family will get higher monthly checks in future years. This increase is due to the social security law that provides for automatic benefit increases as living costs rise.

In 1985 over 7.5 million people received monthly social security checks as the survivors of deceased workers. Included among these people were the unmarried children of many deceased workers, and people who became disabled before reaching age twenty-two. Others receiving benefits were widows and widowers, divorced wives, grandchildren, and the parents of deceased workers. Certain guidelines determine the eligibility and the amounts of the benefits received by each person.

Retirement Benefits

One of the most important features of the Social Security Act is the plan that regulates *retirement benefits*. Retirement benefits are payments made to workers after they retire from their jobs.

To receive full retirement benefits a worker must have worked for a minimum of ten years. The ten years may be worked over a long period of time—they need not be consecutive. Workers can move from one job to another without losing their work credit.

Most people do not count on social security alone to take care of all their financial needs. The retirement plan is not set up to provide all the money needed after retirement. Since most people will need another income, they save money during their working years. They may also receive benefits from their employers' retirement plans. Still others may do part-time work to supplement their social security benefits.

Last March Jo Oliver told her friend Marie, "I've worked for the LaForte Company for thirty-eight years. In June, I'll be sixty-two years old. I'm going to retire. I don't have any children to help me, but I'll have my company retirement and social security. Even if I had children and grandchildren, I wouldn't want to move in with them."

"I see your point," Marie responded, "but if benefits start before age sixty-five, your checks will be smaller. You'd better find out about that."

At the social security office, Jo was told that Marie was correct. If she retired at sixty-two her payments would be less. This was because she'd be getting benefits for a longer time. The earlier she retired, the smaller her benefit checks would be.

Jo was given an estimate of the amount of each social security payment. She also found out at the LaForte personnel office how much her retirement checks would be. Jo looked over her expenses for the past year. She realized that after retirement she would spend less on transportation, lunches, and clothing. By saving on these expenses, she was sure she could manage. After all, she would have company retirement, social security, and a small income from money saved over the past thirty-eight years.

The chart below shows the number of work credits needed to be entitled to full benefits at the age of sixty-two. A healthy worker must be at least sixty-two to collect benefits. The amount of a worker's benefit is based on the worker's average earnings. The age of the worker at retirement is considered in the formula. The following table shows the amounts of expected monthly retirement checks.

Many people work part-time after retiring from their full-time jobs. These people can still draw their social security benefits if they do not earn over a certain amount. The amount of their benefit usually goes down if they are earning some money.

Work Credits Needed To Receive Retirement Benefits	
If you reach 62 in	**Years you need**
1981	7½
1982	7¾
1983	8
1984	8¼
1985	8½
1987	9
1991 or later	10

The social security payments you make while you are working will help you enjoy the years after you retire. Originated in 1935, the social security retirement benefits have proven to be extremely valuable.

Health Insurance Benefits

Many older people living on low incomes can't afford the medical care they need. Private companies do offer medical insurance for older citizens, but this insurance is expensive—many people can't pay the high cost. In 1965 Congress added a plan for hospital and medical insurance to social security. This insurance program is called **Medicare**.

Medicare was originally planned for people sixty-five and over. Since then it has been extended to include more people who need assistance. For example, almost all people needing special treatments or kidney transplants are covered by Medicare. Disabled workers under sixty-five who have had disability payments for twenty-four consecutive months may also be covered under Medicare. Providing health care payments for those over sixty-five is still, though, the major function of Medicare.

The Medicare program covers a percentage of a person's hospital expenses. It also pays part of the cost of doctor bills and other medical services.

Unemployment Benefits

Although not part of the social security system, **unemployment insurance** was created by the Social Security Act and is a type of social insurance. Unemployment insurance pays benefits to workers who have lost their jobs. These payments help families get through the difficult times caused by unemployment. Unemployment insurance also helps prevent a major economic depression, such as the Great Depression in the 1930s.

State governments manage the payment of unemployment insurance. The employers are taxed at a certain rate, creating a fund that is used to make the payments. Although employers pay for the biggest part of unemployment, some states also put money into the fund.

Young workers are more likely than older workers to be unemployed. When factories and businesses are forced to lay off workers, the people with the least seniority are usually the first to lose their jobs. As a young member of the labor force, you should know something about your state's unemployment laws.

Average Monthly Payments To Workers Receiving Benefits
1984

Beneficiary	Low Earnings $6,968-year	Average Earnings $16,019-year	Maximum Earnings $37,800-year
Worker retired at 65	361.00	542.00	699.00
Worker with spouse at 65	469.00	705.00	908.00
Worker retiring at 62	289.00	434.00	559.00
Worker with spouse at 62	424.00	637.00	821.00
Worker disabled at 55	361.00	542.00	699.00
Worker disabled at 55 with spouse and child	549.00	814.00	1,047.00
Widowed mother/father with one child	540.00	814.00	1,054.00
Widowed mother/father with two children	574.00	985.00	1,232.00

These rates do not reflect possible future cost of living adjustments

Each state has its own regulations about who is and is not qualified to receive unemployment benefits. Some fairly common requirements are listed below. The workers must

- become unemployed through no fault of their own.
- register at a public employment office to get a job.
- be willing to take a job similar to the one lost.
- make claims for benefits.
- have made a certain amount of money or worked a certain length of time.

If you need to find out whether or not you are entitled to unemployment benefits, go to your local employment office. The address is in the phone book under the name of your state.

You usually may *not* draw unemployment benefits if you

- are unemployed as a result of a labor dispute.
- quit your job without cause.
- are discharged for misconduct.
- refuse to apply or take a suitable job.
- misrepresent facts or makes fraudulent claims.
- are discharged after conviction of theft.

The amount of earnings and the length of employment are used to calculate the amount of benefits you may receive. The formula used varies from state to state. Generally the benefits received are equal to one-half your weekly salary. In a number of states, your benefits are based on your earnings during a prior twelve-month period. Unemployed workers cannot receive benefits indefinitely. In many states, thirty-nine weeks is the maximum length of time for receiving benefits.

If you work long enough and become unemployed through no fault of your own, you may be eligible for unemployment benefits. You will have to go to your state's local unemployment office to apply.

Make a Decision

You know people who say it is wrong to accept unemployment checks. They say that people should pay their own way, and that they would never take money unless they earned it. You were just laid off, and you need money to live on. Make a decision—will you apply for unemployment compensation, or try to find some other way to get by until you find a job? Give reasons for your decision.

Worker's Compensation

Another social insurance program is known as **worker's compensation**. Worker's compensation is an insurance program that makes payments to workers injured on the job and to the survivors of these workers. Worker's compensation pays medical bills, pensions, and other benefits. In addition to paying for injuries, some job-related diseases, such as black lung disease, also qualify workers for payments.

As with unemployment insurance, worker's compensation programs are administered by the states. Every state has its own program. The laws governing worker's compensation vary considerably from one state to the next. There are also some federal compensation programs.

Employers pay into the funds that are used to make payments in worker's compensation programs. Employers are taxed at a given rate, depending upon the requirements of the state laws. Most people seem to feel that employers should be responsible for job-related injuries to their workers.

If you are injured on the job, report the injury to your employer or supervisor immediately. This is necessary for your physical well-being and required before making a worker's compensation claim. The personnel officer or your employer should help you receive any benefits to which you are entitled.

Your Social Security Number

In Chapter 5 you learned how to apply for a social security card. You probably already have the card that shows your social security number. If you don't, apply now at the social security office in your area.

You need a social security number if your work is covered by the social security law. In fact, you may need to list this number on your job application. The Social Security Administration uses this number to keep track of how much money you pay in social security. The number will also be used to record the number of work credits you have.

As you begin to save some of your money, you will find that banks and other savings companies ask for your social security number. They will report annually to the federal government the amount of interest paid to you on your savings account.

You will also need a social security number for your income tax return. The IRS identifies all people by number. In this way they avoid confusing you with someone else having the same name.

If you enter military service, your social security number will become your identification number. Along with getting social security work credit, you will also get additional credit for active duty.

There are over 230 million people in this country. Many of them have the same name, but no two people have the same social security number. This is why your number will be used to identify you in so many places.

When you apply for a social security number, you will receive two cards. Carry one of these cards in your billfold. Place the other one in a safety deposit box at the bank. If you know your number, you can replace a lost card by going to the local social security office. If you change your name (through marriage, for example), ask for a card with your new name but with the same number.

If you ever find out that your number is incorrect on your check stub or on any other form, get in touch with a social security office promptly. Someone there will help you correct that record. It's important to take care of this so that you are properly credited for your work and tax payments. Of course you will also want to notify your employer.

It's against the law to use someone else's social security number. It's also illegal to give false information on the application for a social security number. Penalties include a fine of up to $1,000, a jail sentence of up to one year, or both.

This little card doesn't look all that important, but it is. You will use your social security card throughout your lifetime to identify yourself. The government, businesses, schools, and various institutions will use your number to keep track of your accounts in your name.

━━━━━ Make a Decision ━━━━━

Your public library uses social security numbers to assign a library card number for each person wanting a library card. A friend of yours who doesn't have a social security card wants to borrow yours to get a library card. You want to help your friend, but you don't think this is legal. What's your decision— lend your card, or not?

The Future of Social Security

The question is often asked, "Who will pay for social security as it grows and becomes more expensive?" Population studies show that many people are living longer. This means that more people qualify for benefits, and that people receive benefits for a longer period of time. Inflation and cost-of-living increases also make the system more and more expensive.

The laws have been changed several times to increase the amount of money paid into the system. The tax rate, which was 6.05 percent in 1978, was 7.05 percent in 1985. If you read Chapter 22, you know that the rate will continue to go up in the next few years.

The wage base for social security has also been raised. This base is the maximum amount of earnings on which social security taxes are paid. In 1978 the wage base was $17,700; in 1985 though, workers had to pay the tax on all income up to $39,600.

Having workers pay a higher percent on more of their earnings increases the amount of social security funds. This helps to pay for the increasing benefits described above.

The social security law was changed again in 1983. Among the many changes were changes in the Medicare rules. Hospitals will no longer be paid on the reasonable cost for patient care. Instead, payments will be made on the basis of predetermined rates. These changes and the increased rates are expected to keep the system financially healthy until the year 2027.

Social security benefits have been a great help to both old and young people. If you haven't already, you will someday receive benefits. When you see the FICA deduction on your paycheck, think of it as an investment. Your money is working for others now—it will work for you later.

Even if you are not now eligible for benefits, you may want to get more information on social security. You may want information for a member of your family or a friend. To get the answer to any social security question, call or write a social security office. To find the address of the office nearest you, look under *Social Security* in the telephone directory.

REVIEW YOUR LEARNING

CHAPTER SUMMARY

Congress passed the Social Security Act in 1935. This act established a plan of social insurance that provides unemployed, disabled, and retired workers, and the families of deceased workers, with monthly payments to help them through difficult times. The social security system also pays health care expenses through a plan known as *Medicare.*

While you are working, you will pay a percentage of your earnings to the social security system. When you retire or become disabled, you will receive benefits. If you die, your family will receive benefits. Your work credits, average earnings, and the type of benefit involved, all affect the amount of benefit to which you are entitled.

Almost everyone needs to have a social security card, which has that person's social security number. Your social security number identifies your account within the social security system. It is also used by banks, the IRS, the military, and many other organizations, to identify individuals. If you don't already have one, apply for a social security card soon.

WORDS YOU SHOULD KNOW

benefits
disability
Medicare
unemployment insurance
work credits
worker's compensation

STUDY QUESTIONS

1. Why was social security needed less by people who lived many years ago than by people today?
2. Who pays for social security?
3. What is the minimum work credit required for disability benefits if you are under twenty-four years of age?
4. How can social security help a child after the death of a parent who had social security insurance?
5. At what age can a healthy worker start drawing social security retirement benefits?
6. Name at least two groups of people who are eligible for Medicare payments.

REVIEW YOUR LEARNING   CHAPTER 23

7. List five common requirements for workers wanting to receive unemployment benefits.
8. List five conditions under which workers usually *cannot* draw unemployment benefits.
9. List at least two cases in which you might need a social security card for something other than social security business.
10. What two things can be changed to increase the amount of money being paid into the social security system?

DISCUSSION TOPICS

1. Discuss the advantages of having a federal social security program.
2. Do you think the maximum amount of cash benefits for retirement is adequate? Why or why not?

SUGGESTED ACTIVITIES

1. If you do not have a social security card, apply for one at a social security office rather than individual state programs.
2. Use an encyclopedia to find information on the social security program of another country.
3. At a social security office, look over the free information that is displayed. Select a folder on the topic of most interest to you. Prepare a two-minute summary of the information. Present it to the class.

Your Changing Role

DO YOU KNOW . . .
- both the advantages and disadvantages of living on your own?
- what factors you should consider in selecting a place to live?
- what you can do to cope with stress?

CAN YOU DEFINE . . .
- intimidation?
- lease?
- security deposit?
- stress
- subletting?
- utilities?

When you get a full-time job and start earning your own money, you will become more and more responsible for your own actions. Many young people look forward to this exciting time of independence and freedom. Others are very much afraid of the new responsibilities. These young people have doubts about their ability to handle the problems they will need to face.

In most cases you don't know how you will respond to the increased responsibilities and demands until you actually confront them. This chapter does, however, provide you with information that will help you be successful when it comes time to take full charge of your own life.

On Your Own

Almost everyone eventually moves away from their childhood home to start a life of their own. Some people leave home even before they finish high school, while others may not move out until they are in their late 20s or early 30s. But sooner or later, most of us do set out on our own.

Your parents or guardians have probably been handling many of life's responsibilities for you. You may not even realize all the responsibilities they take care of. Not until you have to take care of yourself will you realize how many responsibilities are involved in normal everyday living. There will be bills to pay, decisions to make, and in many cases, not nearly enough time to do all that needs to be done.

No book can tell you how to make the countless decisions you must make from day to day. You must live your own life as you choose. This section will, however, cover some of the problems you will encounter when you first go out on your own. It will even help you decide whether it would be best to start out on your own right away or to be patient and wait awhile.

At Home or Your Own Place

One of the first things many young people do when they get their first full-time job is to move away from home. The idea of being free and independent sounds good. To make all of your own decisions and come and go as you please is just what you wanted—right? Many young people *are* happy and successful on their own.

Many others, however, find out too late that they should have waited a little while before moving away from the security and comfort of home.

Before you move away, consider the advantages of living at home. The first and most obvious advantage is that it costs much less to live at home. Even if you pay your family for food and rent, your expenses will almost certainly be less than if you were on your own. There will be lots of expenses you never anticipated. And as a beginning worker you will be among the first to be laid off if your employer must cut back. If you lost your job, would you be able to manage on your own until you found a new job?

Another reason for staying at home is companionship. If you've never lived alone, you don't realize how lonely it can be at times. You may be taking for granted the time you spend with brothers, sisters, and parents.

Before you rush out to get an apartment of your own, stop and think about the advantages of living at home.

A third advantage to living at home is the help you get from family members. Doing the cooking, cleaning, and laundry after a hard day of work can be difficult. If there are people at home who can help you with these chores, living at home will be easier.

The one big advantage to moving away from home is the opportunity to be in complete control of your own life. You can set your own rules and make your own decisions. You will, though, have plenty of time—the rest of your life—to be on your own. Don't be in too big a hurry. Weigh the freedom you will have against the much greater costs, the possible periods of loneliness, and the lack of help in doing day-to-day chores. You might want to wait awhile, until you are a little more sure of yourself and your job, to move out on your own.

Planning Your Move

Once you decide you want a place of your own, you must make some more decisions. Where will you live? How much can you afford to pay? In what type of place—apartment, house, mobile home—will you be most comfortable? What furniture will you need? Will you live alone? Would you prefer having a roommate, and if so, whom would you live with?

In addition to all this decision-making, you must do some financial planning. You learned a great deal about this in Chapter 17. Some specific financial concerns are discussed in the next column. With careful planning and wise shopping, you can improve your chances of finding the right place and an affordable one.

New Expenses. Houses, apartments, mobile homes, and condominiums (dwellings like apartments, but you buy instead of rent) are available in a wide range of prices. You can't start looking for a place to live until you know what you can afford. You will need to figure how much of your take-home pay you want to spend for rent (or for a house payment if you decide to buy). Many experts recommend that your rent be no more than one week's pay, which would be about 25 percent of your monthly earnings.

Of course your rent will not be your only new expense. You will have several initial expenses when you move out. For example, you'll probably have to pay one or two months' rent in advance as a **security deposit.** This is money that a landlord holds as a guarantee against damages. If you don't do any damage, you get the money back when you move out. Although you usually get your money back, you still must budget for it when you move in.

You will also have to pay hook-up charges for **utilities.** Utilities are services, such as electricity, gas, and water, that are provided by public companies. In addition to the necessary utilities, such as electricity and water, you will probably want telephone service. Not only must you budget for the initial hook-up charges, you must be sure you can afford the monthly payments for the utilities. The rent for some apartments includes utilities.

Some other expenses you must plan for are for the furniture, utensils, and supplies that you will have to buy. There will be all sorts of inexpensive things—can openers, silverware, drinking glasses,

Unfurnished apartments are less expensive than comparable furnished apartments, but furniture is expensive. Unless your family and friends loan you a few pieces of furniture, you might need a furnished apartment.

wastepaper baskets—that can add up to a lot of money. You may need to do your laundry at a laundromat. And if you rent a place without furniture, you will probably need to buy several expensive items, such as sofas, chairs, beds, and tables. If you have a lot of money invested in personal belongings, you will also want to buy some renter's insurance.

Is your paycheck going to be enough to pay for all these extra costs? If so, you are on your way. If not, you will need to start saving some money now so you can move out on your own later.

The most important thing is that you plan ahead. Go back to Chapter 17 and follow the guidelines there for budgeting your money. Talk to your parents or friends who are on their own to make sure you are considering every expense.

You must know what you can afford *before* you move out. Three or four months after you've spent lots of money on furniture and utensils, and paid utility hook-up costs, is not the time to find out you can't afford to pay your rent.

Roommates. If you can't afford a place of your own, you may want to share an apartment with a friend. Utility expenses, rent, and food costs can be cut in half if you have a roommate. You may even know two or three people who would be interested in sharing a place. Thousands of people all across the country share apartments with friends and acquaintances so that they can live in apartments they could not otherwise afford.

Another advantage to having a roommate is companionship. If you have been used to living in a large family, you might be lonely by yourself. You will probably want someone to pal around with after working hours. A roommate, or two or three roommates, can mean instant companionship.

There can, though, be some disadvantages to having a roommate. While most experiences go well, many friendships have ended due to the conflicts that arise between roommates. Before you take an apartment with a friend, ask yourself the following questions.

- Will a roommate prevent me from doing the things I want to do?
- How will I get along with this person? Will I want to spend a lot of time with this person? Will this person interfere with my activities with other people?
- Will this person be willing to pay half the expenses?
- What will happen if we can't get along or my roommate loses his or her job and has to move out? Will I be able to afford all the expenses until I get another roommate?

You must answer these questions before you decide to share an apartment. The size, cost, and location of your apartment will depend on whether or not you have a roommate.

Most roommates don't play the drums, but roommates do have habits, hobbies, and friends that will surprise you.

Make a Decision

You've found an apartment that is perfect, but the rent is too much for one person. You know someone who is looking for a roommate, but you have a feeling that you would have a hard time getting along with this person day in and day out. You'd really rather live alone, but to do that you would have to take a place not nearly as nice as the one you want. What's your decision—nice apartment with roommate, or not-so-nice apartment alone? Give reasons for your decision.

Joanne and Anna were friends all through high school. They graduated a year ago and started working full time. They lived at home for nearly another year, then decided they would like to rent an apartment. Neither could afford to live alone, but together they thought they could pay expenses and have money left over.

Joanne and Anna looked at apartments for several weeks and finally decided on an unfurnished apartment. The rent was quite a bit less than that for furnished apartments. Joanne agreed to buy some used furniture, and Anna paid a bigger share of the rent. By the third month in their apartment, Joanne had furnished the place beautifully.

A week later, Anna took a job in another city and moved. Joanne couldn't afford to pay all the rent herself, so she moved back with her family. She stored her furniture in her grandparents' attic. She's still making payments on some of it.

Finding the Best Place

After analyzing your financial situation and making a decision about a roommate, you are ready to begin looking for a place to live. Shopping for a place to live is a consumer activity much like any other. You will want to follow all the suggestions you learned in Chapter 16 for wise, responsible buying.

Where do you begin looking? Probably the best place to start is by asking family members, friends, and co-workers. One of these people might have a place to rent or know of a place that is especially nice for the money.

The most common way to find a place is to read the "For Rent" section of the classified ads in your local newspapers. These ads are frequently divided into two groups—furnished and unfurnished.

Unless you have already made a decision about wanting either a furnished or unfurnished apartment, you may want to compare the values. If the rent is quite a bit less for unfurnished apartments, buying some furniture may save you money. Think about what furniture you will need. Perhaps your

---

GREENBRIAR—Efficiency. All Utilities. Kitchen—Appliances. Furnished—Carpeted. Month to Month. $335. Ph. 452-7332.

GROVE, 602 E.—Efficiency, all utilities paid. $200. Deposit and lease. No pets. Call 829-8682.

HOVEY, 1503—Very nice 2-bedroom duplex, $375.
Ph. 829-4570 or 454-2694

JEFFERSON, E.—3 rooms, carport. Heat, water furnished. $275. Ph. 662-3257.

LOCUST, 310 E.—Small 1-bedroom with all utilities furnished, off-street parking. $240 plus deposit. Ph. 828-2232.

MACARTHUR, 919 W.—Near Miller Park. Clean, 2-bedroom upper, central air. $300, utilities furnished, no pets. Ph. 728-2729, after 6

MAIN, S.—Attractive, large, clean, 2-bedroom, paneled den. Heat, water paid. Ph. 829-5806.

MAIN, 1106 S.—Clean, carpeted 3 rooms, 1-bedroom, off-street parking. No pets. $245.
Ph. 828-2005

MAJOR, 1200—Large, 2-bedroom, heat and water furnished, Near ISU.
Ph. 452-4221

MARKET, 407 E.—Efficiency, all utilities paid, off—street parking. Rent $190, Deposit $100. NO PETS.
Ph. 828-8138.

MARKET, E.—3-room lower, carpeted, parking. Heat, water paid. Lease. $250. Ph. 829-5806.

MCLEAN, 101 S.—Attractive efficiency for lady, utilities paid, quiet, no pets. Ph. 828-7634.

MONROE ST.—Clean, 3 rooms and bath, carpeted, electric, water furnished. Ph. 452-2938.

****
COLLEGE PARK CT.—Several 2 bedrooms, heat and water paid. $325. Ph. 827-4734.

CROXTON—Park setting, 1-bedroom, carpeted, with appliances, water furnished. Ph. 828-1502, or 829-5421.

DUSTIN DR., Normal
2-bedroom townhouse, 1½ baths, basement. $400 plus utilities. Suitable for working people. No pets. Lease, security deposit.
Ph. 663-8468.

EMPIRE, 2104 E.— ½ OFF FIRST MONTH'S RENT. Townhouse, 2-bedroom, 1½ baths, convenient to Veterans Parkway. Heat and water paid. $340-$350. Ph. 827-8576.
★ ApartmentMart★

EMPIRE-TODD—2-bedroom townhouse, laundry hookups, carport, extra storage space. Near Hershey and Empire. Pets O.K., with reference. $450.
● Ph. 454-2338 ●

EMPIRE-TODD—2-bedroom townhouse, 1st floor laundry, washer and dryer, dishwasher, off-street parking, vanity in master bedroom, low , low heating cost. $450. Ph. 454-2338.

****
EMPIRE, EAST—Spacious two-bedroom townhouse with 1½ baths and large kitchen. Close to Eastland Mall. Heat, water and cable TV furnished. $345. Ph. 827-7747 or leave message

EMPIRE-TODD—2-bedroom townhouse, new carpet, carport, vanity in master bedroom. East side. $420. Ph. 454-2338.

****
ENSIGN—Normal. Two-bedroom townhouse with basement. Carpeted, with 1½ baths and central air. $325.
Ph. 827-7747 or leave message

In reading the ads above, you'll notice that no two ads give exactly the same information. Many things you'll want to know are left out. You can save yourself some time by making a list of questions to ask before you go see the apartments.

family or a close friend can loan you some of the pieces you need. In many cases a refrigerator and stove are included even with unfurnished apartments.

If you have no luck finding a place you can afford in the "For Rent" section of the paper, check the Yellow Pages of the phone book. There you will find listings for real-estate agencies. These agencies may have places to rent that aren't advertised. A real-estate agency often charges a fee for renting a place. Find out who—you or the owner—must pay the fee.

In most cases you will find several possible places listed in the newspaper. When you start looking at these places, you may find yourself becoming confused, forgetting which place had this and which had that. They will all start to blend together in your mind after you have looked at several.

Using a checklist to compare specific features will help you decide which place you like best. You can rate each place according to the points on your checklist. The following points are ones you will probably want on your checklist.

Outside Areas. Many people look only at the inside of an apartment and forget to check the outside. Take time to look around the outside of the building. Drive around the neighborhood to get a feel for what it's like. Compare the outside areas of the apartments on the following points.

- **Location and neighborhood**—Do you like the area? Is there enough privacy? What is the condition of the surrounding buildings?
- **Grounds around the building**—Is there a yard? Will you need to mow the grass? Are the grounds free of litter and trash?
- **Exterior quality of the building**—Is the building in good condition? Will you have to get the owner to make repairs?
- **Noise and air pollution**—Is there a lot of traffic noise? Is the air clean? Do there seem to be many children or animals in the area?
- **Parking facilities**—If you have a car, where can you park it? Will this cost extra?
- **Locked mailbox**—A locked box provides safety. Will you have one available?
- **Safety precautions**—Is the outside area safe to walk through, even at night?
- **Transportation**—If you don't have a car, you'll be curious about public transportation. How close is the nearest bus stop or train depot?
- **Recreation**—What sort of recreational facilities are available nearby? Does the apartment complex have a pool, tennis court, or recreation room?

You can usually get a good idea of what an apartment will look like by inspecting the grounds around the apartment building and the neighborhood in which the apartment is located.

Inside Areas. You will spend a great deal of time in the place you choose. Make sure you would feel comfortable. Think about what it would be like to live in each place. Consider the following points.

- **Condition of hall and steps**—Are the halls and steps in good condition? Will you be able to safely use them even when your arms are loaded with groceries? Does it look as though someone cleans regularly?
- **Fire escape**—Are there at least two ways to get out of the building?
- **Cleanliness**—Will you have to do a lot of cleaning before you move in? Does it look as though the present or former occupants took good care of the apartment?
- **Room arrangement**—Do you like the floor plan? If you have a roommate, will your sleeping arrangements give each of you enough privacy?
- **Storage**—Will there be enough room to store everything? How many closets are there? Is there enough cabinet space in the kitchen?
- **Condition of kitchen fixtures**—Do all furnished appliances work? Do cabinet doors and drawers work smoothly?

- **Condition of bathroom fixtures**—Is there a shower, a bath, or both? Does all of the plumbing work properly? Was there plenty of pressure and hot water when you tried the faucets?
- **Condition of windows, screens, and locks**—Is there any broken glass? Do the windows close easily? Do they lock? Do they look as if they would be tight in the winter? Are there screens for the summer? Are there any holes in them?
- **Condition of doors**—How many and what kinds of locks are on the door?
- **Laundry facilities**—If there are machines, do they work? Are they located conveniently or will you have to go to a laundromat?

Rental Terms. You will find that landlords use a wide variety of charging procedures for their apartments. Some include utilities in the rent, some don't. Some require a deposit and lease, some don't. To get the most economical apartment, you must carefully compare the various terms.

- **Rent and due date**—Consider the amount you must pay for what you are getting. Is the place worth this amount? When is the rent due? It may be convenient if it is due a few days after you get paid.

If you find an apartment you like, you'll be eager to say, "I'll take it." Try to be patient and inspect the apartment carefully. A little extra time here could save you a year of misery with leaky faucets, windows that don't open, and lots of other problems.

- **Security deposit**—How much is the security deposit? Does the owner have an inventory of all items and their condition? How soon do you get your money back if nothing is damaged?
- **Availability**—When will the apartment be available? To avoid having empty apartments, landlords advertise vacancies before the apartments are actually vacant. Make sure you know when you can move in.
- **Utility charges**—Sometimes the owner will pay for such utilities as water, garbage collection, heating, and lighting. Because landlords do this in so many different ways, you must be very careful in your comparisons. A $400 apartment with utilities paid may be cheaper than a $300 apartment without utilities paid.
- **Painting and repairs**—These are usually taken care of by the owner. Sometimes the owner will charge less rent if you agree to do some painting or repair work.
- **Pets**—Are you allowed to have pets? Some landlords allow pets, others don't. Make sure the landlord knows you will want to have a pet if that is the case. If there is no written agreement, the owner may forget he or she gave permission for pets.

Leases. A **lease** is a contract between a landlord and a renter that states the responsibilities of both parties. Most leases are binding for one year, although you may be able to negotiate the length of the lease. Some landlords require a lease, others do not. Once you sign a lease you are obligated to pay the rent for the specified time, whether you live in the apartment or not. If you're not sure how long you will need the apartment, a more expensive apartment that doesn't require a lease may be more economical than a cheaper one that does.

In signing a lease you are usually committing yourself to at least one year of financial responsiblity. Don't you think this calls for careful reading of the contract? If you are confused or concerned about some part of the lease, you might want a lawyer to look at it.

As you learned in Chapter 21, you should not sign any contract until you have read it. You should make sure you understand all the terms of the lease. Find the answers to each of the questions below.

- What is the length of time for the lease?
- Can the landlord raise the rent during the period of the lease?
- How much notice must be given before moving? If you pay your rent once a month, you should let the owner know at least a month before you plan to move. This allows the owner time to advertise for another renter.
- May anything you attach to a wall (towel racks, curtain rods, pictures) be taken down if you move?
- May the owner enter during your absence?
- May you sublet the apartment, and if so, under what conditions? **Subletting** is the process whereby the original renter rents the apartment to a second renter, usually with the landlord's approval. If you think you may want to move before the lease is over, whether or not you are allowed to sublet the apartment is an important question.

Apartment Inspection Checklist

If you must pay a security deposit, it's a good idea to make an inventory of all the areas and items in the apartment and their conditions. Then have the apartment owner or manager sign the inventory.

Area	Condition	Area	Condition	Area	Condition
Entrance		**Kitchen**		**Bedroom**	
Door		Doors		Doors	
Light		Walls		Walls	
Doorbell		Windows		Windows	
Living Room		Ceiling		Floor/Carpet	
Doors		Floor		Light Fixtures	
Walls		Cabinets		Closet	
Windows		Counter		Furnishings	
Ceiling		Stove			
Floor/Carpet		Oven			
Light Fixtures		Refrigerator			
Closet		Furnishings			
Furnishings				Heating/Air Cond.	
		Bathroom		Other	
		Doors			
		Wall/Tile			
		Medicine Chest			
		Tub & Shower			
		Sink			
		Toilet			

_____ Date   _____ Owner/Manager

Moving Day

If you do your decision-making and planning carefully, the day will finally come when you are to move into your own place. As with everything else, your moving day will go much easier if you plan it carefully. A poorly planned move can result in wasted time, damaged furniture, and a poor start to independent living.

In most cases the best method for moving depends on how much furniture you have. It will also depend on how far you will be moving and how much you can afford to spend. The easiest method is to hire professional movers, but this can be very expensive.

If you will be moving large, heavy furniture to a second-floor apartment, you may want to hire a professional mover. If you will be moving only dishes, bedding, clothing, and small furnishings, you can probably handle the move yourself. The in-between alternative is to rent a van or truck and ask your friends to help.

If you decide you need a professional mover to move your furniture, you'll need to sign a contract. The contract should detail the exact charge and the mover's responsibility for damage. You will save money by packing dishes and clothing yourself since the mover will charge extra for packing.

There are several things you should take care of before you move. If your new place needs cleaning, do it before you move in. You will be able to do a much better and faster job of cleaning while the apartment is totally empty.

You will also want to make sure that your utilities are hooked up before you move in. Call the gas, electric, water, and phone companies a week or two prior to moving in. You may need to be present when the utilities are hooked up.

Another thing you can do ahead of time is report your new address to the post office. Filling out a change-of-address card before you move will help prevent lost or delayed mail.

Stages of Your Development

Psychologists have identified certain stages people commonly go through in their career and personal development. With each stage there are certain responsibilities. As you move from one stage to the next, your responsibilities will change. Take some time to study the chart below. Look at where you've been, where you are, and where you are going to be.

Stage	Age	Career Development	Life Responsibilities
One	5-10	Learn to identify people by the kind of work they do. Learn this from watching parents and TV	Personal cleanliness, closely supervised household chores, school responsibilities
Two	10-15	Develop work habits that will be with you for a long time	Organize school assignments, added household chores, not so closely supervised
Three	15-25	Learn about self and how to fit into the world, select and prepare for career, begin work, lay foundation for future success	To succeed on job, manage money, responsibility to family
Four	25-55	Grow emotionally and mentally, and produce on the job. Self-improvement through work and continued education	Family and home responsibilities, education for children, may need larger home, two cars
Five	55-65	Prepare for retirement, help newcomers learn	Children grown and establishing own homes, need for smaller home, saving for retirement
Six	65-	Relax and contemplate	Little or no responsibility to job, free to travel

Stress

The time when you first move out on your own will probably be an exciting, fun time in your life. There may be a new job, new friends, new experiences. You will probably be busy and happy, especially if you have followed the career decision-making and planning guidelines you have learned in this book.

You will discover that with freedom and independence come responsibilities and problems. No longer will someone else take care of the things that need to be taken care of from day to day. No longer will someone else be making the difficult decisions about your financial situation and your career. You will be responsible from now on.

Along with increased responsibility, decision-making, and work comes **stress**. Stress is physical, emotional, or mental strain. It is the hardship that your mind and body feel as a result of hard physical and mental work.

Effects of Stress

Some stress is good for you. For example, you may regularly "stress" your body in physical activity, such as tennis or jogging. This stress helps keep your body in good physical condition. In the same way, a certain amount of problem-solving is good mental activity.

The most troublesome kind of stress is emotional stress, which is often caused by frustration. People who are constantly frustrated often become physically or mentally ill from stress. If these people do not reach some of their goals and end the frustration, they risk serious health problems. Emotional stress can even cause mental breakdowns.

Emotional stress affects different people in different ways. Some people get ulcers. Some develop severe headaches. Others appear to age faster than normal. Stress can generally weaken your body and make you more susceptible to many diseases. It can also cause you to lose your self-confidence.

Causes of Stress

As you get older, the possible causes of stress increase. You may need to support a family. There will be pressure on you to "get ahead" in your career. If you are like many people, you will also have to deal with the added pressure of managing a household while working outside the home. All of these factors will contribute to the stress you feel.

Among the main causes of stress are the inability to reach personal goals and problems in human relations. These causes are described below. Although discussed separately, these causes are often related.

Inability to Reach Personal Goals. If you can't do something that you want very much to do, you become frustrated. Almost everyone must deal with some frustration every day. Getting stuck in a traffic jam, not being able to find something you've misplaced, or a failure to solve a problem in the time you thought it would take, are just a few examples. These small, minor frustrations, which are usually beyond your control, can add up to a lot of stress.

The causes of stress are many. Sometimes they all seem to confront you at once.

What are the most common reasons for not reaching your goals? In many cases it's a lack of ability resulting from too little aptitude or training.

Work you can't do well or don't like is extremely stressful. When you consider how much time you will spend doing your job, you can see how this kind of stress can add up.

Many times you can't do what you want because you don't have enough money. Sometimes you simply don't have enough time.

Regardless of the reason for your inability to reach a personal goal, it is frustrating. This frustration leads to stress.

D on was having a very successful career selling insurance. He just seemed to have a knack for persuading people they should buy more life insurance.

After three years of successful sales, Don was promoted. He was made assistant manager in charge of hiring and training new salespeople.

Don found that teaching and motivating other people to sell life insurance was much more difficult than selling it himself. He was a better salesperson than he was recruiter and motivator. He didn't have as much natural ability for the management responsibilities as he did for the sales job.

Don worried that he couldn't handle the added responsibility. He became irritable and jumpy, even on his days away from the job. He began to have frequent fights with his wife. He had to let his frustration out somehow, and she became the easiest target.

Finally, Don began to consider giving up his management position. He thought he would go back to his sales job even though this would be a step backward in the company's organizational structure. It was a difficult decision, but Don knew he and his family would be a lot happier.

The pressures and demands of work schedules can make some people difficult to get along with. These people can create a lot of stress for their co-workers.

Human Relationships. Much of the stress that people experience is caused by their relationships with other people. You will find this especially true in the world of work, where you can rarely choose the people you work with. Even if you practice all the rules you learned earlier for getting along with and being effective with people, you will encounter some difficulties.

Disagreements are almost unavoidable. Even the most open-minded, accommodating people run into conflicts with others. You may even have serious arguments with friends and members of your family. Unless you care little about other people, these personal conflicts will cause a great deal of stress.

A specific cause of stress in human relations is **intimidation.** Intimidation is the use of fear to force someone to do something. You probably know one or two people who try to get their way by threatening others with physical harm or some other sort of injury. This kind of intimidation causes a great deal of stress for the person being intimidated. You will probably encounter people on the job who try to use intimidation to get their way.

Grief is another common cause of stress in human relationships. Grief is unavoidable. If you lose someone close to you, you can't help but feel sad and lonely. These feelings are very stressful.

Coping with Stress

Everyone is exposed to stress—it can't be avoided. To protect your physical and mental health, you must learn how to *cope with* (deal with, handle) a certain amount of stress. Here are some ways to cope with stress.

Exercise Regularly. Vigorous physical activity helps you work off stress. Exercise actually changes your body chemistry. These changes relieve the bad effects of emotional stress. If you seem overwhelmed with stress, ask yourself if you are getting enough exercise each day.

Talk Out Problems. You will usually feel better if you can talk about your problems with a trusted friend or family member. This is an excellent way to handle stress. This method is often overlooked by people who feel they need to sort things out on their own.

Eat Well and Get Enough Sleep. Bad eating habits can cause many types of health problems. Eating lots of junk food can increase the bad effects of stress.

Sleep is important, too. Almost everyone needs seven or eight hours of sleep per night. People who don't get enough sleep are more likely to suffer from stress. If you are having trouble sleeping, see a doctor.

Help Someone. Doing things with and for others can improve your general attitude. Helping others also gets your mind off your own problems for a while. Later, your problems may not seem so big.

Learn to Compromise. No one is right all the time. Sometimes, even when you want your way, it is better to give in. Consider just how important it is that you have your own way. Ask yourself, "Wouldn't it be better to compromise and relieve the stress?"

Some people, though, compromise *too* easily. They are so afraid of conflict that they always give in to other people. This can lead to stress, too. *Never* getting your own way is frustrating!

Don't Self-Medicate. There are many drugs available, both legal and illegal. You may be tempted to use drugs to relieve stress. Don't do this unless your doctor prescribes them for you. The body gets used to the drugs, and soon they are no longer effective. This can lead to taking larger, more dangerous doses.

Taking two different kinds of drugs at the same time can be especially dangerous. They can work together to create an effect greater than those of the separate drugs. This is the cause of many so-called overdose deaths. For example, some people drink alcohol, which is a drug, even though they have taken another drug. This is very dangerous.

Stress "Stop Signs." There are some signals that indicate stress is becoming too much for you to handle. An important part of coping with stress is recognizing these signals. Some of the more common ones are listed below.

- Trouble concentrating on one thing at a time
- Getting angry over little things
- Inability to relax
- Loss of interest in recreation

- Getting tired very easily

If several of these descriptions apply to you, try to relieve the stress yourself. If this doesn't work, ask for help. Talk first with your family. If professional help is needed, a teacher or minister might be able to refer you to someone who is qualified.

Make a Decision

You've noticed yourself being very irritable lately. Just the slightest problem or inconvenience seems to make you angry. You think the pressure at work is getting to you, and you'd like to talk to a professional—someone who knows about stress and how to cope with it. You're not really sick so it seems foolish to see a doctor—maybe you should just try to deal with the problem yourself. What's your decision—seek help, or handle it yourself? Give reasons for your decision.

Coping with Stress

If problems seem to be building up and life looks generally miserable, you may want to make sure you are doing the things that help relieve stress.

Exercise

Talk to a friend

Get plenty of sleep

Help someone

REVIEW YOUR LEARNING

CHAPTER SUMMARY

When you get a job and start earning money, you will have more decisions to make, such as where you will live. The temptation to move out on your own will be great, but there are some good reasons to live at home. If you do decide to move out, you must decide where you want to live and whether or not you will want a roommate. Looking for a place to live is just like any other consumer activity—you should carefully inspect and compare each apartment. Using checklists for the different areas of the apartments will help choose the best place for you.

With freedom and independence come responsibilities and problems, which often result in stress. Your inability to reach personal goals and deal with problems can actually make you physically ill and even cause mental breakdowns. Proven methods for coping with stress include exercising regularly, talking out problems, eating and sleeping right, helping others, and learning to compromise.

WORDS YOU SHOULD KNOW

intimidation
lease
security deposit
stress
utilities

STUDY QUESTIONS

1. What are three advantages to living at home?
2. What is the one major advantage to moving out on your own?
3. What percent of your monthly pay do many experts recommend that you spend for rent?
4. What are at least three possible expenses in addition to rent when you first move out on your own?
5. What are two advantages to having a roommate?
6. What is the most common way to find places to rent?
7. List six rental terms that you should consider and compare before renting an apartment.
8. What are three things you should do before moving into a new apartment?
9. What is the most troublesome kind of stress?

REVIEW YOUR LEARNING

10. Name three possible results of emotional stress.
11. What are the two main causes of stress?
12. List five things you can do to cope with stress.

DISCUSSION TOPICS

1. Would you prefer to live at home or in your own place? Why?
2. Some psychologists say that people deserve credit only for what they achieve after Stage Three of development—our society and family deserve credit for all accomplishments prior to age twenty-five. Do you agree? Why or why not?
3. Some say that the help we can give our children in each stage of life depends upon our own success in those stages. Do you agree? Why or why not?
4. Have you ever experienced any stress? If so, what do you think caused it? What did you do to cope?

SUGGESTED ACTIVITIES

1. Divide a sheet of paper into three columns. In the first column, list all the household items you will probably need if you rent an unfurnished mobile home or apartment. In the second column, next to each item in the first column, name the place where you might get each item. In the third column, write the cost of each item. To make these cost estimates more accurate, check prices in a discount store, a furniture store, newspaper advertisements, and mail-order catalogs.

   What was the total cost of needed household items? How could these items be purchased most economically?
2. Keep a journal of stressful situations for two weeks. Describe each situation as completely as you can. Include the cause of your stress. Describe your method of coping. That is, tell how you tried to relieve the stress. And finally, discuss how successful you were in getting rid of the stress.

Glossary

Note: The numbers in parenthesis after the definitions indicate the chapters in which the words are defined and explained.

A

ability. A skill that has been developed (2).

apprentice. A person who learns to perform a certain job through the guidance and experience of a skilled worker (4).

aptitude. Potential, or knack, for learning certain skills (2).

assertive. Being confident and standing up for one's rights, beliefs, and ideas (8).

assessor. Someone who estimates the dollar value of property for the purpose of levying taxes (22).

attitude. A person's basic outlook on life—the world and the people in it (6).

B

bail. Money deposited with the court so that an accused person can be freed from jail until the trial (21).

balance. An amount of money, such as that in a checking account (18).

bank statement. A printed record of all transactions during a period of time for a certain account (18).

BASIC (Beginners All-purpose Symbolic Instruction Code). A compiler programming language designed to be easy to learn for the non-professional programmer (12).

beneficiary. Person named in an insurance policy to receive the policy's face value (20).

benefits. The money that eligible people receive from insurance policies and programs such as social security (23).

Better Business Bureau. A private agency that tries to improve business practices (16).

binary coding. A two-digit (0 and 1) communication system that is the essential language of computers; also called *machine language* (12).

binding contract. A contract that is legally valid and cannot be broken (21).

body language. Communication to others through physical actions (8).

boot. To load an operating system into a computer (12).

brand names. Company names (16).

budget. A plan for spending (17).

budget deficit. Condition that results from the federal government planning to spend more than it plans to take in (13).

C

cancelled check. A check that has been cashed (18).

capital. Money, or any resource other than land used to produce more wealth (13).

capital goods. Machines and buildings used by producers of goods and services to create more wealth (13).

capitalism. Also called the *free enterprise system;* a system that allows people to own property and make their own economic decisions (13).

career. Work done over a period of years (1).

career cluster. A group of careers that have certain features in common (3).

career consultation. A meeting with someone in a certain career to obtain information about that career (3).

career interest areas. Categories of jobs that are similar according to interests (3).

cash value. The amount of money some life insurance policies pay when cancelled or at the end of a certain period (20).

certificate of deposit (CD). A method of saving or investing money; a written guarantee to the investor that a certain amount of money will be returned, plus interest, on a certain date (18).

chairperson. A person in charge of a meeting (15).

charge account. A financial arrangement allowing people to buy on credit (19).

chips. Tiny strips of silicon upon which electronic circuits have been etched; also called *integrated circuits* (12).

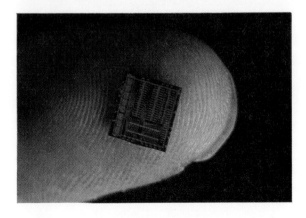

civil laws. Laws that regulate relationships among people; private laws (21).

closed shop. A place of work where the employee must join the union (13).

COBOL (COmmon Business Oriented Language). A compiler programming language developed primarily for business data processing (12).

collateral. Valuable assets a borrower promises as security for a loan (19).

commercial laws. Laws dealing with sales and contracts (21).

commission. A payment that a salesperson receives; usually a certain percentage of total sales (6).

communication. The process of exchanging information (10).

competent parties. According to contract law, people who are responsible for their actions (21).

computer. An electronic device that stores and processes data (12).

computer literacy. Awareness of the role, function, and impact of computers; understanding basic abilities and applications of computers (12).

consideration. A payment given to one party of a contract by another; necessary to make a binding contract (21).

consumer. One who buys and uses goods and services (13).

consumer fraud. Attempts by business people to trick or cheat consumers (16).

contract. A legal agreement between two or more people (21).

convertible. Term used to describe term life insurance policies that can be changed into whole life insurance coverage without interruption or special arrangement (20).

cooperative work experience program. A work plan in which a school and an employer offer part-time, paid experience on the job to the student (3).

corporation. A type of business ownership in which the business is usually owned by a number of people who purchased shares (14).

countersign. To sign a document, such as a contract, in support of another person (21).

coverage. Insurance term that refers to the conditions included in a particular insurance policy (20).

credit. A method of buying in which a business trusts a customer to pay later (19).

credit bureau. An agency that keeps track of whether or not people pay their bills on time (19).

credit cards. Cards that allow a person to make a purchase without the use of money (19).

credit rating. An estimate of the risk involved in giving credit to a certain individual based on that person's credit history (19).

D

data. Facts, such as numbers, words, and symbols (2).

data base. A body of computerized information (12).

data processing. Process of changing bits of data into information people can use (12).

death benefit. The amount of money stated on the life insurance policy that is paid to the beneficiary; face value (20).

debugging. The process of removing errors from a computer program (12).

decimal number. A fraction or mixed number whose denominator is a multiple of 10 (11).

deductible. Money a policyholder must pay for a loss before the insurance company will pay (20).

deduction. Expense that can be subtracted from income on a tax return (22).

defendant. Someone accused of wrongdoing (21).

deficit. A shortage. For example, a trade *deficit* occurs when the value of our exports is less than the value of our imports (13).

demand. The amount of consumer interest in purchasing goods and services at any one time (13).

dependent. Someone supported by a taxpayer (22).

deposit insurance. A type of insurance that guarantees replacement of deposits up to certain limits (18).

difference. The result of subtracting one number from another (11).

digit. The ten basic symbols, 0 through 9, that make up the number system (11).

disability. A physical or mental condition that prevents someone from working (23).

disabling injury. An injury that results in death, permanent physical damage, or inability to effectively perform regular duties or activities (9).

disk drive. A computer hardware device that receives and operates the disk (12).

displays. Temporary computer-generated visualizations on screens or monitors (12).

disposable income. Personal income minus income taxes (13).

distributive processing. Data processing done through a joint effort of one or more micro-computers linked to a mainframe computer (12).

dividends. Profits distributed to stockholders of a business (14).

documents. Permanent computer-generated information printed on paper; hard copy (12).

down payment. A certain amount, usually, 10 or 20 percent of the total purchase price, that is often paid as a first payment (19).

E

economic system. A method of producing and distributing goods and services to the people who need and want them (13).

empathize. To see another's viewpoint; to sympathize with another's situation (8).

employment agency. An organization that brings together a qualified worker and an employer trying to fill a job opening (5).

endorse. To sign a check for the purpose of transferring the right to it to someone else (18).

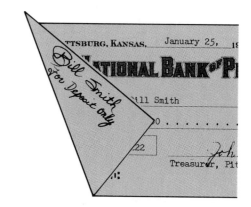

entrepreneur. A person who starts a new business (13).

enunciation. The process of speaking a word clearly and distinctly (10).

Environmental Protection Agency (EPA). A federal agency established to limit air and water pollution and, in general, maintain a healthy environment (9).

estate tax. A progressive tax levied by either the federal or state government on the property and money left by a deceased person (22).

esteem. A person's worth or value as seen by others (1).

excise tax. A federal or state tax levied on manufacturers of certain goods, such as tobacco and alcohol, produced in the U.S. (22).

exemption. A set amount that a taxpayer can deduct from income when filing a return (22).

extemporaneous. Spontaneous and unprepared (15).

exploratory work experience program. An unpaid work plan in which students can try many different kinds of jobs (3).

F

face value. The amount of protection stated on a life insurance policy; death benefit (20).

fatigue. The physical condition of being very tired or exhausted (9).

Federal Reserve System. An agency of the federal government that controls the nation's money supply (13).

Federal Trade Commission (FTC). A federal agency that administers laws designed to protect consumers' rights and prevent unfair business practices (16).

feedback. Visual or verbal communication to speakers in response to their messages (10).

felony. A serious crime (21).

F.I.C.A. (Federal Insurance Contribution Act). A federal law that requires employers to deduct and match a certain percentage of each employee's pay, primarily for the purpose of providing the worker with retirement income (22).

filing. Turning in (usually by mailing) a completed tax return (22).

finance charge. A certain percent of an amount owed; interest (19).

financial responsibility. Obligations concerning money (17).

floppy disk. Magnetic media encased in plastic used in electronic data processing; diskette (12).

Food and Drug Administration. A federal agency that regulates the production and sale of foods and drugs within the U.S. (16).

FORTRAN (FORmula TRANslator). A compiler programming language widely used for math and scientific applications on the computer (12).

franchise. The legal right to sell a company's goods and services in a particular area (14).

free enterprise. An economic system in which people have the right to make their own economic decisions (13).

fringe benefits. Benefits, such as vacations and insurance, that employers offer employees in addition to salary (3).

full employment. A condition where all who want jobs are employed (13).

G

general work experience program. A school program that offers a student part-time, paid work experience that is not necessarily related to a career interest (3).

Gross National Product (GNP). The value of all goods and services produced in the nation (13).

group insurance. Insurance coverage under one policy for several people, usually the employees of a company (20).

H

hard copy. A printed version of information processed by a computer (12).

hardware. Electronic equipment that processes data according to instruction; the components of a computer system, as opposed to the *software* (instructions) for running the system (12).

I

identity. Personal quality or activity by which a person is known (1).

income tax. A tax, either federal or state, levied on a person's income (22).

inflation. An economic condition in which prices rise sharply (13).

inflection. The use of the voice to improve the sound and influence the meaning of a spoken message (10).

initiative. The quality of motivating oneself, doing what needs to be done without outside direction (6).

installment plan. A way of purchasing goods in which the buyer agrees to make regular payments while taking immediate possession of the product (19).

insurance. Financial protection against possible loss, injury, or damage (20).

interest. 1. Money paid by banks to depositors for use of their funds (18). 2. A charge levied by a bank, credit company, or lender for borrowed money or credit; usually a percentage of the amount (19).

interest rate. Percentage used to calculate interest (18).

interests. Activities that a person enjoys doing most (2).

Internal Revenue Service (IRS). A federal agency responsible for collecting taxes (22).

interview. A formal meeting between an employer and a job applicant (5).

intimidation. The use of fear to control someone; a frequent cause of stress (24).

inventory. 1. To make a list of items (16). 2. The total amount of goods in stock at a particular time (14).

itemize. List, such as the listing of deductions on an income tax return (22).

J

jargon. Special words, terms, or phrases describing job-related matters in a particular field (10).

job. Collection of tasks or duties done to earn a living (1).

job leads. Information about possible job openings (5).

juvenile court. A court that handles only those cases involving minors (21).

L

labor. An important resource consisting of workers employed to help producers (13).

labor union. An organization of workers who bargain to obtain higher pay and better working conditions (13).

law of supply and demand. The way in which the relationship between supply (amount of goods and services available) and demand (consumer needs and wants) affects prices (13).

layoff notice. A statement from an employer that an employee's period of employment is over, usually temporarily (6).

lease. A contract that states the terms and responsibilities between a landlord and a tenant (24).

legal system. The combination of laws, processes, and people that protect citizens' rights and safety (21).

levy. To require people to pay, such as *to levy* taxes (22).

liability. In insurance, a type of coverage that pays for another person's losses if the policyholder is responsible (20).

lifestyle. The way a person lives (1).

loan. A lump sum of money that a person receives and promises to repay (19).

lobby. To promote the interests of a special group, such as consumers, to lawmakers (16).

M

machine language. The two-digit coding system, consisting of 0 and 1, which is the fundamental computer language; binary coding (12).

mainframe. A very large computer, which often requires special conditions for operation (12).

marketing. The process of packaging, distributing, advertising, and selling goods and services (13).

marketplace. Anyplace where consumers and producers buy and sell goods and services (13).

media. Material, such as cards or tape, that carries data and can be used as input in computer processing (12).

Medicare. A federal program of hospital and medical insurance (23).

memo. A written message, usually informal, brief, and to specific readers (10).

merit raise. A pay increase based on an employee's outstanding work (7).

micro. A small, personal computer (12).

minimum wage. According to law, the lowest amount of money per hour that employers may pay employees (7).

minor. A person too young to receive all legal rights and responsibilities (21).

minutes. A parliamentary term for the detailed written record of a meeting (15).

misdemeanor. A crime less serious in nature than a felony (21).

modem. A device through which computers can be linked to transfer information; MOdulator-DE-Modulator (12).

money management. The process of using money wisely (17).

monopoly. Almost total control of the buying and selling of certain goods or services; a lack of competition (13).

motion. In a meeting, a formal proposal for action (15).

mutual agreement. Complete understanding and acceptance of terms by both parties to a contract (21).

N

net profit. The amount of money remaining after all expenses are paid from revenues (14).

no-fault insurance. Automobile insurance that requires the insurance company to pay the policyholder's losses from an accident, regardless of who is at fault.

O

Occupational Safety and Health Act (OSHA). Federal legislation that establishes safety and health standards in the work environment (9).

open shop. A place of work where an employee may choose whether or not to join the union (13).

operating expense. Amount of money required to operate a business (14).

ordinances. County and city laws (21).

overtime. A wage 50 percent more than the regular hourly pay; also called *time and a half* (6).

outstanding checks. Checks that have been written but not cashed and recorded by the bank (18).

overdrawn. The condition of a checking account that does not contain enough money to pay for all the checks written on it (18).

P

parliamentary procedure. Established, democratic method of conducting meetings (15).

partnership. A type of business ownership in which the business is owned by two or more people (14).

party. In legal matters, one who enters into a contract (21).

peer pressure. The influence that a group has on the actions and behavior of individuals in the group (16).

percent. A number expressed as a comparison with 100 (11).

peripherals. Equipment and data processing devices that surround the central processing unit and main memory, contributing to the total operation of a computer system (12).

personal data sheet. A brief written description of a person's education, work, experience, and other information related to a potential job; a resume (5).

personal effectiveness. The ability to change situations and influence people (8).

personal income. Wages and all other gain, usually measured in money, received by a person over a period of time (13).

personality. The particular combination of attitudes, interests, values, behaviors, and characteristics that identify a person (2).

plaintiff. Someone who brings charges against another person in court (21).

planning goals. Intermediate goals that help people reach their ultimate career goal (4).

point of order. Under parliamentary procedure, a statement made without permission by a member to question a ruling or enforce a procedure (15).

policy. In insurance, a legal contract between the person buying the insurance and the insurance company (20).

policyholder. A person who enters into a contract with an insurance company to pay certain amounts of money for certain coverage (20).

premiums. The policyholder's payments that make up the cost of an insurance policy (20).

previewing. Reading only those parts of a document that outline or summarize its contents (10).

probation. An evaluation period following conviction of a misdemeanor (21).

producers. Suppliers of goods and services (13).

product. In math, the answer obtained by multiplying (11).

productivity. The ability to produce goods and services (13).

profession. A career that requires specialized training and academic preparation (4).

profit. The amount of money that a business takes in that is more than the amount spent (13).

profit motive. The attempt to make money; the reason that people start and run businesses (13).

profit ratio. Comparison of net profit to total revenue (14).

program. In computer technology, a set of instructions that cause a computer to perform specific tasks; software (12).

progressive tax. A manner of taxing in which the tax rate increases as the amount of taxable income increases (22).

promotion. An advancement to a higher-level job (7).

pronunciation. The way a word sounds (10).

public laws. Laws that regulate relationships between individuals and government (21).

Q

quorum. The minimum number of members needed for a group to conduct official business (15).

quotient. The answer obtained by dividing (11).

R

RAM (Random Access Memory). The larger portion of a computer's main memory; data stored in RAM is lost when the computer is turned off (12).

references. People who will speak in another's behalf (5).

repossess. To take back merchandise previously sold because of inadequate payment (19).

resume. A brief written description of a person's education, work experience, and other information related to a potential job; a personal data sheet (5).

retirement benefits. Money payable from the social security program to an eligible worker after retirement (23).

return. A legal document that states a person's income and expenses during the year for the purpose of determining the amount of taxes owed (22).

revenue. Money obtained from sales of goods and services (14).

ROM (Read Only Memory). The smaller portion of the main memory of a computer that contains permanent instructions that cannot be changed or replaced (12).

S

safety hazards. Potentially dangerous conditions (9).

salary. A fixed amount of pay for a certain period of time (6).

sales tax. A tax, state or local, on goods and services people buy (22).

search warrant. A legal document issued by a judge, giving specific permission to police to search for certain articles (21).

security deposit. Money required by a landlord to cover costs of possible property damage by a renter (24).

self-concept. The way in which a person sees himself or herself; one's own evaluation of one's personal abilities and worth (2).

self-realization. According to Abraham Maslow, the highest level of needs a person is capable of reaching (1).

seniority. The employment status that results from continuous service with one company (7).

severance pay. Payment from an employer who has cut off (*severed*) a person's employment (6).

skimming. Reading through material very quickly to pick out the key points (10).

software. A prepared set of instructions for a computer, as opposed to the *hardware* (components making up the computer system) (12).

sole proprietorship. A type of business ownership in which the business is owned by one person (14).

standard English. A type of English in which the words mean the same to everyone; the type of English successful people use in the world of work (5).

standards. Established levels (9).

stockholders. People who own shares of a business (14).

stress. Physical, emotional, or mental strain (24).

strike. An organized refusal of workers to work for the purpose of obtaining higher pay or better working conditions.

subletting. Renting or leasing property that is already rented (24).

sum. The answer obtained by adding two or more numbers (11).

supervisor. Someone in charge of other workers (7).

supply. The amount of a particular product or service for sale in the marketplace (13).

T

tact. The ability to use actions and words that will not offend another person (8).

taxes. Money citizens pay to maintain a government and provide public services (22).

technology. All ideas, processes, and means used to produce goods and services (13).

term insurance. Life insurance that is payable for a set period of time and does not build up any cash value (20).

termination notice. A statement from an employer that dismisses a person from a job (6).

trade. 1. An occupation that requires manual or mechanical skill (4). 2. The buying and selling of goods and services between parties (13).

tuition. Cost of attending a school (4).

U

unemployment. Condition in which people are willing to work but unable to find a job (13).

unemployment compensation. Money received by eligible people who have recently become unemployed (6).

unemployment insurance. A social insurance program that pays benefits to workers who have lost their jobs (23).

utilities. Public services such as gas, electricity, and water (24).

V

values. The ideas, relationships, and other matters that a person believes to be important (2).

vocation. The work that someone does to earn a living (4).

vocational work experience program. A cooperative work plan by a school and an employer that offers on-the-job experience in the student's specific area of interest (3).

W

wages. Pay received for hourly work (6).

white-collar crime. Corporate crime, including forgery and fraud (21).

whole life insurance. Life insurance coverage that extends for the whole life of the insured and builds up cash value (20).

whole numbers. Numbers that contain no fractions or decimals (11).

work. Productive activity that results in something useful (1).

work credits. Social security measurements to determine qualifications for benefits (23).

work evaluation. A written report of a person's job performance (6).

worker's compensation. An insurance program that pays benefits to workers injured on the job and to the survivors of these workers (23).

W-2 Form. A statement received in January that shows an employee's earnings and deductions during the previous year (22).

W-4 Form. A legal statement that permits an employer to deduct money from a worker's pay (22).

Index

Photo Credits

Alcoa, 30
Allen Products Company, 253
Allied Chemicals, 203
American Industrial Arts Student Association, 237
American Automobile Association, 309, 335
American Petroleum Institute, 203
AMP Incorporated, vii, 152
Appalachia Educational Laboratory, Inc., 98, 129, 137, 312, 329, 343, 379, 381
Apple Computers, Inc., 184, 195, 198, 203
Armstrong Rubber Company/Larry Ciarino, 181
Armstrong Rubber Company/Arthur d'Arazien, 155
Armstrong World Industries, Inc., 319, 322
Ashland Oil, 155
Associated Federal Reporters; Peoria, IL, 329
AT&T Corporate Archive, 155
Bausch & Lomb, 30, 93
Bethlehem Steel, 203, 384
Black Star/Andy Levin, Introduction 1
The Boeing Company, 357
Wendy Boersma, 311
Bradley University/Jim Brey, vi, 44
Burger King, 107
Burlington Coat Factory, 216
Burroughs Corporation, 30
Cameron Iron Works, Introduction 1, 29
Carnation Company, 203
CECO Industries, Inc., 100
Celanese Corporation, 19
Central Illinois Light Company, 113, 140
The Chicago Board of Trade, 208
City of Peoria Board of Election Commissioners, 216, 346
Commercial National Bank of Peoria, 282
CS&A Advertising, 3, 48, 191, 283
Dallas Cowboys, 235
Department of Labor, Mine Safety Health Administration, 206
Department of the Navy, 64
Discover Card Services, Inc., 296
   ("Discover" is a trademark of Sears, Roebuck and Company)

Distributive Education Clubs of America, 237
Duomo/David Madison, 120
Environmental Protection Agency, 143
Mel Erickson Art Service, 5, 8, 16, 17, 21, 28, 71, 75, 80, 85, 86, 93, 95, 97, 101, 106, 108, 109, 110, 112, 114, 115, 116, 123, 126, 128, 130, 138, 139, 154, 197, 204, 225, 252, 258, 259, 286
Fairchild Industries, Inc., 41
FHA/HERO, 237
Janet Featherly, 316
Marc Featherly, 58, 105, 188, 224, 261, 330
Figgie International, 30, 34
Fleetwood Enterprises, Inc., 19, 361
Ford Motor Company, 142, 206
Foster & Kleiser, 253
Frugal Frank, Division of Kinney's Shoes, 228
Future Business Leaders of America, 237
Future Farmers of America, 237
General Dynamics, 343, 345, 359
General Motors, 203
Lorne Green, 253
W.R. Grace & Co., 43
Gromark, 33
Handy & Harmon, 203, 212
Haymeadow Apartments; Peoria, IL, 370, 374, 375
Health Occupations Students of America, 237
Hewlett Packard, 19
Hillenbrand Industries, 35
Hilton Hotels, 39
Hoover Universal, Inc., 36
Honeywell, Inc., 147, 149
IBM, 2, 19, 30
Illinois Central College, 61
Illinois Farm Bureau Graphic Production/Ken Kashian and Al Hasty, 125, 185, 195, 209, 222, 243, 244, 257, 300, 317, 363
Illinois House, 238, 328, 329
Illinois Information Office, 341
Illinois State University, 18
Indiana Pacers, 42
Ink & Image, 297